D0731849

The History of Scepticism from Erasmus to Spinoza

THE HISTORY
OF SCEPTICISM
FROM
ERASMUS TO SPINOZA

Richard H. Popkin

UNIVERSITY OF CALIFORNIA PRESS

BERKELEY   LOS ANGELES   LONDON

University of California Press
Berkeley and Los Angeles, California
University of California Press, Ltd.
London, England

Library of Congress Catalog Card Number 78-6549

This book is a revised and expanded edition of THE HISTORY OF SCEPTICISM
FROM ERASMUS TO DESCARTES (Van Gorcum 1960: and revised edition,
1964, with Humanities Press, Inc.; and Harper Torchbook, 1968). Portions of the
following works are reprinted with the permission of the publishers: *The Complete
Works of Montaigne*, translated by Donald M. Frame (Stanford University Press,
copyright © 1948, 1957, 1958 by the Board of Trustees of the Leland Stanford
Junior University); *Calvin: Institutes of the Christian Religion*, I.LCC, Vol. XX,
edited by John T. McNeill and translated by Ford Lewis Battles (The Westminster
Press, copyright © 1960, W. L. Jenkins); *The Philosophical Works of Descartes*,
translated by E. S. Haldane and G. R. T. Ross (Cambridge University Press,
1931).

1 2 3 4 5 6 7 8 9

With love, to Julie, Jerry, Maggi, and Sue

and dedicated to the memory of Imre Lakatos

CONTENTS

ACKNOWLEDGMENTS

This study has been developed during the last ten years, and represents not only the results of the author's findings, but also the results of the assistance, advice, and encouragement of many people and institutions. It is, therefore, a great pleasure for me to be able to take this opportunity to thank those who have given so generously of their help in various forms.

First of all, I wish to express my thanks to the United States State Department, which awarded me Fulbright Research grants to the University of Paris, 1952-53, and to the University of Utrecht, 1957-8; and to the American Philosophical Society, which awarded me grants in 1956 and 1958 to carry on my research in France and Italy. By means of these grants, I was able to have the opportunity to examine and study much material that is not available in this country, and was able to have periods of time away from my teaching duties, so that I could concentrate on preparing this study.

Since the first edition of this work I have had grants from the American Council of Learned Societies, the Alexander Kohut Foundation, the John Simon Guggenheim Foundation, the American Philosophical Society, the Memorial Foundation for Jewish Culture and the National Endowment for the Humanities which have helped me broaden my knowledge and understanding of modern scepticism.

I am most grateful also to the many libraries in the United States and Europe which have allowed me to use their facilities, especially for the Bibliothèque Nationale of Paris, the British Library, the Biblioteek van de Universiteit van Utrecht, the Biblioteca Laurenziana of Florence, the Rijksbibliotheek in The Hague, the University of Amsterdam Library, the Institut Catholique of

Toulouse Library, the Newberry Library of Chicago, the University of California, San Diego Library, the Henry Huntington Library, the William Andrews Clark Library of the University of California, Los Angeles and the Olin Library at Washington University, St. Louis.

To the Philosophical Institute of the University of Utrecht, and to its members, Professors Cornelia De Vogel and Karl Kuypers, I owe a special debt of gratitude for their kindness in arranging to have this study appear in the series of the Institute. I am extremely happy to be able to have this permanent link with the University of Utrecht, where I spent so pleasant and profitable a year in 1957–8, and I only hope that this study will constitute a partial indication of the gratitude I feel to the University of Utrecht and its philosophers.

I am extremely indebted to the State University of Iowa and to the late Dean Walter Loehwing of the Graduate College for their generosity in making time, materials and funds available to me to complete this study.

I owe my initial acquaintance with and interest in scepticism and the role it played in modern philosophy to my teachers, especially to Professors John H. Randall and Paul O. Kristeller of Columbia University and Charles W. Hendel of Yale University. Through the encouragement of Professor Paul Weiss of Yale, I was led to sketch out my views in a series of articles in the *Review of Metaphysics*. I am most grateful to the many scholars who have patiently discussed matters about the history of scepticism with me, and who have advised and encouraged me in this work. Among others, I should like to thank the late Abbé Robert Lenoble, the late Father Julian-Eymard d'Angers, Father Paul Henry, the late Professor Alexandre Koyré, Professor Herbert Marcuse, the late Professor Bernard Rochot, Professors Leonora Cohen Rosenfield, André-Louis Leroy, René Pintard, Jean Orcibal, Henri Gouhier, and Jean Grenier, the late Imre Lakatos, the late Paul Schrecker, the late Giorgio Tonelli, Paul O. Kristeller (who gave me many valuable suggestions concerning the manuscript of this study), Paul Dibon, J. Tans, the late C. Louise Thijssen-Schoute and Elisabeth Labrousse. Many of these people will, no doubt, disagree with some of the conclusions I have come to, but their discussions with me have been invaluable in helping to clarify and develop my ideas. Also, I wish to thank some of my former students and colleagues who have assisted me, particularly Professors Graham Conroy, George Arbaugh, Richard Watson, Florence Weinberg, Philip Cummins, Harry M. Bracken and Theodore Waldman who were at the State University of Iowa when this work was first being written.

I am most grateful to Mr. John Lowenthal and to my wife, Juliet, who have assisted me enormously in editorial matters connected with the manuscript. And I wish to express my thanks to Mrs. Mildred Keller and to Miss Joan Jones for their arduous efforts in typing the final copy of the original manuscript. I wish to thank Melanie Miller for typing the new material for this edition.

Also, I want to express my thanks to the *Modern Schoolman*, the *Journal of Philosophy*, and to the *Archiv für Reformationsgeschichte* for permission to use some of the material I had published in studies previously.

Lastly, and most importantly, I want to thank my family—my wife Juliet, and my children, Jeremy, Margaret, and Susan—for their fortitude and patience throughout all the trials, tribulations and voyages of the author and his manuscript. Without their love, kindness and willingness to sacrifice, this study could never have been completed. I only hope this study is worthy of all the difficulties it has caused them.

I should also like to thank Professors Donald Frame of Columbia University, John Watkins of the University of London, and the various reviewers, among others, who have called my attention to various items requiring revision.

June 25, 1963, La Jolla, California
February 1979, St. Louis, Missouri

PREFACE

Scepticism as a philosophical view, rather than as a series of doubts concerning traditional religious beliefs, had its origins in ancient Greek thought. In the Hellenistic period the various sceptical observations and attitudes of earlier Greek thinkers were developed into a set of arguments to establish either (1) that no knowledge was possible, or (2) that there was insufficient and inadequate evidence to determine if any knowledge was possible, and hence that one ought to suspend judgment on all questions concerning knowledge. The first of these views is called Academic scepticism, the second Pyrrhonian scepticism.

Academic scepticism, so-called because it was formulated in the Platonic Academy in the third century, B.C., developed from the Socratic observation, 'All I know is that I know nothing.' Its theoretical formulation is attributed to Arcesilas, c. 315-241 B.C., and Carneades, c. 213-129 B.C., who worked out a series of arguments, directed primarily against the knowledge claims of the Stoic philosophers, to show that nothing could be known. As these arguments have come down to us, especially in the writings of Cicero, Diogenes Laertius and Saint Augustine, the aim of the Academic sceptical philosophers was to show, by a group of arguments and dialectical puzzles, that the dogmatic philosopher (i.e., the philosopher who asserted that he knew *some* truth about the real nature of things), could not know with absolute certainty the propositions he said he knew. The Academics formulated a series of difficulties to show that the information we gain by means of our senses may be unreliable, that we cannot be certain that our reasoning is reliable, and that we possess no guaranteed criterion or standard for determining which of our judgments is true or false.

The basic problem at issue is that any proposition purporting to assert some knowledge about the world contains some claims which go beyond the merely empirical reports about what appears to us to be the case. If we possessed any knowledge, this would mean for the sceptics, that we knew a proposition, asserting some non-empirical, or trans-empirical claim, which we were certain could not possibly be false. If the proposition might be false, then it would not deserve the name of knowledge, but only that of opinion, i.e., that it might be the case. Since the evidence for any such proposition would be based, according to the sceptics, on either sense information or reasoning, and both of these sources are unreliable to some degree, and no guaranteed or ultimate criterion of true knowledge exists, or is known, there is always some doubt that any non-empirical or trans-empirical proposition is absolutely true, and hence constitutes real knowledge. As a result, the Academic sceptics said that nothing is certian. The best information we can gain is only probable, and is to be judged according to probabilities. Hence Carneades developed a type of verification theory and a type of probabilism which is somewhat similar to the theory of scientific 'knowledge' of present day pragmatists and positivists.

The scepticism of Arcesilas and Carneades dominated the philosophy of the Platonic Academy until the first century before Christ. In the period of Cicero's studies, the Academy changed from scepticism to the eclecticism of Philo of Larissa and Antiochus of Ascalon. The arguments of the Academics survived mainly through Cicero's presentation of them in his *Academica* and *De Natura Deorum*, and through their refutation in St. Augustine's *Contra Academicos*, as well as in the summary given by Diogenes Laertius. The locus of sceptical activity, however, moved from the Academy to the school of the Pyrrhonian sceptics, which was probably associated with the Methodic school of medicine in Alexandria.

The Pyrrhonian movement attributes its beginnings to the legendary figure of Pyrrho of Elis, c. 360–275 B.C., and his student Timon, c. 315–225 B.C. The stories about Pyrrho that are reported indicate that he was not a theoretician, but rather a living example of the complete doubter, the man who would not commit himself to any judgment that went beyond what seemed to be the case. His interests seem to have been primarily ethical and moral, and in this area he tried to avoid unhappiness that might be due to the acceptance of value theories, and to judging according to them. If such value theories were to any degree doubtful, accepting them and using them could only lead to mental anguish.

Pyrrhonism, as a theoretical formulation of scepticism, is attributed to Aenesidemus, c. 100–40 B.C. The Pyrrhonists considered that both the Dogmatists and the Academics asserted too much, one group saying 'Something can be known,' the other that 'Nothing can be known.' Instead, the Pyrrhonians proposed to suspend judgment on all questions on which there seemed to be conflicting evidence, including the question whether or not something could be known.

Building on the type of arguments developed by Arcesilas and Carneades, Aenesidemus and his successors put together a series of 'Tropes' or ways of proceeding to bring about suspense of judgment on various questions. In the sole surviving texts from the Pyrrhonian movement, those of Sextus Empiricus, these are presented in groups of ten, eight, five and two tropes, each set offering reasons why one should suspend judgment about knowledge claims that go beyond appearances. The Pyrrhonian sceptics tried to avoid committing themselves on any and all questions, even as to whether their arguments were sound. Scepticism for them was an ability, or mental attitude, for opposing evidence both pro and con on any question about what was non-evident, so that one would suspend judgment on the question. This state of mind then led to a state of *ataraxia*, quietude, or unperturbedness, in which the sceptic was no longer concerned or worried about matters beyond appearances. Scepticism was a cure for the disease called Dogmatism or rashness. But, unlike Academic scepticism, which came to a negative dogmatic conclusion from its doubts, Pyrrhonian scepticism made no such assertion, merely saying that scepticism is a purge that eliminates everything including itself. The Pyrrhonist, then, lives undogmatically, following his natural inclinations, the appearances he is aware of, and the laws and customs of his society, without ever committing himself to any judgment about them.

The Pyrrhonian movement flourished up to about 200 A.D., the approximate date of Sextus Empiricus, and flourished mainly in the medical community around Alexandria as an antidote to the dogmatic theories, positive and negative, of other medical groups. The position has come down to us principally in the writings of Sextus Empiricus, in his *Hypotyposes* (*Outlines of Pyrrhonism*), and the larger *Adversus mathematicos* in which all sorts of disciplines from logic and mathematics to astrology and grammar are subjected to sceptical devastation.

The two sceptical positions had very little apparent influence in the post-Hellenistic period. The Pyrrhonian view seems to have been almost unknown in the West until its rediscovery in the sixteenth century, and the Academic view mainly known and considered in terms of St. Augustine's treatment of it. Prior to the period we shall deal with, there are some indications of a sceptical motif, principally among the anti-rational theologians, Jewish, Mohammedan and Christian. This theological movement, culminating in the West in the work of Nicholas of Cusa in the fifteenth century, employed many of the sceptical arguments in order to undermine confidence in the rational approach to religious knowledge and truth.

The period I shall treat, 1500–1675, is certainly not the unique period of sceptical impact on modern thought. Both before and after this time interval, one can find important influences of the ancient sceptical thinkers. But, it is my contention that scepticism plays a special and different role in the period from the Reformation up to the formulation of the Cartesian philosophy; a special and different role due to the fact that the intellectual crisis brought on by the Reformation coincided in time with the rediscovery and revival of the arguments of the ancient Greek sceptics. In the sixteenth century, with the discovery of manuscripts of Sextus's writings, there is a revival of interest and concern with ancient scepticism, and with the application of its views to the problems of the day.

The selection of Erasmus as the starting point of this study has not been made because there is any evidence that he was the first to reintroduce Greek sceptical materials, but rather because a problem raised in his controversy with Luther is an example of the crucial issue of the times to which the ancient sceptical arguments and theories were applied.

The stress in this study on the revival of interest and concern with the texts of Sextus Empiricus is not intended to minimize or ignore the collateral role played by such ancient authors as Diogenes Laertius or Cicero in bringing the classical sceptical views to the attention of sixteenth and seventeenth century thinkers. However, the writings of Sextus seem to have played a special and predominant role for many of the philosophers, theologians and scientists considered here, and Sextus appears to have been the direct or indirect source of many of their arguments, concepts, and theories. It is only in the works of Sextus that a full presentation of the position of the Pyrrhonian sceptics appears, with all of their dialectical weapons employed against so many philosophical theories. Neither the presentations of Academic scepticism in Cicero and St. Augustine, nor the summaries of both types of scepticism, Academic and Pyrrhonian, in Diogenes Laertius, were rich enough to satisfy those concerned with the sceptical crisis of the Renaissance and Reformation. Hence, thinkers like Montaigne, Mersenne and Gassendi, turned to Sextus for materials to use in dealing with the issues of their age. And, hence, the crisis is more aptly described as a 'crise pyrrhonienne' than as a 'crise academicienne.' By the end of the seventeenth century, the great sceptic, Pierre Bayle, could look back and see the reintroduction of the arguments of Sextus as the beginning of modern philosophy. Most writers of the period under consideration use the term 'sceptic' as equivalent to 'Pyrrhonian,' and often follow Sextus's view that the Academic sceptics were not really sceptics, but actually were negative dogmatists. (In this connection it is noteworthy that the late seventeenth century sceptic, Simon Foucher, took it upon himself to revive Academic scepticism and to try to defend it against such charges.)

The period of the history of scepticism considered in this volume goes up to Spinoza's irreligious scepticism and his ardent opposition to epistemological scepticism. My reason for limiting the study in this way is that I believe that scepticism chiefly played one role up to this time, and another afterwards. The super-scepticism of Descartes, involved in his demon hypothesis, began a new phase in the history of scepticism that was to be developed by Pascal, Bayle, Huet, and later Hume and Kierkegaard. Also, Descartes' refutation of scepticism made the sceptics turn their attack against his system instead of against their traditional enemies. Hence, the sceptical arguments had to be altered to fit the new opponent, and scepticism in the last half of the seventeenth century changed from being anti-Scholastic and anti-Platonic, to being anti-Cartesian. Spinoza offered what was to be one of the standard answers to modern scepticism. He also carried Descartes' sceptical method into the domain of religious thought, with devastating results. From Spinoza onward one of the main functions of scepticism has been to oppose traditional religion.

When I wrote the original preface to this work fifteen years ago, I foresaw writing a series of studies on the history of the subsequent course of epistemological scepticism covering the major thinkers who play a role in this development from Spinoza to Hume to Kant to Kierkegaard. Much of this material has been examined in studies by myself, my students, and others. So I am not sure how necessary such volumes may be. My own interest has moved towards studying the history of irreligious scepticism. It is my intention to follow this volume with one on Issac La Peyrère and his influence, and another on Millenarianism, Messianism and Scepticism.

In this study, two key terms will be 'scepticism' and 'fideism', and I should like to offer a preliminary indication as to how these will be understood in the context of this work. Since the term 'Scepticism' has been associated in the last two centuries with disbelief, especially disbelief of the central doctrines of the Judeo-Christian tradition, it may seem strange at first to read that the sceptics of the sixteenth and seventeenth centuries asserted, almost unanimously, that they were sincere believers in the Christian religion. Whether they were or not will be considered later. But the acceptance of certain beliefs would not in itself contradict their alleged scepticism, scepticism meaning a philosophical view that raises doubts about the adequacy or reliability of the evidence that could be offered to justify any proposition. The sceptic, in either the Pyrrhonian or Academic tradition, developed arguments to show or suggest that the evidence, reasons, or proofs employed as grounds for our various beliefs were not completely satisfactory. Then the sceptics recommended suspense of judgment on the question of whether these beliefs were true. One might, however, still maintain the beliefs, since all sorts of persuasive factors should not be mistaken for adequate evidence that the belief was true.

Hence, 'sceptic' and 'believer' are not opposing classifications. The sceptic is raising doubts about the rational or evidential merits of the justifications given for a belief; he doubts that necessary and sufficient reasons either have been or could be discovered to show that any particular belief must be true, and cannot possibly be false. But the sceptic may, like anyone else, still accept various beliefs.

Those whom I classify as fideists are persons who are sceptics with regard to the possibility of our attaining knowledge by rational means, without our possessing some basic truths known by faith (i.e. truths based on no rational evidence whatsoever). Thus, for example the fideist might deny or doubt that necessary and sufficient reasons can be offered to establish the truth of the proposition, 'God exists,' and yet the fideist might say that the proposition could be known to be true only if one possessed some information through faith, or if one believed certain things. Many of the thinkers whom I would classify as fideists held that either there are persuasive factors that can induce belief, but *not prove or establish* the truth of what is believed, or that after one has found or accepted one's faith, reasons can be offered that explain or clarify what one believes without proving or establishing it.

Fideism covers a group of possible views, extending from (1) that of blind faith, which denies to reason any capacity whatsoever to reach the truth, or to make it plausible, and which bases all certitude on a complete and unquestioning adherence to some revealed or accepted truths, to (2) that of making faith prior to reason. This latter view denies to reason any complete and absolute certitude of the truth prior to the acceptance of some proposition or propositions by faith (i.e. admitting that *all* rational propositions are to some degree doubtful prior to accepting something on faith), even though reason may play some relative or probable role in the search for, or explanation of the truth. In these possible versions of fideism, there is, it seems to me, a common core, namely that knowledge, considered as information about the world that cannot possibly be false, is unattainable without accepting something on faith, and that independent of faith sceptical doubts can be raised about any alleged knowledge claims. Some thinkers, Bayle and Kierkegaard for example, have pressed the faith element, and have insisted that there can be no relation between what is accepted on faith and any evidence or reasons that can be given for the articles of faith. Bayle's erstwhile colleague and later enemy, Pierre Jurieu, summed this up by asserting, 'Je le crois parce que je veux le croire.' No further reasons are demanded or sought, and what is accepted on faith may be at variance with what is reasonable or even demonstrable. On the other hand, thinkers such as St. Augustine and many of the Augustinians have insisted that reasons can be given for faith, *after* one has accepted it, and that reasons which may induce belief, can be given *prior* to the acceptance of the faith but do not demonstrate the truth of what is believed. Both the Augustinian and the Kierkegaardian views I class as fideistic, in that they both recognize that no indubitable truths can be found or established without some element of faith, whether religious, metaphysical, or something else.

The usage that I am employing corresponds, I believe, to that of many Protestant writers when they classify St. Augustine, Luther, Calvin, Pascal and Kierkegaard together as fideists. Some Catholic writers, like my good friend the late Father Julien-Eymard d'Angers, feel that the term 'fideist' should be restricted to those who deny reason *any* role or function in the search for truth, both before and after the acceptance of faith.[1] In this sense, St. Augustine, and perhaps Pascal (and some interpreters would argue, perhaps Luther, Calvin and even Kierkegaard), would no longer be classified as fideists.

The decision as to how to define the word 'fideism' is partly terminological, and partly doctrinal. The word can obviously be defined in various ways to correspond to various usages. But also involved in the decision as to what the term means is a basic distinction between Reformation Protestant thought and that of Roman Catholicism, since Roman Catholicism has condemned fideism as a heresy, and has found it a basic fault of Protestantism, while the non-liberal Protestants have contended that fideism is a basic element of fundamental Christianity, and an element which occurs in the teachings of St. Paul and St. Augustine. Though my usage corresponds more to that of Protestant writers than that of Catholic ones, I do not thereby intend to prejudge the issues in dispute, nor to take one side rather than the other.

In employing the meaning of 'fideism' that I do, I have followed what is a fairly common usage in the literature in English. Further, I think that this usage brings out more clearly the sceptical element that is involved in the fideistic view, broadly conceived. However, it is obvious that if the classifications 'sceptic' and 'fideist' were differently defined, then various figures whom I so classify might be categorized in a quite different way.

The antithesis of scepticism, in this study, is 'dogmatism', the view that evidence can be offered to establish that at least one non-empirical proposition cannot possibly be false. Like the sceptics who will be considered here, I believe that doubts can be cast on any such dogmatic claims, and that such claims ultimately rest on some element of faith rather than evidence. If this is so, any dogmatic view becomes to some degree fideistic. However, if this could be demonstrated, then the sceptic would be sure of something and would become a dogmatist.

The sympathies of the author are on the side of the sceptics he has been studying. But in showing how certain elements of their views led to the type of scepticism held by Hume, it is not my intention to advocate this particular result of the development of the 'nouveau Pyrrhonisme'. As a matter of fact, I am more in sympathy with those who used the sceptical and fideistic views of the 'nouveaux Pyrrhoniens' for religious rather than secular purposes, and I have tried to bring this out in other studies.

Owing to the difficulties of obtaining some of the source materials in this country, and due to the limited time I was able to work in the great European libraries, I have had to use more translated sources, (translated either at the time or in recent years), than I would have liked to, and in some instances, I have had to rely on citations in modern studies that I have not had the opportunity to check. However, I hope that the reader will consider this study as an initial attempt to see the role of scepticism in modern thought, and that others will go on and make up for whatever defects or deficiencies there may be.

I

THE INTELLECTUAL CRISIS OF THE REFORMATION

One of the main avenues through which the sceptical views of antiquity entered late Renaissance thought was a central quarrel of the Reformation, the dispute over the proper standard of religious knowledge, or what was called 'the rule of faith'. This argument raised one of the classical problems of the Greek Pyrrhonists, the problem of the criterion of truth. With the rediscovery in the sixteenth century of writings of the Greek Pyrrhonist, Sextus Empiricus, the arguments and views of the Greek sceptics became part of the philosophical core of the religious struggles then taking place. The problem of finding a criterion of truth, first raised in theological disputes, was then later raised with regard to natural knowledge, leading to the *crise pyrrhonienne* of the early seventeenth century.

Martin Luther's views and his quarrel with Erasmus may be briefly considered as an indication of how the Reformation spawned the new problem. This is not to suggest that the issue arose only at the time of Luther's break with the Catholic Church. Rather, that time is an arbitrary starting-point for tracing the sceptical influence in the formation of modern thought, a time which points up not only the conflict between the criteria of religious knowledge of the Church and of the Reformers, but also the type of philosophical difficulties the conflict was to generate.

It was only by degrees that Luther developed from reformer inside the ideological structure of Catholicism to leader of the Reformation, denying the authority of the Church of Rome. In his first protests against indulgences, Papal authority, and other

1

Catholic principles, Luther argued in terms of the accepted criterion of the Church that religious propositions are judged by their agreement with the Church tradition, councils, and Papal decrees. In the *Ninety-Five Theses*, and in his letter to Pope Leo X, he tried to show that, judged by the standards of the Church for deciding such issues, he was right, and certain church practices and the justifications offered for them were wrong.

However, at the Leipzig Disputation of 1519, and in his writings of 1520, *The Appeal to the German Nobility* and *The Babylonish Captivity of the Church*, Luther took the critical step of denying the rule of faith of the Church, and presented a radically different criterion of religious knowledge. It was in this period that he developed from just one more reformer attacking the abuses and corruption of a decaying bureaucracy into the leader of an intellectual revolt that was to shake the very foundation of Western civilization.

His opponent at Leipzig, Johann Eck, tells us with horror that Luther went so far as to deny the complete authority of Pope and Councils, to claim that doctrines which have been condemned by Councils can be true and that Councils can err because they are composed only of men.[1] In *The Appeal to the German Nobility*, Luther went even further, and denied that the Pope can be the only authority in religious matters. He claimed instead that all of Christendom has but one Gospel, one Sacrament, all Christians have 'the power of discerning and judging what is right or wrong in the matters of faith,'[2] and Scripture outranks even the Pope in determining proper religious views and actions.[3] In *The Babylonish Captivity*, Luther made even clearer his basic denial of the Church's criterion of religious knowledge:

> . . . I saw that the Thomist opinions, whether they be approved by pope or by council, remain opinions and do not become articles of faith, even if an angel from heaven should decide otherwise. For that which is asserted without the authority of Scripture or of proven revelation may be held as an opinion, but there is no obligation to believe it.[4]

And finally, Luther asserted his new criterion in its most dramatic form when he refused to recant at the Diet of Worms of 1521:

Your Imperial Majesty and Your Lordships demand a simple answer.
Here it is, plain and unvarnished. Unless I am convicted of error by the
testimony of Scripture or (since I put no trust in the unsupported
authority of Pope or of councils, since it is plain that they have often
erred and often contradicted themselves) by manifest reasoning I stand
convicted by the Scriptures to which I have appealed, and my conscience is taken captive by God's word, I cannot and will not recant
anything, for to act against our conscience is neither safe for us, no
open to us. On this I take my stand. I can do no other. God help me.
Amen.[5]

In this declaration of Christian liberty, Luther set forth his new
criterion of religious knowledge, that what conscience is compelled to believe on reading Scripture is true. To Catholics like
Eck, this must have sounded completely incredible. For centuries, asserting that a proposition stated a religoius truth meant
that it was authorized by Church tradition, by the Pope, and by
councils. To claim that these standards could be wrong was like
denying the rules of logic. The denial of the accepted criteria
would elminate the sole basis for testing the truth of a religious
proposition. To raise even the possibility that the criteria could be
faulty was to substitute another criterion by which the accepted
criteria could be judged, and thus, in effect, to deny the entire
framework by which orthodoxy had been determined for centuries.

Once a fundamental criterion has been challenged, how does
one tell which of the alternative possibilities ought to be accepted? On what basis can one defend or refute Luther's claims?
To take any position requires another standard by which to judge
the point at issue. Thus Luther's denial of the criteria of the
Church, and his assertion of his new standard for determining
religious truth, lead to a rather neat example of the problem of
the criterion as it appears in Sextus Empiricus, *Outlines of Pyrrhonism*, II, Chap. IV;

. . . in order to decide the dispute which has arisen about the criterion,
we must possess an accepted criterion by which we shall be able to
judge the dispute; and in order to possess an accepted criterion, the
dispute about the criterion must first be decided. And when the argument thus reduces itself to a form of circular reasoning the discovery of
the criterion becomes impracticable, since we do not allow them [the

> Dogmatic philosophers] to adopt a criterion by assumption, while if
> they offer to judge the criterion by a criterion we force them to a regress
> *ad infinitum.*[6]

The problem of justifying a standard of true knowledge does not arise as long as there is an unchallenged criterion. But in an epoch of intellectual revolution, such as that under consideration here, the very raising of the problem can produce an insoluble *crise pyrrhonienne*, as the various gambits of Sextus Empiricus are explored and worked out. The Pandora's box that Luther opened at Leipzig was to have the most far-reaching consequences, not just in theology but throughout man's entire intellectual realm.

In defense of a fundamental criterion, what can be offered as evidence? The value of the evidence depends upon the criterion, and not *vice versa*. Some theologians, for example Saint Ignatius Loyola, tried to close the box by insisting 'That we may be altogether of the same mind and in conformity with the Church herself, if she shall have defined anything to be black which to our eyes appears to be white, we ought in like manner to pronounce it to be black.'[7] This, however, does not justify the criterion, but only exhibits what it is.

The problem remained. To be able to recognize the true faith, one needed a criterion. But how was one to recognize the *true* criterion? The innovators and the defenders of the old were both faced with the same problem. They usually met it by attacking their opponents' criterion. Luther attacked the authority of the Church by showing the inconsistencies in its views. The Catholics tried to show the unreliability of one's conscience, and the difficulty of discerning the true meaning of Scripture without the guidance of the Church. Both sides warned of the catastrophe—intellectual, moral, and religious—that would ensue from adopting the others' criterion.

One of the Catholic arguments offered throughout the Reformation was the contention that Luther's criterion would lead to religious anarchy. Everybody could appeal to *his own* conscience, and claim that what appeared true to him was true. No effective standard of truth would be left. In the first years of the Reformation the rapid development of all sorts of novel beliefs by such groups as the Zwickau prophets, the Anabaptists and the anti-Trinitarians seemed to confirm this prediction. The Reformers were continually occupied with trying to justify their own type of subjective, individual criterion, and at the same time were using this criterion as an objective measure by means of which they condemned as heresies their opponent's appeals to conscience.

In the battle to establish which criterion of faith was true, a sceptical attitude arose among certain thinkers, primarily as a defense of Catholicism. While many Catholic theologians tried to offer historical evidence to justify the authority of the Church (without being able to show that historical evidence was the criterion), a suggestion of the sceptical defense of the faith, the defense that was to dominate the French Counter-Reformation, was offered by Erasmus of Rotterdam. Erasmus, who had been one of the moving spirits in the demand for reform, was, in the period 1520–1524, pressed more and more strenuously to openly attack Luther.[8] (Erasmus had various reasons for, and means of, evading the issue, but only the ultimate result will be considered here.) In 1524, Erasmus finally published a work, *De Libero Arbitrio ΔIATPIBH*, attacking Luther's views on free will. Erasmus's general anti-intellectualism and dislike of rational theological discussions led him to suggest a kind of sceptical basis for remaining within the Catholic Church. (His reaction to the philosophers at the University of Paris in his student days, and his condemnation, in *The Praise of Folly*, of their intellectual quest *per se*, culminated in the statement 'Human affairs are so obscure and various that nothing can be clearly known. This was the sound conclusion of the Academics [the Academic Sceptics], who were the least surly of the philosophers.'[9] This contempt for intellectual endeavor was coupled with his advocacy of a simple, non-theological Christian piety.)

De Libero Arbitrio begins with the announcement that the problem of the freedom of the will is one of the most involved of labyrinths. Theological controversies were not Erasmus' meat, and he states that he would prefer to follow the attitude of the sceptics and suspend judgment, especially where the inviolable authority of Scripture and the decrees of the Church permit. He says he is perfectly willing to submit to the decrees, whether or not he understands them or the reasons for them.[10] Scripture is not as clear as Luther would have us believe, and there are some places that are just too shadowy for human beings to penetrate. Theologians have argued and argued the question without end. Luther claims he has found the right answer and has understood Scripture correctly. But how can we tell that he really has? Other interpretations can be given that seem much better than Luther's. In view of the difficulty in establishing *the* true meaning of Scripture concerning the problem of free will, why not accept the traditional solution offered by the Church? Why start such a fuss over something one cannot know with any certainty?[11] For Erasmus, what is important is a simple, basic, Christian piety, a Christian spirit. The rest, the superstructure of the essential belief, is too complex for a man to judge. Hence it is easier to rest in a sceptical attitude, and accept the age-old wisdom of the Church on these matters, than to try to understand and judge for one's self.

This sceptical attitude, rather than sceptical argument, grew out of an abhorrence of 'the comedy of the higher lunacy'. It was not based, as it was for Montaigne, on evidence that human reason could not achieve certainty in any area whatsoever. Instead, Erasmus seems to have been shocked at the apparent futility of the intellectuals in their quest for certainty. All the machinery of these scholastic minds had missed the essential point, the simple Christian attitude. The Christian Fool was far better off than the lofty theologians of Paris who were ensnared in a labyrinth of their own making. And so, if one remained a Christian Fool, one would live a true Christian life, and could avoid the entire world of theology by accepting, without trying to comprehend, the religious views promulgated by the Church.

This attempt, early in the Reformation, at sceptical 'justification' of the Catholic rule of faith brought forth a furious answer from Luther, the *De Servo Arbitrio* of 1525. Erasmus's book, Luther declared, was shameful and shocking, the more so since it was written so well and with so much eloquence. 'It is, as if one carried sweepings or droppings in a gold or silver vase.'[12] The central error of the book, according to Luther, was that Erasmus did not realize that a Christian cannot be a sceptic. 'A Christian ought . . . to be certain of what he affirms, or else he is not a Christian.'[13] Christianity involves the affirmation of certain truths because one's conscience is completely convinced of their veracity. The content of religious knowledge, according to Luther, is far too important to be taken on trust. One must be absolutely certain of its truth.[14] Hence Christianity is the complete denial of scepticism. 'Anathema to the Christian who will not be certain of what he is supposed to believe, and who does not comprehend it. How can he believe that which he doubts?'[15] To find the truths, one only has to consult Scripture. Of course there are parts that are hard to understand, and there are things about God that we do not, and perhaps shall not, know. But this does not mean that we cannot find the truth in Scripture. The central religious truth can be found in clear and evident terms, and these clarify the more obscure ones. However, if many things remain obscure to some people, it is not the fault of Scripture, but of the blindness of those who have no desire to know the revealed truths. The sun is not obscure just because I can close my eyes and refuse to see it. The doctrines over which Luther and the Church are in conflict are clear if one is willing to look and accept what one sees. And unless one does this, one is actually giving up the Christian Revelation.[16]

Luther was positive that there was a body of religious truths to be known, that these truths were of crucial importance to men, and that Luther's rule of faith—what conscience was compelled to believe from the reading of Scripture—would show us these truths. To rely on Erasmus's sceptical course was to risk too much; the possibility of error was too great. Only in the certain knowledge of God's command would we be safe. And so Luther told Erasmus that his sceptical approach actually implied no belief in God at all, but was rather a way of mocking Him.[17] Erasmus could, if he wished, hold on to his scepticism until Christ called him. But, Luther warned 'The Holy Ghost is not a Sceptic,' and He has not inscribed in our hearts uncertain opinions, but, rather, affirmations of the strongest sort.[18]

This exchange between Erasmus and Luther indicates some of the basic structure of the criterion problem. Erasmus was willing to admit that he could not tell with certainty what was true, but he was, *per non sequitur*, willing to accept the decisions of the Church. This does not show that the Church had the rule of faith;

rather it indicates Erasmus's cautious attitude. Since he was unable to distinguish truth from falsehood with certitude, he wanted to let the institution that had been making this distinction for centuries take the responsibility. Luther, on the other hand, insisted on certainty. Too much was at stake to settle for less. And no human could give another person adequate assurances. Only one's own inner conviction could justify acceptance of any religious views. To be sure, an opponent might ask why that which our consciences are compelled to believe from reading Scripture is true. Suppose we find ourselves compelled to believe conflicting things: which is true? Luther just insisted that the truth is forced upon us, and that true religious knowledge does not contain any contradictions.

The rule of faith of the Reformers thus appears to have been subjective certainty, the compulsions of one's conscience. But this type of subjectivism is open to many objections. The world is full of people convinced of the oddest views. The Reformation world was plentifully supplied with theologians of conflicting views, each underwritten by the conscience of the man who asserted it. To its opponents, the new criterion of religious knowledge seemed to be but a half-step from pure scepticism, from making any and all religious views just the opinions of the believers, with no objective certainty whatever. In spite of Luther's bombastic denunciations of Erasmus's scepticism, it became a stock claim of the Counter-Reformers to assert that the Reformers were just sceptics in disguise.

In order to clarify and buttress the Reformers' theory of religious knowledge, the next great leader of the revolt against Church authority, Jean Calvin, attempted in his *Institutes* and in the battle against the anti-Trinitarian heretic, Miguel Servetus, to work out the theory of the new rule of faith in greater detail. Early in the *Institutes*, Calvin argued that the Church cannot be the rule of Scripture, since the authority of the Church rests on some verses in the Bible. Therefore Scripture is the basic source of religious truth.[19]

But by what standards do we recognize the faith, and how do we determine with certitude what Scripture says? The first step is to realize that the Bible is the Word of God. By what criteria can we tell this? If we tried to prove this by reason, Calvin admitted that we could only develop question-begging or rhetorical arguments.[20] What is required is evidence that is so complete and persuasive that we cannot raise any further doubts or questions. The evidence, to exclude any possibility of doubt or question, would have to be self-validating. Such evidence is given us by illumination through the Holy Spirit. We have an inner persuasion, given to us by God, so compelling that it becomes the complete guarantee of our religious knowledge. This inner persuasion not only assures us that Scripture is the Word of God, but compels us upon reading Scripture attentively to grasp the meaning of it and believe it. There is, thus, a double illumination for the elect, providing first the rule of faith, Scripture, and second the rule of Scripture, namely the means for discerning and believing its message. This double illumination of the rule of faith and its application gives us complete assurance.

> Such, then, is a conviction that requires no reasons; such a knowledge with which the best reason agrees—in which the mind truly reposes more securely and constantly than in any reasons; such, finally, a feeling that can be born only of heavenly revelation. I speak of nothing other than what each believer experiences within himself—though my words fall far beneath a just explanation of the matter.[21] (Battles translation)

Religious truth can only be recognized by those whom God chooses. The criterion of whether one has been chosen is inner persuasion which enables one to examine Scripture and recognize the truths therein. Without Divine Illumination one could not even tell with certainty which book is Scripture, or what it means. One can, however, by the Grace of God, accept the rule of faith laid down in the *Confession of Faith of the Protestant Churches of France* of 1559, 'We know these books to be canonical, and the most certain rule of our faith, not so much by the common agreement and consent of the Church as by the testimonial and interior persuasion of the Holy Spirit that makes us discern them.'[22] For the elect, Scripture is the rule of faith, and, as was also claimed, Scripture is the rule of Scripture.

The fundamental evidence for the original Calvinists of the truth of their views was inner persuasion. But how can one tell that this inner persuasion is authentic, not just a subjective certainty which might easily be illusory? The importance of being right is so great that, as Theodore Beza, Calvin's aide-de-camp insisted, we need a sure and infallible sign. This sign is 'ful perswasion, [which] doth separate the chosen children of God from the castaways, and is the proper riches of the Saintes.'[23] But the consequence is a circle: the criterion of religious knowledge is inner persuasion, the guarantee of the authenticity of inner persuasion is that it is caused by God, and this we are assured of by our inner persuasion.

The curious difficulty of guaranteeing one's religious knowledge came out sharply in the controversy over Servetus. Here was a man apparently convinced by inner persuasion that there was no Scriptural basis for the doctrine of the Trinity, and convinced that the doctrine of the Trinity was false. But Calvin and his followers were so sure of the truth of their *own* religious views that they condemned Servetus to death as a heretic. The sole defender of Servetus among the Reformers, the scholar Sebastian Castellio of Basel, saw that the way to argue against the condemnation was to attack the Calvinists' claims to certainty. In his *De Haereticis*,[24] written shortly after the burning of Servetus, Castellio tried to destroy the grounds for Calvin's complete assurance of the truth of his religious beliefs, without at the same time destroying the possibility of religious knowledge.

Castellio's method was to point out that in religion there are a great many things that are too obscure, too many passages in Scripture too opaque for anyone to be absolutely certain of the truth. These unclear matters had been the source of controversy for ages, and obviously no view was sufficiently manifest so that everyone would accept it (otherwise why should the controversy continue, 'for who is so demented that he would die for the denial of the obvious?')[25] On the basis of the continual disagreements, and the obscurity of Scripture, Castellio indicated that no one was really so sure of the truth in religious affairs that he was justified in killing another as a heretic.

This mild, sceptical attitude and defense of divergent views elicited a nasty and spirited response. Theodore Beza saw immediately what was at issue and attacked Castellio as a reviver of the New Academy, and the scepticism of Carneades, trying to substitute probabilities in religious affairs for the certainties required by a true Christian.[26] Beza insisted that the existence of controversies proves only that some people are wrong. True Christians are persuaded by the Revelation, by God's Word, which is clear to those who know it. The introduction of the *akatelepsis* of the Academic sceptics is entirely contrary to Christian belief. There are truths set up by God and revealed to us, and anyone who doesn't know, recognize, and accept them is lost.[27]

Castellio wrote, but did not publish, a reply, in which he tried in a general way to show how little we can know, and the 'reasonable' way for judging this knowledge, and then applied his modest standards to the controversies of his time. The *De arte dubitandi* [28] is in many ways a remarkable book, far in advance of its time in proposing a liberal, scientific, and cautious approach to intellectual problems, in contrast to the total dogmatism of the Calvinist opponents.

Castellio's theory is hardly as sceptical as Erasmus's, and certainly does not attain the level of complete doubt of Montaigne's. The aim of *De arte dubitandi* is to indicate what one should believe, since one of man's basic problems in this age of controversy is that he believes some things are that dubious, and doubts some things that are not. To begin with, there are many matters that are not really doubtful, matters that any reasonable person will accept. These, for Castellio, include the existence of God, God's goodness, and the authenticity of Scripture. He offers as evidence the argument from design, and the plausibility of the Scriptural picture of the world.[29]

Then, on the other hand, there is a time for believing, and a time for doubting. The time for doubting, in religious matters, comes when there are things that are obscure and uncertain, and these are the matters that are disputed. 'For it is clear that people do not dispute about things that are certain and proved, unless they are mad.'[30] But we cannot resolve doubtful matters just by examining Scripture, as the Calvinists suggest, since there are disputes about how to interpret the Bible, and Scripture is

obscure on many points. On a great many questions, two contradictory views are equally probable, as far as we can make out
from Biblical texts.[31]

In order to evaluate a matter in dispute, it is necessary to
search for a principle by which the truth will be so manifest, so
well recognized by all, that no force in the universe, that no probability, can ever make the alternative possible.[32] This principle,
Castellio claimed, is the human capacity of sense and intelligence, the instrument of judgment on which we must rely. Here,
he presented a fundamental rational faith that we have the
natural powers to evaluate questions. Even Jesus Christ, Castellio
pointed out, resolved questions by using his senses and his reason.[33] In reply to the anti-rationalists, Castellio offered an answer
much like one of the arguments of Sextus Empiricus:

> I come now to those authors [presumably Calvinists] who wish us to
> believe with our eyes closed, certain things in contradiction to the
> senses, and I will ask them, first of all, if they came to these views with
> their eyes closed, that is to say, without judgment, intelligence or
> reason, or, if rather, they had the aid of judgment. If they speak with-
> out judgment, we will repudiate what they say. If, on the contrary, they
> base their views on judgment and reason, they are inconsistent when
> they persuade us by their judgment to renounce ours.[34]

Castellio's faith in our rational ability to decide questions was
coupled with a scepticism about our employment of this ability in
practice. Two sorts of difficulties exist (which if taken too
seriously would undermine Castellio's criterion completely): one,
that our faculties might not be capable of functioning properly,
because of illness or our voluntary misuse of them; the other, that
external conditions may prevent our solving a problem. A man's
vision may be poor, or he may refuse to look; or his location or
interfering objects may block his vision. Faced with these possibilities, Castellio admitted that we cannot do anything about the
natural conditions that may interfere with judgment. If one has
poor vision, that is too bad. External conditions cannot be
altered. In the light of these practical considerations, we can only
apply our instruments of judgment, our senses and reason, in a
conditional manner, being 'reasonable' in our evaluations on the

basis of common sense and past experience, and eliminating as far as possible the controllable conditions, like malice and hate, that interfere with out judgment.[35]

This partial scepticism of Castellio's represents another facet of the problem of knowledge raised by the Reformation. If it is necessary to discover a 'rule of faith', a criterion for distinguishing true faith from false faith, how is this to be accomplished? Both Erasmus and Castellio stressed the difficulty involved, especially in uncovering the message of Scripture. But Castellio, rather than employing the sceptical problems about religious knowledge as an excuse or justification for accepting 'the way of authority' of the Church, offered those admittedly less-than-perfect criteria, the human capacities of sense and reason. Since the very limitations of their proper operations would prevent the attainment of any completely assured religious knowledge, the quest for certainty would have to be given up, in exchange for a quest for reasonableness. (Thus it is understandable that Castellio influenced chiefly the most liberal forms of Protestantism.)[36]

In the struggles between the old established order of the Catholic Church and the new order of the Reformers, the Reformers had to insist on the complete certainty of their cause. In order to accomplish their ecclesiastical revolution, they had to insist that they, and they alone, had the only assured means of discovering religious knowledge. The break with authority was not in favor of a tolerant individualism in religion, such as Castellio's views would have led to, but in favor of a complete dogmatism in religious knowledge. In order to buttress their case, the Reformers sought to show that the Church of Rome had no guarantee of its professed religious truths, that the criterion of traditional authority carried with it no assurance of the absolute certitude of the Church's position, unless the Church could somehow prove that traditional authority was the true criterion. But how could this be done? The attempt to justify a criterion requires other criteria, which in turn have to be justified. How could one establish the infallibility of the Church in religious matters? Would the evidence be infallible? This type of attack finally led Protestant leaders to write tracts on the Pyrrhonism of the Church of Rome, in which they tried to show that, using the very principles of religious knowledge offered by the Church, one could never be sure (a) that the Church of Rome was the true Church, and (b) what was true in religion.[37] (Perhaps the apex of this type of reasoning was the argument that according to the Church position the Pope and no one else is infallible. But who can tell who is the Pope? The member of the Church has only his fallible lights to judge by. So only the Pope can be sure who is the Pope; the rest of the members have no way of being sure, and hence no way of finding any religious truths.)[38]

On the other hand, the Catholic side could and did attack the Reformers by showing the unjustifiability of their criterion, and the way in which the claims of certainty of the Reformers would lead to a complete subjectivism and scepticism about religious truths. The sort of evidence presented by Erasmus and Castellio became their opening wedge: The Reformers claim the truth is to be found in Scripture, just by examining it without prejudice. But the meaning of Scripture is unclear, as shown by the controversies regarding it not only between Catholic and Protestant readers, but also by the controversies within the Protestant camp. Therefore a judge is needed to set the standards for proper interpreting. The Reformers say that conscience, inner light, or some such, is the judge of Scripture. But different people have different inner lights. How do we tell whose is right? The Calvinists insist that that inner light is correct which is given or guided by the Holy Spirit. But whose is this? How does one tell 'infatuation' from genuine illumination? Here the only criteria offered by Reformers appear to be no other than just their private opinions—Calvin thinks Calvin is illumined. The personal, unconfirmed and unconfirmable opinions of various Reformers hardly seem a basis for certainty in religious matters. (The *reductio ad absurdum* of the Reformers' position in the early seventeenth century states that Calvinism is nothing but Pyrrhonism in religion.)

With each side trying to sap the foundations of the other, and each trying to show that the other was faced with an insoluble form of the classical sceptical problem of the criterion, each side also made claims of absolute certainty for its own views. The Catholics found the guarantee in tradition, the Protestants in the illumination that revealed the Word of God in Scripture. The tolerant semi-scepticism of Castellio was an unacceptable solution in this quest for certainty. (An exception should be noted: the moderate English theologian William Chillingworth first left Protestantism for Catholicism because he found no sufficient criterion of religious knowledge in the Reform point of view, and then left Catholicism for the same reason. He ended with a less-than-certain Protestantism, buttressed only by his favorite reading of Sextus Empiricus.)[39]

The intellectual core of this battle of the Reformation lay in the search for justification of infallible truth in religion by some sort of self-validating or self-evident criterion. Each side was able to show that the other had no 'rule of faith' that could guarantee its religious principles with absolute certainty. Throughout the seventeenth century, as the military struggle between Catholicism and Protestantism became weaker the intellectual one became sharper, indicating in clear relief the nature of the epistemological problem involved. Nicole and Pellison showed over and over again that the way of examination of the Protestants was the 'high road to Pyrrhonism'. One would never be able to tell with absolute certainty what book was Scripture, how to interpret it, what to do about it, unless one were willing to substitute a doctrine of personal infallibility for the acceptance of Church infallibility. And this in turn would raise a host of nasty sceptical problems.[40]

On the Protestant side, dialecticians like La Placette and Boullier were able to show that the Catholic view *'introduces an universal Scepticism into the whole System of Christian Religion.'*[41] Before adopting the 'way of authority', one would have to discover whether the tradition of the Church is the right one. To discover this, an authority or judge is needed. The Church cannot be the authority of its own infallibility, since the question at issue is whether the Church is the true authority on religious matters. Any evidence offered for the special status of the Church requires a rule or criterion for telling if this evidence is true. And so, the way of authority also, it is argued, leads straightaway to a most dangerous Pyrrhonism, since by this criterion one cannot be really sure what the true faith is.[42]

The Reformers' challenge of the accepted criteria of religious knowledge raised a most fundamental question: How does one justify the basis of one's knowledge? This problem was to unleash a sceptical crisis not only in theology but also, shortly thereafter, in the sciences and in all other areas of human knowledge. Luther had indeed opened a Pandora's box at Leipzig in 1519, and it was to take all the fortitude of the wisest men of the next two centuries to find a way to close it (or at least to keep from noticing that it could never again be closed). The quest for certainty was to dominate theology and philosophy for the next two centuries, and because of the terrible choice—certainty or total Pyrrhonism— various grandiose schemes of thought were to be constructed to overcome the sceptical crisis. The gradual failure of these monu- mental efforts was to see the quest for certainty lead to two other searches, the quest for faith—pure fideism, and the quest for reasonableness, or a 'mitigated scepticism'.

Several of the moderates, worn out perhaps by the intellectual struggles of early modern thought, could see the difficulty and suggest a new way out. Joseph Glanvill in 1665 announced that '*while men fondly doat on their* private *apprehensions, and every* conceited Opinionist *sets up an infallible Chair in his own brain, nothing can be expected but eternal* tumult *and* disorder';[43] he recommended his constructive scepticism as the solution. Martin Clifford in 1675, pointed out that 'all the miseries which have followed the variety of opinions since the Reformation have pro- ceeded entirely from these two mistakes, the tying Infallibility to whatsoever we think Truth, and *damnation* to whatsoever we think *error*,' and offered a solution somewhat like Glanvill's.[44]

The crux of the problem was summed up in the debate between the Catholic Père Hubert Hayer and the Protestant pastor David Boullier, in the latter's *Le Pyrrhonisme de l'Eglise Romaine*. Hayer showed that Protestantism leads to complete uncertainty in religious belief, hence to total Pyrrhonism. Boullier showed that the Catholic demand for infallible knowledge leads to discovering that there is no such knowledge, hence to complete doubt and Pyrrhonism. The solution, Boullier insisted, lay in being reason- able in both science and religion, and replacing the quest for absolute, infallible certainty with an acceptance, in a somewhat tentative fashion, of personal certitude as the criterion of truth, a standard which, while it may be less than desired, at least allows for some limited way of resolving questions.[45]

The problem of the criterion of knowledge, made paramount by the Reformation, was resolved in two different ways in the sixteenth century: on the one hand, Erasmus's sceptical suspense of judgment with the appeal to faith without rational grounds; on the other, the 'reasonable' solution of Castellio, offered after admitting that men could not attain complete certainty. This intellectual history proposes to trace the development of these two solutions to the sceptical crisis which had been touched off by the Reformation. Since the peculiar character of this development is, in large measure, due to the historical accident that at the same time that the sceptical crisis arose, the writings and theories of the Greek sceptics were revived, it is important to survey the knowledge of and interest in Pyrrhonian and Academic scepticism in the sixteenth century, and to make clear the way in which, with the rediscoveries of the ancient arguments of the sceptics, the crisis was extended from theology to philosophy.

II

THE REVIVAL OF
GREEK SCEPTICISM
IN THE SIXTEENTH
CENTURY

Information about ancient scepticism became available to Renaissance thinkers principally through three sources: the writings of Sextus Empiricus, the sceptical works of Cicero, and the account of the ancient sceptical movements in Diogenes Laertius's *Lives of Eminent Philosophers*. To fully appreciate the impact of scepticism on Renaissance thought, one would need studies of when these sources became available, where, to whom, and what reactions they produced. Charles B. Schmitt has done this with Cicero's *Academica*, giving a thorough picture of its impact from the late Middle Ages to the end of the sixteenth century.[1] Schmitt has found that the latin term 'scepticus', which gave birth to the French 'sceptique' and the English 'sceptic' appears first in the Latin translation of Diogenes of 1430, and in two unidentifiable Latin translations of Sextus from a century earlier.[2]

It would take painstaking work like Schmitt's to complete the picture of who read Sextus, Diogenes, and sceptical anti-rational Muslim and Jewish authors like Al-Ghazzali and Judah Halevi. Some of Schmitt's results, which came out after the earlier editions of this work, will here be incorporated into our sketch of the main ways of scepticism, especially how its form of Pyrrhonism struck Europe and became central in the intellectual battles of the late sixteenth century. We will begin with the effect of the writings of Sextus Empiricus on Renaissance thought.

Sextus Empiricus was an obscure and unoriginal Hellenistic writer whose life and career are practically unknown. But, as the only Greek Pyrrhonian sceptic whose works survived, he came to have a dramatic role in the formation of modern thought. The historical accident of the rediscovery of his works at precisely the moment when the sceptical problem of the criterion had been raised gave the ideas of Sextus a sudden and greater prominence than they had ever had before or were ever to have again. Thus, Sextus, a recently discovered oddity, metamorphosed into 'le divin Sexte' who, by the end of the seventeenth century, was regarded as the father of modern philosophy.[3] Moreover, in the late sixteenth and seventeenth centuries, the effect of his thoughts upon the problem of the criterion stimulated a quest for certainty that gave rise to the new rationalism of René Descartes and the 'constructive scepticism' of Petrus Gassendi and Marin Mersenne.

It is possible to date quite precisely the beginning of the impact of Sextus Empiricus on Renaissance thought. His writings were almost completely unknown in the Middle Ages, and only a few actual readers of his works are known prior to the first publication in 1562. So far, only two medieval Latin manuscripts of Sextus's works have been discovered: one in Paris, from the late thirteenth century, a translation of the *Pyrrhonian Hypotyposes* (oddly enough, attributed to Aristotle), and the other, a better version of the same translation, in Spain at least 100 years later.[4] Greek manuscripts began to enter Italy in the fifteenth century and gradually were disseminated throughout Europe.[5] Finally, in 1562, Henri Estienne, the great Rennaissance printer, published a Latin edition of the *Hypotyposes*.[6] This was followed in 1569, by a Latin edition of al lof Sextus's works, published by the French Counter-Reformer, Gentian Hervet.[7] (This edition consists of Hervet's translation of the *Adversus Mathematicos*, and Estienne's of the *Hypotyposes*.) The Hervet edition was republished in 1601.[8] But the Greek text was not published until 1621 by the Chouet brothers.[9] In addition, there is substantial evidence that an English translation of the *Hypotyposes* appeared in 1590 or 1591.[10] Another different English translation occurred in Thomas Stanley's *History of Philosophy* of 1655–61, subsequently reprinted three times over the next century.[11] No other editions occurred in the seventeenth century, though Samuel Sorbière began a French translation around 1630.[12] In 1718, an extremely careful edition based on the study of some of the manuscripts was prepared by J. A. Fabricius, giving the original text, and revisions of the Latin translations.[13a] In 1725, a mathematicisn named Claude Huart wrote the first complete French translation of the *Hypotyposes* which was reprinted in 1735.[13b]

The first known reference, so far, of anyone reading Sextus Empiricus is in a letter, discovered by Schmitt, from the humanist, Francesco Filelfo to his friend, Giovanni Aurispa in 1441.[14] No significant use of Pyrrhonian ideas prior to the printing of Sextus's *Hypotyposes* has turned up except for that of Gian Francesco Pico della Mirandola. Disturbed by Renaissance humanistic thought based on pagan ideas, and by the reliance of contemporary Christian theologians on the authority of Aristotle, the younger Pico was attracted in the 1490's by the ideas of Savonarola, and apparently, by some of the anti-intellectual tendencies in this movement.[15] Thus, Gian Francesco resolved to discredit all of the philosophical tradition of pagan antiquity, and during an enforced exile around 1510 set to work on his *Examen Vanitatis Doctrinae Gentium*, published in 1520.[16]

The book begins with a survey of ancient philosophy. In the second part it turns from historical exposition to theoretical discussion of the problem of certainty. Starting with chap. 20 of Book II, there is a lengthy discussion of Pyrrhonism, based on Sextus Empiricus's *Pyrrhoniarum Hypotyposes*, summarizing his views, as well as adding a good deal of anecdotal material. The next book deals with the material in Sextus's *Adversus Mathematicos*, and the last three with the attack on Aristotle.[17] Throughout the work, Pico employed the sceptical materials from Sextus to demolish any rational philosophy, and to liberate men from the vain acceptance of pagan theories. The end result was not supposed to be that all would be in doubt, but rather that one would turn from philosophy as a source of knowledge, to the only guide men had in this 'vale of tears', the Christian Revelation.[18]

Gian Francesco Pico's Christian Pyrrhonism had a peculiar flavor, which probably accounts, in part, for its failure to attract the large, receptive audience that Montaigne obtained in the late sixteenth century. If men are unable to comprehend anything by rational means, or attain any truths thereby, the sole remaining source of knowledge was, for Pico, revelation through prophecy.[19] And so, not content to advocate knowledge, based on faith alone, as presented to us through God's Revelation as interpreted by the Church, Gian Francesco Pico's view could lead to serious dangers in religious thought, by making those with the gift of prophecy the arbiters of truth.

In spite of Strowski's claim to the contrary that the book by Pico della Mirandola had a very great success, and that it dominated sceptical thought in the sixteenth century,[20] the book seems to have had fairly little influence, and failed to serve as a popularization of the views of Sextus Empiricus, as Montaigne's 'Apologie de Raimond Sebond' did later.[21] Villey says that Agrippa von Nettesheim, who will be discussed later in this chapter, used materials from Pico. If this is the case, Agrippa seems to be one of the few to do so.[22] In seventeenth and eighteenth century accounts of the history of scepticism, Pico is merely listed but not discussed in bibliographies on the subject. In Stäudlin's two volumes on the history of scepticism from Pyrrho to Kant, of 1794, Pico gets a couple of sentences, concluding 'and his entire work is not interesting enough to deserve further characterization here.'[23]

Professor Schmitt has taken issue with me on this point. He agrees that Pico's work did not have the impact of the writings of Montaigne, Bayle or Descartes, but he also insists that it was not unknown. Schmitt traces the influence, sometimes slight, sometimes more serious, of Pico's work on Nizolius, Castellani, the translator of Sextus, Gentian Hervet, various minor Italian thinkers, the authors of the Coimbra commentaries, Filippo Fabri, Pierre Gassendi, Campanella and Leibniz. Pico obviously had some influence, but he was not one of those who made scepticism a major issue of the day. Pico's possible influence on the more celebrated sceptic Agrippa von Nettesheim will be discussed later in this chapter. Pierre Villey claimed that Agrippa used material from Pico, but recent research has made it possible to reevaluate this assertion. Montaigne apparently did not know Pico's work.[24]

No one besides Gian Francesco Pico seems to have taken note

of Sextus Empiricus prior to the appearance of Estienne's edition. The learned humanists do not seem to know the name. And even in the area where Sextus shortly was to become quite important, the controversies over the merits of astrology, there are no references to him. The elder Pico della Mirandola, in his treatise on astrology, does not include him among those who wrote against astrology in ancient times.[25]

The few mentions of Pyrrhonism that occur in early sixteenth century literature do not indicate a knowledge of Sextus, but seem to stem from Diogenes Laertius, or some other ancient account of Greek scepticism. The most famous discussion of Pyrrhonism in this period is that in Rabelais, in the Third Book of *Gargantua and Pantagruel*. Panurge asks various learned men whether he should marry. One of those he asks is Trouillogan, the philosopher. After a chapter indicating the difficulty of obtaining a straight answer from Trouillogan, the thrity-sixth chapter presents a dialogue between the philosopher and Panurge. The chapter is entitled, 'A Continuation of the Answers of the Ephectic and Pyrrhonian Philosopher Trouillogan'. After Panurge has been befuddled for a few pages, he gives up questioning Trouillogan. And then Gargantua gets up and says,

> Praised be the good God in all things, but especially for bringing the world into that height of refinedness beyond what it was when I first became acquainted therewith, that now the most learned and most prudent philosophers are not ashamed to be seen entering in at the porches and frontispieces of the schools of the Pyrrhonian, Aporrhetic, Sceptic, and Ephectic sects. Blessed be the holy name of God! Veritably, it is like henceforth to be found an enterprise of much more easy undertaking, to catch lions by the neck, horses by the mane, oxen by the horns, bulls by the muzzle, wolves by the tail, goats by the beard, and flying birds by the feet, than to entrap such philosophers in their words. Farewell, my worthy, dear and honest friends.[26]

The picture of the Pyrrhonist that Rabelais presents is, one might well expect, less that of a sceptical philosopher than of a comic character. Trouillogan does not baffle and confuse Panurge by empolying standard sceptical dialectical gambits, as Moliére's Pyrrhonian philosopher. Marphurius, did to Sganarelle in *Le*

Mariage Forcé in the next century.[27] Rather, Rabelais's Pyrrhonist accomplishes his end by a series of evasions, non-sequiturs, and cryptic responses. The portrait drawn is not based on materials in Sextus Empiricus. And Gargantua's comment appears to have had little basis in fact. There do not seem to have been philosophers of the time who considered themselves Pyrrhonists.[28] The commentators explain Gargantua's remarks in the light of Cicero's *Academica*, which was then being studies, and Agrippa von Nettesheim's *De incertitude et vanitate scientiarum*, which generated some degree of interest at the time.[29] The terminology, however, seems to come from Diogenes Laertius's discussion of Pyrrho.[30]

As we shall see, the extended discussions of scepticism in the early sixteenth century, with the exception of that of Gian Francesco Pico della Mirandola, all seem to be based upon the information in Cicero, Lucian, Diogenes Laertius, or Galen.

Probably the most notorious of those who have been ranked as sceptics in this period is the curious figure, Henricus Cornelius Agrippa von Nettesheim, 1486–1535. He was a man who was interested in many things, but most notably, occult science.[32] A strange work he wrote in 1526, *De Incertitudine et vanitate scientiarum declamatio invectiva* . . . has led him to be classed as an early sceptic. The popularity of this work, its many editions in Latin, as well as Italian, French and English translations in the 16th century, plus its influence on Montaigne, have given Agrippa an undeserved stature among those who played a role in the revival of sceptical thought in the Renaissance.

The book itself is actually a long diatribe against all sorts of intellectual activity, and all types of arts. The purpose, Agrippa tells us in his preface, is to denounce those who are proud in human learning and knowledge, and who therefore despise the Sacred Scriptures as too simple and crude; those who prefer the school of philosophy to the Church of Christ.[33] This denunciation is accomplished by surveying the arts and sciences (including such arts and sciences as dice-playing, whoring, etc.), and announcing that they are all useless, immoral, or something of the sort. Practically no argument occurs, only condemnations of the sins that all human activities are heir to. Knowledge, we are told, was the source of Adam's troubles, and will only cause us grief if we pursue it.

> Nothing cen chaunce unto men more pestilente, then knowledge: this is the very pestilence, that putteth all mankind to ruine, the which chaseth awaie all Innocencie, and hath made us subjecte to so many kindes of sinne, and to death also: whiche hath extinguished the light of Faith, castinge our Soules into blinde darkenesse: which condemninge the truethe, hath placed errours in the hiest throne.[34]

The only genuine source of Truth is Faith, Agrippa announces. The sciences are simply unreliable opinions of men, which are never actually established.[35]

Not satisfied with these pronouncements, Agrippa then discussed each science and art in turn, liberally indicting the villainies of scientists and artists. The grammarians are blamed for having caused confusion about the proper translation of Scripture; the poets and historians are accused of lying; the logicians, criticized for making everything more obscure; mathematicians are castigated for offering no aid in salvation and for failing to square the circle; musicians for wasting people's time; natural philosophers for disagreeing with each other about everything; metaphysicians for having produced heresies; physicians for killing their patients; and theologians are accused of quibbling, and ignoring the Word of God.

What Agrippa advocated instead was that one should reject all knowledge, becoming a simple believer in God's Revelation. 'It is better therefore and more profitable to be Idiotes, and knowe nothinge, to beleve by Faithe and charitee, and to become next unto God, the being lofty & prowde through the subtilties of sciences to fall into the possession of the Serpente.'[36] On this note, the book closes, with a final condemnation of the scientists, 'O yee fooles & wicked ones, which setting apart the giftes of ye Ghost, endevour to learne those things of faitheles Philosophers, and masters of errours, whiche ye ought to receive of God, and the holy Ghoste.'[37]

This example of fundamentalist anti-intellectualism is hardly a genuine philosophical argument for scepticism regarding human knowledge, nor does it contain a serious epistemological analysis.

Some commentators have questioned whether it genuinely represents Agrippa's point of view in the light of his interest in occult science. Others have considered *De vanitate* more a fit of anger than a serious attempt to present doubts about what can be known.[38] A recent study of Nauert has tried to show the relationship of Agrippa's views about the occult and his 'scepticism.' It is indicated that because of his distrust of our human mental capacities, Agrippa sought truth by more esoteric means. On this interpretation, *De vanitate* represents a stage in the development of Agrippa's views, in which faith and the Bible were becoming more central elements in his quest for truth which he felt could not be carried on by reason and science.[39]

However, even though Agrippa's work does not present any sceptical analysis of human knowledge, it represents a facet of the revival of ancient scepticism, and it had some influence in producing further interest in sceptical thought. Agrippa mentions Cicero and Diogenes Laertius among his sources, and may have used Gian Francesco Pico's work.[40] I have found no reference to Sextus Empiricus in his book, though there are some sections which look as if they may have been based on that source.[41] As to influence, Agrippa's book was well known in the sixteenth century, and was used by Montaigne as one of his sources.[42]

Several of the other discussions of sceptical themes in the early sixteenth century indicate the growing interest in Academic scepticism deriving primarily from Cicero rather than the Pyrrhonism of Sextus Empiricus. The concern with Academic scepticism, as presented in Cicero's *Academica*, appears to have developed among those interested in fideistic theology. There were a number of theologians who had denounced the capabilities of human reason and had insisted that knowledge could only be obtained by faith. Cardinal Adriano di Corneto had said in 1509 'that Holy Scripture alone contains the true knowledge and that human reason is incapable of raising itself by its own resources to knowledge of divine matters and of metaphysics.'[43] Thinkers who shared this view could find support in many of the arguments of the ancient sceptics of the later Platonic Academy.

As Busson has shown, figures like Reginald Pole, Pierre Bunel and Arnould du Ferron, utilized some of the ingredients or claims of Academic scepticism in stating their anti-rationalism, and as a prelude to their fideistic appeal.[44] Several works appeared against these 'nouveaux academiciens', and the group seems to have been strong enough to create the impression that Academic scepticism was a force to be reckoned with. Besides Theodore Beza's work against the 'nouveau Academicien' (considered in the previous chapter), the work of Castellio, and Gentian Hervet's discussion of the Calvinists as new academicians in the preface to his edition of Sextus, there are not many other works that deserve notice.[45]

Cardinal Jacopo Sadoleto, Bishop of Carpentras, a friend of Reginald Pole, wrote an answer to Academic scepticism, *Phaedrus sive de Laudibus philosophiae*, probably as a result of his correspondence with Pole on the question of whether anything can be known by rational means.[46] The work was composed in 1533, and first published in 1538.[47] In the first part of the book, Phaedrus presents the views of the Academics, drawn mainly from Cicero, and advocates the fideist thesis. He points out the futility of natural philosophy. God has hidden the secrets of nature, so that we can never know them. Those who think they have discovered something about nature contradict themselves and each other in their principles and theories. We can only know God by Revelation, and not by philosophy. Moral philosophy is as hopeless as natural philosophy. Our aim is to act virtuously, not to discourse and dispute about virtue and good. Similarly, dialectic is useless, just a lot of figures and syllogisms by which one can prove anything one wants, even absurdities. So, Phaedrus contends, we can only learn truth through God's Revelation, and not through philosophy.[48]

The second part of the book gives Sadoleto's answer. In order to discover the truth, one must follow true philosophy; this philosophy is not that of the Schools, but the ancient views of Plato and Aristotle that were being revived by the humanists and Paduans in Italy. This true philosophy does not have the faults, or the uselessness of Scholastic thought, but rather it is the source of true wisdom and virtue. The cornerstone of this wonderful philosophy is reason, and by reason we can discover universals. Such a discovery will remove us from the level of opinions and doubts, and bring us to certain knowledge and happiness. The proper object of reason is truth, including, especially, religious truth. Hence, the quest for religious truth belongs to true philosophy also. Therefore, contrary to the claims of Academic fideists, human reason when properly employed can discover true knowledge, and can attain even the highest knowledge, religious truth.[49]

Cardinal Sadoleto's answer to Academic scepticism is more a panegyric on the merits of ancient philosophy and human reason than an answer to the challenge. His overwhelming faith in the capacities of rational thought does not seem to be based upon any genuine analysis or answer to the arguments of the Academics. Instead, he has tried to shift the locus of the attack, letting the Academics' battery fall on the Scholastics, while blissfully retaining unshaken confidence in man's rational powers, if properly employed.

Both Busson and Buckley assert that Sadoleto was attacking the Pyrrhonists; the occurrence of his attack, in their view, indicates that Pyrrhonian scepticism was well known in France in the early part of the sixteenth century.[50] But, there is nothing in Sadoleto's work to support this contention which seems to be based on a failure to distinguish Pyrrhonism from Academic thought.[57]

Sadoleto's work does not appear to have had much effect. In 1556 a paraphrase of it appeared in Louis Le Caron's *Le Courtisan second*.[52] Some superficial similarities between Sadoleto's book and a subsequent consideration of Academic thought by Guy de Brués (which will be examined shortly), offer suggestive, but inconclusive indications of Sadoleto's influence.[53] The possibility that Montaigne was influenced by Sadoleto, was examined carefully by Villey, and shown to be unlikely.[54]

Another humanist, contemporary with Sadoleto, who appears to have been somewhat disturbed by fideism based on Academic scepticism, was Guillaume Budé. He saw the view as casting doubt not only on the achievements of human reason, but also on the revealed truths:

Oh God, Oh Savior, misery, shameful and pitiless fault: we believe Scripture and Revelation only with difficulty. . . . Such is the result of frequenting cities and crowds, mistresses of all errors, which teaches

us to think according to the method of the Academy and to take nothing for certain, not even what Revelation teaches us concerning the
inhabitants of heaven and hell.[55]

It is hard to tell whom Budé was criticizing, since the Academics
we have met, like Phaedrus, exempt religious knowledge from
their sceptical challenge.

A decade later, a more developed interest in Academic thought
occurs in the circle around Peter Ramus. One of his friends,
Omer Talon, wrote a lengthy favorable account of this type of
scepticism, and its fideistic extension, while another, Guy de
Brués wrote a dialogue purporting to be a refutation of this point
of view. Ramus himself discussed the various sceptical schools of
philosophy, using material from Cicero, Diogenes and elsewhere.
Ramus mentioned Sextus but there is not indication that Ramus
knew his works. Ramus never indicated any real adherence to
Academic scepticism, though he found himself accused of being a
'nouveau academicien'.[56]

In 1548, Omer Talon, published a work entitled *Academica*
which was mainly a presentation of Cicero's account of Academic
scepticism. The aim of Talon's book was, apparently, to justify
Ramus's attacks on Aristotle and Aritotelianism and 'to deliver
opinionated men, slaves of fixed beliefs in philosophy and
reduced to an unworthy servitude; to make them understand that
true philosophy is free in the appreciation and judgment it gives
on things, and not chained to one opinion or to one author.'[57]

To achieve this end, Talon traced the history of the Academic
movement, as set forth in Cicero, from Plato to Arcesilas to
Carneades, and its roots in Socratic and pre-Socratic thought,
and indicated the logic by which the Academics came to the conclusion that one ought not to judge any questions whatsoever.
The Academicians', Talon asserted in accord with Cicero, 'are as
much above other philosophers as free men are above slaves, wise
men above foolish ones, steadfast minds above opinionated
ones.'[58]

This statement of the views of the Academic sceptics, by a man
who seems to have accepted their philosophy, appears to have
been the fullest, and purest presentation of scepticism à la

Cicero. Talon, however, added the new conclusion, which occurs with almost all the nouveaux Academiciens and nouveaux Pyr-rhoniens of the sixteenth and seventeenth centuries, namely the distinction between a scepticism with regard to reason and a religious scepticism.

> What is then to be done? Must we believe nothing without a decisive argument, must we abstain from approving anything without an evident reason? On the contrary; in religious matters a sure and solid faith will have more weight than all of the demonstrations of all of the philosophers. My dissertation only applies to human philosophy in which it is necessary to know first before believing. With regard to religious problems, on the other hand, which go beyond understanding, it is necessary to believe first in order to then reach knowledge.[59]

Once more, sceptical reasoning is joined to a complete fideism about matters of religious belief.

As a result of his friend Omer Talon's work, Peter Ramus found himself accused of being a 'nouveau academicien'. Ramus and Talon agreed in attacking Aristotelianism as an unchristian and anti-Christian view. Talon had gone so far as to label Aristotle as 'the father of atheists and fanatics'.[60] In answer, a professor who taught at the Collège de France, Galland, wrote *Contra novam academiam Petri Rami oratio*,[61] in which he accuses the two anti-Aristotelians of wishing to replace the Peripatetic philosophy with the scepticism of the New Academy. After having defended Aristotle from the charge of irreligion, Galland then accused Ramus and his friend of this crime because of their scepticism.

> All of the other sects, including even that of Epicurus, busy themselves with safeguarding some religion, while the Academy strives to destroy all belief, religious or otherwise, in men's minds. It has undertaken the war of the Titans against the gods. How would he believe in God, he who holds nothing as certain, who spends his time refuting the ideas of others, refuses all credence to his senses, ruins the authority of reason! If he does not believe what he experiences and almost touches, how can he have faith in the existence of the Divine Nature which is so difficult to conceive?

The aim of Ramus and Talon, according to Galland, could only be to attack the Gospel after having ruined all of philosophy.[62]

A few years later another member of the Ramist circle, Guy de Brués, wrote a much calmer criticism of the *nouveaux académiciens* in the *Les Dialogues de Guy de Brués, contre les Nouveaux Academiciens* of 1557. The author came, probably, from a family of jurists in Nîmes, and was born around 1526–36.[63] Around 1555, he assisted Peter Ramus, by translating some quotations from Latin writers for the French edition of the *Dialectique*, and in the *Dialogues*, de Brués employed some materials from Ramus.[64]

The *Dialogues* themselves are peculiar in that the characters discussing the merits of Academic scepticism are four contemporary persons, with whom de Brués was connected, the great poet, Pierre de Ronsard, Jean-Antoine de Baïf, Guillaume Aubert and Jean Nicot, all connected with the Pléiade. Baïf and Aubert argue the sceptics' cause, while Ronsard and Nicot refute it. It is hard to tell if the *Dialogues* relate to an historical setting or discussion among the Ronsard group.[65]

The *Dialogues* consist of three discussions, the first on epistemology and metaphysics, the second on ethics, and the last on law. The sceptics, Baïf and Aubert, argue that ethical and legal views are simply opinions; they outline an ethical relativism about all value considerations. They are answered, rather poorly, by Ronsard and Nicot, but seem quite convinced and happily, too, that scepticism has been refuted. The first dialogue is the most philosophical, while the last two may represent what concerned the author most, as well as an interesting realization of what the application of scepticism to problems of practical ethics might involve.

The philosophical argument for scepticism, carried on by Baïf, in the first dialogue, is based on the ethical claim that men behaving naturally are better off than in a morally ordered world, since moral prescriptions are actually fanciful opinions, which have introduced such unnatural and evil ideas as punishments, private property, etc.[66] Ronsard answers this, insisting that our value standards are based on reason, and that there is no natural, primitive goodness.[67] This Baïf challenges saying that laws are opinions which are not based on rational evidence.[68]

This leads him to a general argument against human rational achievements, based on materials from Cicero and Diogenes Laertius. Baïf's argument is not so much the epistemological analysis of the ancient sceptics as a listing of a diversity of human opinions on all matters. He is willing to abandon a central sceptical idea that the senses are unreliable but insists, even if they should be accurate, scientists and philosophers still disagree about everything; therefore, their views are not objective but only their own opinions. Lists and lists are given to show the variety and contrariety of views on all sorts of subjects.[69] As a result, Baïf suggests that truth can only be found in Scripture.[70] On the basis of this picture of how wise men disagree, Baïf rests his scepticism.

If the argument for scepticism lacks the full force of the ancient sceptic's critique of human reason, the defense of reason is even weaker. Ronsard points out that if scepticism were true, men would be reduced to beasts. But, fortunately, men of sound judgment agree, because their senses, when used properly, are accurate. The common sense and reasoning are able to discover general truths from sense information. Our intellect is able to know real essences, apart from the senses, through some sort of awareness of innate ideas. With this combination of ingredients from Plato's and Aristotle's theories of knowledge, Ronsard defends the thesis that genuine knowledge is possible even though in some matters we may be able to have only good opinion.[71] Baïf gives up his scepticism and accepts this theory, while declaiming, 'O miserable Pyrrho, who has made all into opinion and indifference!'[72] The other two dialogues follow a somewhat similar pattern, both attempting to resolve the sceptical views about variations of opinions, and attempting to convince the sceptics.

Brués, in his dedicatory epistle to the Cardinal of Lorraine and in his preface, said that his aim was to save the youths who would be led away from religion by sceptical doubts.[73] Since the sceptics in the *Dialogues* neither put up a strong defense nor fall before a convincing answer, but simply give in without much resistance, it is hard to see how the work could have achieved its stated purpose. The mediocrity of the answer to scepticism has raised some consideration of the possibility that Brués was really on the sceptic's side, and afraid to say so (though there is no indication that being a sceptic in 1557 would have brought one into serious trouble.)[74] Others have insisted that even if his refutation of scepticism is poor, there can be no doubt that Brués was trying to achieve the orthodox purpose of answering scepticism in order to safeguard religion from the doubters.[75]

But even if we cannot determine the views of the author with any precision, Brués' *Dialogues* are of interest because they show concern with, and the relevance of, sceptical ideas to discussions in the mid-sixteenth century. The work lacks any serious grasp of the force and nature of Greek scepticism, possibly because, as Villey has suggested, Brués did not know 'the irresistible arguments of Sextus', but only the less philosophical presentations of ancient scepticism in Cicero and Diogenes Laertius. The virtue of the work, perhaps lies in the face that, 'Brués sums up in a way the uneasiness and uncertainties that were felt all around and that Cicero's *Academica* helped make clear.'[76] Busson and Greenwood see Brués' efforts as part of a great picture of the early apologists fighting a complex of Renaissance monsters arising from Paduan Aristotelianism, Pyrrhonism, etc.; they ally Brués with a continuous sixteenth century movement fighting all types of 'sceptical' irreligion.[77] More likely is the view that his work represents a provisional exploration into the scepticism that arises from observing the relativity of human opinions and the possible consequences of this in applied morality, a theme which may well have come to mind in the discussions about academic scepticism and the alleged New Academy, in the circle around Ramus and the Pléiade. Brués hardly seems to have the anti-sceptical zeal of his present day admirer, Professor Greenwood.[78]

The impact of Brués' work was, if anything, slight. Busson quotes a P. Boaistuau, in *Le théatre du monde* of 1558, as referring to Brués' book against 'les nouveaux academiciens' as a source.[79] Villey has shown that the *Dialogues* were one of Montaigne's sources.[80]

These several indications of interest in ancient scepticism in the first part of the sixteenth century are what Villey called 'small fires of scepticism which cast a very pale and brief glimmer of light and then quickly disappear.'[81] None of the figures considered were particularly competent as thinkers; none of them seems to have discovered the true force of ancient scepticism, possibly because with the exception of the younger Pico, they knew only the less philosophical presentations in Cicero and Diogenes Laertius, or possibly because they were befuddled by the wealth of disagreements that have always existed among men about all intellectual topics.

At any rate, prior to the publication of Sextus Empiricus, there does not seem to be very much serious philosophical consideration of scepticism. Busson has tried to make the few works dealing with Academic scepticism signs of a vast intellectual movement growing out of the impact of Paduan thought in France.[82] However, although there was no doubt some joint development, the Aristotelianism of the Italian thinkers was far removed from sceptical thought *except for* its final fideistic conclusion. The Paduans were confirmed rationalists, whose views in philosophy were the result of accepting a certain philosophical framework and the rational constructions within it. The sceptics, on the other hand, denied or doubted the entire procedure and basis of the Aristotelians. The sole point of agreement of the two was that the articles of faith could not be supported by rational evidence, and must be believed, not proved. The few discussions of scepticism before 1562 may have occurred historically in the context of Paduan influences, but the ideas stem from ancient discussions about scepticism. Rather than being the culmination of Italian Aristotelianism, as Busson suggests, they appear to be due to isolated rediscoveries about Hellenistic philosophy. Those who write on scepticism do not seem to have studied each other, nor do they seem to be too concerned with serious philosophical analysis of sceptical problems. It is only after the works of Sextus were published that scepticism became an important philosophical movement, especially as a result of Montaigne and his disciples.

In publishing the *Hypotyposes* of Sextus in 1562, Henri Estienne set out his reasons for translating this work and his evaluation of it. The work is dedicated to Henri Memmius, with whom he first jests in a sceptical vein about what he has done. Then, he explains how he came to find Sextus, reporting that the previous year he had been quite sick, and during his illness developed a great distaste for belles-lettres. One day, by chance, he discovered Sextus in a collection of manuscripts in his library. Reading the work made him laugh, and alleviated his illness (somewhat, apparently as Sextus claimed, by scepticism's being a purge). He saw how inane all learning was, and this cured his antagonism to scholarly matters by allowing him to take them less seriously. By uncovering the temerity of dogmatism, Estienne discovered the dangers of philosophers trying to judge all matters, and especially theological ones, by their own standards. The sceptics appeared superior to the philosophers whose reasoning finally culminated in dangerous and atheistic views.

In the light of all this, Estienne suggested in his introduction first, that the work might act as a cure for the impious philosophers of the day, bringing them back to their senses; second, Sextus's book might serve as a good digest of ancient philosophy; lastly, the work should be of aid to scholars interested in historical and philological questions.

Should someone object that it might be dangerous to print the work of one who has declared war on philosophy, Estienne points out that Sextus, at least, is not as bad as those philosophers who are not able to safeguard their dogmas by decent arguments. Since Sextus's reasoning is more subtle than true, there is no reason to fear any disastrous consequences for the truth will shine more brightly for having been attacked by Pyrrhonism.[83]

In contrast to Estienne's rather light-hearted promulgation of what was later called 'that deadly Pyrrhonic poison,'[84] Gentian Hervet gave similar but more somber reasons for his edition in 1569. In his dedicatory epistle to his employer, the Cardinal of Lorraine, Hervet said that he had come across a manuscript of Sextus in the Cardinal's library at a time when he was worn out from his Counter-Reform activities and his work on the Church Fathers. He took the manuscript to read as a divertissement while travelling. Then, he reported, when he had read it with unbelievable pleasure, he thought it was a most important work, since it showed that no human knowledge can resist the arguments that can be opposed to it. The only certainty we can have is God's Revelation. In Sextus one finds many arguments against the pagans and heretics of the time, who try to measure things by reason, and who do not understand because they do not believe. In Sextus one can find a fitting answer to the *nouveaux academiciens* and Calvinists. Scepticism, by controverting all human theories, will cure people from dogmatism, give them humility, and prepare them to accept the doctrine of Christ.[85]

This view of Pyrrhonism, by one of the leaders of French Catholicism was to set the direction of one of its major influences on the next three-quarters of a century. Shortly after the publication of Sextus, however, one finds signs of its being read for philological reasons and as source material about ancient philosophy. One such reader was Giordano Bruno who discussed Pyrrhonism in some of his dialogues.

In the dialogue, *La Cena de le Ceneri*, of 1584, there is a reference to the 'efettici e pirroni' who profess not to be able to know anything.[86] In the dialogue, *Cabala del Cavallo Pegaseo*, of 1585, there are several comments about the *efettici* and *pirroni*. Saulino, in the first dialogue, asserts that these thinkers and others like them, hold that human knowledge is only a species of ignorance, and compares the sceptic to an ass unable and unwilling to choose between two alternatives. He, then, goes on to praise the sceptical point of view, asserting that the best knowledge we can have is that nothing can be known or is known; likewise, that one is neither able to be other than an ass, nor *is* other than an ass. This insight is attributed to the Socratics, the Platonists, the *efettici*, the *pirroniani* and others like them.[87]

In the second dialogue, Saulino draws a distinction between the *efettici* and the *pirroni*, which Sebasto then develops in an appraisal of scepticism. The *efettici* are equated with the Academic sceptics, those who assert nothing can be known, whereas the *pirroni* do not even know or assert this much. The *pirroni* are then portrayed as possessing a higher degree of asininity than the *efettici*.[88] In the subsequent speech by Onorio, some of the information, and the phraseology seems to come directly from Sextus's work.[89] Thus, Bruno appears to have come in contact with Sextus's writings, and to have found the ideas interesting enough to include and comment upon in his discussions of types of theories.

Another Italian writer of the period, Marsilio Cagnati, a doctor of medicine and philosophy, gives a brief discussion of Sextus and his works in his *Variarum Observationum*, of 1587. A chapter[90] is devoted to discussing Sextus's biography, his medical career, whether Sextus was Plutarch's nephew,[91] and whether he was the Sextus referred to by Porphyry. The interest in Sextus appears to be exclusively historical, rather than philosophical. A similar use of Sextus as a historical source occurs in Justus Lipsius' *Manuductionis ad Stoicam Philosophiam*. Here, in discussing the division of philosophers into Dogmatists, Academics and Sceptics, and explaining who the sceptics were and whay they believed, Lipsius referred to the writings of Sextus Empiricus.[92]

There is an interesting work by Petrus Valentia that was apparently little known in its day, but was seriously read in the eighteenth century.[93] In 1596, this author published *Academica*, a quite objective history of ancient scepticism dealing with the Academic and Pyrrhonian movements up to the middle Hellenistic period.[94] Sextus is, of course, one of the principle sources, and Valentia describes this work as one that almost everyone possesses.[95] The Pyrrhonian position is presented only in general fashion, while much more detail and criticism is given of the views of the chief Academic thinkers, Carneades and Arcesilas. At the end of the work, the author explained that he would have discussed these matters at greater length if the Greek text of Sextus had been available to him. The Latin translations, especially those of Hervet, he found inadequate for a serious examination, and so was unwilling to rely upon them.[96] Valentia claimed his survey of ancient scepticism would have two sorts of values, one philological, the other philosophical. It would help in our understanding of several ancient authors like Cicero, Plutarch and Augustine. More important, this survey would make us realize that the Greek philosophers did not find the truth. Those who seek it, ought to turn from the philosophers to God, since Jesus is the sole sage.[97] Hence, not because of the sceptical arguments, but from the study of the history of scepticism, one should presumably, discover the fideistic message, that truth is found by faith rather than be reason.

On the more philosophical side, two serious presentations, one written by Sanchez and the other by Montaigne, of the sceptical point of view appeared about twenty years after the first printing of Sextus. Before examining Montaigne's views, which will be the subject of the next chapter, I shall conclude this survey of sixteenth century scepticism with a discussion of Sanchez's work.

The only sixteenth century sceptic other than Montaigne who

has achieved any recognition as a thinker was the Portuguese doctor, Francisco Sanchez (or Sanches), 1552–1623, who taught at Toulouse. His *Quod nihil scitur*[98] has received much praise and examination. On the basis of it, the great Pyrrhonist, Pierre Bayle, in a moment of overzealousness, said of Sanchez, 'he was a great Pyrrhonist.'[99]

Sanchez was born in 1552 either in Tuy or Braga, of Jewish parents, who had become Christians. Due to the troubles of the time, both religious and political, the family moved to France, to Bordeaux. The young Francisco Sanchez studied at the Collège de Guyenne, then travelled in Italy for a while, and finally took his degrees at Montpellier. He became a teacher of philosophy and medicine at Toulouse, where he was quite successful and famous.[100]

His *Quod nihil scitur* was written in 1576 and published in 1581. This book differs radically from the works considered previously in this chapter, in that it is a philosophical work in its own right; in it Sanchez develops his scepticism by means of an intellectual critique of Aristotelianism, rather than by an appeal to the history of human stupidity and the variety and contrariety of previous theories. Sanchez begins by asserting that he does not even know if he knows nothing.[101] Then, he proceeds, step by step, to analyze the Aristotelian conception of knowledge to show why this is the case.

Every science begins with definitions, but what is a definition? Does it indicate the nature of an object? No. All definitions are only nominal ones. Definitions are nothing but names arbitrarily imposed upon things in a capricious manner, having no relation to the things named. The names keep changing, so that when we think we are saying something about the nature of things by means of combining words and definitions, we are just fooling ourselves. And, if the names assigned to an object such as man, like 'rational animal', all mean the same thing, then they are superfluous and do not help to explain what the object is. On the other hand, if the names mean something different from the object, then they are not the names of the object.[102] By means of such an analysis, Sanchez worked out a thorough-going nominalism.

From considering definitions, Sanchez went on to examine the Aristotelian notion of science. Aristotle defines science as 'disposition acquired through demonstration.' But what does this mean? This is explaining the obscure by the more obscure. The particulars that one tries to explain by this science are clearer than the abstract ideas that are supposed to clarify them. The particular, Socrates, is better understood than something called 'rational animal'. Instead of dealing with the real particulars, these so-called scientists discuss and argue about a vast number of abstract notions, and fictions. 'Do you call this science?' Sanchez asked, and then replied, 'I call it ignorance.'[103]

The method of Aristotelian science, demonstration, is next attacked. A demonstration is supposed to be a syllogism which produces science. But this wonderful method of the syllogism involves a vicious circle, rather than engendering any new information. To demonstrate that Socrates is mortal, one argues from all men are mortal and Socrates is a man. The premises, however, are built up from the conclusion: the particular, Socrates, is needed to have a concept of man and mortality. The conclusion is clearer than the proof. Also, the syllogistic method is such that anything can be proven by starting with the right premises. It is a useless, artificial means, having nothing to do with the acquisition of knowledge.[104]

Sanchez concluded, science could not be certitude acquired by definitions, neither can it be the study of causes, for if true knowledge is to know a thing in terms of its causes, one would never get to know anything. The search for its causes would go on *ad infinitum* as one studied the cause of the cause, and so on.[105]

Instead of that which he regarded as false notions of science, Sanchez proposed that true science is the perfect knowledge of a thing, ('SCIENTIA EST REI PERFECTA COGNITIO.') This notion, he insisted is perfectly clear. Genuine knowledge is immediate, intuitive apprehension of all the real qualities of an object. Thus, science will deal with particulars, each somehow to be individually understood. Generalizations go beyond this level of scientific certainty, and introduce abstractions, chimeras, etc. Sanchez's scientific knowledge would consist, in its perfect form, of experiential apprehension of each particular in and by itself.[106]

But, having cast doubt on whether anything can be known by Aristotle's method, Sanchez then analyzed his own theory of science and showed that, strictly speaking, human beings were incapable of attaining certainty. The science of objects known one by one cannot be achieved, partly because of the nature of objects and partly because of the nature of man. Things are all related to one another, and cannot be known individually. There are an unlimited number of things, all different, so they could never all be known. And still worse, things change so that they are never in such a final or complete state that they can be truly known.[67]

On the human side, Sanchez devoted a great deal of time to presenting difficulties that prevent men from obtaining true knowledge. Our ideas depend on our senses, which only perceive the surface aspects of things, the accidents, and never the substances. From his medical information, Sanchez was also able to point out how unreliable our sense experience is, how it changes as our state of health alters, etc. The many imperfections and limitations, which God has seen fit to leave us with, prevent our senses, and our other powers and faculties from ever attaining any true knowledge.[108]

The conclusion of all this, for Sanchez, is that the only truly meaningful scientific knowledge cannot be known. All that man can achieve is limited, imperfect knowledge of some things which are present in his experience through observation and judgment. Unfortunately few scientists make use of experience, and few people know how to judge.[109]

Sanchez is more interesting than any of the other sceptics of the sixteenth century except Montaigne in that his reasons for his doubts are neither the anti-intellectual ones of some one like Agrippa, nor the suspicion that knowledge is unattainable just because learned men have disagreed up to now. Rather, his claim that *nihil scitur* is argued for on philosophical grounds, on a rejection of Aristotelianism and an epistemological analysis of what the object of knowledge and the knower are like. By and large, Sanchez's totally negative conclusion is not the position of Pyrrhonian scepticism, the suspense of judgment as to whether anything can be known, but rather the more full-fledged negative dogmatism of the Academics. A theory of the nature of true knowledge is asserted, and then it is shown that such knowledge cannot be attained. The Pyrrhonists, with their more thorough-going scepticism, could neither assent to the positive theory of knowledge, nor to the definite conclusion that *nihil scitur*.[110]

Although *Quod nihil scitur* seems to present a view close to that attributed to Arcesilas and Carneades,[111] according to Cicero and Diogenes Laertius, Sanchez also appears indebted to Sextus Empiricus, who is not mentioned in the work. Carvalho suggests that both the style and some of the argument derive from Estienne's translation of Sextus.[112] And one study of Sanchez goes so far as to consider him as a successor to Sextus.[113]

The experimentalism advocated by Sanchez has been taken by some as evidence that he was not a real sceptic, but an empiricist breaking new ground, and preparing the way for Francis Bacon. On this interpretation, Sanchez is portrayed as only using sceptical arguments for the purpose of opposing the then current Aristotelian dogmatists, as Descartes later employed the method of doubt. Having destroyed the enemy, he could develop a new conception of knowledge, empirical science, which these interpreters say, would have appeared in subsequent works.[114] However, I think that Sanchez's own analysis of knowledge casts doubt on this evaluation. Unlike both Bacon and Descartes, who thought they had a means of refuting the sceptical attack, Sanchez accepted it as decisive, and then, not in answer to it, but in keeping with it, he offered his positive programme. This positive programme was offered, not as a way of obtaining true knowledge, but as the only remaining substitute because *nihil scitur*, somewhat as Mersenne later developed his 'constructive scepticism'.[115]

As to influence, Sanchez does not appear to have had very much in his day. Late in the seventeenth century two refutations appeared in Germany.[116] Montaigne probably did not know *Quod nihil scitur*, nor did its author know the *Essais*.[117] The historian of scepticism in the late eighteenth century, Stäudlin, did not find Sanchez particularly exciting.[118] It appears that only in the last hundred years has he risen to being considered 'one of the most keen-sighted and advanced thinkers of the seventeenth century,'[119] or superior even to Montaigne because, 'Sanchez was the only sceptic who at the same time was a positive thinker,' who, as a result, can be portrayed as a precursor of Descartes.[120]

It may be that Sanchez's formulation of the sceptical problem is closer to the modern idiom than that of any of his contemporaries including Montaigne, and in terms of how philosophy developed reads more like a precursor of Bacon or Descartes. (In fact, a recent unpublished English translation I have seen on Sanchez's *Quod Nihil Scitur* almost reads like a twentieth century text of analytic philosophy.)

In the revival of Greek scepticism in the sixteenth century, the thinker who most absorbed the new influence of Sextus Empiricus, and who used this material on the intellectual problems of his time was Michel de Montaigne. His Pyrrhonism helped to create the *crise pyrrhonienne* of the early seventeenth century. The next chapter will show that through Montaigne, Renaissance scepticism became crucial in the formation of modern philosophy, contrary to the view that it was only a transitional moment in the history of thought.

III

MICHEL DE MONTAIGNE AND THE 'NOUVEAUX PYRRHONIENS'

Michel de Montaigne was the most significant figure in the six-teenth century revival of ancient scepticism. Not only was he the best writer and thinker of those who were interested in the ideas of the Academics and Pyrrhonians, but he was also the one who felt most fully the impact of the Pyrrhonian theory of complete doubt, and its relevance to the religious debates of the time. Montaigne was simultaneously a creature of the Renaissance and the Reformation. He was a thorough-going humanist, with a vast interest in, and concern with the ideas and values of Greece and Rome, and their application to the lives of men in the rapidly changing world of sixteenth century France. He was alive, per-haps as no other contemporary, to the vital signficance of the rediscovery and exploration of the 'glory that was Greece and the grandeur that was Rome', as well as to the discovery and explor-ation of the new World. In both of these newly found worlds, Montaigne discerned the relativity of man's intellectual, cultural and social achievements, a relativity that was to undermine the whole concept of the nature of man and his place in the moral cosmos.

Montaigne's personal life was a microcosm of the religous macrocosm of his time for he came from a family divided by the religious conflict. His father was a Catholic, his mother a Jewish new Christian.[1] The elder Montaigne was a man interested in the varying religious and theological currents of the age; he spent much time conversing with such figures as Pierre Bunel; he studied the writings of Raimond Sebond in his search for religious understanding and peace. The young Montaigne was, like his father, a Catholic, but he was deeply interested in the various streams of Reformation and Counter-Reformation thought. At his father's urging, he translated Sebond's suspect work on natural theology. From his own interests he came to known intimately such figures as the Protestant leader, Henri de Navarre, and the great Jesuit Counter-Reformer, Juan Maldonat. During his journeys, Montaigne often stopped to talk with adherents of various religions, and showed an eager interest in their views and practices.[2]

Many sides of Montaigne meet in his longest and most philosophical essay, *Apologie de Raimond Sebond*, that amazing product of his own personal *crise pyrrhonienne*. Although as Frame has pointed out, Montaigne's Pyrrhonism pre-dates and post-dates this essay,[3] it serves as the logical focus of our attention. Villey, in his study of the sources and development of Montaigne's *Essais*, has shown that a large part of the *Apologie* was written in 1575–76, when Montaigne through studying the writings of Sextus Empiricus was experiencing the extreme trauma of seeing his entire intellectual world dissolve into complete doubt.[4] Slogans and phrases from Sextus were carved into the rafter beams of his study, so that he could brood upon them as he composed his *Apologie*. It was in this period that his motto, 'Que sais-je?' was adopted.

The *Apologie* unfolds in Montaigne's inimitable rambling style as a series of waves of scepticism, with occasional pauses to consider and digest various levels of doubt, but with the overriding theme an advocacy of a new form of fideism—Catholic Pyrrhonism. The essay begins with a probably inaccurate account of how Montaigne came to read and translate the audacious work of the 15th century theologian, Sebond.[5] Montaigne's father had been given a copy of the *Theologia naturalis* by Pierre Bunel, who said it had saved him from Lutheranism, a malady, Montaigne added, which 'would easily degenerate into an execrable atheism.'[6] Years later the elder Montaigne found the book and asked his son to translate it into French. (Montaigne jokingly claimed the original was in Spanish with Latin endings.) Thus, Montaigne's translation came into being.[7]

Thereafter, we are told, some of the readers of Sebond, especially the ladies, required some assistance in making out and accepting the message of the work, that all the articles of the Christian religion can be proven by natural reason. Two main sorts of objections had been raised, one that the Christian religion ought to be based on faith and not reason, and the other that Sebond's reasons were not very sound or good. The first point allows Montaigne to develop his fideistic theme, and the second his scepticism. He first alleges to 'defend' Sebond by expounding a theory of Christianity based exclusively on faith; second by showing, à la Pyrrho, that since all reasoning is unsound, Sebond should not be blamed for his errors.[8]

The initial statement of the fideistic message is peculiarly presented. In a rather back-handed manner, Montaigne excuses Sebond's theological rationalism by saying that although he, Montaigne, is not versed in theology, it is his view that religion is based solely on faith given to us by the Grace of God. Nevertheless there is nothing wrong in using reason to buttress the faith, 'but always with this reservation, not to think that it is on us that faith depends, or that our efforts and arguments can attain a knowledge so supernatural and divine.'[9] This leads Montaigne to assert more forcefully that true religion can only be based on faith, and that any human foundation for religion is too weak to support divine knowledge. This, in turn, leads to a digression on the weakness of present day religion because it is based on human factors like custom and geographical location. 'We are Christians by the same title that we are Perigordians or Germans.'[10] But if we had the real light of faith, then human means, like the arguments of Sebond, might be of use. Thus, in order to 'defend' Sebond's thesis that the truths of faith can be demonstrated rationally, Montaigne first made pure faith the cornerstone of religion; then allowed Sebond's efforts second-class status as aids after, but not before the acceptance of God.

To answer the second charge, that Sebond's arguments are so weak they can easily be overturned, Montaigne offered a variety of sceptical arguments.

The means I take to beat down this frenzy, and which seems fittest to me, is to crush and trample underfoot human arrogance and pride; to make them feel the inanity, the vanity and nothingness, of man; to wrest from their hands the puny weapons of their reason; to make them bow their heads and bite the ground beneath the authority and reverence of divine majesty. It is to this alone that knowledge and wisdom belong; it alone that can have some self-esteem, and from which we steal what we account and prize ourselves for.[11]

In order to excuse the weakness of Sebond's reasoning, Montaigne set out to show that nobody else's reasoning is any better, and that no one can achieve any certainty by rational means.

After offering a few anti-rational sentiments from St. Paul, Montaigne began in earnest. Man thinks that he, unaided by Divine Light, can comprehend the cosmos. But he is only a vain, puny creature, whose ego makes him believe that he, and he alone, understands the world, and that it was made and is run for his benefit. However, when we compare man with animals, we find he has no wonderful faculties that they lack, and that his so-called rationality is just a form of animal behavior. To illustrate this, Montaigne chooses examples from Sextus Empiricus, such as that of the logical dog who, supposedly, worked out a disjunctive syllogism. Even religion, Montaigne says, is not exclusively a human possession, but seems to exist among elephants, who appear to pray.[12]

The lengthy, demoralizing comparison of man and beasts was intended to create a sceptical attitude towards human intellectual pretensions. The glories of the animal kingdom are contrasted with the vanity, stupidity and immorality of the human world. Montaigne says that our alleged achievements of reason have helped us to find not a better world than the animals have, but a worse one. Our learning does not prevent us from being ruled by bodily functions and passions. Our so-called wisdom is a snare and a presumption that accomplishes nothing for us. When we look at the entire biological kingdom, and examine the lives of the animals and of man, and then compare them with the boasts of the philosophers about man's mental abilities, we cannot avoid being overwhelmed by the 'comedy of the higher lunacy'. 'The plague of man is the opinion of knowledge. That is why ignorance is so recommended by our religion as a quality suitable to belief and obedience.'[13]

Up to this point, Montaigne's sceptical attack has been little more than the anti-intellectualism of Erasmus's *In Praise of Folly*. The point is now made in terms of the rather disastrous (for the reader) comparison of men and beasts. (Anyone reading all of Montaigne's evidence on this point is bound to be shaken, even if the efficacy of human reason has not actually been disproven.) Later the more philosophical development of his scepticism will follow a brief panegyric on ignorance, and another advocacy of complete fideism. Wisdom (says Montaigne) has never been of any benefit to anyone, whereas Nature's noblemen, the recently discovered residents of Brazil 'spent their life in admirable simplicity and ignorance, without letters, without law, without king, without religion of any kind.'[14] The Christian message is, according to Montaigne, to cultivate a similar ignorance in order to believe by faith alone.

> The participation that we have in the knowledge of truth, whatever it may be, has not been acquired by our own powers. God has taught us that clearly enough by the witnesses that he has chosen from the common people, simple and ignorant, to instruct us in his admirable secrets. Our faith is not of our own acquiring, it is a pure present of another's liberality. It is not by reasoning or by our understanding that we have received our religion; it is by external authority and command. The weakness of our judgment helps us more in this than its strength, and our blindness more than our clearsightedness. It is by the mediation of our ignorance more than of our knowledge that we are learned with that divine learning. It is no wonder if our natural and earthly powers cannot conceive that supernatural and heavenly knowledge; let us bring to it nothing of our own but obedience and submission.[15]

In support of this complete fideism, Montaigne gave what was to be the favorite Scriptural text of the 'nouveaux Pyrrhoniens', St. Paul's declamation in I Corinthians, first chapter 'For it is written, I will destroy the wisdom of the wise, and will bring to nothing the understanding of the prudent. Where is the wise? where is the scribe? For after that in the wisdom of God the world by wisdom knew not God, it pleased God by the foolishness of preaching to save them that believe.'

On this inspiring note, Montaigne raised his second group of sceptical arguments which comprise a description and defense of Pyrrhonism with an explanation of its value for religion. Pyrrhonism is first distinguished from the negative dogmatism of Academic scepticism: the Pyrrhonists doubt and suspend judgment on all propositions, even that all is doubt. They oppose any assertion whatsoever, and their opposition, if successful, shows the opponent's ignorance; if unsuccessful, their own ignorance. In this state of complete doubt, the Pyrrhonists live according to nature and custom.[16] This attitude Montaigne found to be both the finest of human achievements, and the most compatible with religion.

> There is nothing in man's invention that has so much verisimilitude and usefulness. It presents man naked and empty, acknowledging his natural weakness, fit to receive from above some outside power; stripped of human knowledge, and all the more apt to lodge divine knowledge in himself, annihilating his judgment to make more room for faith; neither disbelieving nor setting up any doctrine against the common observances; humble, obedient, teachable, zealous; a sworn enemy of heresy, and consequently free from the vain and irreligious opinions introduced by the false sects. He is a blank tablet prepared to take from the finger of God such forms as he shall be pleased to engrave on it.[17]

Not only had these ancient Pyrrhonists found the summit of human wisdom, but also, as Montaigne and his disciples were to claim for the next century, they had supplied the best defense against the Reformation. Since the complete sceptic had *no* positive views, he could not have the wrong views. And since the Pyrrhonist accepted the laws and customs of his community, he would accept Catholicism. Finally, the complete sceptic was in the ideal state for receiving the Revelation, if God so willed. The marriage of the Cross of Christ and the doubts of Pyrrho was the perfect combination to provide the ideology of the French Counter-Reformation.

Montaigne then contrasted the magnificence of Pyrrhonism with the endless quarrels and irreligious views of the dogmatic philosophers of antiquity. In every field of intellectual inquiry, he found, philosophers have finally had to confess their ignorance, or inability to come to any definite and definitive conclusion. Even in logic, paradoxes like that of 'The Liar' undermine our confidence.[18] Still worse, even the Pyrrhonists become lost in the morass of human intellectual undertakings, for if they assert, as the conclusion of this survey of opinions, that they doubt, they have asserted something positive that conflicts with their doubts. (The fault, Montaigne suggested, lies in the character of our language, which is assertive. What the Pyrrhonists need is a negative language in which to state their doubts, without overstating them.)[19]

When one looks over the sad history of the efforts of the philosophers in all the various areas of their interests, one can only conclude, says Montaigne 'And indeed philosophy is but sophisticated poetry.'[20] All that philosophers present in their theories are human inventions. Nobody ever discovers what actually happens in nature. Instead, some traditional opinions are accepted as explanations of various events, and accepted as authoritative, unquestionable principles. If one asks about the principles themselves, one is told there is no arguing with people who deny first principles. But, Montaigne insists, 'Now there cannot be first principles for men, unless the Divinity has revealed them; all the rest—beginning, middle, and end—is nothing but dreams and smoke.'[21]

At this point, Montaigne is now ready for the philosophical heart of the matter, the Pyrrhonian evidence that all is in doubt. Those who contend that human reason is able to know and to understand things, will have to show us how this is possible. If they appeal to our experience they will have to show what it is we experience, and also that we actually experience the things we think we experience.[22] But, these dogmatists cannot tell us, for example, what heat, or any other quality is; in what its real nature consists. And, most crucial of all, they cannot determine what the essence of our rational faculty may be. The experts all disagree on this matter, both as to what it is, and where it is.[23]

> By this variety and instability of opinions they lead us as by the hand, tacitly, to this conclusion of their inconclusiveness . . . They do not want openly to profess ignorance and the imbecility of human reason,

so as not to frighten the children; but they reveal it to us clearly enough under the guise of a muddled and inconsistent knowledge.[24]

Our sole basis for understanding ourselves is through God's Revelation, 'all that we see without the lamp of his grace, is only vanity and folly.'[25] We are surely not the measures of ourselves nor anything else.

The Academics, in the face of this, try to maintain that although we cannot know the truth about ourselves or other things, we can assert that some judgments are more probable than others. Here, Montaigne insists 'The position of the Pyrrhonians is bolder and at the same time more plausible.'[26] If we could even recognize the appearance of truth, or the greater probability of one judgment than another, then we should be able to reach some general agreement about what a particular thing is like, or probably like. But, with each change in ourselves, we change our judgments, and there is always disagreement either with ourselves or each other. Montaigne appeals, in the style of the tropes of Sextus, to the endless variations in judgments, adding in his fideistic *leit-motif*, 'The things that come to us from heaven have alone the right and authority for persuasion, alone the stamp of truth; which also we do not see with our own eyes, or receive by our own means.'[27] Our own powers, Montaigne shows, change with our bodily and emotional conditions, so that what we judge true at one moment, we see as false or dubious at another. In the light of this, all we can do is accept the Pyrrhonian conservatism, that is, live with the laws and customs of our own society.

> And since I am not capable of choosing, I accept other people's choice and stay in the position where God put me. Otherwise I could not keep myself from rolling about incessantly. Thus I have, by the grace of God, kept myself intact, without agitation or disturbance of conscience, in the ancient beliefs of our religion, in the midst of so many sects and divisions that our century has produced.[28]

When we look at the scientific achievements of man, we see the same diversity of opinions, the same inability to discover any truth. The Ptolemaic astronomers believed the heavens moved around the earth, but Cleanthes or Nicetas, and now Copernicus claim the earth moves. How can we tell who is right? And, perhaps, a millenium hence, another theory will be offered that will overthrow these.[29] Before Aristotle's principles were accepted, other theories were found satisfactory. Why should we then accept Aristotle as the final word on scientific matters? In medicine, Paracelsus argues that previous medical practitioners were actually killing people, but he may be just as bad. Even geometry, the allegedly certain science, has its difficulties, since we can produce geometrical demonstrations (apparently like those of Zeno), which conflict with experience.[30] Recently the discoveries in the New World shake our faith in the laws offered about human behavior.

From this Montaigne went on to dwell upon the theme of Sextus's tenth trope, the variations in moral, legal and religious behavior. Armed with evidence about the savages of America, the cases in ancient literature, and the mores of contemporary Europe, Montaigne drove home the message of ethical relativism.[31]

Then, he drifted into a more theoretical aspect of the Pyrrhonian argument, the critique of sense knowledge, 'the greatest foundation and proof of our ignorance.'[32] All knowledge comes from the senses which give us our most assured information, such as 'Fire warms.' But at the same time, there are certain fundamental difficulties in sense knowledge which can only cast us into complete doubt.

First, Montaigne asks, do we have all the requisite senses for obtaining true knowledge? We have no way of telling, and for all we know we are as far removed from accurately perceiving Nature, as a blind man is from seeing colors. 'We have formed a truth by the consultation and concurrence of our five senses; but perhaps we needed the agreement of eight or ten senses, and their contribution, to perceive it certainly and in its essence.'[33]

But even if we happen to possess all the needed senses, there is a greater difficulty in that our senses are deceptive and uncertain in their operation. The various occurrences of illusions give us reason to distrust our senses. The effects of sense qualities on the passions indicate that we are too easily led to false or dubious opinions by the 'force and vivacity' of sense experiences. Besides, our sense experience and our dream experience are so much alike that we can hardly tell which is which.[34] Montaigne, then, rapidly presents the traditional Pyrrhonian case, that our sense experience differs from that of animals, that each individual's experiences differ under different conditions, our senses differ with each other and with those of other people, and so on. Thus 'it is no longer a miracle if we are told that we can admit that snow appears white to us, but that we cannot be responsible for proving that it is so of its essence and in truth; and with this starting point shaken, all the knowledge in the world necessarily goes by the board.'[35]

We find that by means of various instruments we can distort our sense experiences. Perhaps, our senses also do this, and the qualities that we perceive are imposed upon objects, rather than really being in them. Our various states of health, waking, sleeping, etc. seem to condition our experiences, so we have no way of telling which set corresponds to the real nature of things.

> Now, since our condition accommodates things to itself and transforms them according to itself, we no longer know what things are in truth; for nothing comes to us except falsified and altered by our senses. When the compass, the square, and the ruler are off, all the proportions drawn from them, all the buildings erected by their measure, are also necessarily imperfect and defective. The uncertainty of our senses makes everything they produce uncertain.[36]

The critique of sense knowledge leads to the crescendo of this symphony of doubt, the problem of the criterion. If our sense experiences vary so much, by what standards shall we judge which are veridical? We need some objective basis for judging, but how shall we determine objectivity? 'To judge the appearances that we receive of objects, we would need a judicatory instrument; to verify this instrument, we need a demonstration; to verify the demonstration, an instrument: there we are in a circle.'[37] Besides this circular problem of having to judge the judging instrument by what it judges, there is also a difficulty that will generate an infinite regress, in the search for a basis for knowledge. 'Since the senses cannot decide our dispute, being themselves full of uncertainty, it must be reason that does so. No reason can be established without another reason: there we go retreating back to infinity.'[38]

Thus, we can conclude that our ideas derive from our sense experience. Our sense experience does not show us what objects are like, but only how they seem to us. To judge of objects by our ideas is a most dubious procedure. We can never tell if our ideas, or sense impressions, do or do not correspond to real objects. It is like trying to tell whether a portrait of Socrates constitutes a good likeness, if we have never seen Socrates.

These successive waves of sceptical arguing lead, finally, to the realization that trying to know real being is like trying to clutch water. All that we can do in our present state is to go on in this uncertain world of appearances, unless God chooses to enlighten and help us. Only through the Grace of God, and not through human effort can we achieve any contact with Reality.[39]

In the course of all these wanderings, traversing so many levels and currents of doubt, Montaigne manages to introduce most of the major epistemological arguments of the ancient Pyrrhonists, albeit in a rather unsystematic fashion. Except for the critique of signs and inferences, practically all the gambits and analyses of Sextus Empiricus are touched on. Although most of the *Apologie* dwells on the foibles of mankind, their disagreements and variations, and the superiority of beasts to men, the culmination of the essay is the uncovering of the bottomless pit of complete doubt. The analysis of sense experience, the basis for any knowledge we might have, leads to the problem of the criterion, which leads in turn to a vicious circle or to an infinite regress. So that, finally, we realize that none of our views has any certain or reliable foundation, and that our only course is to follow the ancient Pyrrhonists and suspend judgment. But, coupled with this rambling yet forceful unfolding of *la crise pyrrhonienne*, Montaigne constantly introduces his fideistic theme—complete doubt on the rational level, joined with a religion based on faith alone, given to us not by our own capacities but solely by God's Grace.[40]

The *Apologie* treats the three forms of the sceptical crisis that were to trouble the intellectuals of the early seventeenth century, finally extending the crisis from theology to all other areas of human endeavor. First Montaigne dwells on the theological crisis, pressing the problem of the rule of faith. Because of our rational inability to discover, or justify, a criterion of religious knowledge, he offers total scepticism as a 'defense' of the Catholic rule of faith. Since we cannot tell by rational means which standard is the true one, we therefore remain in complete doubt and accept tradition; that is, we accept the Catholic rule of faith.

Secondly, Montaigne extends the humanistic crisis of knowledge, that type of doubt engendered by the rediscovery of the great variety of points of view of ancient thinkers. In the light of this vast diversity of opinion, how can we possibly tell which theory is true? This sort of learned scepticism is made more persuasive by Montaigne, not only by quoting ancient authors, as previous sceptics had done, but by coupling the impact of the rediscovery of the ancient world with the discovery of the New World. On the other side of the Atlantic Ocean another cultural universe existed, with different standards and ideals. On what basis could we ever judge whether the outlook of the noble savages was better or worse than our own? The message that the merits of all human opinions are relative to the cultures in which they have been produced was put forth by Montaigne, as a new type of sceptical realization, one that was to have far-reaching effects even four centuries latter.

The third, and most significant sceptical crisis precipitated by Montaigne was the crisis of scientific knowledge. In an age when the whole scientific outlook of Aristotle was under attack, the extension of the religious and humanistic crises to the scientific world threatened to destroy the very possibility of any knowledge whatsoever. Montaigne's last series of doubts, the most philosophical level of his Pyrrhonism, raised a whole series of problems, about the reliability of sense knowledge, the truth of first principles, the criterion of rational knowledge, our inability to know anything except appearances, and our lack of any certain evidence of the existence or nature of the real world. These problems, when seriously considered, undermined confidence in man's ability to discover any science in Aristotle's sense—truths about the world which are certain.

In spite of Busson's claim that Montaigne's total scepticism was not new, but was just a repetition of his sixteenth century predecessors',[41] there is a crucial novelty in Montaigne's presentation that makes it radically different from, and more important than that of any other sixteenth century sceptic. Unlike anti-intellectuals like Erasmus, Montaigne developed his doubts through reasoning. Unlike his sceptical predecessors who presented mainly a series of reports on the variety of human opinions, Montaigne worked out his complete Pyrrhonism through a sequence of levels of doubt, culminating in some crucial philosophical difficulties. The rambling musings of the *Apologie* have a method in their madness, a method of increasing the fever of doubt until it destroys every possible stronghold of rational activity.[42]

The occurrence of Montaigne's revitalization of the Pyrrhonism of Sextus Empiricus, coming at a time when the intellectual world of the sixteenth century was collapsing, made the 'nouveau Pyrrhonisme' of Montaigne not the blind alley that historians like Copleston and Weber have portrayed,[43] but one of the crucial forces in the formation of modern thought. By extending the implicit sceptical tendencies of the Reformation crisis, the humanistic crisis, and the scientific crisis, into a total *crise pyrrhonienne,* Montaigne's genial *Apologie* became the *coup de grâce* to an entire intellectual world. It was also to be the womb of modern thought, in that it led to the attempt either to refute the new Pyrrhonism, or to find a way of living with it. Thus, throughout the seventeenth and eighteenth centuries, Montaigne was seen not as a transitional figure, or a man off the main roads of thought, but as the founder of an important intellectual movement that continued to plague philosophers in their quest for certainty.[44]

Before leaving Montaigne, a word must be said on the vexing problem of his intentions. In the course of the centuries in which he has played so major a role in the intellectual life of the modern world, probably second only to that of Erasmus, Montaigne has been read both as a total sceptic, doubting everything, even the religious tenets he pretended to defend, and more recently as a serious defender of the faith. ('Montaigne not a Christian! Is it possible that this has ever been said!')[45] It is not possible here to evaluate the evidence offered on both sides, but a few observations can be made that will be developed later in this study.

The fideism of Montaigne is compatible with either interpretation. Whether Montaigne was trying to undermine Christianity or defend it, he could have made the same *non sequitur* that he did, namely, because all is doubt, therefore one ought to accept Christianity on faith alone. Such a claim was made by Hume and Voltaire, apparently in bad faith, and by Pascal and Kierkegaard, apparently in good faith.[46] The type of Christian Pyrrhonism stated by Montaigne and his disciples was taken by some Church leaders as the best of theology, and by others as rank atheism.[47]

I believe that all we can do, in evaluating the alleged fideists, is to make a probable guess, based on their character and activities, as to their sincerity. The present day scholars who find the Christian Pyrrhonism of the seventeenth century *libertins* fraudulent, while accepting Montaigne's as authentic, have a difficult problem. The views of all concerned are almost identical. The personalities, as well as one can fathom them at this range, seem capable of both a religious and non-religious interpretation. My own view is that, at best, Montaigne was probably mildly religious. His attitude appears to be more that of indifference or unexcited acceptance, without any serious religious experience or involvement. He was opposed to fanaticism, primarily as displayed by the French Reformers, but at the same time he certainly seems to have lacked the spiritual qualities that characterized such great French Counter-Reformers as St. François de Sales, Cardinal Bérulle or St. Vincent de Paul.[48]

Regardless of what personal convictions Montaigne may or may not have had, his writings were to play an enormous role in the intellectual world of the seventeenth century. The impact of Montaigne's Pyrrhonism occurred both directly through the influence of the *Essais*, which were very widely read and reprinted in the years immediately after their initial publication,[49] and also, through the more didactic presentations of Montaigne's disciples, Father Pierre Charron, and Jean-Pierre Camus, Bishop of Bellay.

Pierre Charron is a neglected figure in the development of modern philosophy, neglected because neither his thought nor his style rose to the heights of that of his mentor, Montaigne, and because of his reputation for *libertinism*. But, in his day, and in the half century after his death, Charron had an influence at least as great as his master's in furthering the break with tradition, and in forming the ideology of both the *libertinage érudit* and the French Counter-Reformation. Because he was a professional theologian, Charron was able to connect the scepticism of Montaigne more systematically with the main anti-rational currents in Christian thought, thereby providing a more thoroughgoing Christian Pyrrhonism by uniting the doubts of Pyrrho with the negative theology of the mystics. Also, since Charron was a learned doctor, he could present the case for the new Pyrrhonism in a way in which it could be studied by those trained in the Schools, rather than in the more rambling, and for its day, more esoteric, method of the French Socrates.

Who was Pierre Charron? He was born in Paris in 1541, one of twenty-five children. Somehow, he managed to attend the Sorbonne, where he studied Greek, Latin and philosophy. After this, he went to Orléans and Bourges to study law, and received the degree of Doctor of Law. He practiced in Paris for a few years, apparently unsuccessfully, since he had no connections at court. He then turned to theology, and became most renowned as a preacher and as a theologian. Queen Marguerite chose him to be her *predicateur ordinaire*, and Henri IV, even before his conversion to Catholicism, often attended his sermons. Charron's career consisted of his being *thélogal* of Bazas, Acqs, Leictoure, Agen, Cahors and Condom, and *chanoine and écolâtre* of the church of Bordeaux. In spite of his immense success, he wished to give up worldly pursuits, and retire to a cloister. However, being 48, he was turned down by two orders because of his age, and was advised to remain in the secular world. In 1589, for better or for worse, after his failure to gain admittance to a cloister, the most important event of Charron's life occurred, his meeting with Michel de Montaigne again.[50] During the remaining three years of Montaigne's life, Charron studied and conversed with him, adopting the sceptical insights of the French Socrates as his own. Montaigne found in the preacher an ideal intellectual heir, and left him a large worldly and spiritual legacy, as well as adopting him as his son. (While Montaigne was alive, the sole gift that we know he gave to Charron was an heretical work, the catechism of the extremely liberal Reformer, Ochino.) After Montaigne's death, Charron revealed the actual extent of his legacy, by showing in his writings the magnificent union of scepticism and Catholicism.[51]

(The principal source for the biographical information regarding Charron and his relations with Montaigne is the 'Eloge' to his works published in 1606 after his death by Gabriel Michel de la Rochemaillet. Recently Alfred Soman has raised serious questions about the accuracy of this account, in large measure because it cannot be checked. Montaigne never mentioned Charron in any document that survives and Montaigne's friends didn't seem to know Charron. Besides the book Montaigne gave him, the only other solid evidence is that Charron left Montaigne's sister and her husband a lot of money in his will.

From re-examiing the data Soman argues that Charron was actually a middling theologian with no serious place in the world of letters. He could only get protection from an off-beat bishop, Claude Dormy. And his works only became significant in the 1620's. More data might help determine if the official version is correct, or if Soman's suggested revision is.)[52]

Charron undertook two vast works after Montaigne had passed away. In 1594, at Bordeaux, his theological opus, *Les Trois Veritez*, appeared; it was an attack on atheists, pagans, Jews, Mohammedans, and most of all, Calvinists. The bulk of it is an answer to the Reformer, Duplessis-Mornay. The following year, after a rejoinder had come out, Charron published a much expanded edition. The other work, his philosophical opus, *La Sagesse*, appeared in 1601, a book which derives in great measure from Montaigne's *Essais*. Charron died in 1603 while preparing a revised, and slightly more moderate version of *La Sagesse*. A bitter battle was put up by his theological and philosophical opponents to prevent its being reissued, but nonetheless, in 1604, the enlarged edition appeared, to be followed by a great many printings in the early part of the seventeenth century.[53]

The *Trois Veritez* was intended primarily as a Counter-Reformation tract against Calvinism, but in order to set the stage for the main scene, Charron discussed the first truth, that God exists. Here, he presented a 'Discourse on knowledge of God', in which he linked Montaigne's fideism to the tradition of the negative theologians. He argued that God's nature and existence were unknowable because of 'our weakness and the greatness of God'.[54] The infinitude of God surpasses all possibility of knowledge, since to know is to define, to limit, and God is beyond all limitations. The greatest theologians and philosophers know neither more nor less concerning God than the humblest artisan.[55] And, even if God were not infinite, the feebleness of man is such that we still could not know Him. Very briefly, Charron mentioned some of the standard reasons, mainly drawn from the changing history of human opinions, that cast doubt on our ability to know anything natural or supernatural, and then declared, 'O sorry and paltry that is man and all his knowledge, O foolish and mad presumption to think of knowing God.'[56] The only possible way of knowing God, is to know Him negatively, knowing what He is not.[57] Positively, 'True knowledge of God is a complete ignorance of Him. To approach God is to be aware of the inaccessible light and to be absorbed by it.'[58]

Once having joined the negative theologian's contention that God is unknowable because He is infinite, to the sceptic's claim that God is unknowable because of man's inability to know anything, Charron employed this double-barrelled fideism to attack the atheists.[59] Their evidence that God does not exist rests on definitions of God, from which absurd conclusions are drawn. But their definitions are simply examples of human presumption, measuring God in human terms. Their conclusions are worthless, since the atheists cannot, and do not, know what they are talking about.[60]

The rest of the *Trois Veritez* is a typical Counter-Reformation tract in which Charron in his tedious fashion tried to show that one has to believe that God exists, that Christianity is the true religion, and that the Catholic Church is the true Church. The argument is primarily negative, showing the unreasonableness of other views in the light of historical evidence, such as miracles and prophecies. The chief negative attack is presented against the Calvinists, arguing that outside the Church no religious truth can be found, no reading of Scripture validated, and that only in accepting the Church's authority can any unique rule of faith be found. The proposed alternatives of inner light and Scripture are denied; the former because it is private, unclear and uncertain, and the latter because the sense of Scripture is indefinite unless interpreted by the Church. Scripture is solely a set of words, whose true meaning can only be divined by a true judge, the Church.[61] Charron concluded with an exhortation to the Schismatics, in which they were accused of 'insupportable pride', and 'too great presumption' for judging that the religious tradition of so many centuries is wrong, and that another ought to replace it.[62] In casting doubt on Catholicism, the Calvinists have the effrontery to make their own weak, miserable mental capacities the criterion of religious truth. Calvinism, according to Charron, is the most dangerous form of dogmatism in that it tries to make man the measure of the most important matters, and insists that the human measuring rods must be preferred to all others. Man, without certitude supplied by the Church through its tradition and authority, will fall into complete doubt, because man's own weaknesses, when unaided by other supports, naturally engender scepticism. Hence, by destroying the only solid foundation of religious truth that we have, the Calvinists make religion rest upon human judgment which is always dubious, and leave us with no certainty at all.[63]

The underlying theory of this Catholicism which is based only on complete scepticism is made much more explicit in Charron's philosophical writing, *La Sagesse*, and his defense of it, *le Petit Traicté de la Sagesse*. The major theme here is that man is unable to discover any truth except by Revelation, and in view of this, our moral life except when guided by Divine Light, should be based on following nature. This treatise of Charron's is little more than Montaigne's *Apologie* in organized form. In so ordering it, Charron presented what was one of the first philosophical writings in a modern language. Also, because it developed a theory of morality, apart from religious considerations, Charron's work represents one of the important steps in the separation of ethics from religion as an independent philosophical discipline. Charron's ethics was based on Stoic elements.

The argument of *La Sagesse* commences with the proposition

that 'the true knowledge and the true study of man is man',[64] and that the understanding of man leads in a rather startling way to knowledge of God. Part of this type of self-knowledge comes from the examination of human capacities, first of all the senses, because the Schools teach that all knowledge comes to us by means of the senses. Charron, then, developed Montaigne's critique of sense knowledge, showing that we may not have all the senses requisite for knowledge, that there are sense illusions, that our sense experiences vary with different conditions within us and in the external world. Hence, we have no way of telling which sensations are veridical, and which are not; thus, we have no way of obtaining any certain information by means of the senses.[65]

Our rational faculties are also unreliable. (Most of Charron's case is made out against Aristotle's theory of knowledge, showing that if our reason has only sense information to work with, it is bound to be as unreliable as its source.) Also, even supposedly rational men disagree about everything; in fact, there is no judgment made by man that cannot be opposed by 'good' reasons. We have no standards or criteria that enable us to distinguish truth from falsehood. We believe mainly by passion, or the force of majority pressure. In addition, the great rational minds have accomplished little besides justifying heretical opinions, or over-throwing previous views (as Copernicus and Paracelsus do.) Thus, we might as well face the fact that for all our alleged rationality, we are just beasts, and not very impressive ones. Instead of looking for truth, we ought to accept Montaigne's dictum, that 'There are no first principles for men, unless the Divinity has revealed them: all the rest is nothing but dreams and smoke.'[66]

In the second book of *La Sagesse*, Charron presented his *discours de la méthode*, the means for avoiding error and finding truth, if man's mental capacities are so weak and unreliable. We should examine all questions freely and dispassionately; keep prejudice and emotions out of decisions; develop a universality of mind, and reject any and all solutions that are at all dubious.[67] This sceptical attitude 'is what gives more service to piety, religion and divine operation than anything else',[68] by teaching us to empty ourselves of all opinions, and to prepare our souls for

God. When one applies the Charronian method of systematic doubt, until one has thoroughly cleansed the mind of all dubious opinions, then he can present himself 'blank, naked and ready' before God.[69] At this point the Revelation can be received to be accepted on faith alone. The advantage of this Pyrrhonian training is that 'an Academic or a Pyrrhonian will never be a heretic.'[70] Since the effect of the method of doubt is the removal of *all* opinions, the practitioner cannot have the wrong opinions. The only views he might have are those which God chooses to impose upon him. (If someone suggests that besides having no unorthodox views, the Charronian Pyrrhonist might well have no views at all, and end up an *indifferent* rather than a Christian, Charron answered that it was not a matter of choice; God, if He pleased, would force the decision.)[71]

The sceptical sage, having purged himself of all opinions, lives, apart from God's commands, by a *morale provisoire*, by living according to nature. This natural morality makes one a noble savage, but cannot make one a perfect human being. The Grace of God is necessary to achieve complete virtue. But, short of this aid, the best we can do in our ignorance, is to reject all supposed knowledge, and follow nature. This programme, though insufficient to give us salvation, at least prepares us for Divine aid. And, until such assistance is given, we do the best we can by being sceptical and natural.[72]

Thus, according to Charron, Pyrrhonism provides the intellectual basis for fideism. The realization of the inability of man to know anything with certainty by the use of his own faculties rids one of any false or doubtful views. Then, unlike the Cartesian *cogito* which is discovered in one's mind and overturns all uncertainty, the act of Grace provides the sole basis for assured knowledge. As long as God is active, supplying the revealed truth, man is safe in his total natural ignorance. One can toss away all rational supports in the quest for certainty, and await those from Heaven. If one accepts, as Charron apparently did, the view that God, through the Catholic Church, supplies a continuous revelation, one can undermine any evidence or standards employed to justify a rule of faith, and never lose the faith.[73]

Maryanne C. Horowitz has challenged my interpretation of

Charron's view of the source of wisdom.[74] She has insisted that a careful textual analysis shows that Charron was a Neo-Stoic. I think we would agree that Charron was very eclectic. He borrowed in large measure from Montaigne, but also from Du Vair and other classical and contemporary Stoics. Many of the writers of this period, as the late Julien Eymard D'Angers[75] pointed out, used Stoic ideas and materials. Nonetheless, what was taken as the message and meaning of Charron was the Christian Pyrrhonism. (The evidence of why he changed certain passages does not indicate that he was trying to alter his views but that he was trying to get his book approved.)[76]

Charron's complete Christian Pyrrhonism was taken, as we shall see shortly, as a two-edged sword. Many French Counter-Reform leaders saw it as an ideal philosophical basis for their position vis-à-vis the Calvinists.[77] Others perceived an insidious corrosion of all belief, natural or supernatural, in Charron's argument. Once led to doubt, the sceptic would continue to the point where he doubted everything, even the Christian truths, until he became a *libertin* and a generation later, a Spinozist. Thus, the anti-Charronians could see his work only as the 'breviary of the libertines.[78] Charron, himself, may have been a sincere fideist rather than 'a secret atheist'.[79] At least his long theological career and his pious *Discours Chretien* suggest this. But whatever his own personal views may have been, Charron was to have an influence, second only to Montaigne's, on both the avant-garde of seventeenth century French intellectuals and the orthodox theologians of the time. Those who tried to denounce him in the earth seventeenth century, were to find that a most strange alliance of powerful defenders stood guard over the memory of Father Pierre Charron.[80]

Another early disciple of Montaigne was Jean-Pierre Camus, 1584–1654, who became a doctor of law at eighteen, a priest a few years later, and the Bishop of Bellay at the age of twenty-five. He became the secretary of St. François de Sales, and spent much of his life writing pastoral novels and attacking the monastic orders. His most philosophical work, *Essay Sceptique*, was written prior to his religious life when he was only nineteen. Although he was later embarrassed by its light tone, it contained his basic fideistic point of view. Even though he later came to condemn Montaigne's style and literary form, he never gave up Montaigne's ideas, and even defended his mentor against the charge of atheism.[81]

The *Essay* was written when 'I was then fresh from the shop of Sextus Empiricus.'[82] It is an attempt of a rather novel sort to bring about Pyrrhonian suspense of judgment in order to prepare one for the true faith. As Pierre Villey has pointed out, 'The fear of Protestant rationalism is at the base of the scepticism of Camus,'[83] hence, by undermining human rational pretensions, he advanced a fideistic defense of Catholicism.

The presentation of the case for scepticism by Camus is unique, though, as he was the first to admit, the content 'has been only a pure abridgement of Sextus Empiricus', and the style is an imitation of Montaigne's.[84] Rather than rambling through the various themes of Pyrrhonian philosophy, as Montaigne did, or welding them into a battery of arguments, primarily against Aristotelianism, as Charron did, Camus created a vast structure of Hegelian thesis, antithesis and synthesis. The thesis is Academic scepticism—nothing can be known; the antithesis is dogmatism—something can be known; and the synthesis—'sceptical indifference', the Pyrrhonian suspense of judgment.

Most of the work, 300 pages of it, is devoted to the thesis. After a general attack on the bases of human knowledge, especially sense knowledge, using the familiar arguments of Sextus and Montaigne, Camus bombarded the individual citadels of dogmatism, the various sciences. Taking each science in turn, Camus tried to show that there are theoretical difficulties which make it impossible to obtain any certain knowledge, that there are insoluble practical problems, and sufficient reasons, in each case, for doubting that the sicence in question has any value. This wide-ranging discussion covers astronomy, physics, mathematics, logic, jurisprudence, astrology, politics, economics, history, poetry, grammar, and music among other disciplines. (Once again Copernicus is introduced to show that even the most accepted first principles are denied by some people.)[85] The material employed varies from arguments of Sextus, and anecdotes of Montaigne, to various observations culled from the contemporary sciences.

After developing the thesis, a half-hearted attempt is made in 50 pages to defend the antithesis, that is, to show that there is scientific knowledge. The previous battery of objections is admitted to be correct but not decisive. Some effort is made to explicate Aristotle's theory of knowledge and his account of sense errors and illusions. The general theme is that even if the sciences are full of questionable claims, there are scientific truths that no sane man doubts; that fire is hot, that there is a world, that $2 + 2 = 4$, etc.[86]

Then, Camus turned to the synthesis, Pyrrhonism, supposed to result from the two previous parts of his *Essay*. In twenty-five pages, he briefly sketched the nature of complete scepticism, and the basic arguments on which it is based—the problem of the criterion, the uncertainty of our senses, and the disagreements of the dogmatists. He showed the Pyrrhonian view on various sciences, and then said that he was not going to repeat all the detail from the first part, suggesting if one were interested, he read Sextus Empiricus.[87] (A reissue of the 1569 edition had just appeared.)[88]

Throughout the *Essay*, a fideistic note is constantly sounded, declaring that faith without reasons is best, since it is not erected on some shaky foundation which some new Archimedes may easily overthrow. The only truths men know are those it has pleased God to reveal to us, 'all the rest is nothing but dreams, wind, smoke, opinion.'[89] We ought to suspend judgment and accept the revelation with humility. 'The ancient faith' is our only basis; it cannot mislead us for it comes from God. Those who refuse to accept this Catholic fideism, and try to develop a rational road to Faith, produce only errors, heresies and Reform theories. These are the fruits of man's vain claim that his reason can find the truth. The solution to man's problems is to develop the Pyrrhonian suspense of judgment, which brings us to God in that, recognizing our weakness, we are content to believe what God tells us.[90]

Though Camus was an important figure in the seventeenth century, and his works were printed often, he does not seem to have had a great influence on the rising tide of Pyrrhonism of the time. He represents the orthodox acceptance of Christian Pyrrhonism, but his work played little or no role in the *crise pyrrhonienne* of the era. For it was Montaigne, Charron and Sextus who undermined the assurances of the philosophers, who served as the inspiration and source for the sceptics, and about whom the battles against the sceptical menace took place. Even Bayle, always on the lookout for sceptical heroes, remembered Camus for his sallies against the monks, rather than for his presentation of Pyrrhonism in the form of the Dialectic.[91]

The new Pyrrhonism of Montaigne and his disciples, dressed up in fideistic clothing, was to have tremendous repercussions in the intellectual world, in theology, in the sciences and in the pseudo-sciences. We shall turn next to the indications of these influences, before examining the *nouveaux Pyrrhoniens* in their glory, as the intellectual avant-garde of France.

IV

THE INFLUENCE OF THE NEW PYRRHONISM

In the late sixteenth and early seventeenth centuries the influence of the revival of ancient Pyrrhonism was noticeable in several areas of intellectual concern.

Charles Schmitt has shown that Pyrrhonian themes came up in the questions debated at Oxford.[1] A case that may be typical of what happened to many young English intellectuals at the beginning of the seventeenth century, is that of Joseph Mede, 1586–1638. He was at Christ's College, Cambridge from 1602–10, and studied philology, history, mathematics, physics, botany, anatomy, astrology and even Egyptology (whatever that may have been at the time). In spite of all this learning 'his philosophical reading led him towards Pyrrhonism.' But he could not accept the possibility that mind might not know reality, and might only be dealing with delusory ideas of an external world.[2]

Young Mede saved himself from the labyrinths of a total Pyrrhonism by an effort of will, first trying to find truth in physics, and then turning to studies of texts about the Millenium in the Bible. Mede became professor of Greek at Cambridge, and his masterpiece, *The Key to the Apocalypse* made him a leading figure in Millenial thinking well into the nineteenth century.[3]

Mede's case, which is probably not unique, shows how Pyrrhonism was triumphing over accepted views at the outset of the seventeenth century. Perhaps the most significant influence was that on the theological battles of the period, where the arguments and views of Greek scepticism were found most useful. The Pyrrhonian arsenal proved to be an excellent source of ammunition with wihich to devastate opponents, as well as the basis of a fideistic theory on which to justify the stand of the French Counter-Reformers.

The dialectical use of Pyrrhonism, old and new, is typified in the report about the great English Protestant controversialist, William Chillingworth, 1602–1644. Chillingworth had moved from Protestantism to Catholicism, and then to Anglicanism, both times because of the force of arguments showing that each of these theologies led to total uncertainty in religious matters. Aubrey, in his life of Dr. Chillingworth, tells us that,

> My tutor, W. Browne, haz told me, that Dr. Chillingworth studied not much, but when he did, he did much in a little time. He much delighted in Sextus Empeiricus. He did walke much in the College grove, and there contemplate, and meet with some cod's-head or other, and dispute with him and battle him. He thus prepared himselfe beforehand. He would alwayes be disputing; so would my tutor. I thinke it was an epidemick evill of that time, which I think now is growne out of fashion as unmannerly and boyish.[4]

This use of Pyrrhonism as a weapon in disputation is reflected in Chillingworth's writings, as for example, in the pattern of argumentation used in his *Discourses*.[5] In an age of controversy one can easily imagine the good use to which the style of debate offered by Sextus and his new followers could be put.

The employment of Pyrrhonism both as a means of destroying the theological opponent and as a defense of one's own faith appears in the writings of some of the major figures of the Counter-Reformation in France. For about seventy-five years after the Council of Trent, there seems to have been an alliance between the Counter-Reformers and the 'nouveaux pyrrhoniens', an alliance aimed at annihilating Calvinism as an intellectual force in France. The success of this *entente cordiale* was, no doubt, due to the fact that during this period the dominant views in Catholic theology in France were primarily negative and Augustinian; they were against scholasticism, rationalism and Calvinism, rather than for any systematic and coherent intellectual defense of the faith.[6] As we shall see, this alliance was not based only on a temporary agreement of the sceptics and the orthodox Catholics in ideas, but also was an alliance of personal friendships and mutual admirations.[7]

In the mid-sixteenth century, the Calvinist movement in France grew very rapidly, and in a few short years the country was embroiled in a civil war both militarily and intellectually. In order to save the citadels of French thought from falling into the hands of the Reformers, strong measures had to be taken. One of these measures was to put Pyrrhonism to work in the service of the Church. The first step taken in this direction was the publication in 1569 of the writing of Sextus Empiricus in Latin by the leading French Catholic, Gentian Hervet, the secretary of the Cardinal of Lorraine. As has been mentioned earlier, Hervet, in his preface, boldly stated that in this treasury of doubts was to be found an answer to the Calvinists. They were trying to theorize about God. By destroying all human claims to rationality through scepticism, Hervet believed that the Calvinist contentions would be destroyed as well. Once one realized the vanity of man's attempts to understand, the fideistic message that God can be known only by faith, not by reason, would become clear.[8]

The avowed aim of Hervet, to employ Pyrrhonism to undermine the Calvinist theory, and then to advocate Catholicism on a fideistic basis, was to become the explicit or implicit view of many of the chief battlers against the Reformation in France. By adapting the pattern of argument of the sceptics to the issue at hand, the Counter-Reformers constructed 'a new machine of war' to reduce their opponents to a 'forlorn scepticism' in which they could be sure of nothing. Beginning with the great Jesuit theologian, Juan Maldonat, who came to teach in Paris in the early 1560's (Maldonat was a friend of Montaigne and Hervet, and appears to have shared some of their fideistic ideas),[9] a type of dialectic was developed, especially by the Jesuit controversialists, for undermining Calvinism on its own grounds by raising a series of sceptical difficulties. One finds this style of argumentation, in whole or in part, in various writers trained at, or teaching in the Jesuit colleges, especially those of Clermont and Bordeaux; such writers as St. François de Sales, Cardinal du Perron, Cardinal Bellarmine, and Fathers Gontery and Veron, for example.

The attack begins with the problem of the criterion raised by the Reformation; how do we tell what is the rule of faith, the standard by which true faith can be distinguished from false faith? Luther and Calvin had challenged the Church's criterion, the appeal to the Apostolic tradition, written and unwritten, to the writings of the Church Fathers, to the decisions of Popes and Councils. But how do we tell if Luther and Calvin are right? All they offer is their opinion that because the Church can and does err in matters of faith, therefore, the Catholic rule of faith is unsafe and unreliable. But, then, as St. François de Sales observed in his *Controverses*, written in 1595,

> If then the Church can err, O Calvin, O Luther, to whom will I have recourse in my difficulties? To Scripture, they say; but what will I do, poor man that I am? For it is with regard to Scripture itself that I have trouble. I do not doubt whether or not I should adjust faith to Scripture, for who does not know that it is the word of truth? What bothers me is the understanding of this Scripture.[10]

Who is going to tell what Scripture says? It is here that a dispute exists, not just between Catholics and Reformers, but between Luther, Zwingli and Calvin as well. If the Church errs, why turn to one person rather than another in order to find the rule of faith? As St. François de Sales put the problem,

> But the absurdity of absurdities, and the most horrible folly of all, is this, that while holding that the entire Church has erred for a thousand years in the understanding of the Word of God, Luther, Zwingli, Calvin can assure themselves of understanding it well; even more that a simple parson, preaching as the Word of God, that the whole visible Church has erred, that Calvin and all men can err, dares to pick and choose among the interpretations of Scripture that one that pleases him, and is sure of it and maintains it as the Word of God; still more, that you others who hearing it said that everyone can err in matters of religion, and even the whole Chruch, without wishing to search for other views among the thousand sects which boast of understanding well the Word of God and preaching it well, believe so stubbornly in a minister who preaches to you, that you do not want to hear anything different. If everybody can err in the understanding of Scripture, why not you and your minister? I am amazed that you do not always go around trembling and shaking. I am amazed that you can live with so much assurance in the doctrine that you follow, as if you could not [all] err, and yet you hold it as certain that everyone has erred and can err.[11]

This initial version of this style of argumentation was intended to show that as soon as the Reformers had admitted that the Church could err, thus denying the traditional rule of faith, they could then be reduced to sceptical despair. If the alternative criterion of true faith is Scripture, then, according to St. François de Sales, Cardinal du Perron, Pierre Charron, Bishop Camus and others, no one can tell by Scripture alone what it says or means. All the Reformers have to offer are the dubious opinions of Luther, Calvin, and Zwingli.

This dialectical weapon was welded into the perfect machine of war by two ardent debaters of the Jesuit order, Jean Gontery and François Veron. The latter, whose presentation we shall examine, was one of the fabulous characters of the Counter-Reformation. Originally a teacher of philosophy and theology at La Flèche (when Descartes was a student there), Veron became so successful at debating and demoralizing Protestants, that he was freed of his duties as a teacher, and later from those of his order, so that he could be the official arguer for the Faith for the King of France. He was given free rein to attend Calvinist meetings and services, and to debate with Reformers, anywhere and anytime always with the King's protection. Thus he rapidly became the scourge of the French Protestants who tried desperately to avoid him and his attacks.[12]

Veron's method, which he attributed to St. Augustine, was to show, step-by-step, both that the Calvinists have no basis for calling any of their views articles of faith, and that a systematic application of a series of sceptical objections to the Reformers' rule of faith will drive them into a complete and utter Pyrrhonism. The core of Veron's reduction of Calvinism to total scepticism was an attack upon the use of rational procedures and evidence to justify any statement of a religious truth. Veron insisted that he was *not* claiming that our rational faculties or achievements were doubtful, but only that they ought not to serve as the foundation or support of the faith, which is based on 'the Word of God alone set forth by the Church'.[13]

The argument begins by asking the Calvinists, 'How do you know, gentlemen, that the books of the Old and New Testament are Holy Scripture?'[14] The question of canonicity raises a peculiar difficulty. If the Calvinists hold that Scripture is the rule of faith, then how are we to judge which work is Scripture? Calvin's answer, that it is by the inner persuasion of the Holy Spirit, first of all, admits that something other than Scripture is the rule of faith, and second, raises the problem of the authenticity of inner persuasion, that is, how to distinguish it from madness, false enthusiasm, etc. In order to do this, one would need a criterion for judging the veracity of inner persuasion. Both Pierre Charron and St. François de Sales had earlier pointed out the weakness of the appeal to inner persuasion.

> Now let us see what rule they have for discerning the canonical books from all of the other ecclesiastical ones. "The witness", they say, "and inner persuasion of the Holy Spirit." Oh God, what a hiding place, what a fog, what a night! We are not in this way very enlightened in so important and grave a matter. We ask how we can know the canonical books. We would very much like to have some rule for detecting them, and we are told of what takes place in the interior of the soul that no one sees, no one knows, except the soul itself and its Creator.[15]

In order to accept inner persuasion as the rule of Scripture, one would have to be certain it was caused by the Holy Spirit, that it was not just fantasy.

But, even if one could tell which book is Scripture, how could one tell what it says, and what we are supposed to believe? The text, as one of the later Catholic users of Veron's *Victorieuse Methode* said, is just 'waxen-natur'd words not yet senc't nor having any certain Interpreter, but fit to be plaid upon diversly by quirks of wit.'[16] And so, since the sacred writings are only words, with no instructions for reading them, one needs some rule for interpreting them. Once again, the Calvinist rule of faith, that Scripture is the rule, has to be abandoned. A retreat to inner persuasion is open to the same objections as before, that inner persuasion is unverifiable or may be illusory.

If the Calvinists say in their own defense, that they are reading Scripture reasonably, and drawing the obvious logical interferences from what it says, then they are obviously targets for 'the machine of war.' First of all, any alleged reading is uncertain and may be mistaken, unless there is an infallible rule for interpretation. To go beyond the words to draw inferences, as Veron claimed the Calvinists had done in deriving all their articles of faith, is definitely an un-Scriptural procedure. The Bible does not itself state that it is to be interpreted in this fashion, nor does it state any rules of logic. Nowhere have we any warrant for the assertion that truths of religion are to be based upon logical procedures.[17] The Reformers cried out that reasoning is a natural capacity given to man, and, also, that Jesus as well as the Church Fathers reasoned logically.[18] Veron replied that the rules of logic were set down by a pagan, Aristotle, and nobody appointed him judge of religious truth, though he may be the arbiter of valid argumentation. Neither Jesus nor the Church Fathers claimed their views were true because they were derived by logical procedures, but rather they called them true because they were the Word of God.[19] Some of the Reformers countered by attributing the rules of inference to Zeno, rather than Aristotle, to which Veron replied, 'A great objection! that it be Zeno or some other. Are they better judges of our controversies?'[20] When Pierre du Moulin, one of the leading French Protestants, countered in his *Elements de la Logique Françoise* that logic is not based on the opinions of some ancient Greeks, 'For there is a natural logic, which man naturally makes use of without bringing in anything artificial. Even peasants make syllogisms without thinking about them,'[21] Veron cried out 'poor supposed religion based upon the rules of Zeno's logic, or upon the strength of a peasant's reasoning!'[22] Something as unreliable as the natural reasoning of a peasant could hardly supply an absolutely certain basis for the faith. Finally, Veron pointed out, the application of the principles of inference was sometimes faulty; that is, people sometimes drew the wrong inferences. How could we be completely sure in *any given instance*, that a logical error had not been committed.[23] (Checking the reasoning by the rules of logic, leads to the problem Hume raised in the *Treatise*; how can you be sure the checking has been accurate?)[24]

The core of Veron's case against arriving at religious truth by reasoning from the text of Scripture was summarized into what he called his eight 'Moyens'. (1) Scripture does not contain any of the conclusions reached by the inferences of the Reformers. (2) These inferences are never drawn in Scripture. (3) By drawing inferences, one makes reason, rather than Scripture the judge of religious truths. (4) Our reason can err. (5) Scripture does not teach us that conclusions arrived at by logical procedures are articles of faith. (6) The conclusions reached by the Reformers were unknown to the Church Fathers. (7) The conclusions are, at best, only probable, and are built upon bad philosophy or sophistry. (8) Even a necessarily true conclusion drawn from Scripture is not an article of faith.[25] (Because 'nothing is an article of faith which is not revealed by God.')[26]

The kind of sceptical crisis Veron was trying to create for his Calvinist opponents was somewhat different from that of Montaigne and Charron. They, in their wholesale Pyrrhonism, tried to undermine any rational capabilities of mankind, and thereby cast doubt upon, along with everything else, the reasons of the Protestants for their faith. Veron instead, was quite careful not to advocate a 'scepticism with regard to reason' or a 'scepticism with regard to the senses'. But, he insisted on developing a scepticism about the *uses* of sense and reason in religious matters and their proper application in any given instance. In this manner, he tried to show that once the Reformers had given up the infallible judge, they could have no assured faith, because they had no defensible rule of faith. Each criterion of religious knowledge that they were driven to adopt, Scripture, inner persuasion and reason, was shown to be extremely dubious as a rule of faith, but not necessarily dubious for other purposes. And, the final conclusion of this bombardment by 'the machine of war', according to Veron was, 'O confused Babylon! O how uncertain is the supposed religion with regard to all the points in controversy.'[27] The Calvinists were cut adrift from any certainty in religious knowledge, because they had no standards for determining true religious knowledge which could not be undermined by Veron's type of scepticism.

The hardpressed Calvinists tried many ways of fighting back. By and large, they could only see Veron's attack as a scepticism with regard to both sense and reason, and therefore thought the solution to the difficulties proposed lay in destroying scepticism. Hence, several of the Reformers either tried to show the complete and catastrophic Pyrrhonism that would result from the use of

Veron's method, or to show that there is true knowledge about the world, based upon the employment of our natural faculties of sense and reason.

One of the great Protestant arguers, Jean Daillé, held that in raising doubts about the reliability of our reasoning faculties in their application to specific problems, one is opening up a type of scepticism that can be just as well employed with regard to any of our rational knowledge. If reason is sometimes deceptive, how can we be sure it is not in error with regard to mathematical and physical truths, and even such obvious truths as 'Snow is white,' 'Fire burns,' etc. 'Judge what is the desparation of these Methodists' [the users of Veron's method] who are reviving complete scepticism.[28] In order to prevent the Protestants from justifying their faith by Scripture, they destroy everything, their own grounds, science, sense knowledge, and envelop the human race 'in eternal darkness.'[29] Just because the senses and reason are sometimes in error, is no basis for never trusting them, and for not relying on them most of the time. The person who goes from recognizing that our faculties are sometimes faulty, to complete doubt of them had better go to a doctor to have his brain purged with hellebore.[30] Daillé insisted, in the Aristotelian tradition, that our faculties were naturally reliable, and could always be trusted providing the proper conditions prevailed. A man in 'bon sens' could always tell when he had reasoned properly.[31]

In his classic work, *Traicté de l'Employ des Saincts Peres*, Daillé tried to show how shaky the Catholic basis for their faith was, and how the Veronian style of argument would have devastating results if applied to the Catholic sources, the Church Fathers. On the positive side, Daillé claimed, the views of the Protestants were accepted by Catholics as well as Reformers. What was in dispute were additional views that the Catholics derived from the Fathers. Here, a type of scepticism about the meaning of historical documents could be developed. We cannot be sure that the writings of the Fathers are really by them, that they have not been altered, that they meant the same thing to the authors that they mean to us, that the authors believed, or continued to believe what they said, that the authors intended their remarks as necessary truths, or only probabilities, and so on.[32] But, Daillé said, he would not go to such lengths as Veron, and show that one could never be sure of what any Father, Council or Pope said. 'But I leave aside all of the little points, as more proper for the Pyrrhonists and the Academicians, who want to cast all in doubt, than for Christians who seek in the simplicity and sincerity of their hearts for that on which to base their faith.'[33]

Veron answered by accusing Daillé of having missed the point of the method, and of having become Daillé, '*Minister of Charenton, new Pyrrhonian, and indifferent in religion*'.[34] The problem of the application of reason to specific questions does not entail the universal scepticism that Daillé made of it and that Daillé 'has fought against his shadow'.[35] The issues that Veron had raised were twofold. First of all, since the Calvinists had insisted that the Church erred in reading Scripture, and that all men are fallible, how then could they be sure they had not erred in their own particular interpretations of Scripture? This sort of problem does not extend to scientific and mathematical reasoning, Veron said, because there the principles and inferences 'are evident and certain'.[36] But to contend that the same is true in regard to the Protestant reading of Scripture, 'Is not this to be reduced to desperation? What! So many holy Fathers have not possessed common sense, nor any of our predecessors? and the minister alone and his cobbler will have? and will be sure of it? etc. and on this assurance and folly he will risk his damnation?'[37] In this case, it appears the height of presumption and audacity to pretend that only the Protestants, in the last hundred years have been *en bons sens* and have interpreted the Bible correctly, while the entire Catholic tradition has been wrong. And so, Veron continued, the same sort of basis for doubt about Scriptural interpretation does *not* lead to a more general doubt about all our knowledge.

But then the second issue rises again. The fact that our reasonings may be 'evidents & certains' in some matters, does not mean that what is evident and certain is an article of faith. Daillé, 'This ignoramus confuses not being an *article of faith* with being dubious knowledge.'[38] Lots of things, scientific knowledge, evidences of the Christian religion, etc., are not doubtful according to Veron, but, at the same time they also are not articles of faith, and will not be such unless revealed by God.[39]

Daillé's counter-attack, developing a 'machine of war' against the Church Fathers, Veron regarded as really dangerous. The sort of reasons offered could be extended to all books whatsoever, including Daillé's. 'The same doubts could be raised as to whether Daillé's book is by him, or is supposed to be, whether he speaks in his prime, etc.'[40] Since Veron refused to admit that his knowledge of the true religious propositions was based on any evidence, interpretation of documents, or experiences, but was contained only in the revealed word of God, he could observe that Daillé's ways of arguing 'would introduce the sect of the Pyrrhonians, and indifference in religion.'[41]

Another Protestant rose to answer Veron, one Paul Ferry, who felt that the solution to Veron's bombardment lay in the defense of rationality, almost a complete reversal of the initial Calvinist position. After attempting to show that the Calvinist articles of faith are in Scripture (which Ferry actually disproved rather than established, since he pointed out the articles are simply reasonable interpretations of the text.)[42] Ferry defended the use of reason to establish religious truths. His contention was that we have a natural disposition or capacity, our rational faculties, which is a basic feature of our human nature, and which enables us to know things. By means of our 'universal experience' we tell that fire is hot, and other natural truths; by means of our 'first principles' or 'truths which are born with us' we know certain general truths like 'The whole is greater than the part'; and by means of 'judgment' we are able to discern the logical consequences of the truths we know. All this provides an indubitable basis of rationality which is natural in us. To challenge this fundamental natural rationality is to try to destroy our humanity and make us into beasts. Insofar as we have these capacities and abilities, we can then reason from what we know with certitude, and hence reason from religious truths to others.[43]

Veron brushed aside this defense of rationality by saying, 'Who doubts it? but none of this suffices to establish an article of faith, for none of this is the Word of God, and to believe is nothing but to hold something as true because God has said it.'[44] The defense of reason is not the point at issue, but only whether an article of faith can be established by reason. People like Ferry, in glorifying our rational abilities, come close to adopting what Bayle called the Socinian heresy, that reason is the rule of faith.[45] For Veron, reason may be perfectly sound and unquestionable, but this does not overcome a scepticism with regard to its use in establishing the articles of faith. Even theological reasoning, which Veron admitted could be 'necessary and certain', does not make its conclusions religious truths, unless they have also been revealed by God.[46]

The Veronian method was aimed at cutting the Reformers adrift from any criterion for ascertaining the truth of their religious convictions. To make sure that the Protestants could not justify their faith by Scripture, or reasoning from Scripture, he introduced a type of partial scepticism, applying some of the stock Pyrrhonian techniques to bring out the lack of complete certainty in the Reformers' view. Then he concluded, 'poor religion, without certitude, abandoned to the discretion of each particular bungler or other'.[47] By skillful use of the 'new machine of war', the fortress of the Protestants was reduced so that they were left holding a book whose authenticity they could not establish, and of whose meaning they could never be certain; they were left with only the fallible faculties of man to employ for a task that they could not show they were to be used for. Thus, Veron believed, he had shown the doubtfulness of the Reformers' claims, and that *their* method of establishing religious truths would lead to a religious scepticism, and, perhaps to a total Pyrrhonism.

The Protestants, however, saw that the same sceptical approach could be used on its inventor, with the same effective results. The 'new machine of war' appeared to have a peculiar recoil mechanism which had the odd effect of engulfing the target *and* the gunner in a common catastrophe. If the Reformers could not determine infallibly true articles of faith from the text of Scripture by rational means, neither could the Catholics discover any religious truths, since they would be confronted with the same difficulties with regard to ascertaining the meaning and truth of what Popes, Councils, and Church Fathers had said. As far as the Reformers could see, Veron had developed a complete scepticism to defeat them, but was just as defeated as they were by this argument.[48]

Exclude Scrpiture-Consequences, and the Papists are not able to
impugn one Tenet of the Protestants, nor are they in Capacity to prove
the first Article of the Roman Faith, namely, the pretended Infallibility
of their Church. While they wrest such Weapons out of our hands, they
at the same time disarm themselves. And by endeavouring to disserve
the Cause of the Reformed Churches, they utterly undo their own. For
if our Reasonings of this kind be insignificant against them, theirs are
also insignificant against us, and by this same art that they endeavour
to blunt the edge of our Swords, they are bound to throw away their
own.[49]

Both sides could raise sceptical perplexities as to how the others
knew and could be sure that their views were true. Once Veron
had set up his scepticism with regard to the employment of reason
in religious matters, then neither side could, any longer, adduce
satisfactory evidence in defense of its own cause. Instead, they
could concentrate their fire on enlarging the sceptical difficulties
of their adversaries.

But, Veron's 'machine of war', so much admired in its day by
the leaders of the Counter-Reformation, was not simply, as Bredvold has claimed,[50] a strategic use of scepticism to meet the chal-
lence of Calvinism. Rather, I believe, it was the result of another,
and deeper, influence of scepticism in the early seventeenth century, the alliance of Pyrrhonists and Catholics in the advocacy of
fideistic Christianity. In these terms, as we shall see, the Catholics could not be harmed by the sceptical bombardment issuing
from their own guns, since they had no position to defend. Their
view was grounded in no rational or factual claim, but in an
accepted, and unquestioned faith in the Catholic tradition. They
saw, as Maldonat had suggested, that if they once doubted this
faith by traditional acceptance, they, too, would be pulled down
into the same quicksand in which they were trying to sink the
Reformers.[51] And so, one finds an implicit fideism in many of the
French-Counter Reformers which can be, and probably was, best
justified by the explicit fideism of the 'nouveaux Pyrrhoniens'.

Beginning in the sixteenth century with Hervet and Maldonat,
one finds many indications that the leading French Catholic
figures subscribed to a type of fideism whose theoretical development and expression appeared in the writings of Montaigne and

his followers. Hervet, as we have seen, in the preface to his translation of Sextus Empiricus, had insisted on the non-rational
character of the faith, and the need to believe rather than know.
Scepticism would aid Christianity by destroying the dogmatic
philosopher, so that faith alone would remain as the road to religious truth.[52] And Maldonat's friendship with Montaigne seems,
in part, to be based upon a similarity of views. The burden of
Maldonat's theology appears to have been to free religious belief
from dialectical arguments, to deny the presumptions of the
rational man in trying to judge about religious matters. The basis
of Christianity is the faith as set forth in Scripture and tradition.
'It should be enough for us to answer, in one word, that we are
Christians, not philosophers. The Word of God is our stay; and
while we have this clear and plain, we lay little stress on the dictates of mere natural reason.'[53]

Many of the other Counter-Reformers offer no rational defense
of their position, but a fideistic view is suggested by those theologians and philosophers they admire. The Cardinal du Perron,
perhaps the greatest of the French Counter-Reformers,[54] and
himself a convert to Catholicism, spent practically no time in his
controversial writings presenting evidence for his cause, but
devoted himself primarily to pointing out the inadequacy of the
Calvinist theory of religious knowledge. The Cardinal, however,
was a friend of Montaigne's adopted daughter, Mlle. de
Gournay, and a great admirer of the fideistic writings of Montaigne's adopted son, Pierre Charron.[55] A story about du Perron
indicates his evaluation of the merits of human reason in theological matters. He was once invited to dinner by Henri III, and,
at the table, presented a discourse against atheism, offering
proofs of the existence of God. When the king expressed his
pleasure at this, and praised du Perron, the latter said, 'Sire,
today I have proved by strong and evident reasons that there is a
God. Tomorrow, if it pleases Your Majesty to grant me another
audience, I will show you and prove by as strong and evident
reasons that there is no God at all.' The King, apparently not a
fideistic Christian, became angry, and threw his guest out.[56]

Even in the case of the most spiritual of the French Counter-
Reformers, St. François de Sales, there are some signs, though

quite faint, of fideistic leanings. Although St. François condemned those 'of our time, who profess to cast all in doubt,' he
selected as his secretary the Christian Pyrrhonist, Jean-Pierre
Camus, and devoted some time to the spiritual guidance of Montaigne's heiress, Mlle. De Gournay.[57] In St. François's early
writing, *Les Controverses*, he cited Montaigne as one of the very
few contemporary authorities on religious questions. The book as
a whole is definitely not fideistic. But, in defense of miracles, a
possibly ironical passage from the *Essais* is quoted 'to prove the
faith by miracles'.[58]

There are many other indications of the links between the
Counter-Reformers and the 'nouveau Pyrrhonisme'. Apparently,
even to Montaigne's surprise, the Vatican expressed only the
mildest disapproval of the views in the *Essais*, and invited him to
devote himself to writing in defense of the Church.[59] Most of the
disciples of Montaigne in the early seventeenth century received
protection and encouragement from Cardinals Richelieu and
Mazarin.[60] The Bishop of Boulogne, Claude Dormy, was a great
admirer of Charron, and helped to obtain an approbation for *La
Sagesse*. The bishop was so fideistically inclined that he disap-
proved of Charron's few efforts at moderating his Christian
Pyrrhonism in the face of opposition from the Sorbonne.[61] The
King's Confessor, the Jesuit Nicolas Caussin, printed an adaption
of the core of Charron's fideistic scepticism in his *La Cour
Sainte*.[62] The Cardinal Bérulle in his critique of rational knowledge offered a view strikingly like that of Charron.[63] In the
1620's, when Charron had been accused of being a 'secret
atheist',[64] he was defended first by Father Ogier,[65] and then by
the great Jansenist theologian, Saint-Cyran, (Jean Duvergier du
Hauranne). The latter, who said that the Cardinal du Perron had
recommended Charron's theology to him, insisted that it was, by-
and-large, just good Augustinianism, and that Charron's Christian Pyrrhonism was in accord with the best in religious thought
as well as Scripture.[66]

These indications of the approval of the 'nouveau Pyrrhonisme',
and the 'nouveaux Pyrrhoniens' by many of the leading spirits of
the Counter-Reformation in France, illustrate, I believe, the
paramount influence of the revival of Greek scepticism in the

period. The aim of the Christian Pyrrhonism of people like Montaigne and Charron may have been 'to enlarge the distance between reason and revelation' and 'to construct a morality not rational, but rationalistic, in which religion occupies only a secondary place.'[67] But, nonetheless, the scepticism of Montaigne, Charron, Camus, and Sextus Empiricus supplied both a method for fighting Calvinism (also, as the Reformers saw, just as good a method for fighting Catholicism), and a rationale for the use of the method. The sceptical puzzles aid in destroying the opponent, while fideism prevents self-destruction as well. The sceptical theory of religous knowledge advanced by Montaigne and his disciples provided a theoretical framework in which the 'machine of war' could operate without firing at the gunner as well, a framework in which a total scepticism on the rational plane became the preparation for the revelation of the true faith.

Since the type of sceptical method used by the Counter-Reformers could be applied to any theory of religious knowledge, safety and salvation lay in having no theory. They could advocate their Catholicism on faith alone, while demolishing their enemies by engulfing them in sceptical difficulties. By allying themselves with the 'nouveaux Pyrrhoniens', the Counter-Reformers could get their ammunition from the sceptics, as well as a fideistic 'justification' for their own cause. The Calvinists could cry out that both the Protestants and the Catholics would be involved in a common catastrophe, since both had to base their views on documents, pronouncements, and reasoning about them. But, the Catholics seem to have been unaffected by these cries, unaffected, I believe, because they had accepted the claim of the Christian Pyrrhonists that scepticism is the way to God. Man's efforts can be only negative, eliminating false and doubtful beliefs from his mind. Any positive content that remains is supplied by God, not man. As long as God is on the Catholic side, the general doubts of Montaigne, and the applied doubts of Veron, serve only the beneficial function of curing one of false beliefs, and keeping one from false religons. If one gives up the attempt to understand religious matters, one is saved from reaching heretical conclusions. God, through Revelation, keeps one in the true religion. The rational Catholic and the rational Protestant may be demolished by the 'machine of war,' but the man of faith is saved through God, not be reason or evidence. The true believer is at the mercy, as well as under the protection of God.

Any change from the traditional Church would involve a human decision as to what is right or wrong in religion. In order to make such an important decision, one ought to have adequate reasons. Hence, the Counter-Reformers, and their sceptical allies tried to show that the Reformers were making reason the rule of faith. Having accomplished this, they tried to develop either a scepticism with regard to the use of reason in religion, or a scepticism with regard to reason itself. Meanwhile, as far as both the Counter-Reformers and the sceptics were concerned, the true religion was constantly revealed by God, through His Church. By remaining in the traditional camp, and standing on the Rock of Faith, they could blast away at the new dogmatists, the Calvinists, the new defenders of the efficacy of man's rational faculties in determining religious truth. All through the battle the Catholics could rest secure in their fideistic fortress, providing, of course, that God, on their side, sustained them. What Mlle. de Gournay said of her religious beliefs, and of Montaigne's, was, in large measure true also of the French Counter-Reformers. The touchstone, for them, of true religion was

> the Holy Law of our fathers, their tradition and authority. Who can also suffer these new Titans of our time, these climbers who think they will reach knowledge of God by their own means and circumscribe Him, His works and their beliefs within the limits of their means and reason: not wanting to accept anything as true if it does not seem probable to them.[68]

Besides influencing the theological struggles of the time, the revival of Pyrrhonism also had an effect on some of the other intellectual struggles of the later Renaissance, especially those concerned with the pseudosciences of astrology, alchemy, sorcery, etc., and those concerned with the conflict between the Aristotelian sciences and the 'new philosophy'. As early as 1581, one finds a discussion of Pyrrhonism in Jean Bodin's work on *De la Demonomanie des Sorciers*, where as a prelude to discussing his topic, Bodin felt it necessary to deal with the criterion problem, the rule of truth, in order to show that the evidence he had to offer was sound. Three theories of knowledge are outlined, that of Plato and Democritus that only the intellect is the judge of truth, next a crude empiricism attributed to Aristotle, and lastly the total scepticism of Pyrrho (as well, according to Bodin, as that of Nicholas of Cusa). All these views, and especially scepticism, are rejected in favor of a sophisticated empiricism, which Bodin called the common-sense theory of Theophrastus, which allows for truths derived from interpretations of sense experience. On this basis, his evidence about 'demonomanie' is then justified.[69]

Around the turn of the century, the opponents of astrology apparently started introducing material from Sextus Empiricus, especially from his work against astrologers. In 1601, John Chamber opposed the astrologers, and used as part of his source material some items from Sextus.[70] A defender of this 'science', Sir Christopher Heydon published a reply, in which Sextus is listed on the title-page as one of those who will be answered.[71] One of the charges against Chamber is that he did not admit how much of his book was taken from Sextus.[72] Heydon made only a slight effort at refuting Sextus, pointing out that the Pyrrhonists doubted everything, merely cavilled against astrology in the same way as they opposed all sciences, hence they should not now be taken seriously.[73]

A French spiritologist, Pierre Le Loyer, took the Pyrrhonian criticisms of human knowledge much more seriously, and added an eleven page section to his *Discours, et Histoires des Spectres*, answering this view.[74] What apparently disturbed him was that the sceptics challenged the reliability of sense information, for he intended to base his case on a variety of testimonials, apparitions, etc. So, Le Loyer first sketched out the history of ancient scepticism up to Sextus Empiricus, (against whose works, he claimed, 'Francesco Pico, Count of Mirandola, nephew of Gian Pico, the Phoenix of his age, would have written and refuted all the arguments of the Pyrrhonians and Sceptics.')[75] Then, he turned to his refutation of the sceptical critique of sense knowledge, offering essentially an Aristotelian answer, that when our senses are operating properly, under proper conditions, we then perceive true information, and that, when necessary, our intellect can correct our sense reports and hence, discover reliable knowledge about the sensible world.[76]

Other important evidences of sceptical claims being used in the battles against the pseudo-sciences are the attacks on alchemy of Fathers Mersenne and Gassendi. Mersenne, in his *Verité des Sciences* of 1625, presented a dialogue among a sceptic, and an alchemist, and a Christian philosopher, and although the main aim of the work is to attack the sceptic, the latter lands many telling blows against the alchemist by using the standard sceptical materials from Sextus against the alleged science of alchemy.[77] Gassendi, himself an avowed Pyrrhonist at the time, wrote a refutation, at Mersenne's request, of the Rosicrucian theorist, Robert Fludd, in which the sceptical attitude is employed to demolish Fludd's views.[78]

In the wars against Scholastic science, one finds stock arguments from the sceptical tradition being employed. Both Sir Francis Bacon and Gassendi employed some of the criticisms of sense knowledge in their fight against the Aristotelianism of the Schools. In fact, Bacon's type of protest against traditional philosophy and science, was seen by Mersenne as an imitation of the Pyrrhonians.[79] And Gassendi, in his first work, one of the strongest anti-Aristotelian documents of the time, marshalled all the routines of the Pyrrhonian tradition into one vast denunciation, concluding that nothing can be known, and no science is possible, least of all an Aristotelian science.[80] One finds that one of the common characteristics of the 'new philosophers' is their acceptance of the Pyrrhonian critique of sense knowledge, and its employment as a crucial blow against Aristotelianism.

But, scepticism was not always on the side of the angels. At the same time that Pyrrhonian arguments were being employed in order to attack the pseudo-scientists and the Scholastics, some of the sceptics were using the same material against the 'new science' and mathematics. (It should be mentioned that one of the greatest sceptics of the later seventeenth century, Joseph Glanvill, employed his sceptical skill to support his belief in witches, by demolishing the dogmatism of the anti-watch faction.)[81] Those whom I shall call the 'humanistic sceptics', men such as François de La Mothe Le Vayer, and Guy Patin, as well as the pure Pyrrhonist, Samuel Sorbière, seemed to have little or no appreciation of the scientific revolution going on around them, and regarded the new theories as either another form of dogmatism, replacing the former ones, or insisted on suspending judgment on all scientific theories, new or old. Patin, when rector of the medical school of the Sorbonne, opposed any innovations in teaching, and insisted on a Pyrrhonian conservatism, sticking to the traditionally accepted views of the Greeks.[82] La Mothe Le Vayer regarded any and all scientific research as a form of human arrogance and impiety, which ought to be abandoned for complete doubt and pure fideism. The value of scepticism for the sciences, he claimed, was that a proper indoctrination in Pyrrhonism would lead one to give up all scientific pretensions.[83] Sorbière, Gassendi's henchman, wanted to suspend judgment even about scientific hypotheses if they went beyond appearances.[84]

With regard to mathematics, the sceptical atmosphere of the early seventeenth century was apparently strong enough to require that some defense be given for this 'queen of the sciences'. There is a work by Wilhelm Languis, of 1656, on the truth of geometry, against sceptics and Sextus Empiricus.[85] And Mersenne devoted most of his *Verité des Sciences* to exhibiting the vast number and variety of mathematical truths, as the best means for 'overthrowing Pyrrhonism.[86]

By and large, the revival of Greek scepticism seems to have had great influence on the intellectual controversies of the early seventeenth century. Its first and main impact was upon theology, probably because the key issue in dispute, the rule of faith, set up a form of the classical Pyrrhonian problem of the criterion. Also, the fideism involved in the 'nouveau Pyrrhonisme', served as an ideal defense for those who employed the sceptical gambits in the religious controversies of the time. As the science of Aristotle began to lose its authority, and competing scientific and pseudo-scientific theories arose, another area for the application of Pyrrhonian arguments came to the fore. In this latter area, the development of the kind of sceptical crisis that already had appeared in theology, was to occur. The 'nouveau Pyrrhonisme' was to envelop all the human sciences and philosophy in a complete sceptical crisis, out of which modern philosophy, and the scientific outlook finally emerged.

We will turn now to the high point of the 'nouveau Pyrrhonisme', the point at which it was no longer merely an ally of the
Counter-Reformation in France and an aid to anyone fighting in
the scientific controversies of the time, but the avant-garde view
of the new intellectual era dawning in early seventeenth century
France.

V

THE LIBERTINS
ÉRUDITS

In the early part of the seventeenth century, a broader form of the scepticism of Montaigne, Charron and Camus blossomed forth in France, and flourished briefly as the view of the bright young men of the time. The wider popularity and application of the 'nouveau Pyrrhonisme' brought out more sharply its implications for both religious and science. This, in turn, gave rise to a series of attempts, culminating in the heroic failure of René Descartes, to save human knowledge by destroying scepticism.

The sceptics of the early seventeenth century, the so-called 'libertins érudits', were, in part, direct line descendents of Montaigne and Charron, in part, children of Sextus Empiricus, and, in part, simply anti-Aristotelians. Most of them belonged, by virtue of offices secured by Richelieu and Mazarin, to intellectual circles in and around the palace. They were humanistic scholars prepared to push France into its Golden Age, *libertins* prepared to break with tradition and to launch a new tradition.

These figures, Gabriel Naudé, librarian to Richelieu and Mazarin and secretary to Cardinal Bagni; Guy Patin, a learned medical doctor who became Rector of the medical school of the Sorbonne; Leonard Marandé, a secretary of Richelieu's; François de La Mothe Le Vayer, the teacher of the King's brother; Petrus Gassendi, the great scientist, philosopher and priest, who became Professor of Mathematics at the Collége Royal; Samuel Sorbière, the editor of Gassendi's works, and Isaac La Peyrère, the secretary of the Prince of Condé, have been classified as the *libertins* of the intellectual world of their day, the free-thinkers who undermined accepted beliefs. They have been portrayed as subtle, clever, sophisticated men engaged in a sort of conspiracy to undermine confidence in orthodoxy and traditional intellectual authority. Their views have been seen as the link between Montaigne and Bayle and Voltaire in the development of the modern outlook. The 'libertins érudits', opponents of superstition and fanaticism, have been pictured as doubting everything for the purpose of destroying the old ways, and for their own amusement.[1] For example, the Pyrrhonist of Molière's *Le Mariage Forcé*, is the seventeenth century sceptic who paves the way for the complete libertinage of mind and morals of Molière's *Don Juan*.

To make this picture of the intellectual *libertinage* seem as immoral and as risqué as possible, the usual portrayal of this movement has stressed the activities of their informal society, the *Tétrade*, their *débauches pyrrhoniennes* and *banquets sceptiques*, as well as their friendships with such notorious libertines as Père Jean-Jacques Bouchard, and their interest in such 'suspect' Italian philosophers as Pomponazzi and Cremonini.[2] Much has been made too of Guy Patin's letter describing their plans for a *débauche*.

> M. Naudé, librarian of Cardinal Mazarin, intimate friend of M. Gassendy, as he is of mine, has arranged for all three of us to go and sup and sleep in his home at Gentilly next Sunday, provided that it will only be the three of us, and that there we will have a débauche; but God knows what a débauche! M. Naudé regularly drinks only water, and has never tasted wine. M. Gassendy is so delicate that he would not dare drink it, and believes that his body would burn, if he drank it. This is why I can say of one and the other this verse of Ovid "He avoids wine, the teetotaler praises water without wine" As for me, I can only throw powder on the writings of these great men. I drink very little, and nevertheless it will be a débauche, but a philosophical one, and perhaps something more. For all three of us, being cured of superstition and freed from the evils of scruples, which is the tyrant of consciences, we will perhaps go almost to the holy place. A year ago, I made this voyage to Gentilly with M. Naudé, I alone with him. There were no other witnesses, and there should not have been any. We spoke most freely about everything, without scandalizing a soul.[3]

In addition to the revelation that none of the participants were drinkers, there are suggestions that perhaps the 'libertins érudits' were 'esprits forts', capable of the libertinage of Théophile de

Viau and Des Barreaux,[4] which shocked the early seventeenth century, and that they were opposed to the 'mass of humble believers and the simple faithful'.[5] However, an examination of the views of these sceptics will indicate that it is, at best, only in a peculiar sense, or according to a special interpretation of what they were advocating, that they can be classed as dangerous immoral *libertins*.

Neither Naudé nor Patin was a philosopher. They applied an attitude imbibed from ancient and modern scepticism to certain problems, but they did not theorize in order to establish a basis for their attitude. They greatly admired the writings of Montaigne and Charron; Naudé, in his *Advis pour dresser une bibliothèque* had suggested that a library should not be without Sextus Empiricus, Sanchez and Agrippa, among those who had written against the sciences.[6] But the sceptical outlook that appears in Naudé's books and Patin's letters hardly merits the extravagant evaluation given by Sainte-Beuve, when he called Naudé 'the great sceptic', who stands between Montaigne and Bayle,[7] nor, perhaps, the judgment of Pintard, who has described Naudé as 'a learned unbeliever'.[8]

In his earliest work, a defense of some famous people accused of magic, Naudé made his sceptical attitude fairly clear. Both he and Patin were indefatigable humanists, deeply interested in the great authors, past and present. In order to form any judgments about the merits of the opinions of various writers, one must have a 'method', and Naudé suggested that 'unless we acknowledge something as just and reasonable as a result of a diligent examination and of an exact censure'[9] we should not judge. To those who wished to learn to judge reasonably, he recommended reading such excellent critical authors as Charron, Montaigne, and Bacon. As a result of all this careful reading, he said one would probably end up accepting 'The correctness of the Pyrrhonians based on the ignorance of all men.'[10] What such humanistic studies seem to have accomplished for Patin and Naudé was to make them extremely doubtful of currently accepted superstitions, wary of any type of fanatic dogmatism.

With regard to religion, Naudé has usually been seen as an atheist, a man who believed nothing, and Patin, at best, as a sincere Catholic who was unwilling to sacrifice his intellectual standards to Church authority. The collections of alleged remarks by the two men, the *Naudaeana* and the *Patiniana*, contain many comments critical of various religious practices and views. But, there are also signs of an implicit theology in their admiration for so many fideistic writers. (When the Cardinal Bagni asked Naudé what was the best of all books, he said, after the Bible, *La Sagesse* of Charron. The Cardinal is reported to have expressed his regrets at not knowing the work.)[11] I believe that it is almost impossible to determine what the religious views of Naudé and Patin were. They may have been true libertins, or they may have been mild fideists, who stayed on the Catholic side out of fear of Protestant dogmatism.[12] In any case, if Naudé was truly irreligious, actively trying to undermine the Catholic Church, he managed to hide this pernicious side from his employers, Cardinals Bagni, Barberini, Richelieu and Mazarin. And both Naudé and Patin spent their lives in fairly constant association and friendship with leading Church figures.[13]

The more philosophical of the humanistic sceptics was François de La Mothe Le Vayer, known both as 'the Christian sceptic', and the 'epicurean unbeliever'. La Mothe Le Vayer's interest, as shown in his writings, was primarily in developing evidence about variations in ethical and religious behavior in this world. In parctically all of his works, which are based on the views of 'the divine Sextus', a type of blind fideism or pure Christian Pyrrhonism is preached.

La Mothe Le Vayer had inherited the mantle of Montaigne, the keys to the sceptical kingdom, from Mlle. de Gournay. As the spiritual heir of Montaigne, and the interpreter of the new Decalogue of Sextus, he set to work to present the beauty, the wisdom and the practicality of the sceptical *epoche* in learned, humorous discourses. His literary achievements, such as they were (usually pedantic imitations of Montaigne), earned him a membership in the *Acadèmie française*. His intellectual pretensions made him both the hero of those who were sceptically inclined and the protégé of Cardinal Richelieu. Thus, he entered the palace circle as the teacher of the King's brother, the Duc d'Anjou,[14] where his extreme sceptical fideism earned him the wrath of such fanatics as Guez de Balzac, Antoine Arnauld, and René Descartes.[15]

Starting with his *Dialogues* of Oratius Tubero, dated '1506', for peculiar reasons of pedantic perverseness, but published in the early 1630's,[16] La Mothe Le Vayer heaped up evidence in favor of the Pyrrhonian cause, on the variations in moral behavior, the diversity of religions, the vanity of the sciences, the virtues of sceptics and scepticism, etc. His work is neither incisively critical nor highly theoretical, but rather predominantly illustrative. The fideistic message runs throughout all his works. St. Paul's I Corinthians, Tertullian's *credo quia absurdum*, and the views of the negative theologians are sung in unison with the 'golden books' of Sextus Empiricus.[17] The net effect is that of an insipid Montaigne. Unfortunately, La Mothe Le Vayer was neither the personality that Montaigne had been, nor the theoretician that Charron was. He was more erudite than either, but far less exciting intellectually.

The best presentations of his case appear in some of his discourses. In his *Opuscule ou Petit Traitté Sceptique sur cette Façon de Parler, N'avoir pas le Sens Commun*, La Mothe Le Vayer began by asking whether we really know anything. The most obvious things, like the sun, are not understood. Maybe things appear real to us only because of their relation to us, and our faculties. Perhaps, we are in the position of having the instruments for seeking the truth, but no means for recognizing it. Our senses are unreliable, as the tropes of Sextus easily show us, and we have no guaranteed criterion for distinguishing veridical experiences from others, 'since there is only the imagination which judges appearances as seems right to it.' It is only in heaven that any indubitable truths are known, not in human sciences.[18]

The *Discours pour montrer que les Doutes de la Philosophie Sceptique sont de grand usage dans les sciences* develops this last theme, leading to the nihilistic claim that the value of Pyrrhonism for the sciences lies in eliminating the possibility of, and the interest in, scientific research. The crucial sciences of the Dogmatists, logic, physics and ethics, are all in doubt, basically because our nature is too weak to reach knowledge of the divine and eternal without God's help. And so, unfortunately, 'the desire to know too much, instead of making us more enlightened, will case us into the darkness of a profound ignorance.'[19]

Everybody is aware that logic is full of ambiguities, sophisms,

and paradoxes. So, La Mothe Le Vayer presented a series of traditional canards about logic and logicians, without ever coming
to grips with the question of whether or not a sound basis can be
given for doubting the principles and procedures of reasoning.[20]
He then turned to physics, and contended that this entire subject
matter is problematical. The foolish physicists try to know everything, and do not even know themselves. The physicists, whether
they be Democriteans, Aristotelians, or anything else, simply
amass sets of conflicting opinions. The basic difficulty in the
attempt to know the principles of Nature is that Nature is the free
manifestation of God's will, and is not bound by the rules of
Aristotle or Euclid. The only way of comprehending the reasons
why things happen is through knowledge of God. But the physicists, in refusing to recognize that such information can only be
obtained by Revelation, and not by man's weak faculties, insist
upon trying to impose their rules on God's actions and manifestations. God can do anything; hence no necessary conditions or
principles apply to His activities. Thus, no necessary knowledge,
or science (in this metaphysical sense), is possible. The attempt to
discover principles of Nature is actually a kind of blasphemy, an
attempt to restrict and limit God's freedom. But the physicists,
like the rest of us, prefer 'to blame Nature, and perhaps its
author, than to admit our ignorance.'[21] And in ethics, it is also
the case that there is no reliable knowledge. All ethical standards
are relative to conditions, cultures, etc.[22]

   In the light of all these reflections (and that is, by and large,
what they are, rather than conclusions of rational arguments),
one may recognize the doubtfulness of all human intellectual
activities and achievements.

> It is not therefore without reason that we have maintained in this small
> discourse that the doubts of Sceptical Philosophy are of great value in
> the sciences, since instability and uncertainty are obvious there to the
> extent that we have said. In fact the general system composed of Logic,
> Physics and Ethics, from which all human studies borrow their con-
> siderable features, is nothing but a mass of opinions contested by those
> who have the time to examine them a little.[23]

For La Mothe Le Vayer, unlike his contemporaries, Descartes
and Bacon, the value of the method of doubt lies in clearing away

the sciences as well as scientific interest. What remains is the suspension of judgment on all matters, and the Divine Revelation. 'O precious Epoche! O sure and agreeable mental retreat! O inestimable antidote against te presumption of knowledge of the Pedants!'[24]

This wonderful suspense of judgment is totally non-dogmatic. It is not based upon the assumption that nothing can be known. The Pyrrhonists are not avowing that they have discovered one certain and indubitable principle, that everything is uncertain. The complete sceptics are uncertain even of this. Rather than having a negatively dogmatic theory, their doubts consume even that and leave them in a complete suspense of judgment, even about the merits of being doubtful about everything.[25]

This total scepticism has two advantages; first that it undermines the pride and confidence of the Dogmatists, and secondly, that it is closest to true Christianity. Of all the ancient philosophies, 'there are none of them which come to terms so easily with Christianity as Scepticism, respectful towards Heaven and submissive to Faith.'[26] After all, wasn't St. Paul preaching pure scepticism as the way to God?[27] The perfect Pyrrhonist has been cleansed of all errors, and is ready to receive the Word of God.

> The soul of a Christian Sceptic is like a field cleared and cleansed of bad plants, such as the dangerous axioms of an infinity of learned persons, which then receives the dew drops of divine grace much more happily than it would do if it were still occupied and filled with the vain presumption of knowing everything with certainty and doubting nothing.[28]

The Christian sceptic leaves his doubts at the foot of the altar, and accepts what Faith obliges him to believe.[29]

The Pyrrhonist who doubts all, even the Word of God, is causing his own downfall. Such a rejection of God's Grace would not be the result of scepticism, but the willful act of a particular sceptic.[30] And it would leave him in the sad position of Pyrrho, forever excluded from salvation. In spite of the virtue of the sceptical sage, as well as of his disciple Sextus, they lacked any Divine Illumination, and hence were doomed forever.[31]

The *libertins érudits* were a bit worried that their associate Isaac La Peyrère was applying scepticism to the Bible in his *Men*

Before Adam, written in 1641 and published in 1655. Naudé, Patin, La Mothe Le Vayer and Gassendi were all leery of supporting La Peyrère's claim that the Bible is not the accurate history of all humanity, but just of the Jews. La Peyrère's scepticism about the Bible will be discussed in Chapter XI.

The anti-intellectual and destructive scepticism of La Mothe Le Vayer, coupled with a completely irrational and anti-rational Christianity, has usually been interpreted as the height of *libertinage*. Although La Mothe Le Vayer might not have contributed much to the theory of the 'nouveau Pyrrhonisme', he carried the general pattern of its position to the absurd extreme, denying completely the value of any intellectual activities, and insisting on the totally blind character of faith. Almost all of the interpreters have concluded that his motive must have been to make religious belief, especially that of the Christian, appear so ridiculous that one would give it up entirely.[32] On the other hand, some of the commentators have recognized that La Mothe Le Vayer's theology is quite similar to that of Pascal and Kierkegaard, and is essentially, if slightly accentuated and exaggerated, the same as that of Montaigne.[33]

Thus, it has been difficult to assess the sincerity of La Mothe Le Vayer. Beginning with Balzac and Arnauld in the seventeenth century, down to such contemporary critics as Pintard, Grenier and Julien-Eymard d'Angers, there has been a rather uniform judgment that this so-called 'Christian sceptic' was really a 'concealed sceptic' who lacked the religious fervor of Pascal, or the possibly orthodox intent of Montaigne.[34] The critics have pointed out that the logic of La Mothe Le Vayer's position is such that once one had abandoned all rational standards, one would have no basis for choosing to be a Christian. But, this is true of the entire history of sceptical Christian Fideism, and, as has been indicated in previous chapters, is the case for a great many sixteenth century sceptics and Counter-Reformers. If one doubts that we have any rational means for distinguishing truth from falsehood, one has removed the basis for giving reasons for beliefs. Does this sort of scepticism, even with regard to theology, imply any sort of religious scepticism? I do not believe that it does. If there are no grounds for belief, how does one determine

whether one *ought* to believe or not? Hume and Voltaire appear
to have decided not to believe since the evidence for belief was
lacking. But this is just as much of a non sequitur as choosing to
believe. The principle that one should believe only those propositions for which there is adequate evidence does not follow from
any sceptical reflection, though it may be a principle widely
accepted by 'reasonable' men. The principle of Tertullian also
does not follow from a consideration of the reasons that there are
for doubting. Complete scepticism is a two-way street, from
which one can exit either into the 'reasonableness' of the Enlightenment, or the blind faith of the fideist. In either case, the sceptical argument would be the same.[35]

In pointing out that a great variety of sceptical thinkers have
said approximately the same thing that La Mothe Le Vayer did,
and that some have been famous for their disbelief, and some for
their belief in Christianity, the problem becomes one of finding
adequate standards for determining sincerity or intent. Julien-
Eymard d'Angers, in his excellent essay on 'Stoïcisme et 'Libertinage' dans l'oeuvre de François La Mothe Le Vayer' has found
'evidences' of his non-religious intent in his style and his use of
examples.[36] Jean Grenier has found 'evidences' in the flavor of his
writings.[37] René Pintard has found 'evidences' in his career, his
associations, etc.[38] Others, like Tisserand, have been satisfied by
his resemblance in attitude to an eighteenth century 'rationalist'.[39]

But, it is my opinion that all the information about La Mothe
Le Vayer is compatible with either the interpretation of him as an
'epicurean unbeliever' or as a 'Christian sceptic'. His style is no
more ironical or anti-Christian than Kierkegaard's, nor are his
examples any more blasphemous. The flavor of the works is, in
good measure, dependent on a prior guess as to how to interpret
them. The biography of La Mothe Le Vayer is not illuminating,
since he was a friend of many of the religious people, as well as of
many of the irreligious. So, we are left with the problem of making some sort of reasonable guess as to his motivation and intent.

In spite of the long tradition classifying La Mothe Le Vayer as
one of the key figures in the *libertinage* of the seventeenth century, I think it is perfectly possible that the continual emphasis on
Christian scepticism in his writings was intended as a sincere

view, at least as sincere as that of Montaigne and Charron. In this, I know I stand alone except for the eighteenth century editor of La Mothe Le Vayer's *Dialogues*, L. M. Kahle.[40] But, it seems perfectly possible that the point of the so-called *libertinage érudit* was not to destroy or undermine Christianity, but to serve as a buttress for a certain type of liberal Catholicism as opposed to either superstitious belief, or fanatical Protestantism. By judging these seventeenth figures by what articles of faith they assert, contemporary critics may be introducing some present day standards that did not then apply.

In an age when fideists like Jean-Pierre Camus could be leading churchmen, and a wide range of tolerance existed inside the Church (after all, Sextus was never put on the Index, and Montaigne not until 1676), it seems perfectly possible that various liberally minded people might have felt more at home inside the Church, than in the dogmatic world of the Reformers. They might well have adhered to some sort of 'simple Christianity' which both they and the Church of the time found an acceptable formulation of the Christian message, a formulation actually more ethical than religious. Further, men like La Mothe Le Vayer, Naudé, Patin, all extremely learned, and wise in the ways of the politics of ecclesiastical organizations, might well have had contempt for the credulity of simple men, and for the working of the religious organization to which they belonged, without condemning what they may have regarded as the core of Christianity.

What I am suggesting is that the so-called *libertinage érudit* might be an erroneous interpretation of certain movements in France in the seventeenth century. If one is now prepared to grant the possibility that the revival of scepticism in the sixteenth century was more anti-Protestant than anti-religious, and can be regarded as compatible with Catholicism, the outlook of La Mothe Le Vayer, Naudé and Patin may be better understood as a continuation of a sixteenth century development rather than as a malicious or delightful (depending on one's perspective) distortion of a previous tradition. They may not be as deep, incisive, or perceptive as their predecessors, but this does not prevent them from being in the same tradition.

In contrast to the humanistic sceptics, who carried on their doubts almost oblivious to the intellectual revolution going on around them, there wre also some sceptically-minded thinkers, who presented their case in the light of the scientific discoveries of the time. Montaigne, Charron, Camus, Naudé, Patin, and La Mothe Le Vayer criticized science, but usually understood by this either the Renaissance conception of the Scholastic scientist, the Aristotelian, or the motley group of Renaissance alchemists, astrologers, numerologists, pantheists, etc. Some of the humanistic sceptics knew and admired personally such heroes of the scientific revolution as Galileo. But, their usual notice of what was to become the 'new science' was to comment briefly on Copernicus or Paracelsus, not as discoverers of new truths, but as peculiar figures who denied accepted theories, thus suggesting that if even the most accepted scientific theories could be challenged, nothing in the sciences should be accepted as true.

On the other hand, thinkers like Leonard Marandé, Petrus Gassendi, and Gassendi's disciple, Samuel Sorbière, had scientific interests, and were participants in the formation of 'the new science'. Their scepticism did not involve undermining and rejecting all science, without any real comprehension of the monumental revolution in scientific thought going on around them. Rather, their scepticism was developed in the light of these new ideas.

Marandé, a secretary of Cardinal Richelieu, presented his scepticism with regard to the sciences in his *Jugement des actions humaines*, of 1624, dedicated to his employer.[41] Much of the argument in the book appears to be drawn from, or based upon, Sextus Empiricus. The general theme of the work is to show why we are incapable of discovering scientific knowledge, in the sense of knowledge of things as they really are. Accepting the Aristotelian thesis that our scientific reasoning is dependent upon our senses, Marandé began his attack with a critique of sense knowledge. Our senses give us conflicting information; they alter the information they bring us, etc. Illusions, such as that which occurs when one presses one's eyeball, indicate that we have no way of distinguishing veridical perceptions from illusory ones.[42] So, we can only conclude, 'our senses [are] too feeble to study and understand what is the truth. They can not even represent images to us; because there is no relation nor resemblance of the true to the false.'[43] We either accept our feeble senses, with their reports about images whose relations to objects are indeterminable, or we will have to give up scientific reasoning altogether. All that we perceive are pictures, not things. And, as Berkeley later pointed out, our sense information is only a set of ideas, so how can we know about external objects? Thoughts and things are completely different, so how can we judge the truth of things from our unreliable sense reports? Hence, 'Our knowledge is only vanity.'[44]

In order to have a genuine science, we need some assured principles, but none such are revealed to us. The principles that philosophers agree on are only 'false presuppositions',[45] immaterial ideas by which they want to measure material things.[46] Those who would employ mathematical principles and concepts to gain scientific knowledge are only making their results more dubious. Mathematics is about imaginary objects, so how can it be applied to physical things which do not have the same properties? There are no physical points, without length, width, or depth, and so on.[47] Mathematical conclusions and sense information conflict, as in the case of angle of contact between a circle and a tangent.[48] And mathematicians, as well as other scientists, disagree. For example, some say the earth is fixed; others, like Copernicus, that it moves. Both sides are rational principles, so how do we tell who is right? Every scientific claim has been disputed, and we have no criterion for judging which is true, and which false.[49]

In religion, we ought to accept the Revelation on faith. But we have nothing so assured on which to found the sciences. Most scientific principles are justified by appealing to common consent or agreement. Even something as basic as '1 + 1 = 2' is accepted on this ground. However, common consent is not a trustworthy standard of scientific truth, since somthing that was commonly accepted could be false. In fact, nothing is agreed to by everyone, since there are always the Pyrrhonists who doubt everything.[50] One can only conclude, 'We possess nothing more certain than doubt. And, for myself, if I doubt the arguments and the principles of the sciences which we have discussed above, perhaps I doubt still more the arguments I have offered against them.'[51]

This Pyrrhonism, and Pyrrhonism of Pyrrhonism, of Marandé represents an attempt by someone acquainted with the scientific progress of the day to develop a *crise pyrrhonienne* with regard to all science, new or old. A more far-reaching, and more fully matured attack along these lines appeared in the same year, 1624, written by one of the heroes of the scientific revolution —Pierre Gassendi.

Gassendi, (or perhaps Gassend).[52] was one of the prodigies of the early seventeenth century. He was born in 1592 in Provence, went to college at Digne, and by the age of 16 was lecturing there. After studying theology at Aix-en-Provence, he taught theology at Digne in 1612. When he received his doctorate in theology, he became a lecturer in philosophy at Aix, and then canon of Grenoble. Quite early in life, Gassendi began his extensive scientific researches, assisted and encouraged by some of the leading intellectuals of Aix, like Peiresc. The philosophy course that he taught led Gassendi to compile his extended critique of Aristotelianism, the first part of which appeared as his earliest publication in 1624, the *Exercitationes Paradoxicae adversus Aristoteleos*. This was followed by several scientific and philosophical works, which gained Gassendi the greatest renown in the intellectual world and brought him into contact with the man who was to be his life-long friend, Father Marin Mersenne. In 1633, Gassendi was appointed Provost of the Cathedral of Digne, and in 1645, Professor of Mathematics at the Collège Royal in Paris. Gassendi retired in 1648, and died in 1655.[53]

In spite of his tremendous role in the formation of 'the new science' and 'the new philosophy', Gassendi's fame has survived mainly for his criticisms of Descartes' *Meditations*, and not for his own theories, which throughout the seventeenth century had rivalled those of his opponent. He is also remembered for the part he played in reviving the atomic theory of Epicurus. But by and large, until quite recently, Gassendi's status as an independent thinker has been most neglected. Perhaps this is due in part to Descartes' judgment of him, and in part to the fact that he usually presented his ideas in extremely lengthy Latin tomes, which are only now being translated into French.[54]

But Gassendi, in his life time, had an extremely important intellectual career, whose development, perhaps more than that of René Descartes, indicates and illustrates 'the making of the modern mind.' Gassendi started out his philosophical journey as a sceptic, apparently heavily influenced by his reading of the edition of Sextus brought out in 1621, as well as by the works of Montaigne and Charron. This phase of 'scientific Pyrrhonism' served as the basis for Gassendi's attacks on Aristotle as well as on the contemporary pseudo-scientists, and made Gassendi one of the leaders of the Tétrade. However, he found the negative and defeatist attitude of humanistic scepticism unsatisfactory, especially in terms of his knowledge of, and interest in, the 'new science'. He announced then that he was seeking a *via media* between Pyrrhonism and Dogmatism. He found this in his tentative, hypothetical formulation of Epicurean atomism, a formulation which, in many respects, comes close to the empiricism of modern British philosophy. In this chapter we shall deal with the sceptical views of Gassendi's early writings, and in a later chapter shall discuss his 'tentative Epicureanism' or 'mitigated scepticism'.

Bayle, in his article on Pyrrho, credited Gassendi with having introduced Sextus Empiricus into modern thought, and thereby having opened our eyes to the fact that 'the qualities of bodies that strike our senses are only appearances.'[55] This attack upon the attempts to build up necessary and certain sciences of Nature from our sense experience is the starting point of Gassendi's thought. As early as 1621, he announced his admiration for the old and the new Pyrrhonism.[56] In his lectures on Aristotle at Aix, he began employing the sceptical arsenal to demolish the claims of the dogmatists, and especially those of Aristotle. The *Exercitationes Paradoxicae adversus Aristoteleos*, of 1624, represent the first installment of this sceptical onslaught against those who claim to have knowledge of the nature of things, and who fail to see that all that we ever actually do or can know are appearances. (The book was planned as having seven parts, of which only two ever appeared. It is possible that Gassendi stopped work on it after he heard of the attacks by some of the entrenched philosophers on a few of the anti-Aristotelians in Paris, in 1624–5.)[57] In it, Gassendi asserted bluntly that he much preferred the *acatalepsia* of the Academics and Pyrrhonians to the arrogance of the Dogmatists.[58]

From the outset, Gassendi proclaimed himself a disciple of Sextus, and for him, this involved two main elements, a doubt of all claims to knowledge about the real world, and an acceptance of the world of experience or appearance as the sole basis for our natural knowledge.[59] After presenting his sceptical attitude in the preface, Gassendi criticized the insistence of the Aristotelians on their way of philosophizing. Instead, he called for complete intellectual freedom, including a recognition that Aristotle's doctrines do not deserve any special or privileged position. The Aristotelians have (he said) become merely frivolous diputers instead of searchers after truth. They argue about verbal problems instead of studying experience. They submit servilely to the word of the Philosopher or his interpreters rather than thinking for themselves; a submission one owes to God, but not to a philosopher. Aristotle's views are not so wonderful that they deserve all this respect. To show this Gassendi tried to point out all the errors and doubts that existed in Aristotle's theories.[60]

The second book of the *Exercitationes*, not published till later,[61] contains the heart of the sceptical criticism of Aristotelianism, and of dogmatic philosophy in general. The attempt to discover scientific knowledge, in Aristotle's sense, is doomed to failure because the principles and the definitions can only be gained through experience. The only clear information we have is what we perceive. In order to arrive at real or essential definitions of objects we need some basic concepts by which to understand things, but we actually know only the sensible object. From experience, we cannot induce general propositions or principles, because it is always possible that a negative instance may turn up later. (Although Gassendi was acquainted with Bacon's work, this problem, as well as most of Gassendi's views here, is more likely derived from Sextus' discussions of logic.)[62] Even if we knew some definitions and principles, we could gain no scientific knowledge by means of syllogistic reasoning, since, as the Pyrrhonists had shown, the premises of the syllogism are only true if the conclusion is antecedently known to be true. The conclusion is either part of the evidence for the premises, in which case the syllogism is a circular argument, or the syllogism is inconclusive since one does not know if the premises are true (the problem later raised by J. S. Mill.)[63]

The high point of Gassendi's Pyrrhonian attack occurs in the last chapter, entitled, 'That there is no science, and especially no Aristotelian science.' Here, the tropes of the ancient Pyrrhonists, of Sextus, Agrippa, Aenesidemus and others, were employed in order to show that our knowledge is always restricted to the appearances of things, and can never deal with their real, hidden inner natures. We can tell how things seem to us, but not how they are in themselves. Thus, for example, we know from our experience that honey seems sweet. But we cannot discover if it is *really sweet*.[64] The distinction Gassendi made between apparent qualities, how things seem or appear to us, and real qualities, what properties the object actually has, is one of the earliest clear formulations of the primary-secondary quality distinction in modern philosophy.[65]

Since we can know nothing 'by nature and in itself, and as a result of basic, necessary and infallible causes',[66] no science, in the sense of necessary knowledge about the real world, is possible. All that we can know about nature is how it appears to us, and, as the sceptical arguments show, we can neither judge nor infer the real natures of things which cause or produce the appearances. Variations in sense experience prevent us from being able to define or describe the real objects on the basis of what we perceive. Due to the lack of indicative signs, that is, necessary true inferences from experience to reality, and due to the defects of syllogistic reasoning, we have no way of reasoning from our experience to its causes, or from its causes to their effects. We cannot even establish a criterion of true knowledge, so we cannot tell what would constitute a science. All that we can conclude is nothing can be known.[67]

In all this, Gassendi was challenging neither Divine Truth, which he accepted primarily on a fideistic basis, nor common-sense information, the world of appearances.[68] Rather, he was attacking any attempt, be it Aristotle's or anyone else's, to construct a necessary science of nature, a science which would transcend appearances and explain them in terms of some non-evident causes. In experience, and in experience alone (he said), lay the sole natural knowledge that men could attain. Everything else, whether it be metaphysical or mathematical foundations or interpretations of our sense information, is only useless conjecture. As Gassendi's disciple, Samuel Sorbière, said of him 'This learned man does not assert anything very affirmatively; and following the maxims of his profound wisdom, he does not depart from the Epoche, which protects him from the imprudence and presumption to which all the other philosophers have fallen.'[69]

The early Gassendi was concerned primarily with the destructive side of the sceptical critique of scientific knowledge, attacking any who sought to discover necessary, certain knowledge of things. If such knowledge must be demonstrable from certain premises, or be self-evident, and yet must also deal with something other than appearances, then all that can be concluded is 'nothing can be known'. Starting his attack with Aristotle, Gassendi quickly broadened it to include the Renaissance naturalists, the Platonists, and any philosophers whatever who claimed to know the true nature of things.[70]

On the other hand, while Gassendi called himself a disciple of Sextus, he included in his discipleship an unquestioned acceptance of experience as the source of all knowledge. And, as one of the major figures in the scientific revolution, Gassendi sought to extend man's knowledge through careful examination of nature. In the fields of astronomy and physiology, he made important contributions, describing and discovering facets of the natural world.[71] Later he made perhaps his greatest contribution to modern science by developing the atomic theory of Epicurus as an hypothesis, or mechanical model, for relating appearances and predicting future phenomena.[72] The positive side of Gassendi's thought led him to an attempt to mitigate his initial Pyrrhonism into a type of 'constructive scepticism' and to develop a theory which would lie between complete scepticism and dogmatism.[73] This later view, fully developed in his *Syntagma*, as well as the theory of knowledge of his friend Mersenne, constitutes, perhaps, the formulation, for the first time, of what may be called the 'scientific outlook'. This view will be examined later, and it will be shown to be perhaps the most fruitful result of the impact of Pyrrhonism on modern philosophy.

In evaluating Gassendi, two questions have been debated by many commentators; first, was Gassendi really a sceptic? and second, was Gassendi a *libertin*? The problem of the first of these revolves around what is meant by a sceptic. If a sceptic is supposed to be someone who doubts everything, and denies that we have, or can have, any knowledge, then Gassendi definitely was not a sceptic, especially in his later writings, where he specifically denied these views, and criticized the ancient sceptics.[74] However, there is a more fundamental sense of sceptic, that is, one who doubts that necessary and sufficient grounds or reasons can be given for our knowledge or beliefs; or one who doubts that adequate evidence can be given to show that under no conditions can our knowledge or beliefs be false or illusory or dubious. In this sense, I believe, Gassendi remained a sceptic all of his life. In the chapter dealing with the 'constructive scepticism' of Mersenne and Gassendi, I shall try to show that though both thinkers attack, and claim to answer scepticism, their positive views actually constitute a type of epistemological Pyrrhonism, much like that of David Hume. As the Jesuit writer, Gabriel Daniel, said of Gassendi, 'He seems to be a little Pyrrhonian in science, which, in my view, is not at all bad for a philosopher.'[75]

The other question, about Gassendi's *libertinism*, is more difficult to decide. Gassendi was a priest, who performed his religious duties to the satisfaction of his superiors. He was a fideist, by and large, offering theological views like those of Montaigne and Charron.[76] He was also a member of the Tétrade along with such suspect figures as Naudé, Patin, and La Mothe Le Vayer and went to their *débauches pyrrhoniennes*. He was a friend of some very immoral *libertins* like Lullier and Bouchard.[77] His religious friends found him a most sincere Christian. In view of this apparently conflicting information, French commentators have debated 'le cas Gassendi'. Pintard has recently marshalled the evidence that suggests Gassendi was really a *libertin* at heart.[78] On the other side, Rochot has argued that none of the evidence against Gassendi actually proves his libertinism, and that there is overwhelming evidence to the contrary.[79]

In previous discussions of the question of the sincerity of the other so-called *libertins érudits*, I have tried to show that there is a problem in estimating the actual views of the Christian Pyrrhonists. The majority of reasons for classifying them as either dangerous or exemplary unbelievers are based upon traditional evaluations and guilt-by-association. The traditional estimates were formed by and large by either extremely intense religious thinkers such as Pascal and Arnauld, or extremely anti-religious writers like Voltaire. The information about the lives and views of all the so-called *libertins érudits* is compatible, both philosophically and psychologically with either an interpretation of sincerity or insincerity. But, in the case of Gassendi, it most strains the limits of one's credulity, to consider him as completely insincere. If, as I have previously suggested, it is possible that Naudé, Patin and La Mothe Le Vayer might have been true Christian fideists in the style of Montaigne and Charron, then it is even more possible and likely that Gassendi was, in view of his religious life, the testimonials of his religious friends and friendships, etc. As the Abbé Lenoble has put the problem,

> If one wishes at all costs to penetrate to the inner core of Gassendi in order to determine the reality of his faith and the extent of his 'libertinage' (in which I do not believe), it is necessary to analyze closely the letters of Launoy and Boulliau. Both speak of a profoundly Christian end of his life, and without any anxiety of a repentant libertine. But then how does one judge (again!) the secret heart of these two witnesses?

If one suspects the two witnesses, as well as Gassendi, of lying, 'One here, I believe, runs into a psychological impossibility, unless it is supposed that the two (it would be necessary then to say three) cronies possessed an exceptional cynicism, of which we have, no proof, this time.'[80]

The long tradition of assuming that there must have been duplicity in the writings and actions of the *libertins érudits* depends, it seems to me, on the supposition that no other explanation of their views can be offered. But, as I have tried to indicate, another possibility exists, namely that men like Naudé, La Mothe Le Vayer and Gassendi were sincere Christians (though, perhaps, not particularly fervent ones). In the absence of completely decisive evidence as to the real intentions of these men, why should we assume the worst (or the best?), that they were engaged in a conspiracy against Christendom. The overwhelming number of their intimates and contemporaries found no signs of insincerity. And one of the basic sources of the suspicion of *libertinage* in each case has been the friendship with the others; Naudé was a friend of La Mothe Le Vayer and Gassendi; Gassendi was a friend of Naudé and La Mothe Le Vayer, etc. If we knew definitely (a) that at least one of these men was a genuine *libertin* trying to undermine Christendom, and (b) that the others accepted his friendship because of (a), then the argument of guilt-by-association might be significant. But since it is possible that each of the men in question was a sincere fideist, and quite probable that Gassendi was, then nothing is indicated by the fact that these men, all to some extent involved in the affairs of the Church or the Christian State, with similar avowed sceptical views and fideistic theologies, were close friends. (One might mention that they were all, apparently, intimates of Father Mersenne, who has not, to my knowledge, ever been accused of libertinage.) If one considers the *liberitns érudits* without any preconceptions as to their intent, can we decide positively either from their views, or their careers, or the circle of religious and irreligious figures within which they moved, whether they were the center of a campaign against Christianity, or part of a sincere movement within the Counter-Reformation aimed at undermining Protestantism through the advocacy of fideism?

To return to the historical material, the last of this group of sceptical thinkers of the early seventeenth century whom we shall mention here is Gassendi's and La Mothe Le Vayer's disciple, Samuel Sorbière. He was not an original thinker, but more a parrot of the most Pyrrhonian side of his mentors. Perhaps, in the context of the history of French scepticism, what is different or novel about Sorbière, is that he was both a philosophical sceptic and a Protestant.[81] However, he overcame this peculiarity later in life by becoming a Catholic. Much of Sorbière's success in publication came from printing other people's works, like those of

Hobbes and Gassendi. And, for the sceptical cause, he attempted a French translation of Sextus Empiricus which was never completed.[82]

In the two letters of Sorbière which contain the surviving fragments of his translation of Sextus's *Hypotyposes*, he indicated that he had started this task on leaving college in order to cultivate his knowledge of Greek, and to learn a type of philosophy he had not been taught.[83] He evidently became a complete admirer and advocate of Pyrrhonism and, hence, a disciple of the 'nouveaux pyrrhoniens'. With almost a fanatic consistency, he continued throughout his life to advocate a complete scepticism with regard to all matters that went beyond appearances, and to phrase his observations so that he could not be accused of transgressing the doubts of the sceptics. In a *Discours sceptique* about the circulation of the blood, Sorbière said, 'Permit me then, Monsieur . . . , to remain in suspense of judgment regarding scientific matters. On others, that divine revelation convinces us of or that duty orders us to, you will find me more affirmative. These latter are not in the province or jurisdiction of my scepticism.'[84] Only when he was shown that the circulation of the blood was an empirical theory, and not a judgment of what existed beyond experience, was he willing to accept it. In his account of his voyage to England, Sorbière carefully stated that he was only recounting 'what appeared to him, and not what is perhaps actually in the reality of things.'[85] Bishop Sprat, in his rejoinder for the Royal Society against some of Sorbière's nasty comments, chided him for not maintaining his suspense of judgment on such questions as whether English cookery was bad.[86]

Sorbière appears to have been a man quite well versed in the intellectual movements of his time, seeing them all in terms of a constant Pyrrhonian attitude. With such an outlook, he could only see as meaningful questions those that related to matters of appearance. The rest were only the vain presumptions of the Dogmatists. Sorbière was not a theoretician of the 'nouveau Pyrrhonisme', but rather represented the next generation which absorbed its conclusions and applied them almost automatically to whatever problems it was confronted with.

The French sceptics of the first half of the seventeenth century confronted the new, optimistic age in which they lived and prospered with a complete *crise pyrrhonienne*. As the avant-garde intellectuals of their day they led the attack on the outmoded dogmatism of the scholastics, on the new dogmatism of the astrologers and alchemists, on the glorious claims of the mathematicians and the scientists, on the fanatic enthusiasm of the Calvinists, and, in general, on any type of dogmatic theory. Some, like La Mothe Le Vayer, heaped up information from the classical world and the New World and, of course, from 'the divine Sextus', to undermine the moral sciences. La Peyrère was casting doubts on some of the basic claims of the Bible. Others, like Marandé and Gassendi, used the Pyrrhonian doubts and new information to undermine the natural sciences.

The Reformation had produced a *crise pyrrhonienne* in religious knowledge in the quest for absolute assurance about religious truths. The new Pyrrhonism had begun as a means of defending Catholicism by destroying all rational grounds for religious certainty. From Montaigne and Charron, down to the Tétrade, an abyss of doubts had been revealed, undercutting not only the grounds of religious knowledge, but of all natural knowledge as well. As the Scientific Reformation began, and the system of Aristotle was challenged, the sceptical attack quickly broadened the problem to an assault on the bases of all knowledge. In two orders of human knowledge, revealed and natural, the very foundations were taken away.

Not only had the old problem of the criterion been raised in theology setting men off to justify a 'rule of faith', but the same difficulty had occurred in natural knowledge, forcing men to search for some 'rule of truth.' The 'new science' of Copernicus, Kepler, Galileo and Gassendi has 'cast all in doubt'. The discoveries in the New World and in the classical world had given other grounds for scepticism. And the 'nouveaux pyrrhoniens' showed man's inability to justify the science of Aristotle, of the Renaissance naturalists, of the moralists, and of the new scientists as well. The cumulative attacks of humanistic Pyrrhonists from Montaigne to La Mothe Le Vayer, and of the scientific

Pyrrhonists like Gassendi and Marandé, left the quest for guaranteed knowledge about the 'real' world without a method, a criterion, or a basis. No type of rational inquiry into the truth of things seemed possible, since for any theory, or any dogma, a battery of apparently irrefutable arguments could be put up in opposition. The *crise pyrrhonienne* had overwhelmed man's quest for certainty in both religious and scientific knowledge.

VI

THE COUNTER-
ATTACK BEGINS

In this critical situation, the scientists, the philosophers, and the theologians would either have to fight for survival, or abandon the quest for certainty. Gradually, first in the area of religion, and then in science and philosophy, the menace of Pyrrhonism was recognized, and a counter-attack was begun. Out of this struggle, the modern philosophers emerged as so many Saint Georges, prepared to slay the sceptical dragon; only in this case the dragon was never really slain, and, in fact, managed within a century to consume the various knights who tried to rescue human knowledge.

Involved in this battle was the paradox that no matter how much the sceptics sneered and argued, and pushed one into doubt, not all matters happened to be dubious. In spite of the sceptic's criticisms, the sciences, new or old, seemed to contain some real knowledge about the world. As a result, the struggle, in part, was an attempt to reconcile the force of the doubts of the Pyrrhonists with the rapidly expanding knowledge that human beings possessed. For some thinkers, the battle was not so much a quest for certainty, as a quest for intellectual stability in which doubt and knowledge could both be accepted. For others, it was a Holy War to overcome doubt so that man could be secure in his religious and scientific knowledge.

As is all too often the case, the first dragon-killers were the worst. The first opponents of the 'nouveau Pyrrhonisme' were both naïve and vituperative, and, hence, failed to come to grips with the issues in question. These first antagonists either dwelt upon invective instead of argument, or begged the question by assuming that Aristotle's views were not in doubt and thus, could be recited to the sceptic to make him disappear. The earliest to be aware of the menace of the revival of Pyrrhonism were astrologers like Sir Christopher Heydon, or spiritologists such as Pierre Le Loyer.[1] The latter, as indicated earlier, devoted a brief portion of his book in defense of spectres to answering the sceptical critique of sense knowledge by an appeal to Aristotelian epistemology, a line of defense that we shall find fairly common in this survey of the anti-sceptics of the first half of the seventeenth century.

But the answer to scepticism that really launched the counter-attack was less philosophical and far more bombastic, that of Father François Garasse of the Society of Jesus. Apparently shocked by the *libertinage* of Théophile de Viau, and by the scandalous things he heard in confession, corruptions which people told him they were led to by reading Charron's *La Sagesse*, Garasse started a crusade against the atheistical and *libertin* tendencies of the time.[2] In 1623, he published his *La Doctrine curieuse des beaux esprits de ce temps, ou pretendus tels*, in which a series of sensational charges, he claimed to see through the mask of piety in Charron's Catholic Pyrrhonism, and to see behind it a most dangerous and pernicious irreligion. The 'pretended piety' of Charron is revealed as a real disservice to his country and his faith. The book of over one thousand pages attacks Charron for his impertinence and ignorance in religious matters, using invective as its main weapon.[3]

A disciple of Charron's, Father François Ogier, immediately replied in kind in his *Jugement et Censure du Livre de la Doctrine curieuse de François Garasse*, criticizing Garasse's style, temper, ignorance, etc. Perhaps the most cutting remark in this answer is, 'Garasse, my friend, that which is above us is nothing to us. The works of Charron are a little too high tone for low and vulgar minds like yours.'[4]

Ogier's harsh criticism led Garasse on to stronger attacks. First, in 1624, he charged forth with his *Apologie du Pere Francois Garassus, de la Compagnie de Jesus, pour son livre contre les Atheistes & Libertins de nostre siecle*. Besides abusing his critic, Ogier, Garasse tried to strengthen his attack on Charron, who 'chokes and strangles sweetly the feelings of

religion as if with a silken cord of philosophy'.[5] Two chapters occur
which list the 'Impious and atheistical propositions' and the
'Impious and brutal propositions' drawn from Charron's
Sagesse.[6] Finally, Garasse, in 1625, brought forth his magnum
opus on the problem, *La Somme Theologique des veritez
capitales de la Religion Chrestienne.* In the dedication to
Cardinal Richelieu, the author explained why a new *Summa* was
necessary. 'This title which I place at the head of my works,
having been used for four of five centuries, deserves to be revived,
and since the libertine types have beclouded our times with new
darkness, we must seek for new lights to illuminate the Truth.'[7]
'The terror of the secret atheists' and of the 'incorrigibles and
desparate types' of whom Charron is the worst, required this new
theological undertaking.[8] In order to perform this tremendous
task properly, Garasse attacked the views of any and all kinds of
atheists, all kinds of 'real Troglodytes or village rats'[9] Almost any
type of view other than Garasse's constitutes atheism, from the
views of Calvin to those of the Pyrrhonists. Five classes of atheism
are listed, (1) 'furious and enraged atheism', (2) 'atheism of libertinage and corruption of manners' (3) 'atheism of profanation' (4)
'wavering or unbelieving atheism' and (5) 'brutal, lazy, melan-
choly atheism'.[10] The Pyrrhonists, like Charron, are in the fourth
group. 'Wavering or unbelieving atheism is that vagabond spirit
of the Pyrrhonians, which claims all matters are indifferent, and
does not become impassioned either for or against God, thus
adopts a cold policy of leaving matters undecided.'[11] The people
of this type, monsters who have arisen in the seventeenth
century,[12] are indifferent about religion; they are neither for God
nor the Devil. To them, religion is a matter of convention, not a
serious question. Garasse was not concerned to answer their
arguments for suspending judgment on all matters, but only to
denounce them and to show the horrors of religious indifference.[13]
In fact, Garasse himself was somewhat sceptical of rational
theology, denying that there were any a priori proofs of god's existence, and insisting that the best way to know God was by faith.[14]
But, he refused to believe that this was the sort of view that
Charron and the Catholic Pyrrhonists subscribed to. Instead, he
saw their theory as a suspense of judgment on all matters including religious ones.

The charge by Garasse that Catholic Pyrrhonism, especially that of Charron, was really an atheistical plot, raised a storm of controversy, and put the problem of Pyrrhonism and its refutation at the center of the intellectual stage. Garasse hardly touched on the philosophical issues involved, merely smearing the Pyrrhonists with the label 'Atheist'. In 1625, his *Somme Theologique* had received an official approbation, in which it was stated that the work conformed to the doctrines of the Catholic Church, and that the work was worthy of being published 'to serve as an antidote against the impieties of the present Atheists and Libertines.'[15] But it became apparent immediately that Garasse had challenged the *entente cordiale* of the Church and the 'nouveaux Pyrrhoniens', and has accused the latter of constituting a 'fifth column'. As a result, one of the most dynamic theologians of the time rushed to do battle with Garasse, and forced the condemnation of his *Somme Theologique*.

Jean Duvergier du Hauranne (better known as Saint-Cyran), the French leader of the Jansenist movement, the spiritual head of Port-Royal, and the disciple of Cardinal Bérulle, denounced Garasse in a huge tract, fought against Garasse's views until he forced the Sorbonne to condemn his work, and, finally, brought about the silencing of the bombastic Jesuit. The attack on Garasse, Orcibal has shown, played a vital role in the development of Jansenism in France and was, perhaps, the opening blow in the Jansenist Crusade.[16] Theologicallly, as we shall see, Saint-Cyran was committed to a type of anti-rationalism not far removed from Charron's,[17] and, hence, was willing to make common cause with the Catholic Pyrrhonists.

A tremendous fuss was made about the appearance of Saint-Cyran's monumental four-volume opus of 1626, *La Somme des fautes et faussetez capitales contenues en la Somme Theologique du Pere Francois Garasse de la Compagnie de Jesus.* Signs were put up all over Paris announcing the work. The book itself begins, as Garasse's did, with a dedication to Cardinal Richelieu. Here, and throughout the work, violent charges and accusations are made against the Jesuit who dared to attack 'the secret atheists'. We are told that Garasse 'dishonors the Majesty of God';[18] that 'the author of this Summa Theologica has destroyed the Faith and the Religion in all its principal points';[19] that Garasse's

charges against Charron are such that 'I do not know if the ages
past or those which are to come will ever see, notably in a priest,
such a kind of effrontery, or malice and ignorance dominant to a
similar degree';[20] that Garasse's work is 'a most appalling
monster as a book';[21] and its author is 'the most hideous author
one has ever seen in view of the innumerable falsehoods with
which his books are filled.'[22] Saint-Cyran found it incredible that
a religious order could have permitted the publication of such a
work.[23] Garasse had (he said) advocated heresies, had misquoted,
slandered, been impious, impertinent, had uttered buffooneries.
In the course of his attack, Saint-Cyran further accused his Jesuit
opponent of Pelagianism, Arianism, Lutheranism, Calvinism,
and Paganism.[24]

What troubled Saint-Cyran, besides the vast number of errors
in citations and interpretations of Scripture, the Church Fathers,
and diverse theologians, was Garasse's attack on fideistic Pyrrhonism as a form of atheism. Late in the second volume, when
Saint-Cyran discussed Charron's views, he stated that he had
never known or read Charron's books before he saw them
attacked and vilified by Garasse as the most impious and atheistical works ever produced. But the indications of Charron's
thought that Garasse presented hardly lived up to the description. So, Saint-Cyran tells us, he bought a copy of the denounced
work, and found that, contrary to Garasse's claims, the views of
the Catholic Pyrrhonist were intelligent and sound, worthy of the
praise and esteem that they had received from the best Catholic
thinkers in France, including the eminent Cardinal du Perron.[25]

The anti-philosophical views of the Jansenists, their opposition
to rational theology, and their appeal to an almost purely fideistic
reading of St. Augustine, led Saint-Cyran to discover a good
many of the basic Jansenist claims in Charron.[26] The sceptic's
insistence on the incomprehensibility of God, the feebleness of
human reason, and the danger of trying to measure God by
human standards, Saint-Cyran endorsed as sound Augustinian
Christianity. Without attempting to, or desiring to, defend all of
Charron's views, Saint-Cyran tried to show that the message of
Catholic Pyrrhonism was really the same as what the Jansenists
set forth as orthodox Christianity—the misery and weakness of

man without God. Augustine is constantly cited to justify Charron's picture of the hopeless limitations on the quest for human knowledge, and the need for Revelation in order to know. The very views that Garasse had taken for atheism, Saint-Cyran insisted were sound, traditional Christian views.[27]

As a result of this defense of Catholic Pyrrhonism by one of the most important theologians of the period, Garasse's counter-offensive against scepticism was brought to a complete and drastic end. Saint-Cyran pressed his opposition until the Faculty of Theology of the Sorbonne finally condemned Garasse and his tirades. The report from the Sorbonne indicates that, because of the complaints, they studied and examined the *Somme Theologique* for several months, until finally, in September, 1626, they concluded that this work of François Garasse,

> Ought to be entirely condemned, because it contains many heretical, erroneous, scandalous, rash propositions, and many passages from Holy Scripture and the Holy Fathers badly cited, corrupted and turned from their true sense, and innumerable buffooneries which are unworthy to be written or read by Christians and by theologians.[28]

Though Father Garasse's answer by abuse to Pyrrhonism may have met its appropriate end, his type of counter-attack is reflected in several works of the period, in which no charge is too strong to hurl at the sceptics. Mersenne, without naming any names, called them monsters, unworthy to be called men. And Mersenne's early polemics, dating from 1623 to 1625, are full of all sorts of denunciations and insults, such as the following,

> They call themselves Sceptics, and are libertine people, and unworthy of the name of man that they bear since like baleful birds of the night, not having an eyeball strong enough to bear the bright light of truth, they sacrifice themselves shamefully to errors, and limiting all of man's knowledge to the range of the senses alone, and to the external appearance of things, reduce us unworthily to the most vile state, and to the lowest condition of the stupidest animals and deprive us of all genuine discourse and reason.[29]

Father Jean Boucher, a leading Franciscan, charged the Pyrrhonists with carrying on dangerous, subversive activities.

Boucher's lengthy tome, *Les Triomphes de la Religon Chres-tienne*, of 1628, presents an odd combination of a modified form of Catholic Pyrrhonism, along with a most strenuous denuncia-tion of the views of Montaigne and Charron. The latter are accused of impieties, of writing dangerous, venomous books, whose literary merits hide the serpent lurking inside. The effect of the writing of the two great 'nouveaux Pyrrhoniens' is likened to that of the medical 'Empyriques', who, Boucher tells us, killed five to six hundred persons for every five or six that they cured.[30] But, in spite of the dangerous and insidious effects of the writings of Montaigne and Charron, the type of theological view offered by Boucher is not too different. If religious truths had to be based on natural reason, *'we would not possess anything either assured or solid,* since we see natural judgments not only so diverse amongst themselves, but also the same judging faculty variable and con-trary to itself.'[31] We possess no perfect science because all our knowledge is based on reason and the senses, and the latter often deceive us, and the former is inconstant and vacillating.[32] In order to obtain any infallible knowledge, we must gain it by Faith, through Revelation. Truth is to be discovered in the Bible, and not by using our weak faculties.[33]

A study of Boucher's views by Father Julien-Eymard d'Angers has tried to show that this apparent copy of some of the features of Montaigne's fideism was really the orthodox view of the Catho-lic Church. In order to support this view, stress is laid upon the fact that though Boucher denied there could be any 'evident argu-ments' in matters of religion, he did assert that there were 'proba-ble and persuasive arguments'. Thus, no completely certain evi-dence could be set forth to establish any religious truth, but, at the same time, short of faith, some kind of persuasive or morally certain evidence, could be offered which was adequate either to convince one of, or to support, but not to establish a religious truth.[34] This modified form of fideism is not really different from that of Charron, for whom the certitude of religious truths depended solely on faith, but who also presented a great deal of allegedly persuasive 'reasons' to convince one of these truths. Fideism as a religious epistemology would seem to involve the claim that the guarantee of the truth of religious knowledge comes solely by faith. Such an assertion in no way denies that there may be all sorts of evidences that render this knowledge plausible or probable, or might lead one to believe it. But, the evidences can never be adequate to establish the truth of the religious propositions.

This kind of violent anti-scepticism coupled with an acceptance of fideism like that of the 'nouveaux Pyrrhoniens' also appears in the views of Guez de Balzac, a well-known apologist for the Jesuits. Balzac, in his correspondence, inveighs continually against La Mothe Le Vayer, whom he regarded as an atheist, and against Mlle. de Gournay, who is treated as a vain, presumptious person.[35] But this personal dislike for the living disciples of Montaigne did not prevent Balzac, in his *Socrate Chrestien*, from maintaining a type of Christian Pyrrhonism.

> This Truth [what Socrates was seeking] is none other than JESUS CHRIST: and it is this JESUS CHRIST who has made the doubts and irresolution of the Academy; who has even guaranteed Pyrrhonism. He came to stop the vague thoughts of the human mind, and to fasten its reasonings in air. After many centuries of agitation and trouble, he came to bring Philosophy down to earth, and to provide anchors and harbors to a Sea which had neither bottom nor shore.[36]

Thus, without Jesus, all is in doubt, and by natural means one can only arrive at complete scepticism. Truth depends solely on faith.

Another who joined in denouncing the sceptical menace, was the future member of the *Academie française*, Charles Cotin. But in this case the concern is solely in making clear the horrible, even harrowing effects of the Pyrrhonism of Montaigne and Charron, and not in developing some sort of fideism as well. In his *Discours a Theopompe sur les Forts Esprits du temps* of 1629, Cotin described the terrible state of affairs in Paris, where there are monsters, 'Forts-Esprits', who look like men, but who deny that anything is true, and accept only appearances. These villainous creatures, created through reading Montaigne and Charron, want to reduce us to being mere animals, and subject our souls to our bodies. The result of the views of these 'Forts-Esprits' is rage and despair. And what is most frightful, is that there are an almost infinite number of these monsters now in existence.[37]

Besides the refutations by abuse of Pyrrhonism, the call to

arms of Garasse, Mersenne, Boucher, Cotin and others, philosophical answers to the 'nouveau Pyrrhonisme' began to appear
in large number, starting about 1624, the year of Gassendi's first
publication. These replies can be roughly classified in three categories, though some of the works to be considered fall in more
than one of these; (1) refutations based upon principles of Aristotelian philosophy; (2) refutations which admit the full force and
validity of the Pyrrhonian arguments, and then attempt to mitigate the effects of total scepticism; and (3) refutations which
attempt to construct a new system of philosophy in order to meet
the sceptical challenge.

The Aristotelian type of answer to some of the sceptical arguments had been offered, as has been indicated earlier, by Pierre
Le Loyer in his defense of spiritology. It was also used by such of
the Protestant opponents of François Veron, as Jean Daillé and
Paul Ferry. In trying to show the reliability of some sense information, or the justification of rational procedures, these thinkers
had appealed to Aristotle's theory of the natural functioning of
the senses and reason, and the need for proper conditions for the
employment of our faculties. In the battles against the 'nouveaux
Pyrrhoniens' in the second quarter of the seventeenth century,
more elaborate and complete statements of this Aristotelian type
of rejection of scepticism appeared. One of the clearest examples
of this kind of approach is Pierre Chanet's answer to Charron.

Chanet, a Protestant doctor, published his *Considerations sur
la Sagesse de Charon* in 1643. In the preface, the author indicated
his concern about the reception his book would have since so
many people admired the writings of Charron. But, Chanet realized, he ought not to be afraid since he was only expounding the
opinions everybody accepted, the views of the Schools. The only
people who will disagree, he tells us, are those who take Charron
for Socrates, and the *Apologie de Raimond Sebond* for
Scripture.[38]

The first part of Chanet's work is devoted to refuting certain
peculiar sceptical assertions of Montaigne and Charron dealing
with the similarities of men and animals. They had argued that
man was vain in thinking that he had any special or privileged
place in the scheme of things, or that man had any faculties or
abilities not also shared with beasts. Also they had contended

that there was no reason for supposing that the five human senses constituted the totality of means that natural creatures possessed for gaining knowledge about the world. Chanet attempted to show that the evidence offered to support these claims (mainly anecdotal materials drawn from Plutarch, Sextus and others), could be accounted for without making any of the drastic claims of Montaigne and Charron.[39]

In the second part of his book, Chanet came to grips with the philosophical core of the 'nouveau Pyrrhonisme', the arguments offered to bring about a scepticism with regard to the senses, and a scepticism with regard to reason. In spite of the sceptical tropes about the variations, etc., in our sense experience, there is a basis, Chanet insisted, for asserting 'the Certitude of the Senses'. Sometimes our senses do deceive us, but there are conditions, namely those stated in Aristotle's *De Anima*, which if fulfilled, render the senses incapable of error or deception. If the sense organ is functioning properly, if the object is at a proper distance, and if the medium through which perception takes place is as it ought to be, then no sense errors can occur. Contrary to Charron, who claimed that even under the best of conditions, the senses can be deceptive, Chanet insisted that errors, illusions, or deceptions could only take place if something was abnormal in the organ, the medium, or the location or nature of the object. With his Aristotelian standards, he then proceeded to analyze all the standard examples of sense illusions offered by the sceptics. The problem of the oar which appears bent in water is explained as due to the fact that the milieu is not 'as it ought to be'. The square tower that appears round from a distance is accounted for by claiming that the sense organ, the eye, does not receive rectangular forms well. The double images that one perceives when one's eyeball is pressed are due to the sense organ being in an unhealthy or unnatural state. Perspective problems are explained as the result of perceiving objects from improper distances, and so on.[40] In all this, Chanet never saw that these examples were introduced by Charron as challenges to his criterion of sense knowledge, and not as illustrations of its operation. The issue that the sceptics had raised was, is there any way of distinguishing veridical from non-veridical sense experience? Chanet answered yes, by employing the Aristotelian criterion of sense knowledge. But the sceptics were challenging the criterion, and asking how we could be sure that even perceptions which occurred with healthy, normal sense organs, with specified media, distances, and objects, were veridical? Merely stating a criterion, which, if true, would allow one to classify veridical and deceptive perceptions begs the question, unless one can also show that the Aristotelian standard of sense knowledge is justified.

Next Chanet turned to sceptical difficulties raised with regard to reasoning. Here, as in his claims about sense knowledge, he maintained that though we are sometimes deceived, there are some judgments that are so evident 'that one would have to be mad to doubt this certainty.'[41] A standard of right reasoning exists, namely the rules of Aristotelian logic, and this standard enables us to distinguish what is evident from what is only probable. By means of this standard, we are able to recognize true premises, and employ them to discover other truths. True premises are those that have either been demonstrated from evident truths, or they are so evident that they are indubitable. Hence, with the canons of logic and the self-evident character of truths like 'The whole is greater than the part,' we are able to build up rational scientific knowledge.[42] Once again, Chanet bypassed the sceptical problems raised by Montaigne and Charron by assuming that Aristotle's theories are not in doubt, and then applying them to the difficulties set forth.

In Father Yves de Paris's *Theologie Naturelle*, one finds this type of use of an Aristotelian answer to Pyrrhonism briefly introduced among other criticisms of the *libertins*, whom he portrayed as having suspended judgment on all matters, religious as well as natural. First, the self-referential problem is raised. When the sceptics say nothing is true, all must be doubted, they are forced into a contradiction since they think these very assertions are true. But, then, Yves de Paris asserted, there is a better way to make the sceptics see the error of their ways, namely by showing them the natural knowledge which they cannot reject, our sense information. When our senses are operating in a normal state, under normal conditions, and our rational faculty is properly employed, we have no reason to doubt, and we can know the truth.

So, instead of remaining with 'the torments and hopeless anxieties of these miserable souls', the *libertin* sceptics should recognize that knowledge is possible through proper use of our faculties, and that there is no need for doubt with regard to either natural or revealed information. We have the means to discover scientific truths, and God has informed us of the true religion. So, in these circumstances, scepticism is either stupidity or perversion.[43]

A more elaborate rejection of Pyrrhonism, somewhat in the same vein, appears in the *Apologeticus fidei* by Jean Bagot of the Society of Jesus, in 1644. The opening portions of this work deal directly with the Pyrrhonian and Academic theories in their classical form as presented in Sextus, Cicero, Diogenes Laertius and St. Augustine. Only later are the views of the modern sceptics, especially Charron, treated. Bagot saw the sceptical claims as menancing the faith, and, as he observed in a marginal note, 'Today there are many Pyrrhonists.'[44] After outlining the arguments of the Greek sceptics, Bagot offered his answer, asserting that there are some truths which are based upon the infallible authority who states them, and others whose truth is evident and manifest, providing our rational and sense faculties are properly used under proper conditions. In these terms, the basic arguments of the sceptics are answered, and a detailed theory of truth is worked out.[45]

A modified form of the use of Aristotelian theories to answer scepticism appears in some other thinkers of the period. As we shall see in later discussions, some of the elements of the Aristotelian theory of knowledge were used to reject certain Pyrrhonian claims even by thinkers whose general views were not in the Aristotelian tradition, as in the instances of Father Mersenne and Herbert of Cherbury. In the vast eclectic project of Charles Sorel, *La Science universelle*, many ingredients of the Aristotelian theory are introduced as part of his rebuttal to scepticism, along with several other kinds of answers, some drawn, apparently, from contemporary sources, like the writings of Mersenne.

Sorel was a well-known writer and historian of the period, and a friend of the *libertin érudit*, Guy Patin. The first part of Sorel's

grandiose philosophical work, *La Science des choses corporelles*
of 1634, begins in the style of many of the writings of the new
thinkers of the seventeenth century, bemoaning the low state of
human learning, the uselessness and stupidity of what is taught in
the Schools, and offering a new panacea, *the universal science*,
'In which the Truth about all things in the World is known by the
force of Reason, *And the refutation of the Errors of ordinary Philosophy is found.*'[46] This new science, we are told, will be completely reasonable and certain, and will improve mankind. After
this fanfare, Sorel discussed two types of criticisms of the possibility of a true science of nature: one, which appears to be a kind
of Platonism, denying that there can be any real knowledge of
matters in this world, and insisting that truth is only to be found
in the Heavenly World; the other a scepticism, contending that
we can't really know anything. In view of the initial claims set
forth for *the universal science*, some rather extreme modifications
are stated in relation to the criticisms. Man, Sorel tells us, can
know as much about all things as is necessary for his happiness.
His natural capacities of sense and reason are able to receive
information and judge it. But, in so doing, there may well be
secrets of Nature that have not, or cannot be explained. It may be
difficult to know the essences of incorporeal things; it ma;y be
impossible to know God. However, this does not destroy the
possibility of knowledge, but, rather, enables us to see the falsity
of certain theories that have been offered, as well as allowing us to
know the limits of human knowledge. We can at least know what
we can't know, and hence have a science of our ignorance.[47] Sorel
was willing to settle for a little less than complete knowledge of
everything, in order to justify our assurance in what we are able to
know.

In later portions of his epic presentation of *the universal
science*, Sorel came to grips with the sceptical challenge, which he
felt had to be met in order for us to be able to make proper use of
our faculties and capacities.[48] The Schools and the logic texts did
not have any satisfactory answer, but Sorel felt that he and Mersenne had found one.[49] From studying the Pyrrhonian classics,
like Sextus, and observing that 'there are sometimes libertines

who revive them to the great prejudice of Religion and Human Society,'[50] Sorel set to work to vitiate the force of scepticism, ancient and modern.

In answer to the doubts introduced by the Pyrrhonists about the reliability of our sense knowledge, Sorel offered an Aristotelian reply. The information received by our external senses has to be weighed and judged by our 'common sense' in order to avoid deception. We have a variation in experiences due to the disposition of the sense organs, the temperament of the observer, the location of the object, and the medium through which perception takes place. But our senses are capable of perceiving the qualities of objects as they actually are, and our interior sense, the 'common sense', has the ability or capacity for judging when the senses give accurate reports, and for correcting them when they do not. In all his detailed examination of the examples offered by the sceptics about the differences between human and animal perception, (which he seemed to be willing to accept at face value), and the variations in human perception, Sorel never saw that the point the Pyrrhonists were questioning was whether we have any way of telling when or if our senses are ever accurate. Instead, he assumed that we can and do recognize some veridical perceptions and can then judge others accordingly. Thus, perspective and distance problems cause no trouble, since we have these reliable perceptions, and in using them we learn to judge and correct special perceptions by experience. There may be some unusual circumstances, when it is better not to judge at all, but, by-and-large, we can use these perceptions to evaluate almost every circumstance, and, by employing our 'common sense,' determine what things are actually like from how they appear to us. Then we can disregard all the sceptical cavils about the experiences and views of maniacs, or delirious people, since we know that such people have corrupted sense organs, and thus, see things as other than they are.[51]

The only rationale offered by Sorel for his constant assumption that normal people, with normal sense organs under normal conditions have accurate, reliable sensations, or a normal, natural ability to weigh and judge the reliability of their experience, is that it would be odd and strange if those in perfect condition did not know the truth, and only abnormal people did. But the sceptics were arguing that we have no way of telling whether those conditions that we regard as optimum for observing the world happen to be the right ones for perceiving the real state of affairs. It might be odd if only a couple of idiosyncratic people saw things as they really are, but it is also odd that only people with normal vision do. Sorel, in offering as a resolution of the sceptical difficulties a description of our normal procedures for judging sense information, has not met the problem of how we tell that our normal, natural way of distinguishing reliable perceptions from unreliable ones is in accord with the actual features of real objects.

The same sort of answer, merely embellished or elaborated, was put forth by Sorel to all the other sceptical arguments. Can we tell whether all our experience is just a dream? This problem that Sorel's famous contemporary, Descartes, was to make so much of, is easily dismissed. The normal person, when awake, can tell the difference between dreaming and waking. If somebody dreamt that he ate a large meal, and then awoke and was hungry, he could tell that he had been dreaming. Are we ever acquainted with anything other than the appearances of things? Even if we only perceive surfaces, or appearances of objects, we can judge the inner nature of the object, just as we do in ordinary cases when we judge what is inside from seeing the outside, or when we judge what a whole object is like from seeing its parts. Effects provide an adequate basis for determining causes.[52]

The sceptics who have tried to generate an infinite regress of difficulties about going from effects to causes, to causes of causes, and so on, have created a bogus problem. They have maintained we can only know an object if we know completely why it is what it is, what the causes of all its properties are. Sorel dismissed this problem by first admitting that some things may be unknowable, and others only partially knowable, but we can still have assured knowledge about some matters. Our assured knowledge is all that we require, and can be gained from the pertinent information available to us, and the use of our natural faculties.[53]

We have sufficient information and adequate faculties for developing sciences. The Pyrrhonists deny that we know any certain first principles to use as the premises of our scientific knowledge. They suspend judgment on the most obvious truths, that the whole is greater than the part, that anything including themselves exists, that the sun shines, etc., because they think these are all uncertain. 'One sees finally here how pernicious are their indifferences, and that they tend to subvert all Science, Politics and Religion.'[54] But, we possess first principles which are indisputable, known either by the common experience of all mankind, or 'known by the light of Reason'. By employing our natural reason, we can discover reliable scientific knowledge from these certain principles. The sceptics, in order to challenge our scientific knowledge, have to dispute the reliability of our normal, natural sense organs, our normal 'common sense' and our natural reason or understanding. But we can see that our faculties have the perfections requisite for their function, and hence, we have no reason to be concerned with the objections of the sceptics to the possibility of our obtaining scientific knowledge. There may be difficulties, there may be things we can never now, but if we take great precautions, we can know what is necessary for us well enough, and with complete assurance so that we can establish the Arts and Sciences on a firm basis. Our 'common sense' and the manifest and indubitable first principles are the gateway to knowledge of the truth about objects.[55]

After this appeal to the normal, natural conditions and faculties that enable us to gain true knowledge, Sorel presented one other answer to the Pyrrhonist, the standard problem of the self-contradictory nature of the sceptic's position.[56] The sceptics, Sorel contended, cannot be as ignorant as they pretend, since they look for reasons for their views, and seem to prefer the ones *they* offer to those of the Dogmatists. They are certain that nothing is certain, (a claim that Sextus, Montaigne, La Mothe Le Vayer and others were careful to avoid making); thus, they have found a certain truth, and so cannot be completely in doubt.

We should boast here of having overthrown their foundation, did not their doctrine consists in proving that there is no view which has any foundation, but therefore theirs is then without any basis; and if in order to defend it, they claim that it has some foundation, it is again overthrown by this, since it should not have one according to their maxims.[57]

So, by taking the sceptic's position as a definite assertion, Sorel pointed out the self-referential character of the view, and the dilemma involved. The problem of stating the Pyrrhonian view without self-contradiction is one of the persistent problems recognized by the sceptics, and one of the continual answers offered by the opponents.

By employing elements of Aristotle's theory of knowledge, by insisting on the adequacy of the knowledge that we can gain thereby for our purposes, by conceding some possible limitations on our full and complete understanding of things, and by showing the self-contradictoriness of an assertion of complete scepticism, Sorel thought he had destroyed the Pyrrhonian menace.

An interesting variant of the use of Aristotle's theories to reject scepticism appears in some comments of Sir Francis Bacon (who was himself called an imitator of the Pyrrhonists by Mersenne for his harping on some of the sceptical difficulties in finding true knowledge).[58] In *Of the Advancement and Proficiencie of Learning*, Bacon criticized the sceptics for misrepresenting the problems involved in gaining knowledge through the senses. They had seized (he said) upon the errors and deceptions of the senses in order to 'pluck up Sciences by the roots'. What they failed to see was that the real causes of the errors were the Idols, and that the proper solution to the difficulties was the use of instruments; 'yet assisted by industry the senses may be sufficient for the sciences.'[59] In other words, a set of conditions can be given, in terms of corrections of the unaided senses, which, when coupled with certain internal reforms, will specify when our adjusted perceptions are veridical. But our natural, normal senses are not sufficient to give us reliable knowledge, unless certain aids and instruments are employed. Thus, one ought to adopt a partial or temporary scepticism until all the aids and procedures of the *Novum Organum* can be successfully employed.

'Nor need any one be alarmed at such suspension of judgment, in one who maintains not simply that nothing can be known, but only that nothing can be known except in a certain course and way; and yet establishes provisionally certain degrees of assurance for use and relief until the mind shall arrive at a knowledge of causes in which it can rest. For even those schools of philosophy which held the absolute impossibility of knowing anything were not inferior to those which took upon them to pronounce. But then they did not provide helps for the sense and understanding, as I have done, but simply took away all their authority: which is quite a different thing - almost the reverse.'[60]

The different types of Aristotelian answers to the sceptical crisis share in common, regardless of variations, a view that there are proper conditions either for perceptions or reasoning, and that we have faculties which, when operating properly under these conditions, are able to give us true knowledge. Hence neither a scepticism with regard to the senses nor with regard to reason is called for. The sort of evidence introduced by the sceptics is either false, or deals with abnormal conditions and corrupted faculties.

Those who employed this kind of answer to the Pyrrhonists refused to recognize that the sceptics were challenging the reliability of even our natural faculties, under the best of conditions, and were denying the criteria Aristotle had laid down for deciding when our faculties were functioning properly. It may well be that the Aristotelian system is ingeniously constructed for avoiding the standard sceptical arguments, by either specifying a way of answering the problems on the basis of a standard which is not questioned, or by ruling the arguments out as foolish. Hence, according to the Aristotelians, if one is really in doubt about first principles or the criterion, one is not prepared to philosophize. But, the 'nouveau Pyrrhonisme' was questioning the very system of the Aristotelians, which could not be justified or defended merely by employing the system.

The abusive critics of scepticism failed to meet the problems being raised, and the Aristotelians met them by begging the crucial questions. The former tried to destroy the force of Pyrrhonism by denouncing it. The latter tried to answer the problems by treating them as items to be dealt with within their system, difficulties to be resolved by the criteria they accepted. They did not see that to dispel the sceptical crisis they would first have to establish the basis for their philosophical system before they could show that what was true according to Aristotle's theory was actually true. In the next chapters, we shall examine some attempts to deal with the sceptical challenge by a more serious appraisal of the basic problems raised.

VII

CONSTRUCTIVE OR MITIGATED SCEPTICISM

Another way of meeting the sceptical crisis was the formulation of a theory which could accept the full force of the sceptical attack on the possibility of human knowledge, in the sense of necessary truths about the nature of reality, and yet allow for the possibility of knowledge in a lesser sense, as convincing or probable truths about appearances. This type of view, which has become what many philosophers today consider the scientific outlook, was first presented in the seventeenth century in Mersenne's grandiose attack on Pyrrhonism, *La Verité des Sciences, contre les Septiques ou Pyrrhoniens*, and later, in a more systematic form, by Mersenne's good friend, Gassendi. In such other writers as the English theologian, Chillingworth, and the French Franciscan writer, Du Bosc, one finds the quest for, and a partial statement of, this mitigated scepticism. This attempt to find a *via media* between the completely destructive tendency of the 'Nouveau Pyrrhonisme' and a questionable dogmatism, has ultimately become a crucial part of modern philosophy, in the movements of pragmatism and positivism. But, even though the most theoretical formulations of this mitigated or constructive scepticism probably occurred in the early seventeenth century, a new dogmatism had to develop and be demolished before this new solution to the *crise pyrrhonienne* could be accepted. Only after the presentation of this view by David Hume, and the nineteenth century digestion of it by Mill and Comte, could it become philosophically respectable.

Marin Mersenne, 1588–1648, was one of the most important figures in the history of modern thought, and has been until very recently most neglected and misunderstood.[1] He is remembered principally because of his friendship and correspondence with Descartes, and has usually been classified as a bigoted religious thinker whose saving grace was his friendships, not his ideas. However, this picture hardly corresponds with Mersenne's vital role in the scientific revolution of the seventeenth century.

He was one of the first students to be trained at the Jesuit college at La Flèche, which Descartes attended in a later class. After this, Mersenne entered the order of the Minimes and became a model of Christian piety and wisdom. His literary career commenced in the third decade of the seventeenth century, with the publication of a group of vast polemical works against every conceivable enemy of science and religion—the atheists, the deists, the alchemists, the Renaissance naturalists, the Cabbalists and the Pyrrhonists.[2] After this start, Mersenne devoted the rest of his life to the more constructive task of propagandizing for the 'new science,' exhibiting his love of God through his monumental service to the scientific revolution. He was a man with a voracious interest in scientific and pseudo-scientific questions, ranging from complex problems in physics and mathematics, Hebrew philology and music theory, to such problems as 'How high was Jacob's ladder?,' and 'Why do wise men earn less money than fools?' Mersenne published a large number of summaries, explanations and systems of scientific works, including those of Galileo. He also aided and abetted all the leading workers in the 'new philosophy' including, besides Descartes: Gassendi, Galileo, Hobbes, Campanella, Herbert of Cherbury, the super-heretic, Isaac La Peyrère, and many others. His immense correspondence, which is only now being published, encouraged and informed scientists everywhere.[4] All in all, Mersenne probably contributed more than any other of his contemporaries to increasing knowledge of, and interest in, the tremendous scientific achievements of the age.

The part of Mersenne's contribution that will be of concern here, is the new understanding that he worked out of the significance of scientific knowledge, and the importance of this in the light of the sceptical crisis of the time. The last of Mersenne's huge polemics, *La Verité des Sciences contre les Septiques ou Pyrrhoniens* (1625), attempts to answer the Pyrrhonian arguments, but to answer them in a new way. What Mersenne wanted to establish was that *even if* the claims of the sceptics could not be refuted, nonetheless we could have a type of knowledge which is not open to question, and which is all that is requisite for our purposes in this life. This kind of knowledge is not that which previous dogmatic philosophers had sought, knowledge of the real nature of things. Rather it consists of information about appearances, and hypotheses and predictions about the connections of events and the future course of experience. Scientific and mathematical knowledge for Mersenne did not yield information about some transcendent reality, nor was it based upon any metaphysical truths about the nature of the universe. A positivistic-pragmatic conception of knowledge was set forth, which omitted any search for rational grounds for what is known and denied that such a search could be successful, yet insisted, against the destructive force of compelte Pyrrhonism, that scientific and mathematical knowledge could not seriously be doubted.[5]

La Verité des Sciences, a work of over a thousand pages, begins, as has been indicated earlier, in the style of Garasse. In the dedicatory letter to the king's brother, Mersenne denounced the sceptics in quite extreme terms. They are accused of all sorts of shameful and dangerous views and intentions.[6] Then, in the preface to the book, further charges are made, culminating in the claim that the sceptics are those *libertins* who are afraid to show their real impiety. They, therefore, try to convince everyone that nothing is certain in order to attack indirectly the sciences, religion and morality. Mersenne's purpose in presenting his huge volume was to put a stop to the impetuous course of Pyrrhonism.[7] Any sceptic who reads it will see 'that there are many things in the sciences which are true, and that it is necessary to give up Pyrrhonism if one does not want to lose his judgment and his reason.'[8]

The book itself consists of a discussion between an alchemist, a sceptic, and a Christian philosopher, in which both the Pyrrhonist and the alchemist get their just deserts. The stage is set when the alchemist declares that alchemy is *the* perfect science. The sceptic offers a rebuttal, first by criticizing the claims of the alchemist, then, by presenting an argument for complete scepticism, not solely about the merits of this particular claim to true knowledge, but about the possibility of there being any means whereby human beings can gain knowledge about the real nature of things. A brief general summary of the classical Pyrrhonian case is presented, directed against both Platonic and Aristotelian philosophies. We are unable to know the real essence of things, or the Platonic Forms. All we are ever acquainted with are effects, appearances, and never the ultimate causes or real natures. The causes can be traced back *ad infinitum*, without ever arriving at the object of knowledge, and unless we find out the ultimate causes, we can never actually comprehend even the particular experiences that we are confronted with.[9]

Having allowed the sceptic the first general formulation of his case, Mersenne stepped in, in the character of the Christian philosopher, to give his initial presentation of his type of answer to Pyrrhonism. First of all [he said], the problem raised by the sceptic does not show that nothing can be known, but rather that only a few things, the effects, can be known. If our knowledge is really so restricted, it still has some value of a pragmatic variety, since 'this little knowledge suffices to serve as a guide in our actions.'[10] In order to get along in this world, knowledge of effects is sufficient, since it enables us to distinguish objects, etc. The point being made constitutes the general pattern of Mersenne's answer throughout. The sceptical arguments show there are some things we cannot know, namely the real natures of things that previous philosophers have sought to comprehend. However, in spite of the fact that this sort of metaphysical basis cannot be found, we can know something about appearances or effects, namely how to manage in the world of shadows. The sort of knowledge that Plato, Aristotle, Democritus and some others have claimed to possess, Mersenne was willing to concede cannot be known. But just the same, he maintained, there is a kind of knowledge, radically different, that we do have and which is adequate for our needs in this world.[11]

Thus, the problems of sense variations and illusions that the sceptics developed at such length, may well show that we are unable to know things-in-themselves. Nevertheless, the information about how our experiences differ under different conditions allows us to formulate certain laws about sense observations, for example the laws of refraction. With such laws about appearances we can correct or account for certain sense information and, hence, eliminate any problems about illusions.[12] (It is interesting that Mersenne seems to have been the first one to see that the classical Pyrrhonian claims about the differences between animal experience and human experience are inconclusive since animals do not communicate with us to tell us what they perceive.)[13] In the case of all the reports about variations in religious and moral behavior, Mersenne insisted that since we know both divine and natural rules of conduct, it does not matter how other people and cultures behave.[14]

In general, Mersenne tried to make out the claim that in every field of human interest some things are known, like 'the whole is greater than the part,' 'the light at noon is greater than that of the stars,' 'there is a world,' 'it is not possible for the same thing to both have and not have the same property,' 'evil should be avoided,' etc. There may be no philosophical refutation of the sceptical arguments, but, there are a great many things that are not in doubt. If one is reasonable about matters, one will realize that something is known and one will be happy. If not, he will become completely miserable. One may go so far as to doubt the obvious rules of morality, and become a *libertin*, which leads 'headlong into hell with all of the Devils to be burned forever.'[15]

After taking time out to attack alchemy, Mersenne returned to his war against Pyrrhonism, and developed his general criticism in the form of a detailed commentary and refutation of the *Outlines of Pyrrhonism* of Sextus Empiricus, dealing with almost all of the first book and part of the second. The ten tropes were each presented and answered by pointing out that there are scientific laws about sense variations, such as the principles of optics, and that in spite of all disagreements and differences of opinions, there is common agreement on some matters. No one doubts that fire is hot, or ice is cold, or that an elephant is bigger than an ant. Dreams or hallucinations provide no reason for scepticism, since when awake and in sound mental condition, we recognize our dream life for what it is. When the sceptic pointed out that the ten tropes show that we do not know the essences of things, Mersenne's Christian philosopher shrugged this aside with the comment, 'that is not . . . necessary to establish some truth.'[16] In spite of all the difficulties raised by Sextus Empiricus, we do *not* happen to be in doubt about all matters, and we do have means, like measuring devices, for dealing with some of the troublesome situations that arise. With instruments, and by employing laws that we have discovered about perspective, refraction, the effect of wine on eyesight, etc., we can avoid being troubled by bent oars, pigeons' necks and round towers. By being reasonable, we can find ways of living in spite of all the variations in human behavior. Hence, 'all of the arguments of the Pyrrhonians are nothing but chicaneries and paralogisms, with which one does not have to amuse oneself very long.'[17]

The Pyrrhonist is not silenced by this commonsensical rejection of his arguments. But, instead of rebutting, he offers other claims drawn from Sextus, summarizing the remaining portions of Book I, then introducing some of the key arguments from Book II against the possibility of rational knowledge. Everything is a matter of controversy, and every attempt to establish the truth of a theory leads either to an infinite regress or to circular reasoning. The first point is brushed aside by pointing out that many of the controversies cited by the sceptics depend upon what some stupid person has said. But, as Mersenne argued again and again, some matters never are actually disputed. And no infinite regress occurs in explanation because there are some self-evident matters which can be used as maxims upon which to build up scientific knowledge; this in turn, can be verified by checking experientially the predictions that are made on the basis of what we know.[18]

The sceptic tries to bolster his case by presenting Sextus's attack against syllogistic reasoning. In order for a syllogism to be true, its premises must be true. To show that the premises are true, further evidence is required, leading either to an infinite regress or to employing the conclusions as evidence for the premises. Besides, the premises could not be known to be true, unless the conclusion were antecedently know to be true. And, in order to know that the premises imply the conclusion, one would have to show that there is a connection between the former and the latter, and that there is a connection between the connection and the syllogism. If this were not enough, there are also the problems about the criterion. To determine if something has been demonstrated, both a judge and a criterion of judgment are needed. But on what criterion will it be decided who or what is the judge or the criterion? Until all these difficulties are resolved, we cannot know anything but how matters appear to us.[19]

Mersenne's reply to this critique of rational knowledge consisted of a pragmatic version of Aristotle's theory of the proper conditions for obtaining empirical and intellectual knowledge. Without offering any argument, he pointed out that, in fact, man is the judge, and each sense the judge of its own objects. When we see the sunlight at noon, we know it is day, and no arguments about criteria or judges make any difference. If we employ our faculties properly, we will discover *genuine maxims* that everybody accepts. It is not necessary to show indubitably what the criterion of truth is in order to be sure of these maxims. Without answering the sceptical claims, Mersenne pointed out how, in fact, we decide questions. We use our senses, our rules, our instruments, and we evaluate them by means of our rational faculties.[20]

Similarly, the Pyrrhonian objections to syllogistic reasoning can be ignored. It just is not the case that the conclusions constitute some of the evidence for the premises. The former may suggest the latter, but never establish them. The evidence for the premises is either an induction from materials other than the conclusion, or the self-evidence of the premises. If the sceptic really doubts that there are premises that 'ravish' the understanding and lead it to certain conclusions, can he also doubt that he knows that he doubts? If he doubts this, can he doubt that he doubts, and so on? No matter how the sceptic squirms, he will have to admit that something is true, and hence 'it is necessary to bid an everlasting farewell to your Pyrrhonism.'[21]

The half-way house that Mersenne was trying to construct between the sceptical denial that we possess any knowledge, and the dogmatic claim that we can know the real nature of things is exhibited in a digression that occurs concerning the merits of Francis Bacon's proposals. Bacon was accused of going to both extremes. The Idols are just the old sceptical arguments, and can be disposed of in a commonsensical, practical way. The positive procedures offered by Bacon for discovering the truth are unworkable. Besides the fact that they are not based on actual scientific method, they fail to take into account our total inability to find the true nature of things. Regarding 'whatever phenomena that might be considered in Philosophy, it must not be thought that we could penetrate to the nature of individuals, nor to what takes place inside of them, for our senses, without which the understanding can know nothing, perceive only that which is external.'[22]

On the other hand, as Mersenne closed the first Book of *La Verité des Sciences*, brushing aside the Pyrrhonian arguments about physics and metaphysics, by pointing out again that there are things we can know, and practical ways for dispelling doubts, he declared, 'one must no longer suspend judgment. We should accept the truth in our understanding, as the ornament and the greatest treasure that it can receive, otherwise it will be in eternal darkness and will have no consolation.'[23]

If this acceptance of the force of scepticism, and this proposed pragmatic means of resolving doubts did not suffice to eliminate Pyrrhonism, then Mersenne put forth his ultimate answer to complete scepticism—the vast body of mathematical and physical information that is known. When confronted with this, can one still be in doubt? And so, the last 800 pages of *La Verité des Sciences* is a list of what is known in these subjects, matters on which there is no need for suspense of judgment. As arithmetic and geometry are described, along with some odd problems in the philosophy of mathematics, and the 'theology' of mathematics, the Pyrrhonist gradually discovers that his body of knowledge is 'most excellent for overturning Pyrrhonism which had made me doubt of all things until I had the good fortune to meet you.'[24]

The type of answer that Mersenne presented to scepticism has been described by Lenoble as similar to Diogenes' refutation of Zeno by walking around. Pyrrhonism has been rebutted merely by exhibiting what we know.[25] But the arguments for complete scepticism have been ignored rather than refuted.[26] As Bayle pointed out regarding Diogenes, the appeal to the experience of motion does not constitute an answer to the arguments at issue.[27] Nor does the appeal to the knowledge that we obviously possess constitute an answer to the arguments raised by Sextus Empiricus. But, Mersenne was only too willing to grant this point. The refutation of Pyrrhonism was intended to stop the destructive side of the humanistic sceptics, those who doubted everything and intended to suspend judgment on all questions. The sciences (considered as the study of phenomenal relationships), and mathematics (considered as the study of hypothetical relationships), have given us a kind of knowledge that is not really in doubt, except by madmen. But, the sort of assurances sought by the dogmatic philosophers could never be found for this knowledge. Thus, a fundamental scepticism had to be accepted, a doubt that any certain foundations could ever be uncovered as the grounds for what we know. But, this scepticism should not be extended from a doubt concerning foundations or grounds to a doubt concerning the very matters that, regardless of any sceptical arguments, we do in fact know.

In some of his later writings, when he was not occupied in attacking scepticism, Mersenne made his own 'epistelmological' or 'theoretical' Pyrrhonism quite clear. In *Les Questions theologiques*, he argued that a science of eternal truths is not possible, and that the summit of human wisdom is the realization of our own ignorance. Everything we know is open to some doubt, and none of our beliefs can be adequately founded. The wise man recognizes that he knows no subject with sufficient evidence and certainty to be able to establish it as a science, in the sense of a body of indubitable or demonstrable knowledge.

> For it can be said that we see only the outside, the surface of nature, without being able to enter inside, and we shall never possess any other science than that of its exterior effects, without being able to find out the reasons for them, and without knowing how they act, until it pleases God to deliver us from this misery, and to open our eyes by means of the light that He reserves for His true admirers.[28]

In the *Questions inouyes*, Mersenne asked, '*Can one know anything certain in physics or mathematics?*' And he answered that
we cannot explain the causes of the most common effects, like the
cause of light, and of falling bodies. In fact, we cannot even prove
that the world we perceive is not just mere appearance. Thus,
'there is nothing certain in physics, or there are so few things certain that it is difficult to state them.'[29] In mathematics, the truths
are only conditional. If there are objects like triangles, then
certain geometrical theorems are true.[30]

Mersenne's theoretical Pyrrhonism, plus his vehement opposition to applied scepticism, is brought out further by some comments of his correspondents and friends. They seem to realize
that Pyrrhonism is a very trying subject for Mersenne. Pierre Le
Loyer, who had earlier written against scepticism, accused Mersenne of this view, but carefully softened the blow by adding that
he knew that he was definitely not a Pyrrhonist.[31] Gassendi, who
came to share Mersenne's 'constructive scepticism,' confessed
that he, himself, was a sceptic, and that he knew that this
annoyed Mersenne. But, Gassendi said, they could compromise,
and both live their daily lives on a probabilistic basis.[32] La Mothe
Le Vayer, 'the Christian sceptic', added a note to Mersenne to his
Discours Sceptique sur la Musique, which Mersenne had published as part of one of his own books, in which La Mothe Le
Vayer tried to point out the areas of agreement between Mersenne and the 'nouveaux Pyrrhoniens'.

> I have not made difficulties by playing with you with the ways for sus-
> pending judgment, knowing well that you have never disapproved of
> them within the limits of human knowledge, and that you have never
> blamed the Sceptic, when respectful towards Heaven, and enslaving his
> rationality under the obedience of faith, he has been content to attack
> the pride of the Dogmatists by showing the uncertainty of their
> disciplines. The same sword can be used by a wicked person to commit
> an infamous murder, and can be the instrument of an heroic deed in
> the hands of a virtuous man. He who allows divine matters to be
> treated in a Pyrrhonian manner is as much to be condemned as another
> is to be praised for showing that what is set forth as the greatest of
> worldly wisdom is a kind of folly before God, and that all human
> knowledge is dependent on dreams of the night.[33]

La Mothe Le Vayer and Mersenne could agree in using the sceptical sword to slay the dogmatist, but the former wanted to slay the scientist as well. Mersenne accepted the anti-metaphysical use of Pyrrhonism, but he also insisted, in spite of all the sceptical doubts, on the *truth of the sciences.*

A further item in Mersenne's career illustrates his attitude, his advocacy of Hobbes' political theory as a cure to destructive Pyrrhonism. In 1646, Mersenne wrote to the arch-sceptic, Samual Sorbière, telling him that if he examined Hobbes' *De Cive*, it would make him renounce his scepticism.[34] What Hobbes had discovered, apparently for Mersenne, was a new science, the science of man. If the sceptic saw what could be known in this area, he would no longer advance his doubts, even though it would still be the case that no ultimate grounds could be given for his knowledge, and no knowledge of the real nature of things could be discovered.

Mersenne, unlike Charles Sorel, who borrowed many of Mersenne's ideas, was offering a peculiarly novel type of solution to the sceptical crisis. He did not contend, as Sorel did, that we can have knowledge of the true nature of things, but we cannot know everything about reality. Instead, Mersenne's contention was that, epistemologically, there was no solution to the sceptical crisis. But this did not deny the fact that in practice we do have knowledge, that is, reliable information about the world around us. We may not be able to establish that there really is a world, or that it actually has the properties we experience, but we can develop sciences of appearances which have pragmatic value, and whose laws and findings are not doubtful except in a fundamental epistemological sense. The destructive humanistic sceptic, like La Mothe Le Vayer, who would give up what small guidance we have because of his theoretical doubts is as much of a fool and a menace as the religious sceptic who gives up Christianity because its doctrines cannot be given an absolutely certain rational foundation.

Mersenne had found an answer to the challenge of the 'nouveau Pyrrhonisme', and an answer which was to have a great history in more recent times. The sceptics had raised apparently insoluble doubts as to our ability to find a certain and indubitable basis for the knowledge we have. Instead of trying to resolve the doubts, Mersenne tried to save the knowledge by showing that its reliability and use did not depend upon discovering the grounds of *all* certainty. Scientific achievements do not depend upon some unshakeable metaphysical system; therefore, they ought not to be doubted or discarded because of the absence of such a basis. The dogmatist and the destructive sceptic were both wrong, the former for insisting that we can and must have knowledge of reality, the latter for insisting that everything is in doubt. Between the two views lies a new outlook, constructive scepticism, doubting our abilities to find grounds for our knowledge, while accepting and increasing the knowledge itself. Mersenne's mechanism, his world machine, was not set forth as the true picture of the real world, as it was for his fanatic friend René Descartes, but as a hypothesis for organizing and utilizing our knowledge. Beginning with Mersenne, a new type of scientific outlook had arisen, a science without metaphysics, a science ultimately in doubt, but for all practical purposes, verifiable and useful.[35]

Put in another way, the sceptical crisis results from showing that the sort of certainty the dogmatic philosophers seek is unattainable, because, in terms of their quest, certain insoluble difficulties can be proposed, which prevent the discovery of absolutely true, indubitable knowledge. Thus, as Pascal avowed, as long as there are dogmatists, the sceptics are right. But, if one eliminates the dogmatic standards for genuine knowledge, then the Pyrrhonian attack becomes ridiculous, since it is developed in terms of these strong demands or conditions laid down by the dogmatic philosophers.[36] As soon as Mersenne had shifted the standards of true knowledge from self-evident, indubitable truths or true demonstrations from them, to psychologically unquestioned, or even unquestionable truths (which may be false on the former standards), then the sceptics had lost their opponent, and their attacks, applied to Mersenne's type of knowledge, became ludicrous and wantonly destructive. The 'reasonable' sceptic could abandon his doubts as regards this new conception of knowledge, and join Mersenne in his quest for the most convincing, most useful presentaiton and organization of the information we are all aware of, the development of the picture of the world as a machine.

Petrus Gassendi, a great scientist, a fellow priest, and Mersenne's best friend, gradually adopted this attitude of 'constructive' scepticism, and devoted much of his later writings to working out a philosophy midway between total scepticism and dogmatism.[37] Gassendi's atomism was presented, especially in its final form, as the best explanation of the world of appearance. Much more than Mersenne, Gassendi tried to clarify in detail the epistemological status of his mechanical picture of the world through a serious, careful, systematic analysis of the nature of knowledge. His magnum opus, the *Syntagma*, deals not at all with metaphysics, but does treat at great length what his hero, Epicurus, called 'canonics',—philosophy of logic and theory of knowledge. Here Gassendi examined the views he had originally espoused, those of the Pyrrhonists, and showed why he was abandoning their total doubt about the possibility of knowledge.

After presenting a careful summary of the sceptical theory as it appears in the writings of Sextus Empiricus,[38] Gassendi then, in terms of the problem of knowledge as presented by the Pyrrhonians, tried to defend his own compromise between dogmatism and scepticism. The basic question is, is there an absolutely certain criterion for distinguishing truth from error? Some things are obvious at certain times, e.g. 'It is day', while others are not. The sceptics and everyone else, accept what is evident, or apparent. The problem arises in connection with what Sextus called the non-evident, those things which are hidden from us. Some of these are absolutely non-evident, such as whether the number of stars is odd or even. (This, and most of the illustraitons employed by Gassendi in discussing the problem of knowledge, are drawn from Sextus's analysis of the problem of whether indicative signs exist.) Others are naturally non-evident, but can be known by some signs or intermediaries, as, for instance, the existence of pores in the skin can be inferred from the phenomenon of sweat. Lastly, there are some things that can be known evidently, but, due to temporary conditions, are hidden from us.[39]

The cases of the naturally non-evident things and the temporarily non-evident ones require some instrument or criterion in order for us to know them. The latter, even the sceptics admit, can be discerned by 'suggestive signs', that is, constantly conjoined phenomena, such that when we perceive one, we think of the other. Thus when we see smoke, we are aware that there is a fire, though it may be temporarily hidden from us. The Pyrrhonists regard this kind of knowledge of the non-evident by means of suggestive signs as valuable in practical life.[40] However, there is a complete opposition between the sceptics and the dogmatists concerning the signs by which we may discover the naturally non-evident. The sceptics doubt that there is any criterion, and that we can know things other than how they appear to us. The dogmatists insist that the truth of things can be discovered by us through indicative signs.[41]

Gassendi criticized the dogmatic view because it exaggerated the power of the human mind. The secrets of nature, of things-in-themselves, are forever hidden from us. But, at the same time, the sceptics have also gone too far. A way to knowledge can be found between the two opposing camps. It is obvious that something exists, and that some things can be, and are, known. So, total doubt is uncalled for. Even the sceptics agree that we know appearances. But, also, we are capable of knowing something about the nature of reality by means of the criteria by which we can discern a type of indicative sign. The senses allow us to know the visible or apparent sign, and our reason enables us to interpret it, and thereby discover the hidden unperceived object. Though the senses are sometimes unreliable and erroneous, by careful reasoning we can correct their errors. The test as to whether we reason rightly and discover true knowledge, lies in experience, through verifying predictions. The sceptical quibbles about the value and foundation of reasoning are of no importance, since there are certain unquestioned principles of reasoning which are sufficiently evident to use as a basis for our inferences.[42]

This answer to scepticism, like Mersenne's, does not deny the force of Pyrrhonism as applied to the knowledge the dogmatists seek, the knowledge of the true nature of things, 'the actual quality that is in the object,'[43] and the reasons why objects have these properties. In fact, the very sort of necessary information the Stoics claimed to gain by indicative signs,[44] Gassendi and the sceptics believed was unattainable. But, Gassendi thought there was a less imposing, but still useful type of indicative sign, one that taught us the causes of appearances in scientific terms. From experience, through careful reasoning, we can discover laws or reasons that explain why we have the perceptions we do, why honey seems sweet to us, why we see certain colors.[45] In terms of the variations in our experience, we can formulate some truths about the ways objects appear to us under different conditions, laws about the causes of the variations in what we perceive. Gassendi was unwilling to conclude that since we cannot know the essential nature of things, therefore we can know nothing beyond either what appears to us or the observable regularities in these appearances. Between knowledge in the dogmatists' sense, and the appearances and suggestive signs of the Pyrrhonians, there exists a level of scientific knowledge. This knowledge is based upon a studiously careful scrutiny of appearances, and rational interpretations and explanations of these appearances, not in terms of the nature of the real objects which produce them, but in terms of the conditions which make our experience possible and intelligible. Thus, sceintific explanation, which for Gassendi is in terms of an atomic theory, accounts for our experience of sense qualities, but does not tell us anything about the nature of things-in-themselves, except how they appear in relation to us. This is the type of scientific object which Gassendi wished to protect from the doubts of the sceptics. We construct, or learn about these objects from the indicative signs in experience. We then describe these scientific objects (the atoms) in terms of the qualities found in experience. And, finally, we authenticate this atomic explanation in terms of verifiable predictions about experience.[46] Gassendi's atomism may not have borne much fruit, in terms of scientific discovery, or satisfactory scientific explanation, but it was at least a constructive result from his Pyrrhonism, unlike the destructive anti-scientific attitude and theory of his good friend, La Mothe Le Vayer.[47]

When Gassendi was confronted with a dogmatic theory, a

metaphysical picture of the structure of the universe and our knowledge of it, then the Pyrrhonian basis of his thought came out clearly and sharply, not as a disguised equivalent of scepticism as it did in Mersenne, but as a blunt avowal of complete epistemological Pyrrhonism. Thus, when considering the views of Aristotle, Herbert of Cherbury, Descartes, or even the mathematical physicists, whom he took to be Platonists or Pythagoreans, Gassendi advocated total scepticism about the world beyond appearance. His earliest work, directed against Aristotle, concluded: *nihil sciri*.[48] His comments on Herbert's *De Veritate*, both to the author and to their mutual friend, Diodati, again assert this fundamental Pyrrhonism. 'The truth, in my view, is well-hidden from the eyes of men and Monsieur Herbert seems to me to have gone a little too fast and to have had a bit too high an opinion of his view when he so indecently condemned the arguments of the Sceptics.'[49] Gassendi explained to Herbert that like the sceptics, he, Gassendi, knew only about such appearances as the sweet taste of honey, and could explain these in terms of natural, experiential qualities. But beyond this, unfortunately, we can never and will never know the truths of reality. Those who claim to uncover these ultimate verities failed to convince him. 'But, concerning what you think to be the truth of the thing, or the intimate nature of honey, this is what I ardently desire to know, and what remains still hidden for me, despite the almost infinite number of books which have been published up to the present with the pretention of communicating to us, what they call, a demonstrative science.'[50] Similarly, his vast writing on Descartes, the *Fifth Objections*, the *Institutio* and the comments on the logic of Descartes in the *Syntagma*, all stress first the obviousness of the sceptical side of the *Meditations*, that is of the First Meditation, and next that the positive side of Descartes' theory, its claim to true knowledge of reality, is grossly exaggerated, and really leads only to a most dubious view. If we try to obtain true knowledge of things solely from the clear and distinct ideas in our understanding, Gassendi insisted, we are always liable to error, since what seems clear and distinct to us at one time, may not appear so later. Because of our weakness, we should realize that we can never take adequate precautions to assure ourselves that we have not been deceived when we attempt to build solely upon our ideas. Instead, we should turn to nature, to experience, for our guidance, and we should limit our quest for knowledge to what can be discovered on this basis.[51]

Gassendi's extreme caution, his constant reliance on experience and tradition, inhibited him as a creative scientific thinker,[52] but allowed him to formulate quite fully a scientific outlook devoid of any metaphysical basis, a constructive scepticism that could account for the scientific knowledge that we do, or can possess, without overstepping the limits on human understanding revealed by the Pyrrhonists. The *via media* that he and Mersenne developed could supply an adequate rationale for the procedures and discoveries of science, without having to furnish an unshakeable foundation for the new edifice of scientific knowledge. Even though Gassendi worked out his new physics in great detail, it probably failed to become the new world-picture and the new ideology partly because of certain limitations in its author's temperament, a lack of the boldness and audacity that was to characterize such monumental explorers of the new world machine as Galileo and Descartes. Gassendi was extremely conservative, unwilling to leap beyond the experiential information and the intellectual traditions of mankind.[53] He was unwilling to break with the qualitative world of ordinary experience, or throw overboard the heritage of human wisdom in order to pursue a new insight and a new frame of reference.[54] Having less comprehension of the nature of mathematics than did Mersenne, Gassendi was sceptical of the role that it could play in our understanding of nature, and feared that the mathematical physicists were a new brand of metaphysicians, trying to portray the real nature of things in mathematical terms, like the Pythagoreans and Platonists of antiquity.[55]

But, whatever his limitations might have been, Gassendi, perhaps even more than Mersenne, had accomplished one of the more important revolutions of modern times, the separation of science from metaphysics. Building his new outlook on a complete Pyrrhonism with regard to any knowledge of reality, or the nature of things, he was able to develop a method, and a system of the sciences which, of all those of the seventeenth century,

comes closest to the modern anti-metaphysical outlook of the
positivists and the pragmatists. Rochot, in his many studies of
Gassendi's atomism, and his place in the history of scientific and
philosophical thought, shows him to be a most important link between Galileo and Newton, in moving from a conception of the
'new science' as the true picture of nature to one wherein it is seen
as a hypothetical system based solely on experience, and verified
through experience, a conception in which science is never
thought of as a way to truth about reality, but only about
appearance.[56]

This attitude of mitigated or constructive scepticism of Mersenne and Gassendi also appears in more embryonic form in
some of their contemporaries. The Franciscan writer, Jacques Du
Bosc, who was, apparently, once a follower of the 'nouveau Pyrrhonisme,' found that scepticism was praiseworthy as an antidote
to dogmatism, but that as a philosophy it was at least as
dangerous as what it opposed. What was needed was some in-
between view, which he called 'l'indifférence'. The Pyrrhonist 'in
fleeing from the too much, he has fallen into the too little; in fleeing from the fancy for knowledge, he has fallen into the fancy for
ignorance.'[57] Du Bosc accepted the sceptic's critique of traditional philosophy as sound, but his conclusion as excessive. The
middle ground, 'l'indifférence' or 'la médiocrité' is found in a sort
of self analysis, in realizing that we are half-way between the ignorant brutes and the all-knowing angels.[58] By a kind of spiritual
training, we develop a criterion for discerning intellectual and
religious truths.[59] Thus, though admitting the full force of the
Pyrrhonian barrage, Du Bosc still insisted there was a way to
some positive and important knowledge, especially theological
and moral. This kind of mitigated scepticism has been analysed
recently by Julien-Eymard d'Angers as a foreshadowing of the
philosophy of Blaise Pascal.[60]

Another indication of this acceptance of the Pyrrhonian arguments, along with a constructive solution appears in the writings
of the liberal English divine, William Chillingworth. After he had
mastered the message of Sextus Empiricus, and had seen how the
sceptical reasonings undermined the quest for certainty of both
Catholics and Protestants alike, he had returned to the Protestant
fold, and had tried to justify this position in terms of a kind of

probabilism built on the acceptance of an ultimate Pyrrhonism. This moderate view regarding religious knowledge, somewhat like that of Castellio, was to play an important role in developing the basis of the quasi-empirical philosophy of various Anglican theologians such as Wilkins and Tillotson.

Chillingworth saw that the Catholics were demanding a type of certainty, infallible knowledge, as the basis of religion, and that such certainty was unattainable not only in this area, but in any other as well. But, once this had been recognized, the conclusion was not complete doubt on all matters, but, rather, an acceptance of a lesser degree of evidence, moral certainty. Our senses may sometimes deceive, our reasoning may sometimes be faulty, our judgments may not be infallible, and we may not be able to find a demonstrative basis for what we know, but, just the same, we have sufficient assurances so that we can utilize the information that we possess to form reasonable, and morally certain judgments.[61] The person who wants more certitude than this is a fool. 'For, as he is an unreasonable Master, who requires a stronger assent to his Conclusions than his Arguments deserve; so I conceive him a forward and undisciplin'd Scholar, who desires stronger arguments for a conclusion than the Matter will bear.'[62] Once one has recognized that there is no infallible or mathematical certainty to be found regarding scientific or religious matters, then, one does not suspend judgment, but, instead, one proceeds to judge problems according to the degree of assurance that can be obtained. This theory of Chillingworth's contains the seeds of a long tradition which was to develop later in the seventeenth century in England as the commonsensical, practical solution to the sceptical crisis.[63]

Mitigated or constructive scepticism represents a new way, possibly the closest to contemporary empirical and pragmatic methods, of dealing with the abyss of doubt that the crisis of the Reformation and the scientific revolution had opened up. (It was novel for its time, though it obviously echoes some of the attitudes of Greek thinkers like Carneades.) For some, the age of Montaigne and of Luther and Calvin had set off a quest for certainty, a search for an absolutely certain foundation for human knowledge. For others the quest was only for stability, for a way of living once the quest for infallible grounds for knowledge had been abandoned, and for a way of living that could accept both the unanswerable doubts of the 'nouveaux pyrrhoniens' and the unquestioned discoveries of the intellectual new world of the seventeenth century. Mersenne and Gassendi sought to reconcile the sceptical triumph over the dogmatists with the mechanistic triumph over Aristotelianism and Renaissance naturalism. They found such a reconciliation not in a new dogmatism, or a materialistic metaphysic, but in the realization that the doubts propounded by the Pyrrhonists in no way affected *la vérité des sciences*, provided that the sciences were interpreted as hypothetical systems about appearances, and not true descriptions of reality, as practical guides to actions, and not ultimate information about the true nature of things. The *crise pyrrhonienne* fundamentally could not be resolved, but, at least, it could be ignored or abided with, if one could relegate the doubts to the problems of dogmatic philosophy, while pursuing scientific knowledge as the guide to practical living. The *crise pyrrhonienne* would have disastrous consequences if one accepted the conclusion of the destructive humanistic sceptics and extended one's doubts to science and even religion. But, it could have beneficial results were it restricted to the epistemological sphere as a means of eliminating the dogmatists' hopeless pursuit of absolute certainty, while leaving the scientist or the theologian free to discover truths about appearances.

This attitude of constructive or mitigated scepticism is in sharp contrast to either the new metaphysical views of some of the 'new scientists' like Galileo, Campanella and Descartes, or the scientistic attitude that was to develop in the Enlightenment. Although Galileo, Campanella and Descartes might occasionally assert, for tactical reasons, that their theories were only hypothetical,[64] and that there was a level of knowledge about essences that man could never know,[65] at the same time, they seem to share a conviction that man is capable of attaining true knowledge about the real world, and that the mechanistic picture of the universe is an accurate description of the way nature actually operates. In the view of Galileo and Campanella, God has given us the faculties to attain knowledge of the nature of things. However, our knowledge is only partial, unlike His complete knowledge. Nonetheless, we have no reason to question or doubt what we know, and we have no reason to restrict our knowledge to appearances, rather than reality.[66] The sceptical crisis seems to have bypassed these thinkers, and left them only with doubts about the Aristotelian quest for certainty, but not with the quest itself.

Descartes criticized Galileo for being too modest in his claims, and not seeing that the truths of the new science rest upon a certain metaphysical foundation which guarantees their applicability to reality, and which provides the complete assurance which separates these discoveries from opinion or probable information. In approving of Galileo's use of the mathematical method, Descartes commented,

> I agree entirely with him in this, and I hold that there is no other means for finding the truth. But it seems to me that he lacks much in that he continually makes digressions, and does not stop to explain a matter completely; which show he has not examined things in an orderly way, and that, without having considered the primary cause of nature, he has only sought the reasons for some particular effects and thus that he has built without a foundation. Now inasmuch as his way of philosophizing is closer to the true one, to that degree can one more easily recognize its faults, just as it can better be ascertained when people go astray who sometimes follow the right road, than when those go astray who have never entered upon it.[67]

In the case of all three of these thinkers, Galileo, Campanella and Descartes, though there might be some disagreement as to the foundation for the truths of the 'new science', there is no doubt that the 'new science' is true, and true about the real nature of the physical world. There is no epistemological Pyrrhonism, but rather a kind of realism. Science is not the constructive issue of complete doubt, but a kind of knowledge that is not open to question either on the theoretical or philosophical level.

A century later a type of philosophical view was to become prevalent which in another way missed the *via media* of the constructive or mitigated sceptics. The scientism of various Enlightenment figures like Condillac and Condorcet was to regard Pyrrhonism as a kind of learned ignorance which might have been justified in the dark, metaphysical age of the early seventeenth century, but which had no place in the enlightened era of the eighteenth century. The reasons for doubting, supposedly, had now passed into oblivion, since the progress of science had unveiled the true, real world.[68]

But, as Mersenne and Gassendi had seen, the achievements of science in no way disproved Pyrrhonism, unless the sceptic were foolish, or impious enough, to doubt the discoveries of the scientists, as well as the grounds for them. The latter were open to question, and had been undermined by the onslaught of the 'nouveau Pyrrhonisme'. But the former were as convincing and as reliable as ever. The truth of the sciences is not at issue, but this truth, for the mitigated sceptics, could only be appreciated in terms of the *crise pyrrhonienne*, and not as a rational, philosophical answer to it.

The success of constructive scepticism as the core of the modern empirical and pragmatic outlook, the recognition that absolutely certain grounds could not be given for our knowledge, and yet that we possess standards for evaluating the reliability and applicability of what we have found out about the world, had to await the rise and fall of a new dogmatism. Though Mersenne and Gassendi were widely read and approved of in their day, the acceptance of their type of philosophical view as a major outlook did not come until attempts were made to end the *crise pyrrhonienne* by erecting a new intellectual foundation for human certitude. For a time the constructive sceptics were cast into the shadows, while a new metaphysical drama was played out on the center of the stage, while new systems were proposed to give an answer to the sceptical challenge. After new systems like those of Herbert of Cherbury, Jean de Silhon and René Descartes had met the fate of the older ones, then, constructive scepticism could be absorbed into the mainstream of philosophy.

VIII

HERBERT OF CHERBURY AND JEAN DE SILHON

Neither Herbert of Cherbury nor Jean de Silhon appreciated sufficiently the extent to which the 'nouveau Pyrrhonisme' had undermined the foundations of human knowledge. But each saw that it had to be dealt with, and dealt with in a new way. The former proposed an elaborate method to discover truth; the latter tried to present some fundamental truths that could not be doubted. And, as the greatest of the opponents of scepticism, René Descartes saw, each failed in a crucial way because he failed to comprehend the basic problem at issue.

Edward, Lord Herbert of Cherbury (1583–1648), was ambassador to France from 1618 until 1624,[1] where he came in contact with both the current of sceptical ideas, and the attempts being made to counteract it. It is likely that at this time, he also came to know Mersenne, who is thought to have translated Herbert's book into French,[2] and Gassendi, to whom he is known to have presented a copy of his work.[3] He was also friendly with the diplomat, Diodati, who was a member of the *Tétrade*, the society of *libertins érudits*. While Herbert was in Paris, he showed his manuscript to Grotius, who was familiar with the writings of Sextus Empiricus.[4] Finally, in 1624, after years of work on his masterpiece (which had been started in 1617, even before his Paris embassy), filled with fear and trembling about its possible reception, Herbert received what he regarded as a sign from above, and published *De Veritate*.[5]

This book begins with a picture of the sorry state of contemporary learning, the chaos of beliefs, and the many controversies. There are people who say we can know everything, and there are

those who say we can know nothing. Herbert insisted he belonged
to neither of these schools, but, rather, held that *something* can
be known. What is needed in order to recognize and evaluate the
knowledge we have is a definition of truth, a criterion of truth,
and a method of finding truth. When we have found all of these,
we will have no patience with scepticism because we will understand that there are certain conditions under which our faculties
are able to know objects.[6]

The first proposition of *De Veritate* is announced baldly,
'Truth exists.' Herbert tells us, 'The sole purpose of this proposition is to assert the existence of truth against imbeciles and
sceptics.'[7] Having taken his stand in opposition to the message of
the 'nouveaux Pyrrhoniens', Herbert proceeded to show what
truth is, and how it can be attained. There are four types of
truths, the truth of things as they really are in themselves (*veritas
rei*), the truth of things as they appear to us (*veritas apparentiae*),
and lastly, the intellectual truths, the Common Notions by which
we judge our subjective truths, the appearances and concepts,
(*veritas intellectus*). The first class of truth is absolute; it is 'the
thing as it is,'[8] and it is this that we are seeking to know by means
of the three conditional classes of truth, those involved with the
knower rather than the object itself. Starting with the information we have as to how the object appears to us, our task is to
discover a standard or criterion by which to determine when our
subjective information conforms to the truth of the thing-in-itself.
What we know from appearances can be deceitful or misleading
as a guide to what the real object is like. The appearance, as
such, is always genuine; that is, it appears the way it appears. But
it is not necessarily an indication of what the truth of the thing
itself may be.[9] Similarly, the concepts we form on the basis of the
experiences we have are entirely our own and may or may not
coincide or correspond with the things they are supposed to be
concepts of. 'If the sense organ is imperfect, or if it is of poor
quality, if the mind is filled with deceitful prejudices, the concept
is wholly vitiated.'[10] So, the last class of truth, the truth of
intellect, is required in order 'to decide in virtue of its inborn
capacity or its Common Notions whether our subjective faculties
have exercised their perceptions well or ill.'[11] By this standard or

criterion we can judge whether there is conformity between the truth of the thing and the subjective truths of appearance and concept, and hence, whether we possess objective knowledge.

In a cumbersome fashion, Herbert then proceeded to detail, step-by-step, the method for arriving at the different classes of subjective or conditional truth, for recognizing the Common Notions or criterion for assessing if the subjective truths conform to the truth of things, and lastly for applying all this machinery to the search for truth. Since at each level there are difficulties that have been raised by the sceptics, a careful statement has to be given of the conditions for ascertaining each class of truth. Herbert first offered four conditions that the object must meet to be knowable, presenting some of these as Common Notions, universally admitted or innate truths. These conditions specify that what is to be known must fall within the range and have the characteristics that our faculties and capacities can deal with. Then, in order that the appearance of the object can be brought into conformity with the object a further series of conditions is laid down, largely following Aristotle's analysis of the means for obtaining true perception. Rules are presented which specify when the object is in such circumstances that we can obtain a proper likeness or appearance of it. Many of the illusory or deceptive cases of perception brought up by the sceptics can be explained and accounted for as due to the absence of one or more of the conditions.[12]

When a proper object of knowledge is perceived under these conditions so that a true appearance can be obtained; then we are able, under specifiable conditions, to obtain a true concept of the thing. The appearance, presumably, is 'in a precise external conformity with its original,'[13] and what is now required is a means for ascertaining when our internal idea of the object conforms exactly to the true appearance. Other views of Aristotle are offered concerning the proper conditions of the sense organ, and the proper method for concept formation. These eliminate difficulties raised by the sceptics based upon the ideas we form of things when there is some defect in our organs of sensation and reason, such as jaundice influencing colors, or drukenness influencing our concepts of things.[14]

It is Herbert's contention that when the conditions of true appearance and true concepts are fulfilled, we are then in a position to obtain unquestioned intellectual truths. The appearance conforms to, or corresponds to, the object. The concept conforms to, or corresponds to, the appearance. Then the intellect can come to true knowledge about the object by judging that the concept relates to the thing itself. 'It is important to notice that the intellect is never deceived when a real object is present, or when the true rules of conformity are fulfilled . . . when a real object is present, even though it is drawn from memory, and the true conditions are fulfilled, I maintain that the intellect asserts truth even in dreams.'[15]

The basis for this great assurance that something can be known about the real world is the theory of Common Notions. Our faculties of sense and reason alone, no matter how well they were operating, would be insufficient to guarantee us any truth about objects, since by these faculties alone we could never tell whether we were in the plight the sceptics describe, living in an illusory mental universe, or, at least, one whose objectivity we could never determine, or whether we were in possession of some truths about the world. The bridge between the world revealed to us by our subjective faculties and the real world is the Common Notions which enable us to judge the veracity of our picture of the world. It is these innate truths by which 'our minds are enabled to come to decisions concerning the events which take place upon the theatre of the world.' It is only by their aid that the intellect 'can be led to decide whether our subjective faculties have accurate knowledge of the facts.' And, it is by employing them that we are able to tell truth from falsehood.[16]

What are these treasures, these Common Notions? 'Truths of the intellect, then, are certain Common Notions which are found in all normal persons; which notions are, so to say, constituents of all and are derived from universal wisdom and imprinted on the soul by the dictates of nature itself.'[17] What is not known by the aid of these innate ideas 'cannot possibly be proved to be, in the strict sense, true.'[18] These fundamental truths of the intellect cannot be denied except by madmen, idiots, or others who are incapable of comprehending them. If we are sane, we must accept them, unless we prefer to be forever uncertain.[19] The first, and basic, test as to whether some proposition is one of these indubitable Common Notions is whether or not it commands universal consent. If it does, then nothing could ever convince us of its falsity. Unless this standard is accepted, there is no stability in the present turmoil of conflicting opinions in religion and science. 'The wretched terror-stricken mass have no refuge, unless some immovable foundations of truth resting on universal consent are established, to which they can turn amid the doubts of theology or of philosophy,'[20] Thus, Herbert proclaimed, 'In my view, then, Universal Consent must be taken to be the beginning and end of theology and philosophy.'[21] God has providentially given us all these truths; hence, they are trustworthy, as well as being the only basis that we possess for gaining knowledge of the real world.

Several passages suggest that Herbert's scheme for discovering the truths that are universally accepted in simple empirical inspection. To find the Common Notion of Law, we are told, we must investigate, and discover those laws 'which are approved of by the whole world.'[22] The cases that Locke was to bring up against Herbert's theory were anticipated and dealt with in advance. Idiots and madmen do not have to be examined, since the Common Notions are found only in normal people. (This, of course, creates a problem Herbert did not recognize, namely, how do we tell who is normal? If it is by whether one consents to a Common Notion, then how does one tell these innate truths to begin with?) Similarly, infants and embryos are discounted from the survey, because they are regulated unconciously by God.[23] But, by examining normal, mature people everywhere, we find that there are some ideas that are shared by everybody, such as that there is a first cause, and a purpose to the world.[24] Why we have these Common Notions, we cannot tell, any more than we can explain why we have the sense experiences we do. All we can observe is that we have them, and that they are universal. 'Anyone who prefers persistently and stubbornly to reject these principles might as well stop his ears, shut his eyes and strip himself of all humanity.'[25]

With the Common Notions we are able to arrive at a conviction, at mathematical certainty, which we could not accomplish otherwise. Those who try to gain knowledge by the external senses cannot 'pierce beyond the outer shell of things,' and might just as well 'take food through one's ears.'[26] But, our innate ideas, our natural instinct, our Common Notions, provide a basis for attaining certianty. Our logical reasoning and our interpretation of experience as a source of information about the real world, have as their foundation these principles, and these principles are so fundamental that they cannot be doubted without destroying all possibility of knowledge. Thus, Herbert tells us, 'for these Notions exercise an authority so profound that anyone who were to doubt them would upset the whole natural order and strip himself of his humanity. These principles may not be disputed. As long as they are understood it is impossible to deny them.'[27]

Without going further into Herbert of Cherbury's ponderous theory, we can see it as an attempted answer to the problem of knowledge raised by the sceptics, which contains an elaborate method for establishing accurate or true appearances and concepts, and then offers the Common Notions as the long-sought criterion for judging the truth of our most reliable information. Every normal person possesses the standard, or the rule of truth. (If he is not aware of it, he can find it all described and codified in *De Veritate*.) Hence, all that one has to do is first, make sure that the proper conditions of perception and concept formation have been met, and then employ the proper Common Notion or Notions, thereby gaining knowledge which conforms to the thing itself. Hence, although all our ideas are subjective, we have a criterion by which we can judge when they have objective reference, and thus can discover some genuine truths. The rule of truth is guaranteed by its universality and by the conviction of certainty it implants in us, and by the fact that any questioning of the standard would have the disastrous consequences of destroying the very possibility of any objective knowledge.

This new system for meeting the *crise pyrrhonienne* is obviously open to sceptical objections at almost every level. It can, and has been challenged whether there are any Common Notions, any principles upon which there is such universal agreement. The ancient Pyrrhonists tried to show that every fundamental belief, whether it be in logic, metaphysics, science, ethics, etc. has been contested by someone. Herbert might ignore this with the comment that the controversialists must have been madmen. But, this raises the further sceptical problem, how does one tell who is mad and who is not, without begging the whole question at issue? Even if one could accept the claim that there are Common Notions that everybody accepts, one could still remain sceptical of Herbert's general scheme about objective knowledge. Why should what we all accept, be decisive in discovering what the real world is like? Even if we could establish reliable standards for judging the accuracy of data (though one could question why Herbert's conditions are the right ones), and we had accurate concepts (though one could question again whether Herbert's claims are right), and we all agreed on how to apply them, what would this tell us about the truth of things-in-themselves? Herbert's appeal to our feeling of certainty, and our need for accepting his scheme if we are to have any real knowledge, begs the question. Even if we agree to his theory about truths of appearance, truths of concepts, and truths of intellect, we still cannot tell whether there can be any truths of things. And, until we can determine the latter, how can we ascertain if the procedures advanced by Herbert culminate in the discovery of genuine knowledge about the real world?

Although Herbert of Cherbury's antidote to scepticism was apparently well received in its day,[28] it was subjected to devastating criticisms long before Locke by Gassendi and Descartes. The former attacked it as an indefensible dogmatism which had actually failed to conquer the sceptics, while the latter attacked it for being an inadequate dogmatism which failed to refute Pyrrhonism because it had failed to come to grips with the fundamental problem at issue.

Two versions of Gassendi's objections have come down to us, one a rather polite letter to Herbert, which was never sent, raising some basic questions, and the other, written to their common friend, Diodati, containing a nasty denunciation. The second appears to represent Gassendi's true opinion of Herbert's new philosophical system for meeting the sceptical challenge, namely that the scheme is a maze of confusions accomplishing nothing. First,

Gassendi expressed his shock that so many people, including the Pope, had praised *De Veritate*. (But as we shall see shortly, Gassendi, in his letter to Herbert, heaped extravagant compliments upon the author and his book.) The truth which Herbert claimed to have discovered, Gassendi declared was unknown and unknowable. Without knowing what truth may actually be, one can discern that Herbert has not found it, and has not answered the sceptics. Just as one can tell that the king is neither in Aix nor Marseilles, without knowing definitely where he is, one can see that there is something wrong with Herbert's schemes without having a counter-dogmatism to substitute for it.[29] All that one can say of the new system is that it 'is only a kind of dialectic which can well have its advantages, but which does not prevent us from being able to make up a hundred other schemes of similar value and perchance of greater one.'[30]

Having made these comments, Gassendi then briefly formulated a sceptical difficulty which he believed brought to nothing all the efforts of Herbert of Cherbury. According to his scheme, the criterion or standard of truth is natural instinct and our interior faculties (the Common Notions), by which each of us can judge the true nature of things. But, if this is the case, how can we account for 'the great contrariety of opinions that are found on almost every subject?' Every person is convinced by his own natural instinct and interior faculties. If he uses Herbert's means to account for disagreement, each will declare that the other 'is not sound and whole,' and each will believe this on the basis of his own truths of intellect. So they will arrive at an impasse, since each will naturally think he is right, and appeal to the same internal standards. They will have no criterion for determining whose views are true, for, 'Who will be the judge of it and will be able to prove that he has the right not to be taken as one of the parties?'[31]

As long as there are disagreements on practically every matter, the same sceptical problem that had arisen in the Reformation will plague Herbert's philosophy as well. Each individual can find the truth of things subjectively, according to standards within himself, but who is to judge the truth when different people disagree and are each subjectively convinced? Herbert insisted that there was universal agreement on certain basic matters, except for the views of idiots, infants, etc. But, then, who or what can be the judge of sanity, mental health, mental maturity, if the conflicting parties each claim to possess these qualities? Therefore, Gassendi concluded, Herbert's scheme was incapable of determining the truths of nature, since it was based on so feeble and inconstant a standard as natural instinct, or inner conviction.[32]

Gassendi's other letter, addressed to the author himself, develops in much more elaborate and comprehensive form a similar kind of criticism. It says, in effect, that Herbert has not refuted scepticism, and that basic sceptical difficulties could be raised that undermine the value of Herbert's complex scheme. After flattering the author inordinately, calling him 'England's treasure', who has arisen to succeed Francis Bacon, Gassendi showed that once the traditional sceptical distinction had been made between the truth of things-in-themselves, and the truth of appearances, then Herbert's scheme would not help in the slightest to extend our knowledge from appearances to reality. All that we are aware of is how things appear, that honey seems sweet and fire hot. To try to go beyond the knowledge of these appearances exhibits an unfortunate quality of mind, because, as yet, only God knows the real nature of things. All the machinery of *De Veritate* does not reveal truth to us in its purity, but rather only shows more about the conditions under which it appears to us, the conditions under which we gain adequate and useful knowledge about experience, but not the conditions under which we discover the unconditioned *veritas rei*. As he pointed out to Diodati, the theory of Common Notions did not really solve anything, since, first of all there is no universal agreement on matters, and secondly we have no standards or criteria for determining whose Common Notions are the measure or rule of truth. Therefore, the sceptical crisis remains, and all that we are able to do is seek truths of appearance, while ignoring Herbert's grandiose scheme of types of truth, conditions of truth, Common Notions, etc., which would not aid us at all in ascertaining when our experience and concepts relate to, or conform to, the real world.[33]

Another, and possibly more incisive, criticism of *De Veritate* was given by René Descartes, who, unlike Gassendi, was most sympathetic with its aim of refuting scepticism, and hence, more conscious of its fundamental failure. Mersenne had sent Descartes a copy of Herbert's book in 1639, and received a detailed discussion of the work. The work, Descartes observed, deals with 'a subject on which I have worked all my life,' but 'he takes a very different route than the one that I have followed.' The basic point of difference between Descartes's work and Herbert's is that the latter was attempting to find out what truth is, while the former insisted that he never had any doubts or difficulties on this score, because truth 'is a notion so transcendentally clear that it is impossible not to know it.'[34]

The fundamental problem in Herbert's approach, as Descartes saw it, was that if one did not antecedently know what truth is, one would have no way of learning it. Why should we accept Herbert's results unless we were sure that they were true? If we could tell that they were true, we would already have to know what truth was in order to recognize that the scheme of *De Veritate* was a method for measuring or discovering truth. The problem being raised is similar to that of Plato's *Meno* and to one of the criticisms against the Calvinist 'way of examination'—how can one find the truth by means of some set of operations unless one knows what one is looking for?[35] The only knowledge one can gain in this area is that of word usage; how the term 'verité' is employed in French. But no definition aids in knowing the nature of truth. This notion, like several other fundamental ideas such as figure, size, motion, place and time, can only be known intuitively. When one attempts to define them, 'one obscures them, and one becomes mixed up.' The man who walks around a room understands what motion is better than the person who learns the definition from a textbook. And so with truth, supposedly. The man who has experienced or has known a truth can better understand the problem of knowledge than the person who sets down a lot of definitions and procedures for discovering a truth. Herbert had many measuring devices, but could not tell what they measured. Descartes started with the awareness of a truth, and constructed his measure of truth from it. Herbert might have had a criterion, but could not tell if it were the criterion of truth. Descartes possessed a truth, the *cogito*, to test his criterion with.[36]

As to Herbert's criterion itself, Descartes found it open to serious objection. Herbert 'takes universal consent as the rule of his truths.' But many people ('for example all those that we know') can agree on the same errors, so that universal consent is not a reliable standard. Descartes' rule of truth, natural light, is the same in all men, and if they use it, they will all agree on the same truths. But, since practially no one uses his natural light, it is quite likely that much of what people agree on now is doubtful or erroneous, and that some truths that can be known have never yet been recognized, or thought of.[37] Further, natural instinct, which Herbert used as a fundamental source of the Common Notions, is not necessarily a reliable guide that ought to be followed. That part of our natural inclination that derives from our bodily or animal nature can be misleading, whereas only the natural instinct that is the natural light is trustworthy.[38] Thus, the standard introduced by Herbert, based on common consent and natural instinct, can yield unfortunate results. Universal errors are prevalent, and our animal natures can lead us to believing all sorts of things which are not, or may not, be true.

From two different sides, that of the mitigated sceptic and the complete dogmatist, Herbert of Cherbury's answer to scepticism was found wanting. Gassendi saw that the new scheme did not discover the truth of things, and led actually to a kind of scepticism since there was, in fact, no universal agreement on anything. Descartes saw that Herbert had started in the wrong place, and offered an inadequate criterion. To defeat scepticism, one must know what truth is, and not seek it by a lot of procedures whose relation to the quest cannot be determined. And, one must possess a criterion of truth which cannot confuse the true and the false or the doubtful.

If Herbert had not offered a satisfactory solution to the *crise pyrrhonienne*, others were willing to attempt it. Two years after the first publication of *De Veritate*, Jean de Silhon, a curious eclectic figure, entered the field. He was one of the bright young men who aided Richelieu and Mazarin in building the new France, and he was a friend of René Descartes and Guez de Balzac, and of many of those who were trying to destroy the monsters menacing religion. Silhon's answer to scepticism appeared as part of a large apologetic programme, striking out against the enemy already within the gates, against the atheism that was rampant around him. The answer Silhon offered is interesting not only in terms of its place in the history of the counter-attack against the 'nouveaux Pyrrhoniens', but also for some striking similarities to Descartes' thought that occur within it, as well as for some ideas that Pascal may have drawn from it.

The general plan of Silhon's work can best be understood in terms of the apologetic movement of the time. There are doubters of the true religion everywhere. In order to defend the faith, it is not enough to point out what God requires that we believe. One must first establish that there is a God and that we possess an immortal soul. But before one can arrive at these basic truths, one must first eliminate one of the causes of irreligion—scepticism. The Pyrrhonists deny the very possibility of knowledge; hence, before the two basic truths of religion can be known, one must first show that knowledge in general is possible, and next that this particular knowledge can be attained. Thus, the apologetic goal can only be achieved after the Pyrrhonism of Montaigne[39] has been refuted.[40]

Before examining Silhon's answer to Pyrrhonism, I would like to add a few words, parenthetically, on the strange interpretation offered by the famous French scholar, Fortunat Strowski, who accused Silhon of being a freethinker like Naudé. The only apologetic element Strowski could perceive was that Silhon was apologizing for the politics of his master, Richelieu. Strowski classed Silhon with the worst villains of the period because, he said, first that Silhon was a 'mediocre writer', (which while true hardly shows that he was insincere) and second that he was a plagiarist, pilfering ideas from Descartes' unpublished works ('Silhon pilfers from him without shame'). But, even if this were true, it would hardly provide evidence of *libertinage*. Further, as we sall see, there is grave difficulty in determining whether Silhon or Descartes was responsible for their common ideas. At any rate, nothing in Silhon's text, or our knowledge about him suggests that he was really against or indifferent to the apologetic cause, but rather that in his own, perhaps feeble way, he was trying to stem the tide of scepticism and irreligion.[41]

Silhon's campaign began in 1626 with the publication of his *Les Deux Veritez*, a title reminiscent of Charron's. At the outset, in his *Discours Premier*, Silhon attacked the opinion accepted even by some Christians, that there is no science of anything, and that all can be doubted. Christians have the Scriptures which inform them that visible things can lead to invisible truths, and hence they ought not to be sceptics. And philosophers are aware 'of propositions and maxims invested with so much clarity, and carrying in themselves so much evidence, that at the same time they are conceived, one is convinced of them, and that it is impossible that there be an understanding which could reject them.'[42] As examples of such truths, Silhon offered 'everything is, or is not. That everything that has being either gets it from itself or has received it from another. That the whole is greater than its parts, etc.'[43] From these we are able to draw inferences.

The Pyrrhonist, if he is not yet convinced, either knows there can be no science, and hence has a science consisting of this truth, or he does not know there can be no science, and hence has no reason to make the claim. 'As for this chain and string of doubts of Mr. Montaigne in favor of Pyrrhonism, it accomplishes the contrary of his design, and wishing to prove that there is no knowledge, in order to humble the vanity it often inspires us with, he makes our understandings capable of an infinite progress of acts.'[44] The last point offered by Silhon was similar to one of Herbert's, namely the appeal to the naturalness of our reasoning abilities, our natural inclination to accept rationality. Assuming that these tendencies have been implanted in us by Nature, would they have been implanted in us—if they did not lead to truth?[45]

In his first effort to defeat the Pyrrhonists, Silhon fell far short of the mark—either begging the question or missing the point. The Pyrrhonist was questioning not that certain propositions seem true, but whether we have adequate evidence that they are. He was trying to avoid the positive contention that nothing can be known, but would suspend judgment on the question instead. And finally, the Pyrrhonist could easily question Silhon's assumption that our faculties are the result of a benevolent Nature, and hence can be trusted.

After this initial sally against Pyrrhonism, Silhon began to see that his case might not be adequate to the task of defeating scepticism, if the opponent were really determined. So, in his second book of 1634, *De l'Immortalité de l'Ame*, a much more searching

and interesting argument is offered, reflecting perhaps his
acquaintance witht he young René Descartes,[46] or possibly his acquaintance with such live Pyrrhonists as La Mothe Le Vayer.[47]
After 100 pages devoted to the Machiavellians' theory that the
doctrine of immortality is an invention for reasons of policy,
Silhon, in his *Discours Sescond*, presented a *'Refutation of Pyrrhonism and of the reasons that Montaigne sets forth to establish
it.'*[48] The purpose in discussing scepticism was the same as
before; in order to show that God exists, and that the soul is
immortal, it is first necessary to show that knowledge is possible.
If one doubts our knowledge, then one might doubt that the
Revelation comes from God, and, then, all certitude would
vanish. The doubts that the sceptics cast upon our sense knowledge have grave consequences for a Christian, since his religious
knowledge depends upon such signs from God as the miracles of
Jesus, which are known through the senses.[49] Hence, 'If the
Christians who have protected Pyrrhonism had foreseen the consequences of this error, I do not doubt that they would have
abandoned it.'[50] Even Montaigne, Silhon suggested, did not actually fully believe in Pyrrhonism but was only attacking the presumption of people who tried to reason out too much.[51]

The attack on Pyrrhonism which will show that it is 'an extravagant view, and an insupportable error in ordinary reason, and
contrary to experience,'[52] begins with an extended version of the
point that to assert that there is no science of anything, is self-
defeating. If this is known to be true, then we have knowledge,
and if it is not, then why should we assume ignorance to be the
measure or rule of all things. If the proposition 'There is no
science of anything' is either self-evident or demonstrable, then
there is at least one science, namely that one that contains this
true principle.[53] At this point, after going over old ground, Silhon
observed that Montaigne had not fallen into this trap, since Montaigne's Pyrrhonist was too dubious and irresolute to affirm even
that nothing can be known. But this defense, Silhon contended,
leads to a ridiculous infinitude of doubts as to whether one is
certain that one ought to doubt that one doubts, and so on. Anyone possessing common sense and reason can see that one either
has to have 'a final experienced certain and infallible knowledge'[54]

by which one understands both evidently and necessarily, either that one knows something, or one does not, or else one has doubts. And, at this point, Montaigne's defense will have ended.

But, supposing that Pyrrhonism is a reasonable view, let us consider whether our senses and our understanding are as weak and fallacious as the sceptics claim. We have, as Silhon had previously claimed in his *Deux Veritez*, basic principles that as soon as they are presented to our understanding 'it comprehends them and takes hold of them without any difficulty,'[55] e.g. everything is necessary or contingent; the whole is greater than its parts, etc. Only people determined to deny everything, can deny these truths. The rest of us can use these as the fundamentals for developing sciences.[56]

Silhon then proceeded to develop the last part of his answer from his previous volume. Nature would have made a great mistake if we possess this violent inclination to know, and knowledge is impossible. Our arts and sciences for finding truth would be superfluous were there no truth. There cannot be sciences or arts of impossible things, and, thus, if we have sciences and arts they must then have possible aims. The fact that we have rules of logic for finding truths, and distinguishing them from falsehoods would seem to require some knowledge from which to construct the rules, just as the drawing of maps of the New World requires its having already been discoverd.[57] Thus, in this question-begging fashion, Silhon insisted that since we have a criterion that we accept as true, we must possess truth; however, he did not see that the criterion could still be challenged unless we already knew some truth and could show that the standards in use really were the proper measures of it.

After this, Silhon took up what he regarded as 'the chief argument of Montaigne', the deceptiveness of our senses. If there is nothing in the intellect that was not first in the senses, and the senses are faulty or deceptive, then all our reasoning is unsure. Silhon listed the sort of evidence used by Montaigne—illusions, illness, madness, dreams, and then asked if Montaigne were right.[58] If he were, this would amount to blasphemy, since it would deny the goodness and competence of our Maker. We must believe in the reliability of our senses, for 'The confusion is too

great to think that God did not know how to prevent it, and it
would be too injurious to His Goodness, and counter to the
infinite testimonies that we have to His Love, to think that He has
not willed it.'[59] The wisdom and goodness of God require that our
senses be accurate. But, then, how are Montaigne's cases to be
accounted for? Silhon explained illusions as due to misuses of our
senses, in terms of Aristotle's analysis. If the senses are functioning properly, and employed under proper conditions, they do
not err. Illusions are all 'fortuitious and rare cases, these are
things accidental to sight and contrary to the order that nature
has set up for its operation.'[60] Reason and reliable sense operation can eliminate any possibility of deception when one perceives
a bent oar, etc. The problem of dreams can also easily be solved.
Rational people can tell the difference between sleeping and
waking, and hence there is no real difficulty. When they wake up,
they can tell that their previous experience was part of a dream.
The same is true for the odd experiences had when drunk, or
sick.[61]

At this point, Silhon smugly announced that he had refuted the
claim that all our knowledge is deceptive and uncertain. But,
possibly from his conversations with Descartes, Silhon realized
that a really 'tough-minded' sceptic would not hvae been convinced by this alleged refutation of Montaigne. In order to satisfy
the most determined of Pyrrhonists, Silhon had one final
argument, 'here is certain knowledge, no matter in what sense it
is considered or whenever it is examined, and of which it is impossible that a man who is capable of reflection and reason can
doubt and not be certain.'[62] This certain knowledge is that each
person can tell that he is, that he has being. Even if his senses are
deceptive and even if he cannot distinguish hallucinations, imag-
inings and dreams from actual experiences, a man cannot be deceived in judging 'that he is' and it be the case 'that he is not'.[63]
Having presented what appears to be either an anticipation of, or
a borrowing from, Descartes' refutation of scepticism, Silhon
then explained why a man cannot deny his own existence. The
explanation indicates that he had missed the crucial nature of the
cogito almost entirely. Silhon declared God can make something
out of nothing, 'But to make that which does not exist, act as if it

does, involves a contradiction. This is what the nature of things will not allow. This is what is completely impossible.'[64]

Thus, according to Silhon, the undeniability of our own existence is not due to the truth of the *cogito*, which is indubitable. Its undeniability depends on its derivation from a metaphysical claim that whatever acts, exists. If I thought I existed, and yet did not, this would be a contradiction of the metaphysical law, and, apparently, not even God is allowed to contradict it. Even in Silhon's final presentation of his case, in his *De la Certitude des Connoissances humaines* of 1661, after he had ample opportunity to study Descartes' writings, he still derived his *cogito* from the principle that operation or action supposes being, and not even God can make what does not exist, act.[65]

In his answer to scepticism, Silhon appears to have seen that the truth or certitude of one's own existence was significant, and also, that this truth could be used to establish God's existence.[66] But, he did not understand why, or how this crucial certitude refuted scepticism, and hence he failed to begin the revolution in thought that Descartes's publication three years later was to accomplish. By deriving the *cogito* from a metaphysical maxim that he had never shown must be true, he allowed the sceptic the same rejoinder he could raise against all of Silhon's types of refutations of Pyrrhonism; namely, how do we know that the premises being employed ar true, how do we know that the rules of logic do measure truth and falsity, that our sense faculties are the product of a benevolent Creator, that our senses are accurate under certain conditions, and that whatever acts, exists? Unless Silhon could offer proof of his premises, the sceptic could continue to raise his doubts. At best, all that Silhon had accomplished by adding the *cogito*, was to single out one curious fact (though it is almost lost in the morass of Silhon's text), that it seems impossible to deny one's existence. And, if this had to be admitted, then there would be at least one thing the sceptic could not challenge.[67] But it was left to his brooding friend, René Descartes, to see the immense implications of the *cogito*, and to construct a new dogmatism from it.

Silhon's own positive theory of knowledge is quite eclectic and unexciting, except for a couple of elements that were to play a role in the struggles against Pyrrhonism, especially in the views of Blaise Pascal. In order to maintain that we can know genuine truths, Silhon modified the Aristotelian dictum, *nihil in intellectu . . .*, by maintaining that truth involves universals, not sensed particulars, and that infallible and certain truths can be attained without any sense information, since 'our Understandings are neither as poor nor as sterile as some believe.'[68] There are some principles which have no need of 'other illumination in order to be known,'[69] and which no one can refuse to consent to. These can be used to gain further knowledge by means of *demonstrations physiques*, in which the conclusions are connected with the certain principles 'by an indissoluble link', and in which the conclusions emanate from the principles and receive 'the influence and light from all the principles on which they depend'.[70]

Unfortunately, the sort of complete certitude resulting from *demonstrations physiques* is quite rare, and so, Silhon introduced a lesser degree of certainty, that of *demonstrations morales*, to account for most of what we know. Unlike the most certain kind of knowledge, which cannot be doubted, this other kind is conclusive, 'but not evidently so, and where the understanding does not see clearly enough to not be able to doubt of it, nor to take an opposite view if the will desires to, and if some passion leads it this way.'[71] The weight of all the materials, authorities and opinions produces a conviction in a *demonstration morale*, but never produces *l'évidence* which would be needed to attain complete certitude. Since this weaker type of demonstration is only formed when all the available information has been examined, no *demonstration morale* could conflict with other knowledge we already possessed. If there were conflicting information, one would not be able to come to any conclusion. Therefore, a *demonstration morale*, though not absolutely certain, yields a type of certainty which is reliable enough to give us true knowledge, unless *per impossible*, all the information available to us could somehow be part of a conspiracy to lead us astray, 'it is impossible that Demonstration Physique ever deceive . . . it will also never happen that Morale fail.'[72]

Any one capable of rational discourse, who is free from prejudices inculcated by education and custom, and who weighs the information available carefully, will come to the same conclusion by means of the *demonstrations morales*. If, in spite of this, one is still worried that these demonstrations may be convincing but deceptive, he should realize that this type of knowledge has been given to us by God, in His Wisdom and Goodness, in order to resolve most of the problems that confront us. To challenge the reliability of this sort of knowledge is to blasphme against God, and to accuse Him of allowing our most rational form of behavior to lead us astray on grave and important matters.[73] And, it is by means of *demonstrations morales* that we are led to the Christian religion. If one examines the historical, ethical, and Scriptural information available, 'After having considered all these matters, there is no understanding which has a little common sense, and is not carried away by passion, which can infer anything but that it is only the Christian religion that has come immediately from God.'[74] The Jews are too prejudiced by custom and education; the Protestants are too argumentative and do not look at the evidence. But those who are reasonable can seen that only Christianity is supported by *demonstrations morales*, and that these types of demonstrations are sufficient to justify our actions until God reveals the truth in all its firmness to us.

The last feature of Silhon's positive theory deals with the problem of decision when we do not have sufficient information to construct either type of demonstration. Our choice here is based upon something similar to Pascal's wager. If both 'God exists' and 'God does not exist' are equally dubious, and 'The soul is immortal' and 'The soul is mortal' are equally dubious, one would choose to believe the religious alternatives, because, though they are not capable of either type of demonstration, there is no risk involved if they ar false. But if they are true, there would be a risk in the non-religious alternative.[75]

Silhon concluded by pointing out that though we may not like it, we are such that we will have little knowledge based on *demonstrations physiques*, and we cannot change this state of affairs. We have to live our lives by means of *demonstrations morales*, which make our lives a trial, since it is only by our will, which makes us assent, that we are led to important truths like the Divinity of Jesus, the truth of the Christian religion, and the immortality of the soul.[76]

Silhon's answer to scepticism is probably even less satisfactory than Herbert of Cherbury's. He appealed repeatedly to either the fact that certain things were taken for granted, or to the claim that to raise doubts at certain points would amount to blaspheming against the Wisdom and Goodness of God. But the sceptic could easily question the metaphysical premises or the question-begging arguments offered by Silhon, unless Silhon could show that propositions he took for granted had to be true. Even the *demonstrations physiques* could be challenged, either by denying the self-evidence of the principles used as premises, or by denying that they were really demonstrative. The *demonstrations morales*, by their author's own admission, fall short of the certitude required in order to vanquish the Pyrrhonist, unless one accepts Silhon's views about the source of our faculties and Divine Benevolence. And, here, the sceptics from ancient to modern times had raised sufficient doubts to require some basis for asserting the Divine origin and guarantee of our sensual and rational capacities. Silhon's friend, René Descartes, evidently realized how far such an attempt to refute scepticism had missed the mark, for he undertook to answer the sceptical crisis by assuming not the best, but the worst state of affairs, that our faculties are corrupt, deceptive, and possibly demonically organized.[77] And, Pascal, who apparently admired Silhon enough to borrow some of his ideas, saw that the possibility of refuting Pyrrhonism depended upon the origin of our nature, whether it is created by a good God, an evil demon, or by chance. Only if we could establish the first, could we trust our faculties, and, unfortunately we cannot do so except by faith.[78]

Even in presenting his important new answer to scepticism, the *cogito*, Silhon had failed to realize either the force of what he was opposing, or the crucial character of the undeniable truth that he had discovered. Descartes, in two letters which may be about Silhon's *cogito*, indicated what was lacking here. In considering the suggestion that our existence can be established from the fact that we breathe, Descartes insisted that nothing else but the fact that we think is absolutely certain. Any other proposition is open to some doubt as to whether it is true.[79] But the *cogito*, Descartes pointed out in a letter to either the Marquis of Newcastle or Silhon, is not 'an achievement of your reasoning, nor a lesson that your teachers have given you,' but, rather 'your mind sees it, feels it, and touches it.'[80] One does not arrive at the *cogito* on the basis of other propositions, which are all less certain and open to doubt, but one encounters the truth and force of the *cogito* in itself alone. Silhon, at best, had seen that the sceptic could not deny the *cogito*, and hence he could not deny that something was true. But he did not see what it was that was true, or what this might show.

Both Herbert of Cherbury and Jean de Silhon laboured mightily in constructing new answers to the 'nouveaux Pyrrhoniens'. But in failing to grasp the full force of the sceptical crisis, they also failed to offer any satisfactory solution to it. The heroic effort to save human knowledge was to be made by their great contemporary, René Descartes, who saw that only by admitting the full and total impact of complete Pyrrhonism, could one be prepared to meet the serious problem at issue.

IX

DESCARTES
CONQUEROR OF
SCEPTICISM

In Descartes' reply to the objections of Father Bourdin, he announced that he was the first of all men to overthrow the doubts of the Sceptics.[1] More than a century later, one of his admirers said, 'Before Descartes, there had been Sceptics, but who were only Sceptics. Descartes taught his age the art of making Scepticism give birth to philosophical Certainty.'[2] This picture of Descartes' role as an opponent of the 'nouveau Pyrrhonisme,' and of his philosophy as a new dogmatism issuing from the abysses of the doubts of his sceptical contemporaries has received scant attention in the vast literature concerning the origins and characteristics of Cartesianism. Although the traditional interpretation of Descartes saw him as the scientific enemy of scholasticism and orthodoxy fighting to found a new era of intellectual freedom and adventure, this is gradually giving way to a more conservative interpretation of Descartes as a man who tried to reinstate the medieval outlook in the face of Renaissance novelty, and a thinker who sought to discover a philosophy adequate for the Christian world view in the light of the scientific revolution of the seventeenth century.[3] Little attention has been given to Descartes' intellectual crusade in terms of the sceptical crisis of the time. Gilson has indicated that Descartes borrowed from Montaigne and Charron; Brunschvicg showed that some elements of Cartesian thought can best be comprehended by comparison with the views in the *Apologie de Raimond Sebond*.[4] But, except for the recent studies of Dąmbska and Gouhier,[5] there is very little literature dealing with the relations of Descartes' thought and that of his Pyrrhonian contemporaries.

In contrast to this, one finds that Descartes himself expressed great concern with the scepticism of the time; that he indicated a good deal of acquaintance with the Pyrrhonian writings, ancient and modern; that he apparently developed his philosophy as a result of being confronted with the full significance of the *crise pyrrhonienne* in 1628–29, and that Descartes proclaimed that his system was the only intellectual fortress capable of withstanding the assualts of the sceptics. When and how Descartes came into contact with sceptical views is hard to tell. But he seems to have been well aware not only of the Pyrrhonian classics, but also of the sceptical current of his time, and its ever-increasing danger to the cause of both science and religion. He wrote in his answer to Father Bourdin, 'Neither must we think that the sect of the sceptics is long extinct. It flourishes to-day as much as ever, and nearly all who think that they have some ability beyond that of the rest of mankind, finding nothing that satisfies them in the common Philosophy, and seeing no other truth, take refuge in Scepticism.'[6]

It has been said that the course of study at La Flèche included consideration of how Aristotelian philosophy could answer the Pyrrhonian arguments.[7] And Descartes was a student there during the time that François Veron taught philosophy and theology and possibly even the use of sceptical materials against opponents.[8] Early in his life, Descartes had read Cornelius Agrippa, and by the time of the *Discours* seems to have been well versed in the writings of Montaigne and Charron.[9] In replying to the objections submitted by Mersenne, Descartes had remarked, 'I had long ago seen several books written by the Academics and Sceptics.'[10] During the period of the formation of his philosophical views, 1628–1637, he appears to have looked at La Mothe Le Vayer's *Dialogues d'Orasius Tubero*, of 1630, and to have been greatly distrubed by this Pyrrhonian work[11] (in fact, he was almost as outraged by this as he became later when he, himself, was accused of being a Pyrrhonist).

Not only was Descartes acquainted with some of the sceptical literature, he was also deeply aware of the *crise pyrrhonienee* as a living issue. He had examined, as we have seen, the attempt to resolve it by Herbert of Cherbury. He was a friend of both Mersenne and Silhon who were constantly dealing with the problem of answering sceptical arguments. He may well have read their works, and he could not have avoided hearing their views. Also, the evidence of the autobiographical sections of the *Discours* and of Descartes' letters, indicates that around 1628-9 he was struck by the full force of the sceptical onslaught, and the need for a new and stronger answer to it. It was in the light of this awakening to the sceptical menace, that when he was in Paris Descartes set in motion his philosophical revolution by discovering something 'so certain and so assured that all the most extravagant suppositions brought forward by the sceptics were incapable of shaking it.'[12]

Unfortunately, we do not have enough information about the visit to Paris that produced this world-shaking result. But we do possess an intriguing and suggestive clue. Sometime, probably towards the end of 1628, Descartes was invited to a meeting at the home of the Papal Nuncio, Cardinal Bagni (whom the *libertin érudit* Gabriel Naudé was soon to serve as secretary). A large number of the leading *savants* of the time, including Mersenne, were there to hear a talk by a strange chemist, Chandoux, an expert on base metals, who was executed in 1631 for counterfeiting currency.[13] Chandoux gave a speech that must have been fairly typical of the views of many of the avant-garde at the time, denouncing scholastic philosophy. His views on the subject, we are told, were somewhat like those of Bacon, Mersenne, Gassendi and Hobbes.[14] And, on this occasion, 'Chandoux gave a great speech to refute the way philosophy is usually taught in the Schools. He even set forth a fairly common system of philosophy that he claimed to establish, and that he wanted to appear as new.'[15] Whatever Chandoux said, whether it was Pyrrhonistic or materialistic, almost everyone present applauded his views, except Descartes. Cardinal Bérulle, the founder of the Oratory, noticed this, and asked what Descartes thought of the speech 'which had seemed so lovely to the audience.'[16]

According to the account we have, Descartes spoke first in favor of Chandoux's anti-Scholasticism. Next he went on to attack the fact that the speaker and the audience were willing to accept probability as the standard of truth, for if this were the case, falsehoods might actually be taken as truths. To show this, Descartes took some examples of supposedly incontestable truths, and by some arguments even more probable than Chandoux's, proved that they were false. Next, he took what was alleged to be a most evident falsehood, and by probable arguments made it appear to be a plausible truth. Having been shocked with this evidence of how 'our minds become dupes of probability,' the audience asked Descartes if there were not 'some infallible means' to avoid these difficulties. He replied by telling them of his *Methode naturelle*, and by showing them that his principles 'are better established, truer, and more natural than any others which are already accepted by scholars.'[17]

Cardinal Bérulle, perhaps the most important religious thinker of the Counter-Reformation in France, was much taken with Descartes' talk, and invited him to come to see him and discuss this subject further. Descartes came and told the Cardinal why he believed that the commonly employed methods in philosophy were useless, and what he thought ought to be done instead. Bérulle was very pleased and urged Descartes to go and apply his method to the problems confronting mankind in their daily pursuits.[18]

The Chandoux episode and the meeting with Bérulle may well have been the occasion for the commencement of Descartes' quest. Indications are that prior to the period 1628-9, he had not concerned himself with metaphysical questions.[19] He had arrived in Paris a successful young scientist and mathematician who had already exhibited some of his amazing theoretical abilities and thereby caught the eye of some of the prominent people in the field. In Paris he saw Mersenne, possibly was introduced to his circle which included all the prominent 'nouveaux Pyrrhoniens' and discovered how the best minds of the day either spent their time advocating scepticism, or accepted only probable, and possibly uncertain views, instead of seeking absolute truth. The philosophical and scientific studies he had had at college, like the new views of his contemporaries, provided no certainty. Everything was open to question, to dispute, and only probabilities served as the foundations for the arious theories being offered.[20] This being the case, the meeting with Chandoux became the mircocosm of the plight of the whole learned world. Gathered together were some of the wisest and most erudite people of the time, and they could only applaud someone who decried the old views and offered them probabilities instead. Descartes rose to show them the enormous consequences, to give them a living lesson in scepticism. If only probabilities served as the basis for views, then one would never discover the truth, because one could not distinguish truth from falsehood any longer. The criterion, the rule of truth, was gone. What the Reformation was supposed to have accomplished in religion (according to the French Counter-Reformers), reducing all views to mere opinions to be judged by their plausibility, had also occurred in philosophy and science. And the Cardinal Bérulle who had sought and found a clear and certain path to religious truth in his *Méditations* could appreciate and encourage a new truth seeker, who was to construct a theory in many ways similar to Bérullianism in philosophy.[21]

Descartes left Paris and went into Holland to work out his solution to the *crise pyrrhonienne* in solitude. In the *Discours de la Méthode*, he tells us that although he had long realized that there were difficulties and uncertainties that beset all human knowledge, he had not 'commenced to seek the foundation of any philosophy more certain than the vulgar' until this time. Up to this moment, Descartes reports, he had only confessed his ignorance 'more ingenuously than those who have studied a little usually do,' and had doubted 'many things which were held by others to be certain.'[22] To search for the truth, he went off to his retreat in Holland to meditate. His few letters from this period tell us that he was working on a metaphysical treatise about divinity. From science and mathematics, he had turned to theological metaphysics in order to find the unshakable foundation for human knowledge. The Reformation, the scientific revolution, and the onslaught of scepticism had crumbled the old foundations that used to support the entire framework of man's intellectual achievements. A new age required a new basis to justify and guarantee what it had discovered. Descartes, in the tradition of the greatest medieval minds, sought to provide this basis by securing the superstructure, man's natural knowledge, to the strongest possible foundation, the all-powerful, eternal God. The sceptical crisis was to be overcome by a new theology serving an old purpose.

Theological mechanism, Bérulle's theocentricism combined with a rational materialism, would provide the new rock to replace what had turned out to be mud, clay, or even quicksand.

If Descartes' flight to metaphysical theology was to be his proposed solution to the collapse of human knowledge into probabilities, opinions, and doubts, the means for bringing people to see the true metaphysical and theological nature of reality was first to lead them to apprecaite 'the misery of man without God'. The bewilderment of the learned men at the Chandoux meeting was probably a stage on the way to the method of doubt. What appeared most certain was shown to be dubious. What appeared most dubious was shown to be certain. The basis for a complete scepticism was provided in order to shock the audience and get them to seek for absolute certainty.

An autobiographical passage in the *Discours* suggests that it was in 1628 or 1629 that Descartes began his philosophical revolution, probably by applying his method of systematic doubt to the whole edifice of human knowledge in order to discover a certain foundation for what is known.[23] The method, as we shall see, starts off as little more than a reinforced systematic application of the doubts of Montaigne and Charron. In the *Discours*, the *Meditationes* and *La Recherche de la Verité*,[24] a procedure is set forth for developing a *crise pyrrhonienne* possibly even more forceful than that developed by any of the Pyrrhonists ancient or modern. Starting with the rule,

> To accept nothing as true which I did not clearly recognize to be so: that is to say, carefully to avoid precipitation and prejudice in judgments, and to accept in them nothing more than what was presented to my mind so clearly and distinctly that I could have no occasion to doubt it.[25]

Descartes then went on to reveal the extent to which occasions for doubt could arise. The rule itself is quite similar to that earlier proposed in Charron's *La Sagesse*, but in applying it, Descartes showed that the levels of dubiety far surpass the simple and mild ones hitherto introduced by the sceptics.[26]

The first two levels raise only standard reasons for doubting.

The sense illusions, which the 'nouveaux Pyrrhoniens' dwelt upon so much, indicate that there is some basis for questioning the reliability or veracity of our ordinary sense experience. The possibility that all of our experience is part of a dream, the second level, allows us to construct an occasion for doubting the reality of any other objects that we know of, and even the reality of the world itself. On both of these levels, the standard sceptical problems suffice for us to describe a state of affairs in which the usual beliefs that we have regarding our ordinary experience may be doubtful, or even false. And, if we therefore apply the rule, just these two kinds of doubts 'lead us straight to the ignorance of Socrates, or the uncertainty of the Pyrrhonists, which resembles water so deep that one cannot find any footing in it.'[27]

But the next level, the demon hypothesis, is much more effective in revealing the uncertainty of all that we think we know. This possibility discloses the full force of scepticism in the most striking fashion, and unveils a basis for doubting apparently never dreamed of before.[28] If perchance, there is a *malin génie* who is capable of distorting either the information that we possess or the faculties that we have for evaluating it, what then can we be sure of? Any criterion, any test of the reliability of what we know is open to question because either the standard or the application of it may be demonically infected. Unlike Silhon and Herbert of Cherbury and the Aristotelians, Descartes was willing to consider the most radical and devastating of sceptical possibilities, that not only is our information deceptive, illusory, and misleading, but that our faculties, even under the best of conditions, may be erroneous. If this were the case, then no matter how careful we might be in examining our information, and in evaluating it, we could never be certain that we were not being led astray by the only means at our disposal for gaining knowledge. Silhon had drawn back at the brink of the demon possibility, rejecting it as blasphemy against our Maker. But Descartes had seen that unless one increased the fever of doubt to this highest level, and then could overcome it, nothing could be certain, since there would always be a lingering, haunting doubt which would infect everything that we know and render it all, in some measure, uncertain.

The overwhelming consequences of a belief in demonism, of a scepticism with regard to our faculties themselves, were clear to Descartes. In the *Discours*, a mild version of this kind of super-Pyrrhonism had been set forth, without introducing the *malin génie*. The mere fact that our senses sometimes err, that our reason sometimes produces paralogisms, and that Descartes, like anyone else, was subject to error, led him to reject all that he had previously accepted as demonstratively true.[29] In the First Meditation, Descartes pointed out that it is possible that 'I am deceived every time that I add two and three, or that I count the sides of a square, or when I judge things still more simple, if one can imagine anything simpler than that.'[30] The possibility of our being constantly deceived by some evil agency raises doubts about even the most evident matters and any standards of evidence we may have. As Pascal and Hume saw, the highest point in sceptical doubt had been reached.[31] Once it had been suggested that the reliability of our most rational faculties was questionable, man had been transformed from a repository of truth into a sink of uncertainty and error.[32] In his comments on the *malin génie*, in the conversations with Burman, Descartes is reported to have noted that here he made of man a great doubter and threw him into every possible objection, every possible reason for doubting.[33] Only when scepticism had been carried to this extreme, to engender a *crise pyrrhonienne* greater than that ever dreamed of by the 'nouveaux Pyrrhoniens,' could one overcome the force of scepticism. Unless one were willing to pursue the possibility of raising doubts to the end, one could never hope to discover any truth untainted by doubt or uncertainty.

In the *Regulae*, written by 1628, apparently before Descartes' attempt to resolve the *crise pyrrhonienne*, he had insisted that 'Arithmetic and Geometry alone are free from any taint of falsity and uncertainty,' and that intuition, the undoubting conception of an unclouded and attentive mind, is most certain, and deduction 'cannot be erroneous when performed by an understanding that is in the least degree rational.'[34] As Descartes travelled the road to demonism, he passed, as Gilson said, 'from the scientific plane to the purely philosophical one and substitutes for a simple critique of our knowledge a critique of our means of knowing.'[35]

It is not that Descartes was denying or doubting the self-evidence of our mathematical or most certain knowledge, but rather he was showing that as long as we might be demonically infected, what appeared self-evident to us might be false. The simple starting place of the *Regulae*, that reason, in intuiting and deducing, was infallible, and hence that mathematics was indubitably true, was now challenged by a scepticism with regard to our faculties, and a scepticism with regard to our ability to use them. As long as we might be the victims of some force or agent who purposely misleads us, what we consider most certain, what we are unable to doubt (psychologically), may actually be false or dubious.[36] In introducing this level of doubt, creating the possibility of the *malin génie*, Descartes overthrew the mathematical intuitionism of the *Regulae* as the foundation of all certainty. The *crise pyrrhonienne* had been pressed to its farthest limit. Not only had all the opinions and theories of all previous thinkers been cast in doubt, but also those of the young René Descartes. But from this voyage into the depths of complete scepticism, Descartes was to find a new metaphysical and theological justification for the world of human rationality.[37]

Before considering how the method of doubt is supposed to lead us to certainty and not to total suspense of judgment, I should like to mention briefly a possible historical source of the demon hypothesis, and why this sort of scepticism with regard to our faculties might have struck one as a forceful and serious idea at this time. One of the great events of the 1630's was the trial at Loudun of a priest, Grandier, accused of infesting a convent with devils. The case, and the evidence presented at the trial of Grandier in 1634 aroused a good deal of interest in the demoniac, as well as in the standards of evidence by which such matters can be judged. Some problems that may well have come to mind in considering the question of whether Grandier had the power to infest others with devils were, if he had such power, (a) could he ever be apprehended, since, presumably, his force could be exercised upon anybody trying to halt his nefarious activities; and (b) could any reliable testimony be presented against him by his victims, since he, presumably, could influence and deceive them? In order to evaluate the testimony presented against Grandier by the members of the convent, the Sorbonne had to rule on the knotty problem of whether testimony given under oath by devils, (that is, those Grandier supposedly placed in his victims), could be true. In the light of the issues about the reliability of evidence, Descartes may have seen that if there can be a demonic agent in the world, apart from Grandier's case, a serious ground for scepticism is involved. And if the matter were considered on the larger plane of human reasoning in general, rather than the particular plight of the inmates of the convent at Loudun, a startling possibility emerges—namely, that whether we know it or not, we may all be victims of demonism and be unable to tell that we are victims, because of systematic delusion caused by the demonic agent. A more extensive examination of the issues discussed in the learned world as a result of the Loudun trial may throw some light on the source and significance at the time, of Descartes' great contribution to sceptical argumentation.[38]

But, to return to Descartes' method of doubt, in what manner does it differ from the standard sceptical arguings of Charron, La Mothe Le Vayer, and others, except in ingenuity? The series of types of doubt offered in the more systematic presentations of Pyrrhonism, step-by-step indicate the doubtfulness of various beliefs, opinions, and views that we have. Each such indication, according to the classical sceptical theory, is to be followed by a suspense of judgment on the truth or falsity of the matter under consideration. Statements of the Pyrrhonian position of Montaigne, Charron and their successors, propose a stronger reaction, that views and opinions be rejected by the mind, if they are in the slightest degree dubious, until this piecemeal rejection results in the mind becoming a *carte blanche*. This process of emptying the mind, Gouhier, in his excellent and important article on the method of doubt, makes into another and crucial methodic element in Descartes, the method of negation, which he contends separates the Cartesian development of doubt from that of the sceptics, and leads to the ultimate conquest of scepticism in the *cogito*. According to Gouhier, Descartes, in intensifying the doubting method so that whatever is in the slightest degree open to question is considered as if it were false, was able to develop a means of separating the apparently evident and certain from the truly evident and certain. By making his test so severe, changing ordinary sceptical doubt into complete negation, Descartes thereby set the stage for the unique and overwhelming force of the *cogito*, so that by no act of will is one able to resist recognizing its certitude. Only by forcing oneself to doubt and negate to the greatest degree possible, can one appreciate the indubitable character of the *cogito*.[39]

The negative method as well as the method of doubt occurs, to some extent, though not with the same driving force, in the mental elimination process proposed by some of the 'nouveaux Pyrrhoniens'. But, as Descartes saw, perhaps the most crucial difference between the procedure of the sceptics and that of Descartes, lies in the purpose for which the method is employed, and the results that are to be achieved by its use. The sceptics, according to Descartes, doubt only out of perversity. They are people 'who only doubt for the sake of doubting, and pretend to be always uncertain'[40] and gain 'so little from this method of philosophizing, that they have been in error all their lives, and have not been able to get free of the doubts which they have introduced into philosophy.'[41] Their claim that by the achievement of complete doubt and mental blankness, they would be prepared to receive truth by Revelation was apparently not taken seriously by Descartes. As far as he could see they had accomplished nothing with their doubts, and had accomplished nothing only because they had deliberately wished to remain in complete uncertainty. But, 'Although the Pyrrhonians have found nothing certain as a result of their doubt, this does not mean that they could not do so.'[42] If one doubts in order to achieve certainty, then something of monumental importance can issue from the sceptic's method. As an eighteenth-century Cartesian put it, 'The Sceptic or Pyrrhonist doubts everything: because he foolishly wishes to close his eyes to all light,' but to doubt as Descartes did, 'is not to be a Pyrrhonist, but it is to be a philosopher. It is not to unsettle human certitude, but to strengthen it.'[43]

The 'nouveaux Pyrrhoniens' might insist that they were being misrepresented, since their aim, too, was to find certain knowledge. But they hoped to find it miraculously, to have it suddenly delivered to them by God. Descartes, on the other hand, expected to locate the fundamental and indubitable truths, the foundations of human knowledge, within the mind, buried or hidden under the debris of prejudices and opinions. He expected to locate these by the very process of doubting, and not by a *deus ex machina* after doubting. The sceptics did not believe we were in possession of any truths, while Descartes was convinced that we were, but were also unable to see them. By doubting and negating, those opinions and beliefs that, at present, blind us, he said, could be removed so that truth would shine forth.

What will produce this moment of revelation, this recognition of genuine certain truth, for Descartes, is the sceptical method properly and diligently applied. The first stage of doubting will engender a *crise pyrrhonienne*. The various levels of doubt of the First Meditation will leave one free of all false or questionable views, and also completely uncertain of everything, in a 'forlorn scepticism'. But just at this darkest moment, and because one has plunged into this 'sink of uncertainty', the solution is found in the *cogito*, and scepticism is completely overthrown. In the *Discours*, Descartes said,

> I resolved to assume that everything that ever entered into my mind was no more true than the illusions of my dreams. But immediately afterwards I noticed that whilst I thus wished to think all things false, it was absolutely essential that the "I" who thought this should be somewhat, and remarking that this truth, 'I think, therefore I am' was so certain and so assured that all the most extravagant suppositions brought forward by the sceptics were incapable of shaking it, I came to the conclusion that I could receive it without scruple as the first principle of the Philosophy for which I was seeking.[44]

The very process of carrying doubt to its utmost extreme provides the overthrowing of complete scepticism; thus, the Pyrrhonian onslaught becomes its own victim. The method that was supposed to eliminate all manifestations of the disease of dogmatism terminates in eliminating itself as well, by discovering one unshakeable truth that no sceptical ingenuity can render dubious to the slightest degree.

The *cogito* functions not, as some of the critics claimed, as the conclusion of a syllogism[45] (as it did for Silhon), but as the conclusion of doubt. Just by pushing scepticism to its limit, one is confronted with a truth that one cannot doubt in any conceivable manner. The process of doubting compels one to recognize the awareness of oneself, compels one to see that one is doubting or thinking, and that one is here, is in existence. This discovery of true knowledge is not miraculous, not a special act of Divine Grace. Instead the method of doubt is the cause rather than the occasion of the acquisition of knowledge. Its truth, as we shall see, is the result of Divine intervention, but not of a sudden, new intervention, but rather of a continuous and permanent act of Grace which sustains our mind with its innate ideas, and with its natural light that compels us to accept as true that which we are unable to doubt. Thus, the method of doubt leads naturally to the *cogito*, and not supernaturally to truth as the 'nouveaux Pyrrhoniens' claimed.

The discovery of one absolutely certain truth, the *cogito*, may overthrow the sceptical attitude that all is uncertain, but, at the same time, one truth does not constitute a system of knowledge about reality. To discover or justify knowledge about the nature of things a series of bridges must be built once the experience of being confronted by the *cogito* has provided the solid, firm point of departure. However, the one truth produced by the method of doubt is not a premise from which all other truths follow. Rather it is a basis for rational discourse which makes it possible to recognize other truths. The experience of the *cogito* turns on the inner light so that we can now see what other propositions are true. Without the dramatic reversal of doubt that occurs in the discovery of the *cogito*, we would not be able to tell that statements like '2 + 3 = 5' are really true, because we could still manage to question them. What, in effect, the *cogito* accomplishes by producing illumination, is that it also reveals the long-sought standard or criterion of truth, and therewith the ability to recognize other truths, which in turn allows us to build up a system of true knowledge about reality. (It is interesting in this regard that in Descartes' formal presentation of his theory, appended to the replies to the second set of objections to the *Meditations*, the *cogito* is not offered as a premise, axiom or postulate, but the method of doubt is offered as a mental process which will make it possible to tell that the axioms and postulates are true.)[46]

By inspecting the one truth, the criterion of truth is found. As Descartes has said about Herbert of Cherbury's system, only if one knew *a* truth could one then proceed to construct a theory of truth. We are assured of the truth of the one case we are acquainted with solely because it is clear and distinct.

> Certainly in this first knowledge there is nothing that assures me of its truth, excepting the clear and distinct perception of that which I state, which would not indeed suffice to assure me that what I say is true, if it could ever happen that a thing which I conceived so clearly and distinctly could be false; and accordingly it seems to me that already I can establish as a general rule that all things which I perceive very clearly and very distinctly are true.[47]

In the *Principles*, these properties of clarity and distinctness are explained; clarity being that which is present and apparent to an attentive mind, that which commands our mental attention, and distincness, the clarity which differentiates this awareness from all others.[48] The *cogito* strikes us so forcefully with its clarity and distinctness that we cannot doubt it. If something could be clear and distinct and yet false, we might be deceived even by the *cogito*, but this cannot be the case as the very experience of it reveals.

With a criterion of truth we can discover the premises of a metaphysical system of true knowledge, which in turn provides the foundation of a physical system of true knowledge. The metaphysical system will supply us with a justification or guarantee of the criterion. Not only are we such, that whatever we discover is clear and distinct we accept as true, but also it can be shown that, in reality, whatever is clear and distinct *is* true. So, the first step in all this, is to set forth the clear and distinct principles which allow us to reason from our intellectual truths to truths about reality. The axiom, that the objective reality of our ideas requires a cause in which the same reality is contained not objectively, but formally or eminently,[49] provides the first crucial bridge from truths in the mind to truths about something beyond our own ideas, the first bridge from a subjective awareness of one truth about our ideas, the first bridge from a subjective awareness of one truth about our ideas to a knowledge of reality. The support offered for this initial stage in the reconstruction of true knowledge, and this burial of scepticism is (a) that it is clear and distinct, and (b) that this axiom is necessary if we are to be able to know anything beyond the world of our ideas.[50]

Having provided a causeway from ideas to reality, this is then used as the means for establishing the existence and the nature of God. The idea of God requires a cause having at least the same properties formally or eminently, that is, the cause as independent real object has at least the same essential characteristics as the idea. Thus, the perfections in our idea of God must also be perfections of God.[51] The theocentric vision of Cardinal Bérulle becomes transformed from idea to object, with all truth dependent on the Will of this all-powerful Deity who must exist as the cause of the idea of Him that we possess clearly and distinctly.

From the *cogito*, to the criterion of truth, to the connecting link between the ideas in our minds and objective reality, finally, to God, Descartes has created a structure which will ultimately support our knowledge of nature, but only after reinforcing our inner certainty by attaching it to the Divine Will. The omnipotent Deity must be made the final basis for guaranteeing our certitude. If, as the bridge-building indicates, we are certain of various matters because they are clear and distinct; that is, we cannot doubt of them no matter how hard we try now that we have been illumined by the *cogito*; and this inner certitude about our ideas convinces us that there must be an objective God upon whom we are totally dependent for our being and knowledge, then whether our inner certitude is justified objectively (that is with reference to the real world), is up to God and not ourselves.

This series of realizations leads to a higher scepticism, a super-Pyrrhonism that must be overcome in Heaven and not in the mind of man. Perhaps the demonism that destroyed our faith in reason in the First Meditation, is an aspect of the Divine World! Perhaps God wills us to believe, in fact, forces us to believe, all sorts of things which are untrue! Perhaps God is a deceiver, a demon! The road from complete doubt, to the *cogito*, to objective reality may have been the final closing of a trap which shuts us off from all knowledge save that of our own existence, and leaves us forever at the mercy of an omnipotent fiend who wants us to err at

all times and all places. This terrifying possibility that could
transform the Cartesian dream of a rational paradise on earth
into a Kafka-like hell in which all our attempts to discover true
knowledge of reality would be demonically frustrated, requires a
cosmic exorcism, a harrowing of Heaven.[52]

Descartes eliminates the possibility that the Deity possesses
demonic features by stressing the character of *our* idea of God. If
the idea of God cannot include demonic elements, then what is
clear and distinct about the idea must be true about the object,
God Himself.

> . . . I recognize it to be impossible that He should ever deceive me; for
> in all fraud and deception some imperfection is to be found, and al-
> though it may appear that the power of deception is a mark of subtilty
> or power, yet the desire to deceive without doubt testifies to malice or
> feebleness, and accordingly cannot be found in God.[53]

Descartes did not consider the possibility that it may be the
demon, rather than God, who has supplied him with his idea of
God, and who has compelled him to come to anti-demonic conclusions about the moral nature of the Deity. But, with this conception of God, based on the clear and distinct idea of Him,
Descartes was now ready to march on triumphantly to his
promised land, the new world of dogmatism where knowledge of
truth and reality could be completely assured, since 'I now have
before me a road which will lead us from the contemplation of
the true God . . . to the knowledge of the other objects of the
universe.'[54]

Therefore, since God cannot deceive, and He is my Creator,
and I am created with the faculty for judging that whatever is
clearly and distinctly conceived is true, then my faculty of judging
is guaranteed. Not only do I have to believe that whatever I clearly
and distinctly perceive is true, but also, by the Grace of God in
His Goodness, it is actually true. With this monumental assurance Descartes could now dissipate the doubts of the First Meditation about rational knowledge. The demon having been exorcised from Heaven and Earth, there then remained no question
about the truths of mathematics. Once the criterion of clear and
distinct ideas had been founded on God's guaranteed honesty,

the initial doubts, the intial Pyrrhonism, vanished, for one could now tell what was true, what constituted evidence, and so forth. From here on, all is relatively safe and easy. Mathematical truths are clear and distinct. We are compelled to believe them, and in this compulsion we are secure since God is no deceiver. The relationship of these truths of nature can also be discovered by our trust in God. We can be sure that there is a physical world to which the truths about pure extension apply, since God would not make us think so unless there was in fact such a world beyond the reach of our ideas.[55]

The atheist is not able to have this security about the objective truth of his clear and distinct ideas, because he does not have a God to guarantee what he thinks he knows. In answering Mersenne's claim that an atheist can know a mathematical truth clearly and distinctly, Descartes declared,

> I do not deny, I merely affirm that, on the other hand, such knowledge on his part cannot constitute true science, because no knowledge that can be rendered doubtful should be called science. Since he is, as supposed, an Atheist, he cannot be sure that he is not deceived in the things that seem most evident to him, as has been sufficiently shown; and though perchance the doubt does not occur to him, nevertheless it may come up, if he examines the matter, or if another suggests it; he can never be safe from it unless he first recognizes the existence of a God.[56]

Hence, no matter what truths an atheist may be aware of, he can never be completely certain they are true since he can never eradicate the possibility that he is deceived no matter how sure he may be. No secular guarantee or basis of certainty can be found. In a secular world there is always a haunting possibility of demonic deception or self-deception even in the most evident matters. Thus, in a world apart from God, every 'truth' can still be considered as doubtful (in that it may possibly be false), and no 'true science' can be discovered. Only God can dissipate all doubts if He is no deceiver, and hence only God can guarantee that the truths we know in mathematics and physics are more than mere semblances of truth in our minds.[57]

So, all in all, from the despairing depths of the First Meditation Descartes believed he had been able to accomplish a complete overturning of scepticism, marching from complete doubt to complete assurance. This amazing change of state was possible only because Pyrrhonism had been taken sufficiently seriously. In doubting to the limits of human capacity, the force of the *cogito* could emerge as a tidal wave, sweeping away the *crise pyrrhonienne* and carrying the newly illumined person into the realms of solid unshakeable truth. Each stage on the way to absolute truth after the *cogito* strenghtened the escape from scepticism, and made more secure the stages already passed. The criterion led to God, God to the complete guarantee, and the complete guarantee to knowledge of the mechanistic universe. Only by having walked through the valley of complete doubt could one be swept on to the peace and security of the world seen as a theodicy, our ideas and our truths seen as Divine fiats, forever guaranteed by our realization that the Almighty cannot deceive. When the journey of the mind to God was completed, Descartes could write without hesitation in the *Principles*,

> *That we cannot err if we give our assent only to things that we know clearly and distinctly.*

> But it is certain that we shall never take the false as the true if we only give our assent to things that we perceive clearly and distinctly. Because since God is no deceiver, the faculty of knowledge that He has given us cannot be fallacious, nor can the faculty of will, so long at least as we do not extend it beyond those things that we clearly perceive. . . . And even if this truth could not be rationally demonstrated, we are by nature so disposed to give our assent to things that we clearly perceive, that we cannot possibly doubt of their truth [*while we perceive them this way*].[58]

And he could tell the student, Burman, that no one could be a sceptic if he looked attentively at his innate ideas, because it would be impossible to doubt of them.[59]

This dramatic answer to the *crise pyrrhonienne* met the problem that the Reformation had posed at its deepest level, and, in effect, offered a Reformer's solution on the level of rational rather than religious knowledge. The challenge of Luther and Calvin had set off the quest for a guarantee of the certitude of one's basic beliefs and principles. The Reformers and their opponents could each show that the other's views had no defensible foundation and could be infected with sceptical difficulties. The extension of this type of problem into natural knowledge revealed that the same sort of sceptical crisis existed in this realm as well. Any philosophical foundation could be questioned, a foundation demanded for the foundation, and so on.

The Reformers, especially the Calvinists, offered as a defense of their beliefs the claim that by 'la voie d'examen' one would discover a religious truth, the true faith, which would reveal its criterion, the rule of faith, which would in turn reveal its source and guarantee, God. The illumination involved in the discovery of religious truth was twofold, on the one hand one was illumined by the truth, and on the other, by Divine Grace one was able now to recognize it as a truth. The illumination, the inner light, provided a complete assurance, conviction or subjective certainty. And, it was claimed, the very experience of this overwhelming assurance convinced one that what one felt so certain about was also objectively true, that is, it corresponded to the actual state of affairs in the universe.[60] One knows that one has found the true faith, and one knows this because it is the faith measured by the rule of faith, Scripture, which one knows is the rule of faith because it is the Word of God, which He has made us capable of recognizing and understanding. The basic, unquestionable beginning is the subjective certainty of, or total conviction in, the religious truth. In order to guarantee that this complete assurance is not merely a personal feeling or madness, it has to be shown that what one is assured of is objectively true, and is not just what one subjectively believes to be true. Thus the quest is to find 'skyhooks' to attach to this subjective certainty so that it can be transformed from an internal individual experience into an objective feature of the world. And somehow, the personal assurance that one has found the true faith, which can be checked by his true rule (of which he is subjectively certain), and which comes from God, is transformed from his unquestioned opinion or belief, into objective truth by the subjective experience of the illumination of the truth and its source. The religious experience both convinces him of certain religious truths and verifies the truths, so that they are both what he believes completely and what is true. The same mental event in which he gains his assurance somehow transcends itself and reveals to him God, the source of the event, who then guarantees that the content of the event, the religious truths, are not only personal beliefs, but also truths that He has ordained.

In Descartes' answer to scepticism one finds the same sort of Reformation development, and the same attempt to objectify subjective certitude by attaching it to God. The Cartesian 'voie d'examen' is the method of doubt, the examination of what we believe. By moving from the partial Pyrrhonism of doubting the reliability of our senses, to the metaphysical Pyrrhonism of the dream hypothesis, doubting the reality of our knowledge, to the total Pyrrhonism of the demon hypothesis, doubting the reliability of our rational faculties, we finally discover the *cogito*, a truth so subjectively certain that *we* are incapable of doubting it at all. This is the first aspect of the illumination—there is truth. The second is the realization of the source of truth, of the guarantee of truth. The *cogito* leads us to the rule of truth, the rule to God, and God provides the objective assurance of our subjective certitude. Having started on the way to truth by experiencing the illumination of the *cogito*, one ends by realizing that the indubitability of all clear and distinct ideas is not only a psychological fact that one accepts and lives with, but is a God-ordained fact, and hence objectively true. Not only does one believe, and psychologically must believe, any clear and distinct propositions, but one is now guaranteed that what one believes corresponds to what is objectively the case. What I know to be true in the world of *my* ideas (i.e., what I am subjectively certain of), becomes what is true in the real world independent of what I think, feel or believe. My personal truths become the objective truths known by God because of God's guarantee that what I have to accept as true (subjectively) is true (objectively).

Employing the psychological feeling of subjective certainty as the beginning of the resolution of the sceptical crisis incurs the risk of making all trans-subjective knowledge dubious. Luther and Calvin were accused of taking their own personal opinions and their feelings about them; then, trying to found the entire structure of religion on subjective facts, on their own mental lives. By insisting that there is a guarantee that what is subjectively certain is true not only for the individual, but absolutely and objectively, the Reformers declared that they had avoided the pitfalls of scepticism. And Descartes, in starting his Reformation in philosophy had to follow the same path. In the drama of the *cogito*, he 'undermines the bases of Pyrrhonism'.[61] But, in order to make this more than a personal victory about the ideas in his mind and his feelings about them, the unshakeable assurance of Descartes had to be linked to a source that could guarantee its objective truth as well. To be victorious, what Descartes thought was true had to be true; what he was subjectively certain of had to correspond to the objective state of affairs.

Descartes' revolutionary overturning of scepticism and his vindication of objective knowledge may have been the most forceful solution of the *crise pyrrhonienne*. But it was precisely in the movement from subjective certainty to objective truth that Descartes and his philosophy, as well as Calvin and Calvinism, met their most serious opposition, opposition that was to change the Cartesian triumph into tragedy. The enemies fought to show that though a truth might have been found, the heroic effort of Descartes was either no effort at all, or was a complete failure, leaving the *crise pyrrhonienne* unsolved and insoluble at the base of all of modern philosophy.

X

DESCARTES SCEPTIQUE MALGRÉ LUI

Descartes, having presented his triumphant conquest of the sceptical dragon, immediately found himself denounced as a dangerous Pyrrhonist and as an unsuccessful dogmatist whose theories were only fantasies and illusions. The orthodox, traditional thinkers saw Descartes as a vicious sceptic because his method of doubt denied the very basis of the traditional system. Hence, no matter what he himself might say, Descartes was considered the culmination of two millenia of Pyrrhonists from Pyrrho of Elis onward, all of whom had tried to undermine the foundations of rational knowledge. Those of sceptical inclination, while unwilling and unanxious to claim Descartes as their own, wished to show that he had achieved nothing, and that all his claims were only opinions, not certitudes. So they challenged every advance beyond the *cogito* (and even the *cogito* itself), in order to drown the heroic Descartes in a sink of uncertainty. The dogmatists pressed their attack against the First Meditation, for herein lay the most powerful Pyrrhonian argument which, once admitted, they saw could never be overcome. The sceptics attacked the remainder of the Meditations as a doubtful non-sequitur to the First Meditation. On both sides, the same sort of bombardment that had reduced the Reformers to Pyrrhonists was set off against the New Dogmatists, the St. George who claimed to have slain the sceptical dragon. The step from subjective certainty about ideas in the mind to objective truth about the real world was denied, and even the starting place was shown to be naught but one man's opinion. If the opinion of Calvin was insufficient to establish religious truth, the opinion of Descartes was equally insufficient to establish philosophical truth.

Almost immediately following the first publication of Descartes' philosophy, critics appeared who accused the author of having thrown in his lot with the Pyrrhonists. Beginning with Pierre Petit and Father Bourdin, in France, and Gisbert Voetius and Martinus Schoockius at Utrecht, the charge was made that Descartes had given away too much at the outset, and had adopted a scepticism from which nothing certain could actually emerge. With his method of doubt, he had overturned all the acceptable evidence that we possess. He had rejected common sense, experience, and authority; hence, had eliminated any possibility of there being a secure foundation for our knowledge. Since such a scepticism was dangerous not only to philosophy, but also to religion, Descartes, the sceptic and the atheist, must be destroyed.[1]

As early as 1638 one finds an unidentified critic writing to Descartes to complain that the rules of his *morale* and his *méthode* are too sceptical and that, like the doubts of the Pyrrhonians, they will not lead to any basic truths.[2] During this same period, Petit wrote his objections, which tried to show that Descartes had inverted the whole process of knowing things, and, in effect, would make them all unknowable.[3] Unfortunately, we lack Petit's complaints about the method of doubt. But the portion we possess indicates the general point of view from which it was argued that Descartes was casting all in doubt. The contention of Petit was that the highest and most final knowledge that we can have, is knowledge of God, which, from our point of view, is the most unclear and indistinct. We have to commence with the information available to us in our present state, the facts of sense experience, which are the clearest to us, and build up our knowledge from there. If we first have to know God in order to be sure of anything else, all that we know would be cast into doubt, and genuine knowledge would be impossible, since it is beyond our limited, finite capacities ever to comprehend God by rational means.[4]

Father Bourdin, a leading Jesuit teacher at Paris, used the First Meditation and part of the Second as the basis for launching an attack to show that Descartes' method was that of a complete sceptic, and therefore could never achieve any certainty, but only destroy it. Bourdin's criticisms, coming, as they did, from a member of the order that had trained him, bothered Descartes greatly. In his letter of protest to the Jesuit Provincial, Father Dinet, Descartes cried out against Bourdin, against his abuse, his denunciations of Descartes, and his condemnations of him in class. But Descartes claimed that Bourdin's central charge was that the author of the *Meditations* had engaged in excessive doubt; 'he has not objected to anything in me but that I carried doubt much too far.'[5]

Bourdin's criticisms, as contained in the *Seventh Objections* to the *Meditations*, are intended to make Descartes' views ridiculous by presenting them in a humorous light. But, although Bourdin is often guilty of misunderstanding, misrepresentation and misquotation, his attack against the method of doubt and the positive views developed immediately after the *cogito*, indicated some of the problems that, in effect, reduced the Cartesian effort to Pyrrhonism. The two chief charges are, first, that the Cartesian method is entirely negative, casting away all former means of pursuing the truth, and offering nothing in its stead; and second, that because of its negative character, the method cannot attain any certainty.

This first contention is summed up in this poignant passage;

> it [the Method] *takes away our previous instruments: nor does it bring any to occupy their place. Other systems have logical formulae and syllogisms and sure methods of reasoning, by following which, like Ariadne's clue, they find their way out of labyrinths and easily and safely unravel matters that are intricate. But this new method on the contrary disfigures the old formula, while at the same time it grows pale at a new danger, threatened by an evil Spirit of its invention, dreads that it is dreaming, doubts whether it is in a delirium. Offer it a syllogism; it is scared, at the major whatsoever that may be. 'Perhaps,' it says, 'that Spirit deceives me.' The minor? It will grow alarmed and say it is doubtful. 'What if I dream?' How often have not things appeared certain and clear to a dreamer which, after the dream is over, have turned out to be false?' What finally will the method say as to the conclusion? It will shun all alike as though they were traps and*

*snares. 'Do not delirious people, children, and madmen believe that
they reason excellently, though wanting anything like sense and judgment? What if the same thing has happened to me? What if that evil
Spirit casts dust into my eyes? He is evil, and I do not yet know that
God exists and is able to restrain that deceiver.' What will you do
here? What is to be done, when that method will declare, and obstin-
ately maintain, that the necessity of the conclusion is doubtful, unless
you first know with certainty that you are neither dreaming nor crazy,
but that God exists, is truthful, and has put that evil Spirit under
restraint? What is to be done when the method will repudiate both the
matter and the form of this syllogism?—'It is the same thing to say
that something is contained in the concept or nature of some matter
and to say that it is true of that matter. Yet existence, etc.' What about
other things of this kind? If you urge them, he will say: 'Wait until I
know that God exists and till I see that evil Spirit in bonds.' But you
will reply: 'This has at least the advantage that, though it brings forward no syllogisms, it safely avoids all fallacies.' That is capital; to
prevent the child from having catarrh we shall remove its nose! Could
other mothers have a better way of wiping their children's nose?*[6]

The method, according to Bourdin, rejects all the tools of
previous philosophy, and especially those of Aristotelianism. But
when even sense information and the syllogism have been rendered dubious, what is left? Every possible means that we might
employ to gain knowledge can be attacked by the sense problems,
the dream problem, or the demon hypothesis. Descartes' method
may keep us from erring, but, Bourdin insisted, it will also keep
us from knowing. The older methods, which Descartes scorned,
had been tested and found certain enough. What he offered
instead was a completely destructive method, which was also
open to question. The grounds Descartes offered for doubting,
his levels of scepticism, could be challenged. Are we certain that
the senses deceive? That waking and dreaming can be confused?
That there may be a demon? The evidence presented by Descartes
is highly suspicious. It consists of pointing out what happens
occasionally, or how sick and mad people behave. If we are not
really sure of these very doubts, why give up the tried and true
path, to run head-long into a total Pyrrhonism from which nothing certain can follow?[7]

The second contention is that once having accepted the complete scepticism of the First Meditation, Descartes's method cannot lead to any certain truth because it has denied every possible avenue to truth. The conquest of Pyrrhonism in the Second Meditation is a fraud and a fake because of *'the suicidal procedure of the Method,* [because] *of the way in which it cuts itself off from all hope of attaining to the light of truth.'*[8] Over and over again, Bourdin examined and re-examined the *cogito* and the 'truths' that followed after it, to show the upstart Descartes that none of this could survive untainted after the method of doubt had been adopted. Every step Descartes took in a positive direction could be shown to be doubtful on his own standards, since he might be deceived, or he might be dreaming. Whatever appears clear and distinct to Descartes may not actually be so, if the method of doubt is taken seriously. Once we have assumed the possible inaccuracy of our reason, our senses, or our principles, we realize that any conclusion we come to may be erroneous, no matter how forcefully it strikes us, or how much we may believe it. Hence, the *cogito* establishes nothing that we can be absolutely sure is certain, nor do any of the arguments that come after it, since they all can be rendered dubious merely by rediscussing the reasons for doubt, and by applying them to these points.[9]

If Father Bourdin struck at Descartes' rejection of accepted philosophical method, and sought to show that the innovator was trapped in a scepticism of his own making, the most notorious opponents, Voetius and Schoockius, developed this line of criticism to an even greater degree. As much as Descartes was disturbed by the abuse he received from the Paris Jesuit, he was even more upset by the outpourings of the gentlemen from Utrecht. Gisbert Voetius was the rector of the great Dutch university there, and Schoockius his disciple. Both of them were bent first on driving out Cartesian influences from their institution, where one of Descartes' first converts, Regius, was teaching.[10] After ridding the university of the immediate danger, they then went on to expand their criticism to the author of this new philosophy himself, publishing an attack on the Cartesian theory.

In 1643, these two Dutch opponents put out a work, *Admiranda Methodus Novae Philosophiae Renati Des Cartes*, apparently mainly the work of Voetius.[11] In the preface, Descartes is linked with some of the most dangerous enemies of religion—the Sceptics, the Socinians and the Atheists.[12] Then, in the text, Descartes is accused of having adopted the way of life of the Pyrrhonists, and of presenting an inadequate argument against both scepticism and atheism.[13] Finally, in the fourth section, the crucial criticism is raised, that the philosophy of Descartes leads directly to a type of Pyrrhonism called semi-scepticism, semi because Descartes does make some positive claims. ('Indeed, I do not wish our friend, René, to be a Sceptic publicly; it suffices that he be one secretly.')[14] As with Bourdin, the contention is that the method of doubt undermines all our secure bases for knowledge, such as our senses, our judgment, and our reliance on God. In making the difficulties that occur in knowing also apply to the reliability of knowledge itself, Descartes has made everything dubious. The Aristotelians, like Schoockius and Voetius, granted that there are problems involved in attaining true and certain knowledge, but (they say) if we accept the means available to us, starting with our sense information, and so on, then we can proceed successfully. Descartes (in their opinion), however, took the problems so seriously that he destroyed the only ways we have of eliminating them; hence, he ended up actually teaching us only scepticism or complete doubt.[15]

It is interesting to note that nine years later, when Schoockius wrote a full-scale study of scepticism, in which he examined the history of this movement, its principles, and the bases for overthrowing it, Descartes was not vilified as a Pyrrhonist. The roots of scepticism were traced back to pre-Socratic thought. Then, relying heavily on material from Sextus, Schoockius surveyed the development of the Academic and Pyrrhonian views. Among the modern sceptics, he discussed Nicolas of Cusa, Sanchez, Cornelius Agrippa, and Gassendi, mentioning Francesco Pico in the section on those who have written against scepticism.[16] In the discussion of answers to scepticism, the *cogito* was brought up and presented as a truth that the sceptics could not avoid.[17] However, Schoockius went into great detail to show that the *cogito* is not the most basic truth, but that it presupposes others, the principles of sound traditional metaphysics.[18] And, in his own analysis and rejection of scepticism, which is directed against the arguments in Sextus, an Aristotelian answer is presented, in which, contrary to the Cartesian theory, the validity of sense information is made *the* basic contention.[19]

The traditionalist opponents of Descartes hammered at the theme that Descartes, intentionally or not, had created a total scepticism by his method. He rejected the Aristotelian path to knowledge by doubting first the source of all our information, the senses, and second the basic principles and truths by which we reason. By using the method, the clearest and soundest knowledge that we possess is tossed aside as uncertain and possibly false. Once this has been accomplished, there are no means left for attaining any indubitable truths, because the data, the principles and the standards that men have employed have all been removed.

Descartes cried out against this criticism, protesting violently about the accusations of scepticism made by Father Bourdin and Voetius.[20] Not only did they misrepresent his views (he said), but they failed to realize that the principles they were using, those of Scholastic philosophy, were open to question, and that only after one had rejected all the dubious principles could one then proceed to discover something that was certain.[21] However, the opponents could, and did, point out that if all the known principles were as doubtful as Descartes pretended in the First Meditation, then there was no way and no hope of ever emerging from the sceptical despair that Descartes had introduced. In a mock dialogue, written at the end of the seventeenth century by the French Jesuit, Gabriel Daniel, Aristotle is made to show that Descartes had denied that self-evidence could be taken as a mark of truth, since, according to the First Meditation, $2 + 3 = 5$ might be false. And, Daniel argued that the demonic scepticism that preceded the *cogito* undermined the truth value of the criterion (since acceptance of it might be the result of demonic action), and undermined the proof that God exists, since that depends upon the criterion's being reliable. In fact, we cannot even tell whether God or the demon (whichever the source may be) has made *cogito, ergo sum,* a true proposition or a false one. So, Daniel has Aristotle say, after surveying the sceptical debacle that results from taking the First Meditation seriously, 'Upon his Principle, I'll doubt, not only as a *Sceptick,* but now I'll doubt in earnest.'[22]

If the traditionalists tried to destroy Descartes by showing that the First Meditation undermined everything and created a total, incurable *crise pyrrhonienne*, others of a more sceptical bent concentrated on the resolution, the new dogmatism that was supposed to issue from the illumination of the *cogito*. These thinkers attempted to show that the alleged truths of Cartesian philosophy could be rendered doubtful, by the very doubts that he had introduced at the outset, and that each step that was taken after the dramatic revelation of the *cogito* had to be abandoned, until Descartes' triumph was turned into a tragedy. All the absolute, certain, clear and distinct truths, the entire beautiful system of theocentric mechanism became simply the opinions and illusions of René Descartes. The bridges that were supposed to connect the subjective certainties of the author, with the objective truths of and about this divinely run universe, were demolished, and it was shown that Descartes could never move securely a step beyond the cogito, if he could get that far.

Without entering into the criticisms of the *cogito*, especially those developed by the late seventeenth century Pyrrhonist, Bishop Pierre-Daniel Huet (who dissected the beginning of the Second Meditation so deftly, that he finally transformed *I think, therefore I am* into *I thought, then perhaps I was*),[23] the objections offered by Gassendi and Mersenne[24] suffice to overturn, or render doubtful, the monumental conclusions arrived at by Descartes. A central theme of these criticisms is to question whether the fact that Descartes claimed to be certain, to perceive clearly and distinctly that the propositions he advanced were true, sufficed to make them true. Perhaps, they suggested, in spite of how Descartes felt about these propositions, it might still be the case that they were false.

Gassendi dwelt at length in his objections on the old saw of the Counter-Reformers, that the world is full of fools who are absolutely certain, but who are also wrong, and by implication, perhaps the great René Descartes is one more of these unfortunate individuals. In considering the Cartesian criterion of truth, that whatever is clearly and distinctly perceived is true, Gassendi pointed out first that many great minds, who apparently, saw some things clearly and distinctly, had concluded that we could never be sure that anything was true. Secondly, our personal experience should give us qualms, since many things that at one time we believed we perceived clearly and distinctly, and accepted as certain, we later rejected. The only thing that seems to be clear and distinct and true is that what appears to somebody, appears. Even in mathematics, some propositions that were taken as clear and distinct have turned out to be false. The endless controversies that go on in the world suggest, thirdly, that '*Each person thinks that he clearly and distinctly perceives that proposition which he defends.*'[25] It is not the case that these people are just pretending that they really believe the propositions they argue for, but they are so sure that they are willing to go to their deaths for their views. Hence, what this seems to indicate is that clarity and distinctness are inadequate criteria for determining what is true, unless there is a further criterion for distinguishing what is really clear and distinct from what apears to be so.[26] (This, of course, would generate a need for an infinite number of criteria to distinguish what *appears* to be really clear and distinct from what really is clear and distinct, and so on.)

The point being raised here by Gassendi is essentially that which Catholic leaders like St. François de Sales employed to attack the Reformers. If one's position rests upon one's subjective assurance that one is right, cannot one be, in fact, wrong? The Calvinists insisted that the inner light, or the compulsive quality of the truth made them absolutely certain. But the Counter-Reformers argued that this is not enough, since it is always possible that what one thinks is true, feels must be true, finds indubitable, and so on, may be one's private fantasy. All that the Reformers have to put forward is what Calvin thinks is true, what Luther thinks is true, and what each individual member thinks is true. But, no matter how certain they may all feel, they are only measuring truth by their own private assurances, unless they can, somehow, make it a rule that what they are assured of is actually true.[27]

As Gassendi had tried to show, Descartes' Reformation in philosophy stood or fell at this same point. Descartes fought back by insisting, at the outset, that he did not care what various people might believe, or how firmly they believed it, since 'it can never be proved that they clearly and distinctly perceive what they pertinaciously affirm.'[28] If serious, unprejudiced people will take the trouble they will always be able to distinguish for themselves what they only *think* they clearly and distinctly perceive from what, in fact, they really *do* so perceive.[29] Those unfortunates who do not perceive anything clearly and distinctly will have to remain sceptics until they have this experience. But once they do, their doubts will completely evaporate, 'For owing to the mere fact of having perceived anything clearly they would have ceased to doubt and to be Sceptics.'[30]

All this does not answer the problem, but, like the solution of the Calvinists, is merely a reiteration of the idea that subjective certainty is true, and anyone who experiences it will believe this. It merely reaffirms Descartes' contention that there is something in the clarity and distinctness of an idea or proposition that commands complete assent, and one knows immediately when he is confronted with this type of a situation. The natural and overwhelming compulsion to assent to clear and distinct ideas becomes the ultimate guarantee of their truth.[31] In making this the warrant of their truth, Descartes seems to be stressing still further subjective, psychological experience as the basis of certitude rather than any objective features of the ideas or what they may refer to. As long as the case for the criterion of clarity and distinctness is founded primarily on the intuitive awareness and experience of being confronted with something one is unable to doubt, then, the objection of Gassendi, and the attack of the Counter-Reformers can be applied, casting doubt upon the foundations of Cartesian philosophy. Each central principle introduced by Descartes as clear and distinct can be questioned—is it really true, or is it just that Descartes thinks it is true?

To fortify his position, Descartes moved from the individual's subjective assurance of the criterion to making God the judge, who would confirm and guarantee the rule of truth, and the truths measured by the rule. But, both Mersenne and Gassendi offered devastating objections to the philosophical maneuver that transformed this personal subjective assurance to certainty into objective truth, objections which could only be dealt with by conceding that in a most fundamental sense, the Cartesian system had not and could not overcome the *crise Pyrrhonienne*. Similarly, sceptical critics used the so-called Arnauld circle, to show that the objective guarantee of the New Philosophy was still open to question.

Mersenne raised the question of whether it was certain that God cannot lie or deceive, and pointed out that there have been theologians who have held that God has already done this. Even if God should not be a deceiver, perhaps, we deceive ourselves under even the best of conditions, since we are fallible. For, '*But what evidence is there that you are not deceived and cannot be deceived in those matters whereof you have clear and distinct knowledge?*;[32] As others had pointed out, there are people who have been deceived about matters that they thought '*they perceived as clearly as the sun.*' Unless it can be shown that the principle of clarity and distinctness is really clear and distinct and true, so that we cannot be deceived or deceive ourselves in using it, '*we cannot yet make out that there is a possibility of certitude in any degree attaching to your thinking or to the thoughts of the human race.*'[33]

In replying to this challenge of both the criterion and its guarantee in God's honesty, Descartes treated the objection as a basic attack on the very possibility of our attaining true knowledge. Perhaps, the truths we accept *because* they are clear and distinct are not true. But our clear and distinct conceptions cannot be deceptive because God is perfect, and cannot be a deceiver (which we know from our clear and distinct idea of God). Once we have become aware of God's existence, the extreme doubts and problems raised in the first Meditation ought to disappear, for, according to Descartes, he has found 'what seems to me [a good sceptical attitude!] the only basis on which human certitude can rest.'[34] The explication of what this foundation of all certainty is, is most revealing indeed.

To begin with, directly we think that we rightly perceive something, we spontaneously persuade ourselves that it is true. Further, if this conviction is so strong that we have no reason to doubt concerning that of the truth of which we have persuaded ourselves, there is nothing more to enquire about; we have here all the certainty that can reasonably be desired. What is it to us, though perchance some one feigns that that, of the truth of which we are so firmly persuaded, appears false to God or to an Angel and hence is, absolutely speaking, false? What heed do we pay to that absolute falsity, when we by no means believe that it exists or even suspect its existence? We have assumed a conviction so strong that nothing can remove it, and this persuasion is clearly the same as perfect certitude.[35]

In the very statement of the case, Descartes had admitted that a type of sceptical problem exists with regard to the kind of certainty that we can attain. This problem, whether Descartes so desired or not, allows for the construction of a possible state of affairs in which all of our most assured knowledge could be false. If it is possible that the truths that we are most persuaded of may be false on some absolute standard, then can we ever be sure that what we subjectively must accept as true is objectively, or absolutely true? Here Descartes both introduces this sceptical possibility, and admits that we have no way of eliminating it. All we have is 'a conviction so strong' that doubt is impossible for us, and this is what constitutes our certitude. But as long as it is possible that such belief, persuasion, or conviction does not correspond to the Divinely ordained or known truths, everything we know or believe may be false. At the outset of his conquest of scepticism, Descartes had insisted that one should reject any propositions if there was any reason at all for doubt. Here a monumental reason for doubt is presented, namely that for all we can tell, in spite of all assurances we may possess or feel subjectively, everything we know or believe may 'absolutely speaking' be untrue. The absolute standard, that which God or an angel employs, may yield diametrically opposite results from those of our standard of clarity and distinctness. Thus Descartes has unintentionally allowed a wedge to be driven in that separates our subjectively known truths, guaranteed by our natural belief, or complete conviction, from the objective truths of God's world. We can no longer have any guarantee that the two types of truths correspond.

Having developed this complete scepticism within his system, Descartes then argues, in this reply to Mersenne, that it is not important since we have all the assurance reasonable men could wish. Our subjective certainty suffices because it is actually all that we ever have. We cannot tell if our truths are 'absolutely speaking' true or false. And since we cannot tell, and we do not believe the possibility that what we know may actually be false, we can ignore it, and rest content with our truths whose certainty is assured by our complete conviction or belief in them, and our psychological inability to doubt them.

Descartes had begun his conquest of Pyrrhonism by insisting that whatever is in the slightest degree dubitable must be treated as if it were false, and be completely rejected. But after this striking beginning, he ended by saying that we have to accept what we are forced to believe as true and certain, even though it may actually be false. Perhaps because he may have realized how far he had fallen from the heavenly heights of true knowledge in his concession to his friend Mersenne, Descartes tried in the comments that followed to recover his lofty position, but only succeeded in reinforcing the fundamental sceptical problem that had been revealed in his system. He attempted to argue that complete certitude could be found in the clear perceptions of the intellect, like the *cogito*. He asserted that as soon as one tried to doubt them, one would find that he had to believe they were true. This situation arises only with regard to clear and distinct ideas of the intellect. (Hence, the people who are sure of all sorts of other things, completely sure, do not matter, since they are not basing their assurance on the foundation of all certainty.) But, in spite of what Descartes might say, this only shows, at best, that there are propositions that we, with our human faculties and limitations, are not actually able to doubt. The propositions may still be false on God's standards. This possibility Descartes, then, tried to eliminate by asserting, 'Again there is no difficulty though some one feign that the truth appear false to God or to an Angel, because the evidence of our perception does not allow us to pay any attention to such a fiction.'[36] Thus, although we can state a reason for doubting all of our clear and distinct perceptions, we cannot take this reason seriously because of the overwhelming impact of these perceptions. Our subjective certainty is so great, that we are constitutionally unable to entertain the possibility that what we know is objectively or absolutely false. Once Descartes had put the matter in this fashion, it becomes crystal clear that he had not slain the sceptical dragon, because, whether one could psychologically entertain it or not, an incurable doubt existed within his system that would forever prevent him from establishing any true knowledge, in the sense of necessary knowledge about reality.

This point becomes more striking in Descartes' comments on

the objections of Gassendi, when he dealt with what he called the 'objection of objections', which, though he does not attribute it to Gassendi, he notes is very similar to Gassendi's criticisms. This objection is that, perhaps, all our mathematical knowledge, even though clear and distinct, relates to nothing outside of the mind, and, therefore, the whole of Cartesian physics may be just imaginary and fictitious. Descartes interpreted this as amounting to the sweeping suggestion that everything we can understand or conceive of is just a creation of our mind and has no relation to reality.[37] Unless this possibility could be excluded we would be involved in another form of the *crise pyrrhonienne*, the second level of scepticism of the First Meditation, in that, even if we accepted our clear and distinct perceptions as true, we could never tell if they were true about anything more than our thoughts. Hence, our own knowledge would reduce to statements about how things seem to be, or how we thought of them. But we would be unable to know anything about the objective universe, the things-in-themselves.

Descartes' answer to the 'objection of objections' is to point out the frightful consequences that would ensue if we took it seriously. If it were the case that all we could ever know were the thoughts in our minds, that we might have invented, 'it follows that nothing exists which we can comprehend, conceive or imagine, or admit as true, and that we must close the door against reason, and content ourselves with being Monkeys or Parrots, and no longer be Men.'[38] But this is precisely what the Pyrrhonists claimed must happen. We have to shut the door on reason because we are completely unable to find any objective certainty, any bridge between our subjective knowledge, indubitable as it may be, and knowledge about the real world. Descartes had constructed all his links from the *cogito*, to the criterion, to the clear and distinct axiom that allowed one to reason from the content of an idea to its real cause, to God, and to truth about the universe. The 'objection of objections' pointed out that this entire rational structure might be naught but a set of beliefs that we were compelled to accept as true, which we could never relate to any real world outside of us, nor guarantee as absolutely true. Descartes, the supposed conqueror of scepticism, could only look at his new impending *crise pyrrhonienne*, and declaim, in the style of Cassandra, how catastrophic it would be if this crisis could not be avoided. But, no matter how disastrous it might be, Descartes had no means left in his philosophical system to prevent it. He could only announce that he would not give in, and that, for better or worse, justified or not, he intended to stay with his personal, complete subjective assurance. Like the Calvinists, he was willing to risk eternal damnation because of his subjective certainty, the truths of which he was personally convinced, (even though they might be false or imaginary).

Another way in which the sceptical opponents attacked the Cartesian 'triumph,' saying that Descartes' system left in doubt whether we could have objective knowledge about the real world, was by embellishing the argument called 'the Arnauld circle'. The sceptical problem involved here is neatly brought out in a statement of it in Bayle's *Dictionary*,[39] where it says of Descartes,

> One of his first principles of reasoning, after he had doubted of every-thing, seems to be too circular to be safely built upon; for he is for proving the Being of a God from the Truth of our Faculties, and the Truth of our Faculties from the Being of a God. He had better have supposed our Faculties to be true; for they being the instruments, that we make use of in all our proofs and deductions, unless we suppose them to be true, we are at a stand, and can go no farther in our proofs. So that the way of supposing seems to be more rational than that of doubting.[40]

Arnauld had pointed out the apparent circularity of establishing the criterion of clear and distinct ideas from the existence of a non-deceiving God, and the existence of this Deity from our clear and distinct ideas of Him.[41] The sceptical version merely extends the difficulty by contending that we must first employ our faculties to prove that God exists, but that it is not until after this proof has been worked out that we can tell whether the faculties were reliable. Hence, only by begging the question of whether our faculties are safe to use, can we ever justify the knowledge gained by them.[42]

The opponents, traditionalists and sceptics alike, argued that, given that Cartesian starting-point, complete doubt, each step could be challenged, so that the progress of the mind to God became a series of dubious steps, each more doubtful than its predecessor, culminating not in a complete guarantee of all that went before, but in a vicious circle, vitiating any force that might have existed in the previous reasoning that was employed. The doubts of the First Meditation weakened the claims about the criterion, which in turn rendered the proof of the existence of God doubtful, which further made the contention that God is no deceiver open to question. And if the last had not been established as completely certain, then God's final guarantee of all the steps could not be given, or, at least could not be known rationally.

The crucial point that had to be secured, but could not be, was the first bridge from the *cogito*, the doctrine of clear and distinct ideas, the criterion on which all the following steps depended. Arnauld, when he came to write the *Port-Royal Logic*, saw that the very possibility of ever achieving any objective knowledge depended upon maintaining this link from subjective certainty to objective truth about reality. Otherwise, no matter how sure we were of anything, we would still be hopelessly lost in the *crise pyrrhonienne*.

> And this principle [*All that is contained in the clear and distinct idea of a thing, can be truly affirmed of that thing*] cannot be disputed without destroying all of the evidence for human knowledge and establishing a ridiculous Pyrrhonism; for we can only judge of things by the ideas that we have of them, since we have no means of conceiving of them than in so far as they are in our minds, and that they are only there by their ideas. Now, if the judgments that we make in considering these ideas did not concern things-in-themselves, but only our thoughts . . . it is obvious that we would have no knowledge of things, but only of our thoughts. Consequently, we would know nothing of things that we are convinced that we know most certainly, but we would only know that we think them to be such and such, which would certainly destroy all the sciences.[43]

But if the Cartesian conquest of Pyrrhonism depended on the establishing of the criterion of clear and distinct ideas, and its use as the bridge from ideas to reality, this is precisely where the opponents had driven Descartes back into a complete scepticism. The problem is sharply stated in Malebranche's comments on the passage quoted above from the *Port-Royal Logic*. The great Oratorian proclaimed that this view 'then establishes this ridiculous Pyrrhonism, since its principle can be disputed and with good reason.'[44] It can be argued that the principle is true only if things do actually conform to our ideas, but 'that is what is not certain.' We have no way of telling antecedently, as the sceptics have always pointed out, if our thoughts conform to reality. 'It is then not certain that the thing does conform to your idea, but only that *you think it so.*'[45] As long as we try to reason from our ideas to things, we will be trapped in a *crise pyrrhonienne*. All we will be able to do is reiterate over and over again that we think our ideas are true of reality, that we believe this completely, but we will never actually be able to assert more than that it seems to us to be the case that what we perceive clearly and distinctly is true about reality. Whether it *is* so, will forever remain a mystery.

Thus, from all sides, philosophers attacked the Cartesian triumph to turn it into a Pyrrhonism in spite of itself. If the First Meditation were taken seriously, they argued that nothing whatsoever would follow. If one started with the Second Meditation, with the *cogito*, every step forward could be undermined, and the whole beautiful system reduced to merely the opinion of René Descartes who would never be able to determine if it were true. At every turn the sceptical dragon that he was supposed to have slain, would rise up and attack him. In the same way that François Veron had reduced the Reformers to a state of sceptical despair, holding a book whose meaning they could not fathom, and whose truth they could not establish, Descartes' opponents tried to reduce the Father of Modern Philosophy to a man, who, at best, had only knowledge and experience of the *cogito*. But what this meant, or why it was true, or what else was true, he would never find out. Every road he took to or from the *cogito* leads directly to complete Pyrrhonism.

Descartes tried to fight back, insisting, on the one hand, that the principles that led him to true knowledge could not be questioned, and on the other, that the doubts of the First Meditation could not be taken seriously. But, the opponents showed over and over again that the standard sceptical difficulties could be raised against the constructive achievements of Descartes, and, using the Cartesian method of doubt, everything that appeared after the *cogito* could be challenged. Descartes had either taken the sceptics too seriously, or not seriously enough. He had either inadvertently joined their number, or he had not established his philosophy on a foundation so solid that it could not be shaken by some of the standard gambits from the arsenal of Sextus Empiricus.

Descartes protested that his sceptical phase was only feigned, that he never had the doubts of the First Meditation, and that no serious, attentive, unprejudiced person could have them, as long as he was aware of some clear and distinct ideas.[46] The doubts, he said, were put forth for therapeutic and dramatic effect, to make the reader see first the weakness of what he now believed, and then the strength of Descartes' principles. He had no intention of inculcating scepticism, but was feigning the disease in order to show more forcefully what its cure was.[47] The very fact that he came to positive conclusions showed that he did not regard everything as doubtful.[48]

But Descartes' insistence on his noble intentions and accomplishments does not solve the problem. No matter why the First Meditation appears, it, if taken seriously, carries the march of Pyrrhonism to such a point, that it cannot be answered. Not only have doubtful procedures been eliminated, but all possible ones as well. As Hume wisely observed a century later,

> There is a species of scepticism, *antecedent* to all study and philosophy, which is much inculcated by Des Cartes and others, as a sovereign preservative against error and precipitate judgment. It recommends an universal doubt, not only of all our former opinions and principles, but also of our very faculties; of whose veracity, say they, we must assure ourselves, by a chain of reasoning, deduced from some original principle, which cannot possibly be fallacious or deceitful. But neither is there any such original principle, which has a prerogative above others, that are self-evident and convincing: or if there were, could we advance a step beyond it but by the use of those very faculties, of which we are supposed to be already diffident. The Cartesian doubt, therefore, were it ever possible to be attained by any human creature (as it plainly is not) would be entirely incurable; and no reasoning could ever bring us to a state of assurance and conviction upon any subject.[49]

Possibly because he was weary of explaining why he had raised
the doubts he did, Descartes, in a letter to Princess Elisabeth,
observed that though he believed it was necessary to go through
all this once in one's life, one ought not to dwell on such matters
all the time.[50]

Thus, Descartes was left with this choice; either he had propounded a method to discover absolute certainty, a method which
could conquer scepticism by taking it seriously, or he was just one
more dogmatist who refused to question his principles and could
not establish them. If the former, whether he liked it or not, he
was driven into a *crise pyrrhonienne*, and could not actually
escape from the scepticism his method engendered. If the latter,
he had never actually even commenced an answer to Pyrrhonism,
because, like so many of his contemporaries he had not seen that
every dogma he accepted was open to question unless evidence
could be given for it. All that Descartes could do finally was
appeal to the fact he could not doubt his dogmas; therefore, he
was forced to believe they were true, and further, he was going to
insist, that they were true. At this point, the sceptic, Sorbière,
disowned any connection between the glories of the 'nouveau Pyrrhonisme' and the dogmatism of René Descartes, allegedly built
up for scepticism.

> It does not suffice, as you know well, Monsieur, to deserve the modest
> name of Sceptic or Academician, that someone has doubted one sole
> time in his life nor that he has assumed that terrible tumult of
> opinions, from which he has claimed to have saved himself by a uni-
> versal purgation, and by a total overturning of all of our ideas, which is
> completely impossible, or from which it would be very difficult for
> human reason to recover. It is not necessary to do so much to be
> counted a sceptic, but it must be done more seriously and constantly.
> The Epoché should be taken in small doses, and should be employed
> for the health of the mind, like a sweet and benign remedy which saves
> us from poorly directed opinions, and not like a poison which eradi-
> cates everything up to the first principles of our reasoning.[51]

In Descartes' effort and failure to solve the *crise pyrrhonienne* lay
one of the crucial issues of modern thought. The Reformation
controversy had opened a Pandora's box in seeking the foundations of certain knowledge. The revival of Greek scepticism, the

rediscovery of Sextus Empiricus, had collided with the quest for
certainty. Each side could use the Pyrrhonian weapons to undermine the rational basis of the assertions of the other. Each side
could force the other to rest its case in an unjustifiable belief, or
faith, of which it could only be said that one was sure it was right,
but one could not prove it. The extension of this problem from
religion to philosophy led to Descartes' heroic effort. The 'nouveaux Pyrrhoniens', as well as Descartes, showed that the basic
claims of Aristotelian philosophy were open to question, but the
sceptics and the scholastics showed that doubts could also be
raised about Cartesianism. Both traditional philosophy, and the
new system rested ultimately on an indefensible set of assumptions, accepted only on faith.

Descartes, viewing the progress of Pyrrhonism, could see that
his contemporaries had failed to destroy the dragon unloosed
from the texts of Sextus Empiricus, because they underestimated
the strength of the beast. The only way the dragon could be slain
would be if one could discover one truth so indubitable that no
Pyrrhonism, human or demonic, could shake it. Thus, the *cogito*
slew the monster, and triumphed over all doubt. But could a
guarantee be found for the *cogito*, and the consequences developed from it? Both might be indubitable, but was this because *I*
think them so, or because they are so? If the former, as Malebranche later pointed out, we are back in Pyrrhonism. If the
latter, we are back in an unprovable dogmatism. Every effort of
Descartes' to substantiate the second alternative, either gave up
the triumph over scepticism by denying the force of the original
doubts, or announced the failure by being unable to show that the
cogito was more than subjectively certain (as in his replies to Mersenne and Gassendi); thereby granting that his system was just
one more set of unproven and unprovable premises, rules, and
conclusions. The bridges from subjective certainty to objective
truth also turned out to be only subjectively certain.

The victory of the Second Meditation required the super-Pyrrhonism of the First. But this then renders success impossible. To
abandon the initial doubts, however, transforms Descartes from
a conqueror of scepticism to just another dogmatist to be destroyed by the sceptics of the second half of the seventeenth century—Huet, Foucher, Bayle and Glanvill. Descartes could not

sustain both his full realization of the problem raised by the 'nouveau Pyrrhonisme' and his solution. As long as he could see how devastating were the difficulties raised by Sextus and his modern disciples, the problems of the reliability of our information and our faculties, of the reality of our knowledge, and of the criterion, he had cut himself off from any solution other than the certain truth, *cogito ergo sum*. But once he lost the sceptical vision of the First Meditation (if he ever really had it), then his accomplishment could be undermined by the arguments of the 'nouveaux Pyrrhoniens' and himself.

After Descartes, modern philosophy had to reckon with the *crise pyrrhonienne*. If one tried to ignore it, one would leave all one's basic assumptions and all of one's conclusions open to question, to be attacked by some new Pyrrhonists. To live with the crisis meant accepting that in a fundamental sense our basic beliefs have no foundation and must be accepted on faith, be it animal, religious, or blind. We could observe and insist that even with complete scepticism, we do have a certainty that enables us to gain a kind of knowledge and understanding.

Pascal stressed our plight, caught between a total Pyrrhonism that we could not avoid, and a nature that made us believe nonetheless.[52] Even the most sceptical of all the Pyrrhonists, the great Pierre Bayle, admitted, 'I know too much to be a Pyrrhonist, and I know too little to be a Dogmatist.'[53] One major way in which this was resolved in the seventeenth and eighteenth centuries was by the development of 'mitigated scepticism'. This solution, formulated in embryo by Castellio and Chillingworth, and in detail by Mersenne and Gassendi, was to be further developed by the sceptics Foucher, Glanvill, and finally by David Hume. They were to show a way by which theoretical Pyrrhonism could be reconciled with our practical means for determining truths adequate for human purposes. Others could gape in horror at the rapid progress of Pyrrhonism,[54] and debate learnedly about the source of this monstrosity, where Job, or Solomon or the Devil had spawned it.[55] But Pyrrhonism was to remain a spectre haunting European philosophy while philosophers struggled to find a way either to overcome complete theoretical doubt, or to discover how to accept it without destroying all human certitude.[56]

XI

ISAAC LA PEYRÈRE AND THE BEGINNING OF RELIGIOUS SCEPTICISM

To continue to delineate the drama of the epistemological *crise pyrrhonienne*, one could survey the battle which raged between the later Cartesians and the later sceptics, especially Simon Foucher, Pierre-Daniel Huet, and Pierre Bayle. One could also follow the sceptical themes as they entered English philosophy in Hobbes, Boyle and Locke, the full-fledged scepticism of Glanvill, and then Berkeley's heroic efforts to refute scepticism, and the collapse of his efforts into Hume's Pyrrhonism.

All of this has been studied at least in part by myself and others. Another and equally significant scepticism that grows out of some of the same roots, and which forms a critical aspect of modern thought from the Enlightenment onward is religious scepticism—doubts concerning the truth of basic elements of the Judeo-Christian tradition.

We have seen that from the time epistemological scepticism of the Sextus-Montaigne-Charron variety was first opposed, the claim was raised that doubts of such a fundamental character would lead to doubts about religion. Sceptics were charged with being atheists, though no one could produce an orthodox religious doctrine or belief which sceptics denied. The slam-bang attack of Garasse merely led to the strongest defense of Christian Pyrrhonism by the Jansenist leader, Saint-Cyran.[1]

The critical problem was to come from another source, the application of scientific "Cartesian" method to the Bible itself, originally for special religious purposes. The person who is credited with starting modern critical (and sceptical) Bible scholarship, is Isaac La Peyrère, 1596?–1676. La Peyrère came to Paris in 1640, and became a secretary to the Prince of Condé. La Peyrère became involved with leading thinkers of the period, including the nouveaux Pyrrhoniennes. He was close to Mersenne, Grotius, Gassendi, La Mothe Le Vayer, Patin, Boulliard, and Hobbes, as well as leading figures in the Lowlands such as Claude Saumaise of Leyden and Ole Worm and Thomas Bangius of Denmark.[2]

La Peyrère is often described as an atheist in the literature.[3] Paul Kristeller and I have tried to show that the term 'atheist' in the late sixteenth and early seventeenth centuries is used pejoratively, and it does not really describe anybody's position if the 'atheists' were supposed to have denied God's existence and the Judeo-Christian picture of the nature and destiny of man. Critical thinkers had varying interpretations, and doubts about aspects of the truth of the over-all religious story. But atheism as a denial of the existence of a God active in history and as a denial of the Biblical account as the true picture of how history began and is progressing, is a mid-seventeenth century view that develops from La Peyrère's heresies and his scepticism applied to religious materials.[4]

La Peyrère seems to have been far from an atheist when he developed his view. He came from a Calvinist family in Bordeaux. In his early life he got into trouble with the Calvinist synod. The documents are too vague to tell what doctrines he was supposed to have held then. He was accused of atheism and impiety, but in 1626 was acquitted with strong support of sixty pastors. By 1640 and 1641 he had written his two major works, *Du Rappel des Juifs* and *Prae-Adamitae*.[5] Taking the works as a whole into consideration, in addition to related correspondence and the unpublished manuscripts, I think one has to come to the conclusion that La Peyrère held to an unusual Messianic theology, but not that he was an atheist. He was certainly an unbeliever in some of the key doctrines of Judaism or Christianity, but he was also a mystic believer in his own theology[6] (derived in part from Guillaume Postel).[7]

Among La Peyrère's many heretical theses (he later abjured over one hundred) were the claims that Moses did not write the Pentateuch; that we do not now possess an accurate text of the Bible; that there were men before Adam; that the Bible is only the history of the Jews, not the history of all mankind; that the Flood was only a local event in Palestine; that the world may have been going on for an indefinite period of time; that the only significant history is that of the Jews; that the history of the Jews began with Adam, and Jewish history is divided into three great periods: (a) the election of the Jews covering the period from Adam to Jesus, (b) the rejection of the Jews, covering the time from Jesus to the mid-seventeenth century, and (c) the recall of the Jews that is about to occur; that the Messiah expected by the Jews is about to appear; and lastly that everybody will be saved no matter what they have believed.

The order in which La Peyrère worked out his theology is not known, but apparently the pre-Adamite theory, and the theory of the polygenetic origins of mankind were early ingredients. La Peyrère had his whole 'System of Theology based on the assumption that there were men before Adam' worked out by the time he became a functioning member of the *libertin érudits* in 1640 and 1641. He used scientific and historical evidence that he got from the others to buttress his case.[8] It was this that triggered off a genuine scepticism about religious knowledge.

Before turning to those efforts of La Peyrère that led to Spinoza and modern Biblical criticism, I should like briefly to sketch what I believe to have been La Peyrère's actual theology. The key point in his theological vision is the centrality of Jewish history in the world. The pre-Adamite theory, which we will see was worked out in terms of the Biblical text, of pagan historical documents, and of contemporary anthropological data, is basically aimed at separating the pre-Adamites (who encompass everyone except Jews) from the Jews. The pre-Adamite world was a Hobbesian world— nasty, brutish and short—with nothing of significance going on. When God created the first Jew, Divine History begins. And although the Jews alone were the actors in this, the rest of mankind participated in this by 'mystical imputation'. In the first stage of Jewish history—the election of the Jews, from Adam to

Jesus—the Bible is strictly speaking just of Jewish events. Hence the Flood only took place in Palestine. The sun stood still just where Joshua was, etc.

In the second stage of Jewish history, the Jews were rejected. From Jesus to the present, the Jews are no longer the bearers of Divine history. The Gentiles have been grafted onto the Jewish stock.[9] And, now, at long last the Jews are to be recalled. They will become Jewish Christians, will rebuild Palestine, and will be the court of the Jewish Messiah, who will rule the world with the King of France.[10]

From this brief sketch of La Peyrèrean theology one may be able to discern how his major heresies emerged. First, since other people who read the Bible did not see it as La Peyrère did, he had to challenge the Mosaic authorship and the accuracy of the text. (This is not the actual order in which he developed his points.) How do we know that Moses is the author of the Pentateuch? 'It is so reported, but not believed by all. These Reasons made me believe that those Five Books are not the Originals, but copied out by another.'[11] La Peyrère's evidence, the basis for modern Bible criticism, was to point out the conflicts and repetitions in the text, notably that section which was supposedly written by Moses about the death of Moses. La Peyrère concluded, 'I need not trouble the Reader much further to prove a thing in itself sufficiently evident, that the first Five Books of the Bible were not written by Moses, as is thought. Nor need any one wonder after this, when he reads many things confus'd and out of order, obscure deficient, many things omitted and misplaced, when they shall consider with themselves that they are a heap of Copie confusedly taken.'[12]

Thomas Hobbes in the *Leviathan* is usually credited with being the first to deny the Mosaic authorship. The date of Hobbes' text is 1651, ten years after La Peyrère had written his manuscript, and Hobbes is much more cautious, saying: 'But though Moses did not compile those books entirely, and in the form that we have them, yet he wrote all that which he is there said to have written'.[13]

The significance of questioning the Mosaic authorship of the Bible for Judeo-Christianity is tremendous if it is taken seriously.

First, the ultimate guarantee of revealed information is that it comes from Moses who got it from God Himself. If the link with Moses is broken, then a serious scepticism with regard to religious knowledge claims can ensue. If Moses is not the Biblical author, then who was, and what authority did he have to insure the veracity of what he reported?

The challenge to the authenticity of the Biblical text has like sceptical results. If one doubts the authenticity of one passage, by what criterion does one justify accepting any other passage? La Peyrère asserted that the Bible was inaccurate in claiming Adam as the first man, and inaccurate in claiming that all people now on earth are descendents of the seven survivors of Noah's Flood. La Peyrère based his charge of inauthenticity on internal evidence in the Bible, about people who are not descendents of Adam, such as Lilith and Cain's wife; on the evidence of pagan history in relation to Biblical history; and finally on the discoveries of people and cultures all over the world in the sixteenth and seventeenth centuries who appear to have no relation to the Biblical world.[14]

This sort of internal inconsistency was known long before La Peyrère, including the fact that Moses could not have written about his own death. (The discovery is usually credited to Rabbi Ibn Ezra of the twelfth century.) In 1632 Spinoza's teacher, Rabbi Menasseh ben Israel, published the first volume of a work, *The Conciliator*, in which he took various alleged contradictory passages in Scripture, and offered all sorts of ways in which one could reconcile the passage without raising any doubts about the Bible itself.[15] What Menasseh was doing was typical of the Rabbinical tradition as well as that of the Church Fathers. La Peyrère obviously did not want a way of harmonizing Scripture with his data. Rather he wanted to raise a basic kind of religious scepticism about Scripture in order to justify his own religious views.

The evidence from pagan history had, of course, been known to the Jews and Christians of antiquity. They knew that the Egyptians, the Greeks, the Babylonians all claimed a history of far greater duration than Biblical history. A party line answer to all of this data was developed and is forcibly stated by St. Augustine and by Judah Ha-Levi, namely that all these cultures were lying about their claims to antiquity, and since they hadn't had the Revelation, they did not know what was really the case.[16]

Instead of taking this way out, La Peyrère coupled the pagan historical data with the new explorers' data, and argued that on the basis of all of this, the pre-Adamite hypothesis (denying a critical Biblical claim) is the best way of reconciling Scripture with the known facts about mankind. The Mexicans and the Chinese have data that shows that their histories antedate Biblical history. The varieties of mankind posed a genuine question of whether they could all have a common ancestry in the seven survivors of the Flood. A polygenetic explanation would make more sense, according to La Peyrère. And not only would it reconcile the data with the Bible, it would also make it possible to convert the Chinese, the Mexicans, etc., who knew that their own history antedates the Bible.[17]

La Peyrère developed his sceptical case as a way of justifying his own Messianic theory about the recall of the Jews and the arrival of the Jewish Messiah. He may not have realized the sceptical implications of what he was saying, though his friends claim they had pointed it out to him.[18] After showing his manuscript to scholars in France, Holland, and Scandinavia, and adding new evidence gleaned from his travels,[19] he showed the work to Queen Christina of Sweden, who after her abdication was living in Brussels, next door to La Peyrère.[20] Queen Christina liked the work very much and either she told La Peyrère to get it published, or she paid for the publication.[21] La Peyrère went to Amsterdam, and his version of how the book got published is more comical though probably less accurate. He said that it happened through no fault of his own. When he got to Amsterdam, he had to carry his manuscript around with him because he had no place to leave it. In Amsterdam, he said, 'I fell into a crowd of Printers' who wanted to publish his work. Since the manuscript was bulky, and he couldn't carry it everywhere he went, but was afraid of losing it, La Peyrère said: 'I found myself obliged because of this to avail myself of the kindness of the Amsterdam printers, and of the freedom I had for publishing the book.'[22]

The book came out and was immediately denounced in Holland, Belgium and France. If La Peyrère did not see the sceptical implications of his theory, his critics did. The first condemnation came from the President and the Council of Holland and Zeeland on November 26, 1655 (about two months after the book appeared) in which the *Prae Adamitae* is charged with being scandalous, false, against God's Word, and a danger to the state.[23] In Namur, where La Peyrère was then living, the Bishop on Christmas Day, 1655, had La Peyrère condemned in all of the Churches in his diocese 'as a Calvinist and as a Jew'.[24] Within a year of the publication of the book at least a dozen answers were written, and an evergrowing list of 'refutations' was produced during the ensuing century.[25]

The refutations, such as that of the Protestant minister from Groningen, Samuel Desmarets, stressed the fact that *all* of the authorities—Jewish, Catholic and Protestant—disagreed with La Peyrère.[26] (Desmarets also claimed there was a danger to society in La Peyrère's views, because a sect of pre-Adamites had been found in Amsterdam. This claim about the sect has been repeated in later encyclopedias, though there is no evidence such a sect existed.)[27]

The authors of the first refutations were more shocked by La Peyrère's rejection of the Word of God than by the sceptical implications of his views. But soon, especially after Spinoza's use of La Peyrère's Bible criticism, the sceptical side was clearly seen. Before then the General of the Jesuits could tell La Peyrère that he, the General, and the Pope laughed much when they read *Prae-Adamitae*.[28] The overall tenor of most of the early refutations from that of Grotius in 1643[29] onward is to claim that La Peyrère's views are a great danger to religion, and are contrary to all the Church Fathers, all the Doctors of Theology of the Middle Ages, all of the present day Christian scholars of all persuasions, and all of the rabbis from Talmudic times to the present. A few critics tried to spell out the kind of danger involved.

The great Bible scholar, Richard Simon, who knew La Peyrère well, and seemed to enjoy his company at the Oratory, in his correspondence with La Peyrère hardly seems shocked at the latter's views. Simon casually mentioned in a letter of May 27, 1670, 'It seems to me that your reflections are going to ruin the Christian religion entirely.'[30] A stronger claim was made by an unsympathetic reader, Sir Matthew Hale. He said that the belief that La

Peyrère's interpretations of the Bible 'were true would necessarily not only weaken but overthrow the Authority and Infallibility of the Sacred Scriptures.'[31] And the Catholic writer of theological encyclopedias, Louis Ellies-DuPin, declared, 'Of all of the paradoxes that have been advanced in our century [the seventeenth] there is no one, in my opinion with more temerity, nor more dangerous, than the opinion of those who have dared to deny that Moses was the author of the Pentateuch.'[32] Ellies-Du Pin listed Hobbes, La Peyrère, Spinoza and Richard Simon as those who hold this view.[33] Ellies-Du Pin clearly saw the scepticism about revealed religion that would result, and regarded this as the greatest sceptical menace of the time. On the other hand the Protestant Bible scholar, Louis Cappel (whom La Peyrère had consulted), insisted that if Scripture were not completely clear, then any interpretation was possible and total Pyrrhonism would result. And, if the interpretation of Scripture was only a human one, then again complete scepticism follows.[34]

A century later one of the leading sceptics with regard to religion, Tom Paine, could look back and see the monumental effects of doubting the Mosaic authorship. 'Take away from Genesis the belief that Moses was the author, on which only the strange belief that it is the word of God has stood, and there remains nothing of *Genesis*, but an anonymous book of stories, fables and traditionary or invented absurdities or downright lies.'[35]

A Jewish controversialist, David Levi of London, who argued against both Joseph Priestley and Tom Paine, claimed in his second answer to Priestley that 'if a Jew once calls in question the authenticity of *any part* of the Pentateuch, by observing that one part is authentic, i.e., was delivered by God to Moses, and that another part is not authentic, he is no longer accounted a Jew, i.e., a true believer.' Levi went on to insist that every Jew is obliged according to the eighth article (of Maimonides' thirteen principles) 'to believe that the whole law of five books . . . is from God' and was delivered by him to Moses. Levi suggested Christians should be under the same constraints regarding the Old and New Testaments, for 'if any part is but once proved spurious, a door will be opened for another and another without end.'[36]

It is hard to tell if La Peyrère realized the fantastic sceptical potential to his ideas. All his life was dedicated to expressing his Messianic views. When in 1656 he was facing complete opposition from the scholarly and theological world, he hoped to sit out the storm in Belgium, but instead was arrested by order of the Archbishop of Malines. He languished in jail, and his powerful employer, the Prince of Condé was unable to get him released. It was suggested to La Peyrère that if he turned Catholic and offered to present an apology in person to Pope Alexander VII, he would be released.[37] As an *habile* courtier he took the suggestion to heart and acted on it. He changed religions and went to Rome, where his friend, Queen Christina had recently arrived as the most important convert of the time. La Peyrère reported that the Pope greeted him warmly, saying 'Let us embrace this man who is before Adam.'[38] Then La Peyrère was given scholarly help to prepare his retraction. On March 11, 1657 in the presence of Cardinals Barberini and Albizzi, he abjured on his knees before the Pope.[39]

His recantation reeks of insincerity. La Peyrère blamed his pre-Adamite theory on his Calvinist upbringing. Calvinists only accept the authority of reason, inner spirit or the reading of Scripture. La Peyrère insisted that as long as he was a Calvinist, he had to accept the pre-Adamite theory, since it agreed better with right reason, and the natural sense of Scripture, and his individual conscience.[40] His opponents declared that his interpretation was in opposition to that of *all* the rabbis, *all* the Church Fathers, and *all* the Doctors of Theology. But the opposition did not present any other evidence against his theory—no arguments nor Scriptural texts.[41] Then, La Peyrère said, to judge if he were right, or if his opponents were, it was necessary to find some authority or judge. (La Peyrère was operating within the struggle between the Catholics and the Calvinists over the rule of faith.) Who besides the Pope could be this authority or judge? 'His wish shall be my reason and my law.'[42] La Peyrère then declared that he was willing to abjure the pre-Adamite theory and his many other heresies, though he also kept insisting that there was nothing contrary to reason or Scripture in his former views. If the Pope said his views were false, then La Peyrère would abjure the views. But he also claimed, while 'accepting' the Pope's condemnation of his views, that his pre-Adamite theory and what it entailed provided an excellent means of reconciling ancient pagan history with Biblical history.[43] His theory also allowed for the origins of the diverse peoples found all over the world. In fact, La Peyrère said after his abjuration that his pre-Adamite theory was like the Copernican theory. It did not alter any facts in the world. It just changed how they were evaluated.[44]

As we shall see, La Peyrère apparently did not change his views, but remained sceptical about the Bible to the end of his life. What he remained steadfast about was his Messianism. In his *Letter à Philotime* after explaining why he was disowning his Calvinist views, he then expounded again the Messianic vision of *Du Rappel des Juifs*, insisting that the time would not be far off before the Jews and Christians would come together. This time, however, he claimed this great event would be brought about not by the King of France, but by his new friend, Pope Alexander VII. Pope Alexander would complete what Alexander the Great started, presumably bringing all mankind together. Using Kabbalistic interpretations he found more reasons why Alexander VII was the chosen instrument of God. This work ends with a marvelous picture of all of the great things that will happen when the Jews are converted and the Jews and Christians join together.[45]

The Pope was apparently sufficiently impressed by La Peyrère's abjuration and apology that he offered him a benefice to stay in Rome.[46] La Peyrère probably wisely chose instead to go back to Paris and to his master, the Prince of Condé. He became Condé's librarian as well as a lay brother in a seminary of the Oratorians near Paris. In the monastic retreat, we are told that La Peyrère spent most of his time studying the Bible, seeking more ammunition for his pre-Adamite theory and reworking his *Rappel des Juifs*.[47] He published some works on his conversion, a letter to the Comte de Suze urging him to convert to Catholicism, and a book on Iceland that he had written much earlier.[48] Privately he discussed his theories and sought for some way of publishing them. His friends recognized that his head was always full of the pre-Adamite theory.[49]

The greatest Bible scholar of the period, Father Richard Simon, was a fellow Oratorian and knew La Peyrère very well. Simon and La Peyrère discussed some of the latter's bizarre theories by letter and in person. In a letter giving La Peyrère's biography, Simon wrote that all that La Peyrère did in his religious retreat was to read the text of the Bible in order to fortify certain visions he had about the coming of a new Messiah who would re-establish the Jewish nation in Jerusalem.[50] Simon's letters to La Peyrère in 1670 indicate that the latter was constantly on the lookout for more evidence for the pre-Adamite theory. He found that Maimonides mentioned a group, the Sabeans, who claimed that Adam had parents and came from India. He found a story that Adam died of gout, and gout is a hereditary disease. He found a Kabbalistic claim that Adam had a teacher, and a Moslem one that there were a couple of people before Adam. Simon had to straighten him out about what this information was worth.[51]

La Peyrère tried to get his views across to the public by writing the footnotes to Michel de Marolles' French translation of the Bible. In the early parts of *Genesis* La Peyrère put notes to all of the passages that indicated there were people before Adam. But he added to his first long note on the matter,

> This opinion is always rejected, although those who want to establish it do not at all undertake to do so against the authority of the Holy Scripture, to which they render all the respect that is due them. But the Church having judged otherwise, they submit themselves to its decrees, and to the views of all the Church Fathers.[52]

Nonetheless, La Peyrère continued with his notes, getting in his point that the Flood was just a local event, that not all of the people of the world could be survivors of the Flood, and so on. Each time La Peyrère made his point, he added that he accepted the orthodox view. In spite of his cautious formulation, the work was suppressed before the printing was completed. All that remains is the translation and notes up to *Leviticus* 23.[53]

In 1670–71 La Peyrère put together a new version of *Du Rappel des Juifs* which he hoped to get published. He sent it to Richard Simon, who told him that the work could not possibly be published, in part because it contained the pre-Adamite theory, and in part because it contained a theory of two Messiahs which would be rejected by Jews and Christians and would 'completely destroy the Christian religion'.[54] After such frank advice La Peyrère changed the manuscript and sent it to the censor, who rejected it, and refused to give his permission for publication.[55] La Peyrère rewrote the manuscript again in 1673, but still could not budge the censor. The author made one colossal concession. He gave up the pre-Adamite theory while holding on to his Messianic views about the Recall of the Jews, indicating that the latter was more important to him than the former.[56]

La Peyrère died in early 1676. Richard Simon said that La Peyrère had not done anything in the Oratory that would make any one question the purity of his religion. On the other hand another friend of La Peyrère's, Jean François Morin du Sandat, wrote Pierre Bayle that La Peyrère was very slightly Papist, but very full of his idea of the pre-Adamites, which he discussed with his friends secretly up to his death. Morin concluded his report by saying 'La Peyrère was the best person, the sweetest, who tranquilly believed very few things.'[57] Simon heard that La Peyrère, on his death bed, was pressed to retract his pre-Adamite and Messianic theories, but avoided doing so, and finally uttered the words from the letter to St. Jude, 'Hi quaecunque ignorant blasphement.'[58]

After La Peyrère died one of his friends wrote as his epitaph:

Here lies La Peyrère, that good Israelite,
Hugenot, Catholic, finally Pre-Adamite
Four religions pleased him at the same time
And his indifference was so uncommon
That after eighty years, and he had to make a choice
The Good Man departed and did not choose any of them.[59]

La Peyrère's influence was very great. Refutations of his views kept coming out for another hundred years. Aspects of his views were taken up by some hardy souls, and some of his views were espoused by those trying to justify racism in the New World.[60] One could list a very disparate group from Richard Simon, Spinoza, and Vico,[61] to the eighteenth and nineteenth century anthropologists,[62] to Napoleon Bonaparte,[63] to a Professor Alexander Winchell in America who in 1880 wrote a work entitled

Pre-Adamites or a Demonstration of the Existence of Man before Adam, with photographs of some pre-Adamites.[64] The task of assessing La Peyrère's influence will be part of another study.[65] Here I should just like to show his role in inspiring and developing religious scepticism. By the middle of the nineteenth century, the Reverend Thomas Smyth said 'When, however, in modern times, infidelity sought to erect its dominion upon the ruins of Christianity, Voltaire, Rousseau, Peyrère, and their followers introduced the theory of an original diversity of human races, in order thereby to overthrow the truth and inspiration of the Sacred Scriptures.'[66]

La Peyrère's role in causing further doubts about the Bible came about primarily through his influence on Richard Simon and on Spinoza. Simon knew La Peyrère well in the years when he was working on his *Critical History of the Old Testament* (first published in 1678).[67] With a far greater knowledge of the documents, the languages they were written in, the history of the Jews, of the early Churches, and of other Near Eastern sects, Simon began using all of this material as a club against the Calvinists who professed to gain their religious truth from the Bible alone. Simon raised all sorts of sceptical difficulties about ascertaining the origins of the Biblical text, the authenticity of the present text, and the meaning of this text. In part, Simon raised a genuine historical Pyrrhonism about the Bible (that would apply to any other document as well). In his defense against the outcries about his books, Simon insisted that he believed 'the real Biblical text to be divinely inspired, but he just did not know which of present day versions to be so inspired. Simon also held that the Biblical text could not be by Moses, and most probably was written down over a long period of time, likely an eight hundred year time span. Since then it has been copied and added to, and all sorts of errors, glosses, variants, etc., have crept in. For Simon the task of critical scholarship is to try to separate the Divine Message from the human accretions and variations. Simon's work revealed the overwhelming epistemological and historical difficulties in disentangling the human from the Divine dimension. Though Simon did not share either La Peyrère's Messianism or Spinoza's naturalism, and though Simon did seem to believe that there really was a Divine Message, his efforts greatly helped to transform the study of religion into a secular subject. His Bible scholarship helped spawn the scientific study of the Bible. When his scholarship was combined with a scepticism about religious knowledge and with Spinozistic naturalism then, disbelief in traditional religion followed.[68]

Of La Peyrère's contemporaries, the one whom he seems to have influenced the most is Spinoza. Spinoza owned the *Prae-Adamitae*[69] and used portions of it in the *Tractatus-Theologico-Politicus*.[70] La Peyrère was in Amsterdam for six months in 1655 shortly before Spinoza's excommunication from the Amsterdam Synagogue. No evidence has yet turned up that they met.[71] (Very little is known about Spinoza in this period.) Spinoza's teacher, Menasseh ben Israel, very much admired La Peyrère's *Du Rappel des Juifs*, and in a work written in February 1655 listed the author of that work as one of the very few who knew that the Messiah was coming imminently.[72] A document written by Menasseh's friend, Paul Felgenhauer, indicates that both he and Menasseh had read La Peyrère's *Prae-Adamitae* prior to its publication, and Felgenhauer wanted Menasseh's help in arranging a public disputation with La Peyrère.[73] There is no evidence that the disputation took place, but both Menasseh and Felgenhauer wrote refutations of *Prae-Adamitae*.[74] All of this shows that La Peyrère's theories were known and opposed by a leader of the Amsterdam Jewish community.[75]

The first condemnation of *Prae-Adamitae* was in Holland. In view of the number of condemnations and refutations that took place in 1655–56, La Peyrère, by the time he was arrested, must have been one of the most notorious authors in Europe. And it would seem likely that a young intellectual rebel like Spinoza would have been interested in finding out what all the fuss was about.

What makes this seem much more probable is the recent discovery of the late I. S. Révah concerning Spinoza's excommunication. Révah found that three people were excommunicated in the same week in Amsterdam: Spinoza, Juan de Prado and Daniel Ribera, who were all friends.[76] Prado was ten years older than Spinoza, and Ribera a contemporary. Prado had apparently become an irreligious free thinker before he left Spain for Holland. He had written a work, of which no copy has been found, claiming that the law of nature takes precedence over the law of Moses. (Two refutations of this work by Isaac Orobio de Castro exist, from which one can tell what Prado's claims were.)[77] Records of the charges and investigation of Prado and Ribera have survived, but not of those against Spinoza. Prado used themes from La Peyrère, namely his claim that the world was eternal, and that human history is older than Jewish history. Prado's evidence for the latter was one of La Peyrère's points that Chinese history is at least 10,000 years old.[78] Orobio de Castro in one of his answers to Prado challenges him with suffering from the madness of those who affirm that although it is true that God created the universe, this creation took place thousands and thousands of years ago, and not at the period that we believe on the basis of the Bible.[79]

Theses of La Peyrére appear to have been involved in the excommunication. Spinoza wrote a reply to the excommunication. The reply grew and finally became the *Tractatus*. There he used material from La Peyrère to make out his challenge to the Bible. So La Peyrère may well have directly influenced Spinoza from the time of the excommunication onward.

However, as has been indicated, La Peyrère remained a believer in his strange kind of Messianism. Spinoza (and Prado) we learn from a Spanish spy who was with them at a theological discussion club in 1658–59, held that 'God exists but only philosophically.[80] The rest of Spinoza's career was the working out of the implications of that claim, while also developing a total scepticism of the Academic variety against traditional religion.

XII

SPINOZA'S SCEPTICISM AND ANTI-SCEPTICISM

The position developed in Spinoza's challenge to revealed religion involves a thoroughgoing scepticism about religious knowledge claims, a scepticism that often goes beyond mere doubt to outright denial. Spinoza's scepticism about revealed religion, which appears primarily in the *Tractatus-Theologico-Politicus*, the Appendix to Book I of the Ethics and in some of his letters, grows out of his contact with Isaac La Peyrère's ideas, and out of his application of Cartesian method to revealed knowledge. The result, as is well known, is a devastating critique of revealed knowledge claims, which has had an amazing effect over the last three centuries in secularizing modern man.

At the same time that Spinoza was so sceptical of religious knowledge claims, he was completely anti-sceptical with regard to 'rational knowledge', that is, metaphysics and mathematics.

This attitude, the exact opposite of that of a fideist such as Spinoza's contemporary Pascal, is not necessarily schizophrenic. In fact, a great many modern thinkers would pay homage to Spinoza for being the first to apply rational or scientific methods to religion with properly destructive results, and to refuse to apply these same methods to the scientific or rational world which is in some way self-justifying.

Obviously Spinoza changed the locus of truth from religion to rational knowledge in mathematics and metaphysics. To accomplish this he had to start with a most critical analysis of the claims for revealed religious knowledge. Spinoza, in the Preface to the *Tractatus* stated that before anyone decided that Scripture is true and divine, there should be a strict scrutiny by the light of reason of this claim.[1] When this examination is made, it will be discovered 'that the Bible leaves reason absolutely free, that it has nothing in common with philosophy, in fact, that Revelation and Philosophy stand on totally different footings.'[2] Spinoza will show that this means there is no cognitive content to Revelation. His case is developed partly by the use of La Peyrère's Bible criticism and partly by applying the Cartesian method to religious questions.

Spinoza's investigation starts out analyzing a central knowledge claim of the Judeo-Christian-Islamic tradition, that of prophecy. The definition of this phenomena is that 'prophecy, or revelation is sure knowledge revealed by God to man.'[3] But what kind of knowledge can this be? Ordinary natural knowledge is open to everyone. We acquire it by our faculties which depend on our knowledge of God and His eternal laws. Is prophetic knowledge some kind of secret, special knowledge that does not come through our faculties? After carefully analyzing the possibilities, Spinoza concluded that all the prophets except Jesus were using their imaginations *and* were not putting forth cognitive information that is not available to everybody employing his God-given faculties. To claim that what happened to the prophets to give them their supposed information is somehow the result of the power of God says nothing because all events, including all human knowing, are the result of God's power.[4] Hence 'it follows from the last chapter [on prophecy] that, as I have said, the prophets were endowed with unusually vivid imaginations, and not with unusually perfect minds.'[5] Spinoza also suggested that kind of imagination 'was fleeting and inconstant'.[6]

Then what can one learn from prophecy? Spinoza ruled out knowledge of natural and spiritual phenomena, since this can be gained by normal intellectual processes. On the other hand the imaginative process does not 'in its own nature, involve any certainty of truth, such as is implied in every clear and distinct idea, but requires some extrinsic reason to assure us of its objective reality.'[7] (Here it begins to appear that Spinoza is applying the Cartesian method to Biblical knowledge, as well as using, as he does in this same chapter, La Peyrère's reason for doubting the text of Scripture.)

Prophecy per se, Spinoza then claimed, affords no certainty, and even the prophets themselves had, according to the Bible, to ask for a Divine sign to be sure they had been given a Divine Message. 'In this respect, prophetic knowledge is inferior to natural knowledge, which needs no sign.'[8] At best prophetic knowledge was morally certain, not mathematically certain, which Spinoza explained meant that the knowledge of the prophet did not follow from the perception of the thing, but rested on the signs given the prophet.[9] And these varied according to the opinions and capacity of each prophet. So a sign that would convince one prophet would not necessarily convince another. Then Spinoza went over conflicting prophetic claims and experiences, using some of La Peyrère's data, and further denigrating Biblical prophecy. '. . . Prophecy never rendered the prophets more learned, but left them with their former opinions, and that we are, therefore, not at all bound to trust them in matters of intellect.'[10] After scrutiny of the claims of various prophets Spinoza summed up his case that prophets have no special knowledge, but that God adapted revelations to the understanding and opinions of the prophets. The prophets were ignorant of science and mathematical knowledge, and held conflicting opinions. 'It therefore follows that we must by no means go to the prophets for knowledge, either of natural or of spiritual phenomena.'[11]

Prophecy, one of the central religious knowledge claims on which the theological significance of the Bible rests, is reduced by Spinoza to uninteresting opinions of some people who lived long ago. While Spinoza was so blithely reducing prophetic knowledge to opinion, many theologians in Holland, France and England were starting a new and vital movement by finding the key to interpreting Scripture prophecies. Sir Isaac Newton belonged to this group who were sure that when the key was found, one could understand the prophecies, especially those of *Daniel* and the book of *Revelation* which have not yet been fulfilled.[12] For Spinoza, who must have been cognizant of this great interest in prophetic interpretations amongst the theologians around him, the results of such inquiries could not produce any cognitive knowledge, because such knowledge could be gained by reason alone.

If prophecy produced no special knowledge, the second bastion

of revealed religion, miracles, provided only misinformation and
ground for superstition. Before taking up the cases of alleged
miraculous action, Spinoza casts doubt on the possibility of miracles in general, and of a special Divine law known by religious
information. On the latter front, Spinoza argued that natural
Divine law is 'universal or common to all men, for we have
deduced it from universal human nature,'[13] and such law 'does
not depend on the truth of any historical narrative whatsoever,
for inasmuch as this Divine law is comprehended solely by the
consideration of human nature.'[14] Hence no special law, like the
Mosaic law, has to be sought by non-rational means. The Divine
laws for men can be found from the study of human nature.

With regard to miracles, which were employed by so many theologians as proof of a supernatural realm, Spinoza went beyond
the simple sceptical position that was to be presented in the next
century by David Hume. Hume argued that it was extremely im-
probable or implausible that any event is a miracle. Spinoza
simply argued what amounted to an Academic sceptical claim,
namely that the occurrence of miracles is impossible. The universal laws of nature are decrees of God;[15] 'nature cannot be con-
travened, but that she follows a fixed and immutable order.'[16] So
there cannot be an exception to natural Divine order. There can
just be ignorance of what is going on due to our lack of knowledge
of aspects of the order. As we are supposed to realize from a
rational understanding of God and nature, there cannot be any
real miracles. (If there were we would be living in an orderless,
chaotic world.) It obviously follows that we cannot know God's
nature and existence and providence from miracles, but can
know them from understanding the fixed immutable order of
nature.[17] Having settled the question of miracles in general,
Spinoza then went on to account for the alleged Biblical miracles
in particular.

After denying or undermining the claims of those who have
said that they have found special kinds of truth in the Bible, in
chapter seven Spinoza turned directly to the problem of interpre-
tating Scripture. Some people, he pointed out, 'dream that most
profound mysteries lie hid in the Bible, and weary themselves out
in the investigation of these absurdities.':[18] Instead of going

about interpreting Scripture this way, Spinoza took the most radical alternative, the employment of the Cartesian method. 'I may sum up the matter by saying that the method of interpreting Scripture does not widely differ from the method of interpreting nature—in fact, it is almost the same.'[19] For Spinoza, the method of interpreting nature is basically the Cartesian method. So, therefore, what follows in Spinoza's analysis of the Bible is a combination of a lot of sceptical points, many taken from La Peyrère, plus a Cartesian analysis of Scripture.

It is important to note that Descartes and his followers were very careful to restrict the domain in which the Cartesian method was useful, *and* to exclude its employment in theology and religion. Descartes himself always answered charges that he was unfaithful in his religious views, by insisting that he did not deal with religious topics, and that he accepted the views of the Catholic Church without question.[20] Pascal read Descartes this way and blamed him for dealing only with the God of the philosophers, and not the God of Abraham, Isaac and Jacob.[21]

For a long time historians of philosophy assumed that the Cartesian revolution automatically, or necessarily, led to irreligion and that the reasons Descartes gave for rejecting Scholasticism would apply as well to the rejection of the Judeo-Christian picture of the world. On the other hand, twentieth century French scholars such as Gilson, Gouhier and Koyré have made people realize the possibility that Cartesianism and Christianity are compatible and that Descartes himself may well have been a real religious thinker, trying to ally religion and the new science in a new harmonious relationship.[22]

Opponents of Descartes, especially among the Jesuits and Calvinists, saw potentially dangerous irreligious implications, *if* his method were applied to religion and theory.[23] Neither Descartes, nor those in the next generation who considered themselves Cartesians, made such an application, and they insisted they were orthodox in their religion.[24]

It was Spinoza who was the first to take the drastic step of applying his version of Cartesianism to both theology and Scripture with such dire results. As was mentioned in the last chapter the earliest opinion of Spinoza that we know of is the claim of

Prado and himself that God exists, but only philosophically.[25] Taking this to heart, the method for studying God would be a philosophical one. There is no room left for studying Him in terms of Revelation or alleged supernatural data. Hence Spinoza's method for studying anything, a development of the Cartesian method, applies as well to God Himself.

On this basis Spinoza worked his way through the Bible, examining Scriptural statements to see if they agree with a rational analysis based on clear and distinct ideas of God or Nature. Since, he contended, most matters discussed in the Bible cannot be demonstrated, then they have to be interpreted in other terms, for example, philologically, historically, psychologically, in terms of scientific knowledge. This may explain why such items appear in the book, and why some people might believe them, though we are not able to tell if they are true. Spinoza, as is evident, quickly transformed Scripture from a source of knowledge, to an object of knowledge by using the Cartesian criteria with regard to it. Scripture is then reduced to some odd writing of the Hebrews over two thousand years earlier, and is to be understood in this context.[26]

Taking Scriptural statements literally, and judging them on the basis of clear and distinct ideas of God and the laws of nature, Spinoza asked whether this process yields any demonstrably certain or morally certain information about reality. The most that could be found in Scripture on these criteria were basic moral truths, that could also be found through philosophical examination.[27] (A lot of facts about what the ancient Hebrews did and thought could also be learned, but this was relevant to the study of history, not to the understanding of reality.)[28]

In the all important Chapter XV of the *Tractatus*, entitled 'Theology is shown not to be subservient to reason, nor reason to theology: A definition of the reason which enables us to accept the authority of the Bible,' Spinoza made the results of his analysis quite clear. He began by outlining two alternatives that he was going to reject: scepticism and dogmatism. In this context, Spinoza took the sceptical view to be that reason should be made to agree with Scripture. This amounts to denying the certitude of reason. The other view, dogmatism, holds that 'the meaning of Scripture should be made to agree with reason'.[29]

The dogmatic view Spinoza saw as represented by Maimonides and his followers, who alter and even violate the literal meaning of Scripture. They rewrote or reinterpreted passages to make them meet rational standards. Spinoza insisted, in almost fundamentalist fashion, that every text has to be taken at face value.

For Spinoza, the net result of his method of Scriptural interpretation is that a lot of passages just would not make sense. Instead of cheating about it, as Spinoza contended Maimonides did,[30] there was an at least equally dangerous possibility, that of accommodating reason to Scripture. This, the sceptical view, would destroy all rational criteria (since reason would have to be adjusted to fit a non-rational text, Scripture). 'Who, unless he were desperate or mad, would wish to bid an incontinent farewell to reason, or to despise the arts and sciences, or to deny reason's certitude?'[31]

Spinoza then resolved the problem at issue by insisting that philosophy and theology should be separated, rather than accommodated to each other. Philosophy is judged by rational criteria, by clear and distinct ideas. Theology is to be judged in terms of its one meaningful achievement, the teaching of piety and obedience. It cannot and does not offer proofs of the truth of its prescriptions. Theology, if kept to this role, will be in accord with reason, since what it asks people to do and to believe is supported by philosophical evidence. The truth of theological prescriptions will be decided by philosophy, and theology by itself cannot be considered true or false.

This entails a kind of total scepticism about theology and religion. Their propositions are outside the cognitive (except for those that can be supported by philosophy). It is pointless to question, or even doubt theological or religious propositions, since they are outside the realm where these mental acts are relevant. As the positivists earlier in this century declared that ethical discourse and aesthetic discourse were non-cognitive, and not open to questions about the truth or falsity of value claims, similarly Spinoza had defused the power of theology and religion by removing it from philosophic (in the broad sense that Spinoza uses the term) or cognitively meaningful discussion.

After having so drastically demoted theology and religion, and having cast them out of the rational world, Spinoza tried to make

it sound as if there were still a great role for theology and religion.
He ended chapter xv by declaring,

> Before I go further I would expressly state (though I have said it
> before) that I consider the utility and the need for Holy Scripture or
> Revelation to be very great. For as we cannot not perceive by the
> natural light of reason that obedience is the path of salvation, and are
> taught by revelation only that it is so by the special grace of God,
> which our reason cannot attain, it follows that the Bible has brought a
> very great consolation to mankind. All are able to obey, whereas there
> are but very few, compared with the aggregate of humanity, who can
> acquire the habit of virtue under the unaided guidance of reason. Thus
> if we had not the testimony of Scripture, we should doubt of the salva-
> tion of nearly all men.[32]

Spinoza's analysis of the Bible, using the sceptical points of La
Peyrère about the Mosaic authorship, etc., and applying the critical method of Cartesian science to the content of the document,
played a vital role in launching modern Bible criticism. Spinoza
denied that there was any special Message in the Bible that could
not be learned by philosophical means. And he insisted that
much of the Bible can be better understood in terms of Jewish history, primitive psychology and like subjects. Spinoza's extension
of Cartesian methodology to the evaluation of the Scriptural
framework for interpreting man and his place in the universe, led
Spinoza to conclude that Scripture had no place in the intellectual world. Instead the Bible was just a source of moral action for
those who were not capable intellectually of finding the rational
basis of human conduct.

As extreme as Spinoza's position may seem to be in driving
religious questions out of the epistemic realm, and making the
evaluation and interpretation of them primarily the task of the
social scientist, nonetheless the greatest Bible scholar of the late
seventeenth century, Father Richard Simon adopted many of
Spinoza's techniques for Bible criticism. Simon's first important
work, *The Critical History of the Old Testament* (1678), went
through the history of the documents as they passed from ancient
times to the present, exploring the philological history of the
Hebrew and Greek texts, and the anthropology of the early Jews.
Simon, was a far better scholar than his friend, La Peyrère, or

Spinoza. He insisted that he was not trying to create a Pyrrhonism about the Bible text, since he was sure that there was a Message in the Bible if the text were corrected and properly understood. The tasks of correction and proper comprehension might
take forever, but that did not deny the actual existence of the
Divine Message. When Simon was accused of being a Spinozist,
he replied that he agreed with Spinoza's method of Bible study,
but not with his conclusion.[33]

Others found that they could not be so calm about it. The revolutionary implications of Spinoza's Biblical criticism were immediately apparent. The *Tractatus*, like the *Prae-Adamitae* fifteen
years earlier, was banned in Holland. (Very few books achieved
this distinction in Holland in the seventeenth century.) It circu-
lated with false titles like *Traitté des ceremonies superstitieuses
des Juifs*.[34] On the basis of the book, Spinoza came under attack
as an arch atheist. He apparently wearied of the attacks and
decided not to publish the *Ethics* in 1675, when he finished it,
because he did not want to become embroiled in a fight with the
local pastors.[35]

Some of Descartes' opponents who were sure that Cartesianism
would lead to infidelity and atheism found Spinoza proof of their
fears. For example, Henry More, after he broke with Descartes,
was sure that the latter's theory was just a form of infidelity. He
said that he had heard that in Holland there were Cartesians who
were 'mere scoffers at religion, and atheistical'.[36] Then along
came 'Spinoza, a *Jew* first, a *Cartesian*, and now an atheist'.[37]
The *Tractatus*, More claimed, attacked the bases of Biblical religion.

It was the case that even before the publication of the *Ethics*
with its fullblown naturalistic metaphysics, many realized that
scepticism about revealed religion was explicit in Spinoza's
writing, and realized that his way of treating the Bible would deny
the validity or importance of the Judeo-Christian tradition. The
Tractatus plus the *Ethics* would allow for a totally new perspective on human experience. What Pascal decried as the misery of
man without the Biblical God, was for Spinoza the liberation of
the human spirit from the bonds of fear and superstition.

Spinoza's scepticism about the values of the Biblical world, and his view of how it would be replaced by the rational man, was far beyond what mid-seventeenth century thinkers could accept. For years after Spinoza it was a pejorative insult to call anyone a Spinozist. It took about a century before someone could safely say that he was a follower of Spinoza. But some of the German Enlightenment figures who made this statement still got in trouble.[38] The extremely tolerant Pierre Bayle asserted that Spinoza 'was a systematic atheist who employed a totally new method.'[39] And, according to Bayle, the *Tractatus* was 'a pernicious and detestable book'[40] that contained the seeds of the atheism of the *Ethics*.

What Spinoza accomplished with regard to revealed religion cannot be called Pyrrhonian scepticism, or its theological version, agnosticism. Part of Spinoza's case is carrying forward the doubts about the Biblical text of La Peyrère. But much more of it is denying the cognitive content of Scripture in terms of prophecies, miracles or anything else. This could be classified as negative scepticism or Academic scepticism. Spinoza did not merely doubt the truth claims of Scripture, he denied them except for a moral message. In this denial, it no longer makes sense to consider the contentions of revealed religion as being either true or false. They are outside the realm where proof and doubt apply. They can be studied as part of the history of human stupidity for what they represent historically, sociologically or psychologically, but they cannot be studied in terms of their truth and falsity.

The denial of the worth of revealed religion soon got labelled 'scepticism' and theologians were fighting the sceptics and infidels. Probably the most common usage today of the term 'sceptic' is a religious unbeliever.[41] In this sense, with the qualifications of the last paragraph kept in mind, I think it is fair to count Spinoza as a sceptic about religion, even though his views go well beyond mere doubt to complete denial. If Spinoza was an irreligious sceptic, he was most un- or anti-sceptical in the areas of scientific and philosophical knowledge. As I shall try to show, this is not a sign of inconsistency, but rather encompasses one of Spinoza's basic knowledge claims that applies to all subjects including religion.

Spinoza obviously spent a good deal of time working through Descartes' *Meditations* and his *Principles*, and thereby could not avoid coming in contact with sceptical ideas, and with the problem posed by the sceptics. Other than what he learned about scepticism from Descartes, Spinoza was aware of at least one classical sceptical source, Sextus Empiricus, who is quoted in one of Spinoza's letters.[42] Pierro di Vona, in his article, 'Spinoza e lo scetticismo classico' explored the possibility that Spinoza knew other sources. Di Vona thought it more likely that Spinoza might have known of Cicero or Diogenes Laertius than that he knew of Sanchez, Montaigne or Charron.[43]

For our purposes it does not matter how much Spinoza knew of the sceptical literature since his very negative view is basically found in terms of Cartesian concepts in *The Principles of Descartes's Philosophy*, and the same or similar points are brought up elsewhere. Considering how serious 'la crise pyrrhonniene' was in the middle of the seventeenth century, and especially how serious it was for Descartes, it is somewhat surprising to see how calmly Spinoza faced it, and how simple he found it was to dispose of it. The problem of scepticism comes up at least once in Spinoza's major works. I think his conception of the problem may be discerned by starting with the *Principles of Descartes Philosophy* (1666), examining both what Spinoza said and what Descartes said on the same issue.

At the outset of the *Principles*, Spinoza omitted Cartesian doubt as one of Descartes' means of searching for truth.[44] Spinoza said the effect of Descartes' method was that 'he undertook to reduce everything to doubt, not like a sceptic, who apprehends no other end than doubt itself, but in order to free his mind from all prejudice.'[45] Descartes, we are told, hoped to discover the firm and unshakable foundations of science, which could not escape him if he followed the method. 'For the true principles of knowledge should be so clear and certain as to need no proof, should be placed beyond all hazard of doubt, and should be such that nothing could be proved without them.'[46] It is the existence of such principles (and the intellectual catastrophe if there are none such) that Spinoza will appeal to in his skirmishes with the sceptics, skirmishes because he really wages no large battles with them. What removes all the Cartesian doubts is that one knows 'that the faculty of distinguishing true and false had not been given to him by a supremely good and truthful God in order that he might be deceived.'⁴⁷ In discussing this Spinoza made his fundamental basis of certainty clear.

> For, as is obvious from everything that has already been said, the pivot of the entire matter is this, that we can form a concept of God which so disposes us that we cannot with equal ease suppose that he is deceiver as that he is not, but which compels us to affirm that he is entirely truthful. But when we have formed such an idea, the reason for doubting mathematical truths is removed. For then whenever we turn our minds in order to doubt any one of these things, just as in the case of our existence, we find nothing to prevent our concluding that it is entirely certain.⁴⁸

Spinoza went on to present Descartes' theory, and in the course of the presentation made the centrality of the idea of God obvious. He claimed that there was no point in arguing with people who deny they have the idea. It's like trying to teach a blind man colors. 'But unless we are willing to regard these people as a new kind of animal, midway between men and brutes, we should pay little attention to their words.'⁴⁹ The centrality is shown again as Spinoza presents the propositions that make up Descartes' philosophy. The criterion of truth, 'Whatever we clearly and distinctly perceive is true' follows after 'God is utterly truthful and is not at all a deceiver'.⁵⁰ Descartes had used the criterion to prove that God was not a deceiver. In Spinoza's world the idea of God precludes deception and guarantees that clear and distinct ideas are true.

In Spinoza's own attempt to develop his philosophy methodologically (the unfinished *Treatise on the Improvement of the Understanding*), after he had developed his method for discovering certain truth, he stopped to consider the possibility that there yet remains some sceptic, who doubts of our primary truth, and of all the deductions we make, taking such truth as our standard, he must either be arguing in bad faith, or we must confess that there are men in complete mental blindness, either innate or due to misconceptions—that is, to some external influence.'⁵¹ The classification of the sceptic as mentally blind had already occurred in the *Principles of Descartes' Philosophy*. One wonders what evidence Spinoza could give besides appealing to how clear and certain various truths were to him.

Spinoza was obviously perplexed by his supposed sceptic. He went on to say that he could not affirm or doubt anything. He cannot even say that he knows nothing—in fact, he 'ought to remain dumb for fear of haply supposing something which should smack of truth'.[52] If these sceptics 'deny, grant or gainsay, they know not that they deny, grant or gainsay, so that they ought to be regarded as automata, utterly devoid of intelligence.'[53]

In all of Spinoza's comments so far, it is basically an *ad hominem* argument about the mentality and character of the sceptic or doubter; Spinoza has yet to come to grips with the sceptic's arguments, regardless of whether the sceptic is in a position to affirm or deny them. Later on in the *Improvement of the Understanding*, Spinoza made clear what is at issue. 'Hence we cannot cast doubt on true ideas by the supposition that there is a deceitful Deity, who leads us astray even in what is most certain. We can only hold such an hypothesis so long as we have no clear and distinct idea.'[54] When we reflect on the idea of God, we know He can be no deceiver with the same certitude as we know that the sum of the angles of a triangle equals two right angles. Spinoza, also in the *Improvement of the Understanding* brushed aside the possibility that the search for truth would lead to an infinite regress of seeking a method, and seeking a method for finding the method, etc. Spinoza insisted that

> in order to discover the truth, there is no need of another method to discover such method; nor of a third method for discovering the second, and so on to infinity. By such proceedings, we should never arrive at any knowledge of the truth, or indeed, at any knowledge at all." . . . "the intellect, by its native strength, makes for itself intellectual instruments, whereby it acquires strength for performing other intellectual operations, and from these operations get, again fresh instruments, or the power of pushing its investigations further, and thus gradually proceeds till it reaches the summit of wisdom.[55]

In his later works, the *Tractatus* and the *Ethics* Spinoza made even clearer his reasons for rejecting scepticism as a serious possibility in the rational world of philosophy. (It should be noted that Spinoza infrequently discussed scepticism, and when he did it was usually as an aside.) In the *Tractatus*, in dealing with the proof of the existence of God, Spinoza started off, 'As God's existence is not self-evident'[56] and then added an important footnote that appears at the end of the book where he said, 'We doubt of the existence of God, and consequently of all else, so long as we have no clear and distinct idea of God, but only a confused one. For as he who knows not rightly the nature of a triangle, knows not that its three angles are equal to two right angles, so he who conceives the Divine nature confusedly, does not see that it pertains to the nature of God to exist.' At the end of the note Spinoza declared that when it becomes clear to us that God exists necessarily, and 'that all of our conceptions involve in themselves the nature of God and are conceived through it, *lastly we see that all our adequate ideas are true*' (my italics).[57]

So one can be and is a complete sceptic until one has a clear and distinct idea of God. Everything is dubious (or confused) without the idea of God. Spinoza constantly compared the situation to the mathematical one where if one did not have a clear and distinct idea of a triangle, one would not know what other properties a triangle has. But the situation with the idea of God is far more significant, since all our clear ideas 'involve themselves in the nature of God' and are conceived through Him. And it is through knowing God that we know that all our adequate ideas are true.

Hence, before knowing the idea of God we are, or can be, sceptical of everything. But to overcome this nasty situation does not require Descartes' heroic efforts, but just rational effort, and a rational sense for what is clear and certain, or clear and distinct. Spinoza went on in the text in the *Tractatus*,

> "[God's existence] must necessarily be inferred from ideas so firmly and incontrovertibly true, that no power can be postulated or conceived sufficient to impugn them [like Descartes' demon or his deceiving God]. They ought certainly so appear to us when we infer from them God's existence, *if we wish to place our conclusion beyond the reach of doubt* [my italics]; for if we could perceive that such ideas could be impugned by any power whatsoever, we should doubt of their truth, we should doubt of our conclusion, namely if God's existence, and should never be able to be certain of anything."[58]

Besides offering the argument from catastrophe, namely if we could doubt the fundamental truth that God exists, we could not be sure of anything, and would be reduced to being sceptics, Spinoza also presented a central thesis of his theory of knowledge. All knowledge comes from or is validated by our knowledge of God's existence. This fundamental knowledge is self-validating, since one's rational sense cannot entertain the possible sceptical gambit that God is a deceiver, if one knows the idea of God, and one cannot be forced into an infinite regress about how one knows it. This idea immediately precludes the Cartesian sceptical possibilities because of what the idea is like, or because of what the idea conveys. If we do not have a clear idea of God, then it is not just that scepticism is possible, but rather is the plight of man, since in this situation we 'should never be able to be certain of anything'.

So scepticism is both possible and necessary if one does not know clearly the idea of God. Scepticism is not the result of tropes or arguments, but of ignorance. It is not refuted, but rather replaced by the world-shaking consequences of having a clear idea of God. And such an idea precludes Descartes's further sceptical considerations, that God may be a deceiver. The true and adequate idea of God immediately eliminates that as a possibility.

The sceptic might still ask—how do you know when you have the clear and certain, or the true and adequate idea of God? The idea, for Spinoza, will apparently be self-validating. It will be 'so firmly and incontrovertably true, that no power can be postulated or conceived sufficient to impugn them'. The person who does impugn the idea of God is just ignorant and does not really know what the idea is like. The person who does have the idea, will realize it is true and cannot possibly be false no matter what sceptical considerations are introduced. And one of the reasons why it cannot be false is the argument from catastrophe, namely that this and everything else would become uncertain.

Near the end of Book II, the *Ethics* takes up scepticism more extensively, diagnosing it to be ignorance. Prop. XLIII states 'He, who has a true idea, simultaneously knows that he has a true idea, and cannot doubt of the truth of the thing perceived.' In a note to this proposition, Spinoza said,

'No one who has a true idea, is ignorant that a true idea involves the highest certainty. For to have a true idea is only another expression for knowing a thing perfectly, or as well as possible. No one, indeed, can doubt of this, unless he thinks that an idea is something lifeless, like a picture on a panel, and not a mode of thinking—namely, the very act of understanding. And who, I ask, can know that he understands anything, unless he do first understand it? In other words, who can know that he is sure of a thing, unless he be first sure of that thing? Further, what can there be more clear, and more certain, than a true idea as a standard of truth? Even as light displays both itself and darkness, so is truth a standard both of itself and of falsity.'[59]

Spinoza disposed of one of the basic issues that generated scepticism in Montaigne and which Descartes tried to overcome. An idea is not a lifeless object that one tries to evaluate by criteria, which themselves require justification. Spinoza insisted an idea is a mode of thinking whose truth or falsity shows itself. No infinite regress of methods is required, because having a true idea is the same as knowing something perfectly, and this shows itself from the natural faculties of the intellect. There is no possible sceptical problem because one knows, and knows that one knows, or one is in ignorance. The sceptic who wants to debate Spinoza will just be sent to contemplate whether he knows or understands something perfectly (which amounts to clear and certain knowledge). If the sceptic doubts whether he has such knowledge, he is then dismissed as an ignoramus who does not know what is essential to the debate.

For Spinoza no long elaborate proof against the sceptics is needed since he is claiming contrary to Descartes that the very act of understanding as such makes one aware that he knows and knows that he knows. Though the sceptic claims that such a person could be mistaken, Spinoza insisted this would be impossible if the person had a clear and certain idea. It would be its own criterion. As some of the earlier quotations indicate, the choice for Spinoza is either knowing God and all that follows from that knowledge, or knowing nothing. Since we know something, like a triangle is equal to two right angles, a truth that shows itself in the act of knowing it, we don't have to bother with scepticism, but rather with analyzing our truth to discover what makes it true, namely God. The sceptic knows nothing as he has all his purported doubts. He is in a state of ignorance which only a genuine knowing experience could cure. He may be in the state of suspending judgment, which means 'that he does not perceive the matter in question adequately.'[60] As soon as he does he will give up his scepticism.

Spinoza did not see scepticism as the spectre haunting European philosophy. The quotations I have used are almost the totality of his discussions of the matter. Unlike Descartes, who had to fight his way through scepticism to arrive at dogmatic truth, Spinoza simply began with an assurance that his system was true, and anyone who didn't see this was either truth-blind (like color-blind) or was an ignoramus. The ignoramus can be helped if he can be gotten to improve his understanding, and know something clearly and certainly, or adequately.

Spinoza's epistemological dogmatism is probably the furthest removed from scepticism of any of the new philosophies of the seventeenth century. It is a genuine anti-sceptical theory trying to eradicate the possibility or meaningfulness of doubting or suspending judgment. Spinoza started his sytem at the point which others were trying to get to after they overcame the sceptical menace. Spinoza eliminated the sceptics by first propounding the axiom 'A true idea *must* correspond with its ideal or object'[61] (my italics), and later insisting that people have true ideas. The evidence for the latter claim is personal experience; for the former nothing except that it's an axiom. As an axiom it obviates the need to build bridges from ideas to objects.

For Spinoza there are no real sceptics, only ignoramuses. With his tremendous assurance, based on his clear and certain, and true and adequate idea of God, Spinoza could answer his former disciple. Albert Burgh, who had asked *"How I [Spinoza] know that my philosophy is the best among all that have ever been taught in the world. . . ?"*,[62] by saying 'I do not presume that I have found the best philosophy, I know that I understand the true philosophy.'[63] If Spinoza is asked how he knows this, his answer is that he knows it in the same way as he knows that the three angles of a triangle add up to two right angles; 'that this is sufficient, will be denied by no one whose brain is sound, and who does not go dreaming of evil spirits inspiring us with false ideas like the true. For the truth is the index of itself and of what is false.'[64]

Spinoza's thoroughgoing anti-scepticism about knowledge reinforced his scepticism about religious knowledge. Based on the true and adequate idea of God, which is clear and obvious when one understands it, it is evident that God cannot be the figure represented in popular religion. God's judgments might have been claimed to far transcend our understanding. 'Such a doctrine might well have sufficed to conceal the truth from the human race for all eternity, if mathematics had not furnished another standard of verity in considering solely the essence and properties of figures without regard to their final causes.'[65] Our clear and certain ideas show that God does not have motives, or act for the achievement of purposes. There are no value properties in nature that God is trying to augment. All of the nonsense people say on these matters:

> 'Sufficiently shows that everyone judges of things according to the state of his brain, or rather mistakes for things the forms of his imagination. We need no longer wonder that there have arisen all the controversies we have witnessed, and finally scepticism; . . . men judge of things according to their mental disposition, and rather imagine than understand; for if they understood phenomena, they would, as mathematics attest, be convinced, if not attracted by what I have urged.'[66]

Thus for Spinoza the religious controversies built on ignorance of the idea of God just lead to scepticism. If people approach the problem first through mathematical ideas and then through knowledge of God, they will see how false and how stupid popular religion is. The complete dogmatism of Spinoza then justifies a doubt and finally a negation of popular religion.

Spinoza thought that he had found a way to dispose of any force of scepticism while developing a (or *the*) completely certain system of philosophy. The God of his philosophy would provide the basis for a thoroughgoing scepticism or denial of popular religion, as well as of the theological systems of Judaism and Christianity. The God of his system, once known, would provide the bulwark against any sceptical challenge, since the challenge would be written off as a case of ignorance or truth blindness. The sceptics could keep raising points like 'How you know X is true?' and Spinoza said that truth is the index of itself, so the question is either asked in ignorance or stupidity.

Spinoza's super-rationalism and anti-scepticism were attacked by only one sceptic. (Of course his scepticism with regard to revealed religion was attacked by theologians all over Europe.) Pierre Bayle in the *Dictionnaire historique et critique* devoted his longest article, in fact a book-length one, to Spinoza.[67] This article is usually glossed over as a simple misunderstanding of Spinoza's categories, but Bayle was not one to purposely misread his opponents. To do justice to Bayle's attack on Spinoza would require a very lengthy article if not a book. For present purposes, I think, one of his points is interesting, namely that Spinoza's rationalism would justify the most irrational conclusions. In remarks Q and T, Bayle tried to show that if Spinoza had argued logically he would have seen that there is no philosopher who has less reason to deny the existence of spirits and of hell than Spinoza. Bayle tried to show that it followed from the unlimited nature of the Spinozistic deity that He could, and maybe did, create spirits, demons, etc., as well as an underworld. Bayle's point appears to be that the logic of Spinoza's position cannot rule anything out as a possible component of the world.[68] Hence Spinoza's vaunted rationalism would end up justifying all sorts of irrationalism.

Spinozism survived Bayle and many other attackers. The scepticism with regard to religion coupled with a dogmatic anti-scepticism about knowledge became a model for many of the English Deists and French Enlightenment thinkers who pursued the many sceptical points raised by La Peyrère and Spinoza until they had reached a point where they thought they had abolished traditional religion and tried to do so politically during the Reign of Terror.[69] D'Holbach could, for instance, argue dogmatically for a naturalistic metaphysics while writing *The Three Impostors, Moses, Jesus and Mohammed.*[70]

The combination of religious scepticism and dogmatic metaphysics formed the position of many in the Enlightenment. It was not until Hume that someone appeared who was both a religious sceptic and an epistemological sceptic. The religous scepticism spawned by La Peyrère and Spinoza dominated the avant-garde position in England, France, and then Germany. In the course of a century and a half of religious scepticism the usual defenses of revealed religion were severely weakened. Its adherents were forced to argue for it on faith alone, in spite of sceptical criticisms, as was shown by Hamann, Lamennais and Kierkegaard. The dramatic history of how the Western World lost its religious innocence is thus closely bound up with the rise and the flourishing of religious scepticism in the seventeenth and eighteenth centuries. The application of the revived scepticism to some of the basic claims of the Judeo-Christian religious traditions proved to be one of the devastating uses of sceptical tools. The character and quality of religious belief were severely challenged, and the kind of belief that could survive this challenge was more and more based on a sceptical and fideistic position. And this challenge has remained, even in the last quarter of the twentieth century, one of the major issues that any religious believer has to deal with. The march from epistemological scepticism to religious scepticism has posed some of the basic questions that have shaped our quest for knowledge in both science and religion.

REVIEWS OF THE HISTORY OF SCEPTICISM FROM ERASMUS TO DESCARTES

————, in *The Great Ideas Today*, 1962, pp. 361-363.

Alexander, Ian W., in *French Studies*, XVII (1963) pp. 254-255.

Basson, A. H., in *Philosophical Quarterly*, XIII (1963) pp. 176-178.

Blackwell, Richard J., in *The Modern Schoolman*, XXXIX (1961-62) pp. 391-393.

Chesneau, Charles (Julien-Eymard d'Angers), in *Dix-Septième Siècle*, No. 58-59 (1963), pp. 105-109.

Chesneau, Charles (Julien-Eymard d'Angers), in *Études Franciscaines* (1963) pp. 238-239.

Dąmbska, Izydora in *Ruch Filozoficzny*, XXI (1962), pp. 270-271.

DiVona, Piero, in *Rivista Critica di Storia della Filosofia*, 1962, pp. 218-225.

Doney, Willis, in *The Philosophical Review*, LXXIV (1965) pp. 96-99.

Frame, Donald M., in *The Romanic Review*, LII (1961), pp. 226-228.

Gawlick, Günter, in *Archiv für Geschichte der Philosophie*, XLIX (1967), pp. 86-97.

Gilbert, Neil W., in *Renaissance News*, XIV (1961), pp. 176-178.

Kneale, M., in *Mind*, LXXI (1962), pp. 282-283.

Leroy, André-Louis, in *Revue Philosophique*, CLIV (1964), pp. 115-116.

Lindroth, Sten, in *Lychnos*, 1962, pp. 354-355.

Lyttle, Charles H., in *The Humanist*, Nov.-Dec. 1962, p. 199.

Marshall, Margaret Wiley, in *Western Humanities Review*, XVI (1962), pp. 281-282.

P. (Patterson), C. H., in *The Personalist*, XLIII (1962), pp. 255-256.

Roger, Jacques, in *Isis*, LII (1962), pp. 514-515.

Schmitt, Charles B., in *Philosophy and Phenomenological Research*, XXIII (1963), p. 455.

Tonelli, Giorgio, in *Filosofia*, XV (1964), pp. 327-332.

Von Rohr, John, in *Archiv für Reformationgeschichte*, LV (1964) pp. 136-137.

NOTES

PREFACE

1. Father Julien-Eymard d'Angers discussed some of our disagreements in this regard in his review of this study in XVIIe *Siècle, NO. 58*-59 (1963), pp. 105-09.

CHAPTER I: Intellectual Crises

1. Eck's account of the Leipzig Disputation of 1519 as given in *Documents of The Christian Church*, ed. by Henry Bettenson (New York and London, 1947), pp. 271-272.

2. Martin Luther, *The Appeal to the German Nobility*, as cited in *Documents of the Christian Church*, p. 277.

3. *Ibid.*, p. 277.

4. Luther, *The Babylonish Captivity of the Church*, as cited in *Documents of The Christian Church*, p. 280.

5. Luther at the Diet of Worms, as cited in *Documents of The Christian Church*, p. 285.

6. Sextus Empiricus, *Outlines of Pyrrhonism*, translated by Rev. R. G. Bury (Cambridge, Mass., and London, 1939), Loeb Classical Library, Book II, Chap. iv, sec. 20, pp. 163-165.

7. St. Ignatius Loyola, *Rules for Thinking With The Church*, as cited in *Documents of The Christian Church*, Rule 13, pp. 364-365.

8. Cf. Introduction by Craig R. Thompson to Desiderius Erasmus, *Inquisitio De Fide, Yale Studies in Religion*, XV (New Haven, 1950), pp. 1-49.

9. Erasmus, *The Praise of Folly*, translated by Leonard Dean (Chicago, 1946), p. 84.

10. Erasmus, *De Libero Arbitrio ΔIATPIBH* (Basilae, 1524), pp. a2-a3.

11. *Ibid.*, p. a5ff.

12. Luther, *De Servo Arbitrio*, in Luther's *Werke*, Band XVIII (Weimar, 1908), p. 601.

13. *Ibid.*, p. 603.

14. *Ibid.*, pp. 603-605.

15. *Ibid.*, p. 605.

16. *Ibid.*, pp. 606-610.

17. *Ibid.*, p. 605.

18. *Ibid.*, p. 605.

19. Jean Calvin, *Institutes of the Christian Religion*, 2 vols.

20. *Ibid.*, pp. 36-37.

21. *Ibid.*, p. 37.

22. 'Confession de foi des églises protestantes de France-1559', in Eug. et Em. Haag, *La France Protestante*, Tome X (Paris, 1858), p. 32. See also the *Westminster Confession of Faith*, art. I, which states, '. . . The authority of the Holy Scripture . . . dependeth not on the testimony of any man or Church; but wholly

upon God (who is truth itself) the author thereof. . . . Our full persuasion and assurance of the infallible truth and divine authority thereof is from the inward work of the Holy Spirit, bearing witness, by and with the Word, in our hearts. . . . Nothing is at any time to be added—whether by new revelations of the Spirit or traditions of men. . . . The Church is finally to appeal to them. . . . The infallible rule of interpretation of Scripture is Scripture itself. . . .', as cited in *Documents of The Christian Church*, p. 347.

23. Theodore Beza, *A Discourse, Of the True and Visible Marks of the Catholique Churche* (London, 1582), 44th page (unnumbered).

24. Sebastian Castellio, *De Haereticis* (Magdeburgi, 1554).

25. Quoted from the English translation, *Concerning Heretics*, translated and ed. by Roland H. Bainton (New York, 1935), p. 218.

26. Theodore Beza, *De Haereticis a civili Magistratu puniendis libellus, adversis Martini Bellii farraginem, & Novorum Academicorum sectam* (n.p., 1554), pp. 65-77.

27. *Ibid.*, pp. 65-6 and 75-7.

28. Sebastian Castellio, *De Arte Dubitandi*. The full Latin text appears in *Reale Accademia d'Italia, Studi e Documenti, VII, Per la Storia Degli Eretici Italiani del Secolo XVI in Europa*, ed. D. Cantimori e E. Feist (Roma 1937), pp. 307-403. The material discussed in the text is drawn from the recent French edition, Sebastien Castellion, *De l'art de douter et de croire, d'ignorer et de savoir*, translated by Chas. Baudouin (Genève et Paris 1953).

29. Sebastian Castellio, *Art de Douter*, Livre I, Chap. 1-17, pp. 27-75. Latin text, pp. 307-45.

30. *Ibid.*, Chap. 18, p. 77, Latin text, p. 346.

31. *Ibid.*, Chap. 22, pp. 87-90, Latin text, pp. 354-56.

32. *Ibid.*, Chap 23, pp. 90-1, Latin text, p. 357.

33. *Ibid.*, Chaps. 23 & 24, pp. 90-7, Latin text, pp. 357-62.

34. *Ibid.*, Chap. 25, p. 97, Latin text, p. 362.

35. *Ibid.*, Chaps. 27-33, pp. 103-24, latin text, pp. 366-81.

36. Cf. Earl Morse Wilbur, *A History of Unitarianism*, Vol. I (Cambridge, Mass. 1947), pp. 205-8; Etienne Giran, *Sébastien Castellion et la Réforme calviniste* (Haarlem, 1913), esp. chaps. IX-XI; and Elisabeth Feist Hirsch, 'Castellio's *De arte dubitandi* and the Problem of Religious Liberty', and J. Lindeboom, 'La place de Castellion dans l'histoire de l'esprit', in *Autour de Michel Servet et de Sebastien Castellion*, ed. B. Becker (Haarlen 1953).

37. Cf. Jean La Placette, *De Insanabili Romanae Ecclesiae Scepticismo, Dissertatio qua demonstratur nihil omnino esse quod firma fide persuadere sibi pontificii possint* (Amsterdam 1696); and Johannes A. Turretin, *Pyrrhonismus Pontificus* (Leiden 1692).

38. Jean La Placette, *Of the Incurable Scepticism of the Church of Rome* (London, 1688); (the date on the title page is erroneously 1588), Chap. IX; *Traité de l'Autorité des Sens contre la Transsubstantiation* (Amsterdam, 1700), pp. 24-5 and David-Renaud Boullier, *Le Pyrrhonisme de l'Eglise Romaine* (Amsterdam, 1757), p. 91ff.

39. Chillingworth is discussed in Chapters 4 and 7, and references are given there.

40. Cf. Pierre Nicole, *Les Prétendus Réformez convaincus de schisme* (Paris, 1684), and Paul Pellison-Fontanier, *Réflexions sur les différends de la religion* (Paris 1686). See also Pierre Bayle, *Dictionnaire Historique et Critique*, art. Pellison, Rem. D.

41. Jean La Placette, *Of the Incurable Scepticism of the Church of Rome* (London 1688), verso of p. A2 in Preface.

42. Jean La Placette, *Traité de la Conscience* (Amsterdam, 1695), pp. 366-78; *Incurable Scepticism of the Church of Rome*; Boullier, *Le Pyrrhonisme de l'Eglise Romaine*, pp. 61-3, 68, 88-9, 122, and 213-40; and Bayle, *Dictionnaire*, art. Nicole, Rem. C. and art. Pellison, Rem. D.

43. Joseph Glanvill, *Scir* tuum nihil est: or the Authors Defence of the Vanity of Dogmatizing: Against the Exceptions of the Learned Tho. Albius in his late Sciri* (London, 1665), 6th page (unnumbered) of the preface.

44. Martin Clifford, *A Treatise of Hymane Reason* (London, 1675), p. 14.

45. Boullier, *Le Pyrrhonisme de l'Eglise Romaine*, and Le P. Hubert Hayer, *La Régle Foi vengée des Calomnies des Protestans; et spécialement de celles de M. Boullier Ministre Calviniste d'Utrecht* (Paris, 1761).

CHAPTER II: Renewal of Greek Scepticism

1. Charles B. Schmitt, *Cicero Scepticus* (The Hague 1972).

2. *Ibid.*, pp. 12-13.

3. It was François de La Mothe Le Vayer who called him 'le divin Sexte'. Pierre Bayle, in his article, 'Pyrrhon' in the *Dictionaire historique et critique*, Rem. B., asserted that modern philosophy began with the reintroduction of Sextus (although Bayle has the date about eighty years later than it actually took place.)

4. Cf. Bibliothèque Nationale (Paris), Ms. Fonds latin 14700, fols. 83-132; and Biblioteca Nacional (Madrid), Ms. 10112, fols. 1-30. The latter manuscript was discovered by Professor P. O. Kristeller of Columbia University in 1955.

5. For the history of most of the manuscripts, see Hermann Mutschmann, 'Die Uberlieferung der Schriften des Sextus Empiricus', *Rheinisches Museum für Philologie*, LXIV (1909), pp. 244-83. There are also two Renaissance manuscripts of Latin translations of Sextus; one of the Adversus Mathematicos by Joh. Laurentius, Vatican ms. 2990. fols. 266-381 (Prof. Schmitt has recently published a study of the Laurentius manuscript. See his 'An Unstudied Fifteenth Century Latin Translation of Sextus Empiricus by Giovanni Lorenzi', in *Cultural Aspects of the Italian Renaissance, Essays in Honour of Paul Oskar Kristeller*, edited by Cecil H. Clough [Manchester 1976], pp. 244-261; the other of the *Hypotyposes* and some parts of the *Adversus mathematicos* by Petr. de Montagnana. Biblioteca Nazionale Marciana (Venice), cod. lat. 267 (3460), fols. 1-57. I am grateful to Prof. P. O. Kristeller for supplying me with much important information about these manuscripts.

6. Sextus Empiricus, *Sexti Philosophi Pyrrhoniarum Hypotypωsewn libri III* . . . *latine nunc primum editi, interprete Henrico Stephano* (Paris 1562).

7. Sextus Empiricus, *Adversus Mathematicos* . . . , *graece nunquam, Latine nunc primum editum, Gentiano Herveto Avrelio interprete. Eivsdem Sexti Pyrrhoniarvm HYPOTYPWSEWN libri tres* . . . *interprete Henrico Stephano* (Paris and Antwerp 1569).

8. In the list of editions given by J. A. Fabricius in his *Sexti Empirici Opera* (Leipzig 1718) and (Leipzig 1842), as well as in the list in the article on Sextus Empiricus in the *Biographie Universelle*, Vol. XLII, (Paris 1825), a reprinting of the Hervet edition in Paris in 1601 is mentioned. I have not located an example of this printing, and there is none in either the Bibliothèque Nationale or the British Museum.

9. *Sextus Empiricus,* Σέξτου 'Εμπειριχοῦ τὰ Σωζόμενά *Empirici Opera quae extant . . . Pyrrhoniarum Hypotypwseωn libri III . . . Henrico Stephano interprete. Adversus mathematicos libri X, Gentiano Herveto Avrelio interprete, graece nunc primum editi . . .* This edition was printed in 1621 by P. and J. Chouet, and issued in several cities, including Paris and Geneva.

10. Thomas Nashe refers to such a translation in 1591, and both Nashe and Rowlands quote from it. Cf. *The Works of Thomas Nashe,* edited by Ronald B. McKerrow (London 1910). Vol. III, pp. 254f and 332, Vol. IV, pp. 428–429, and Vol. V, pp. 120 and 122; and Ernest A. Strathmann, *Sir Walter Ralegh, A Study in Elizabethan Skepticism* (New York 1951), pp. 226ff. No copy or further information about this 'lost translation' has yet been uncovered.

The 'lost translation' has been often confused with Sir Walter Raleigh's 'The Scepticke'. This work is a translation of a portion of Sextus, Book I. It is probably not by Raleigh, and only appeared in print in *The Remains of Sir Walter Raleigh,* 1651. For a full discussion of the data on this work, see Pierre Lefranc, *Sir Walter Ralegh Ecrivain, l'oeuvre et les idées,* (Quebec 1968), especially pp. 48–49 and 66–67.

11. The twelfth part of Thomas Stanley's *The History of Philosophy* (London 1656-9), (London 1687) (London 1701), and (London 1743), contains a complete translation of the *Hypotyposes.*

12. Cf. Richard H. Popkin, 'Samuel Sorbière's Translation of Sextus Empiricus', in *Journal of the History of Ideas,* XIV (1953), pp. 617-621. Charles B. Schmitt has found another, and much more complete unpublished French translation by Nicolas de la Toison, dating around 1677. Cf. Schmitt, 'An Unknown Seventeenth-Century French Translation of Sextus Empiricus', *Journal of the History of Philosophy,* VI (1968) pp. 69–76.

13a. Sextus Empiricus, *Opera, graece et latine . . . notas addidit Jo. Albertus Fabricius,* (Leipzig 1718).

13b. Sextus Empiricus. *Les Hipotiposes ou Institutions pirroniennes,* ([Amsterdam] 1725), and (London 1735). Barbier's *Dictionaire des Ouvrages Anonymes* attributes the translation to Claude Huart of Geneva. For further information on this, see Popkin, 'Sorbière's Translation of Sextus Empiricus', in *Journal of the History of Ideas,* XIV (1953), pp. 620-621, and 'A Curious Feature of the French Edition of Sextus Empiricus', in *Philological Quarterly,* XXXV, (1956), pp. 350-2.

14. Schmitt, 'An Unstudied Translation of Sextus Empiricus', pp. 245-46.

15. Prof. Donald Weinstein has called to my attention a sermon of Savonarola's of 11 December 1496, in which it is said that the carnal man who has no intellectual interests or illusions (in contrast to the animal man, who thinks he knows, but actually does not), can be converted to the spiritual life more easily than the animal man. Cf. Girolamo Savonarola, *Prediche Sopra Ezechiele,* edited by Robert Ridolfi (Edizione Nazionale), Vol. I (Rome 1955), Predica V, pp. 61-62.

16. The complete title of this work is Joannis Francisci Pici Mirandulae Domini, et Concordiae Comitis, *Examen Vanitatis Doctrinae Gentium, et Veritatis Christianae Disciplinae, Distinctum n Libros Sex. quorum Tres omnem Philosophorum Sectam Universim, Reliqui Aristoteleam: et Aristoteleis Armis Particulatim Impugnant Ubicunque Autem Christiana et Asseritur et Celebratur Disciplina* (Mirandulae 1520).

The work is reprinted with some minor changes in the *Opera Omnia* of Gian Francesco Pico (Basle 1573), (actually volume II of the works of the great Pico).

17. A detailed study of Gian Francesco Pico's work appears in Charles B.

Schmitt, *Gian Francesco Pico della Mirandola (1469-1533) and his Critique of Aristotle* (The Hague 1967).

18. See, for example, chap. 20 of Book II, and following to Book III.; Chap. 2 of Book III is entitled, 'Quid Sceptici contra disciplinas in universum attulerint, sumptis argumentis ex re quae doctrinae praebeatur, ex docente, ex discente, ex modo doctrinae ubi contra ipsos nonnulla dicuntur, & aliqua dicuntur in laudem Christianae diciplinae.' Cf. Louis I. Bredvold, *The Intellectual Milieu of John Dryden* (University of Michigan Publications, Language and Literature, Vol. XII) (Ann Arbor 1934), pp. 28-29; and Eugenio Garin, *Der Italienische Humanismus* (Bern 1947), pp. 159-61.

19. Cf. Garin, *loc. cit.*, especially p. 160.

20. Fortunat Strowski, *Montaigne* (2nd edition) (Paris 1931).

21. Pierre Villey, *Les Sources & L'Evolution des Essais de Montaigne* (Paris 1908), Vol. II, p. 166. See Schmitt, *Pico*, chap. vi for detailed examination of Pico's influence. Schmitt's recent article, 'Filippo Fabri and Scepticism: A Forgotten Defense of Scotus', in *Storia e cultura al Santo* a cura di Antonio Poppi (Vincenza 1976), pp. 308-312, adds some new information on Pico's influence.

22. Villey, *op cit.*, p. 166 n.1, shows that it is most unlikely that Montaigne used Pico's work. He points out that both authors borrow from Sextus, but usually Montaigne's borrowings are more accurate, and also that Montaigne does not use any of Pico's anecdotes, many of which might have appealed to him had he seen them. 23. Carl Fridrich Stäudlin, *Geschichte und Geist des Skepticismus* (Leipzig 1794), Vol. I, p. 557.

24. C. B. Schmitt, *Pico*, chapter VI.

25. Giovanni Pico della Mirandola, *Disputationes Adversus Astrologiam Divinatricem*, edited by Eugenio Garin, (Edizione Nazionale) (Firenze, 1952), 2 vols. In the list of Pico's manuscripts given in Pearl Kibre, *The Library of Pico Della Mirandola* (New York 1936), number 673 and number 1044 are entitled *Tractatus contra arithmeticos et contra astrologos*. Number 1044 is attributed to Sextus in the Index.

26. François Rabelais, *Oeuvres de François Rabelais*, edition critique publiée sous la direction de Abel Lefranc, texte et notes par H. Clouzot, P. Delaunay, J. Plattard et J. Porcher (Paris, 1931), Tome V, p. 269, I. 112-122.

27. Molière's version of the story is much more true to what Pyrrhonism is, since his sceptical philosopher applies various standard responses out of the Pyrrhonian tradition to the question at issue, should Sganarelle marry? And after showing that he is in doubt about all sides of all questions, and is not sure of anything, Molière embellishes the Rabelaisian situation by having Sganarelle hit Marphurius with a stick. When the Pyrrhonist complains, Sganarelle points out that a sceptic can't even be sure that he is being struck, or that it hurts him. A later commentator on this, Friedrich Bierling, in his *Commentatio de Pyrrhonismo Historico* (Leipzig 1724), p. 23, pointed out that Marphurius should have answered Sganarelle, "it seems to me that you have beaten me, and that is why it seems to me that I ought to do the same to you."

28. Henri Busson, in his Le Rationalisme dans la littérature française de la Renaissance (1533-1601) (Paris 1957), pp. 234-5, used Rabelais as major evidence that Pyrrhonism was a well known and well-established view in France at the time.

29. Cf. n. 26 in *Oeuvres de Rabelais*, T. V., p. 269; n. 19, in Rabelais, *Le Tiers Livre*, ed. Jean Plattard (Paris 1929) (Les Textes Français), p. 285; and Rabelais,

The Urquhart-Le Motteux Translation of the Works of Francis Rabelais, edited by A. J. Nock and C. R. Wilson, (New York 1931), Vol. II, notes, p. lxxii, n. 7 to chap. xxxvi.

30. Cf. Diogenes Laertius, *Lives of Eminent Philosophers*, translated by R. D. Hicks, Loeb ed. (London & Cambridge, Mass., 1950), Vol. II, Book IX, chap. xi, pp. 474-519. Pyrrhonian scepticism is briefly described by the humanist, Guillaume Budé (with whom Rabelais corresponded), in his *De Asse* (Paris 1541), p. cxxii, apparently based on Diogenes Laertius.

31. Only Schmitt has traced the readers, commentators and opponents of Cicero's *De Academica*, finding that it was quite extensively read, and productive of not very sharp replies, some of which were published and some of which exist only in manuscript. See *Cicero Scepticus*.

Ezequiel de Olaso's review article of Schmitt's book, 'Las Academica de Ciceron y la Filosofia Remcentista', in *International Studies in Philosophy* VII (1975), pp. 57-68, provides some further data about Cicero's influence.

32. On Agrippa's interests and stormy career, see Bayle's article, 'Agrippa' in the *Dictionaire Historique et Critique*; Fritz Mauthner's introduction to his translation of Agrippa von Nettesheim, *Die Eitelkeit und Unsicherheit der Wissenschaften und die Verteidigungsschrift* (Munchen 1913), pp. VI-XLV; and Charles G. Nauert Jr., 'Magic and Scepticism in Agrippa's Thought', in *Journal of the History of Ideas*, XVIII, (1957), pp. 161-82 and *Agrippa and the Crisis of Renaissance Thought* (Urbana, Illinois 1965); R. H. Popkin, introduction to Olms photoreproduction edition; of Agrippa's *Opera* and Paola Zambelli's essays, especially 'Corneille Agrippa, Érasme et la Theologie humaniste', in *Douziènne Etage International d'Etudes humanistes*, Tours 1969, Vol. I, pp. 113-59 (Paris 1972), and 'Magic and Radical Reformation in Agrippa of Nettesheim', in *Journal of The Warburg and Courtauld Institutes*, XXXIX (1976), pp. 69-103.

33. Henricus Cornelius Agrippa von Nettesheim, *Of the Vanitie and Uncertaintie of Artes and Sciences*, Englished by James Sanford (London 1569), p. Aiv.

34. *Ibid.*, p. 4r.

35. *Ibid.*, pp. 4v and 5r.

36. *Ibid.*, p. 183v.

37. *Ibid.*, p. 187r.

38. Cf. Mauthner, *op. cit.*, p. xlvii; and Pierre Villey, *Les Sources & l'Evolution des Essais de Montaigne*, Vol. II, p. 176. Mauthner, *op. cit.*, p. xlvi calls it 'a work of anger', while it is labelled 'a revenge on the sciences' in Stäudlin's, *Geschichte und Geist des Skepticismus*, Vol. I, p. 558. Some of the French commentators are generous, and willing to assume that the work is ironic, 'it is an ironic pamphlet against stupidity.' Strowski, *Montaigne*, pp. 132-3. Villey tries to place Agrippa's work in the genre of paradoxical literature of the 16th century. Cf. Villey, *op. cit.*, II, pp. 173-5. The claim in Panos P. Morphos, *The Dialogues of Guy de Brués (Johns Hopkins Studies in Romance Literatures*, Extra Volume XXX) (Baltimore 1953), p. 77, that 'Agrippa's purpose was to defend the Protestant position,' is open to question, since Agrippa apparently remained a Catholic all of his life, and he attacks the Reformers in *Vanitie*, pp. 20r-v.

39. See Nauert, 'Magic and Skepticism in Agrippa', esp. pp. 167-82.

40. Villey, *op. cit.*, II, p. 166 and Strowski, *op. cit.*, pp. 130 and 133 n.1 say so. Paola Zambelli supports this view in her 'A propositis della "de vanitate scientiarium et artium" di Cornelio Agrippa', in *Rivista critica di storia della filosofia*

XV (1960), pp. 166–80. Schmitt carefully examines the evidence and doubts that Agrippa used any of Pico's materials. Schmitt, *Pico*, pp. 239–42.

41. For example, chap. 54 on moral philosophy looks like some of Sextus's discussions on the variety of moral behavior. However, where Sextus gives the example that 'also among the Egyptians men marry their sisters,' *P.H.I.*, 153, and III, 205, Agrippa stated 'Emonge the Athenians it was leeful for a man to marry his owne sister,' *Vanitie*, p. 72. Several instances of this sort occur. (Villey states it as a fact that Agrippa borrowed from Sextus, without offering any examples. Cf. Villey, *op. cit.*, II, p. 176). There are several mentions of Pyrrho by Agrippa, but none indicating much acquaintance with Pyrrhonian sources. Nauert, *op. cit.*, note 30, states that Agrippa does not cite Sextus because his works were not yet in print.

42. Cf. Strowski, *op. cit.*, pp. 130 and 133 n.1; and Villey, *op. cit.*, II, pp. 176 and 178–80. Villey appears convinced that Montaigne's borrowings from Agrippa could have had little to do with the formation of Montaigne's scepticism. For a comparison of the scepticism of Agrippa and Montaigne, see Ernst Cassirer, *Das Erkenntnisproblem in der Philosophie und Wissenschaft der neueren Zeit*, Band I (Berlin 1922), pp. 192–4.

43. Quoted from Corneto's *De vera philosophia* in Henri Busson, *Le Rationalisme dans la litterature française*, p. 94 n.2.

44. *Ibid.*, pp. 94–106. Busson presents Du Ferron as somewhat of a philosophical dilettante and eclectic, rather than a serious fideist. For reasons that are never made clear, Busson continually calls these various views derivative from the Academic sceptics, Pyrrhonism, which creates some confusion regarding how knowledge of and interest in Greek scepticism developed in the sixteenth century, and gives a misleading impression of the strength and length of the Pyrrhonian tradition prior to Montaigne.

45. See Schmitt, *Cicero Scepticus* for a survey of these works.

46. Cf. *Ibid.*, p. 95. There is an interesting discussion of this correspondence in Bayle's *Dictionnaire*, art. Bunel, Pierre, Rem. E.

47. Cf. Jacopo Sadoleto, *Elogio della Sapienza* (*De laudibus philosophiae*), trad. and ed. Antonio Altamura, intro. Giuseppe Toffanin (Naples 1950), p. 206. This work was originally published in Lyon in 1538.

48. Jacopo Sadoleto, *Phaedrus*, in *Opera quae exstant omnia* (Veronae 1738), Vol. III. A summary, which I have followed in part, is given in Busson, *op. cit.*, pp. 100–1. The work is also briefly described in Panos P. Morphos, *Dialogues of Guy de Bruès*, p. 78. The material in *Phaedrus* appears to come from Cicero, and Diogenes Laertius. There is a mention of Pyrrhonism on p. 168, but no indication at all of any acquaintance with the writings of Sextus Empiricus. Busson, in the new edition of his study, cited above, says that, 'These paradoxes are really a resumé of C. Agrippa's *De incertitudine scientiarum*,' but no evidence is offered to substantiate this.

49. The positive views of Sadoleto are summarized in Busson, *op. cit.*, pp. 101–3, where several citations are also given. See also Morphos. *op. cit.*, p. 78. Sadoleto's religious rationalism goes beyond the stated views of those usually classified as Paduans.

40. Cf., Busson, *op. cit.*, p. 233; and George T. Buckley, *Atheism in the English Renaissance* (Chicago 1932), p. 118.

51. An even more far-fetched case is introduced by Busson, *op. cit.*, pp. 233–4, and Buckley, *op. cit.*, p. 118, as evidence that Pyrrhonism was current in France

in the first half of the sixteenth century. They cite the poet, Sainct-Gelays, as having attacked Pyrrhonism in his *Advertissement sur les jugemens d'astrologie*, of 1546. All that Sainct-Gelays said was that there is only one right way, and lots of wrong ones, and lots of different opinions have been offered on various matters. 'This was the reason that the sceptics said that all matters are in dispute, and that there is nothing so obvious nor so agreed upon by all that it cannot be debated and made dubious by apparent reasons, in the way that Anaxagoras exerted himself to prove by sophistical disputation that snow is black.' Melin de Sainct-Gelays, *Oeuvres complètes de Melin de Sainct-Gelays*, edited by Prosper Blancemain (Paris 1873) 3 vols., (Bibliothèque Elzévirienne), Vol. III, p. 248. This observation hardly constitutes an attack on, or even evidence of knowledge of the Pyrrhonian tradition.

52. Louis Le Caron, *Le Courtisan second, ou de la vrai sagesse et des louanges de la philosophie*, in *Les Dialogues de Loys Le Caron, Parisien*, (Paris 1556). This work is described in Busson, *Les Sources et le développement du rationalisme dans la littérature française de la Renaissance* (1530-1601), (Paris 1922), pp. 417-8. On Le Caron, see Lucien Pinvert, 'Louis le Caron, dit Charondas (1536-1613),' *Revue de la Renaissance*, II (1902), pp. 1-9, 69-76, and 181-8.

53. This matter is discussed in Morphos, *op. cit.*, pp. 78-9. The citations in Busson, *Le Rationalisme dans la littérature française*, p. 101, n.2, show that the common illustration of comparing God to the Persian king occurs in other works as well.

54. Cf. Pierre Villey, 'Montaigne a-t-il lu le Traité de l'éducation de Jacques Sadolet?' in *Bulletin du Bibliophile et du Bibliothécaire* (1909), pp. 265-78. The suggestion was made by Joseph Dedieu, 'Montaigne et le Cardinal Sadolet', *Bulletin de littérature ecclésiastique*, ser. IV, Vol. 1 (1909), p. 8-22.

55. Quoted in Busson, *Le Rationalisme dans la littérature francaise.*, p. 143 from Budé's *De Transitu Hellenismi*. Busson, p. 143, n.2, interprets the view Budé is commenting on as Pyrrhonism, again confusing the two types of sceptical theories.

57. Quoted in Henri Busson, *Le Rationalisme dans la littérature française*, p. 235.

58. Cited in Busson, *Le Rationalisme*, p. 236.

59. Cited in *ibid.*, p. 237.

60. Cited in *ibid.*, p. 268.

61. P. Galland, *contra Novam Academicam Petri Rami oratio* (Lutetiae 1551). (There is a copy of this work in the Newberry Library, Chicago.) Busson, *Le Rationalisme dans la littérature française*, pp. 269-71, indicates that Galland held the Paduan position. Thomas Greenwood, in his 'L'éclosion de scepticisme pendant la Renaissance et les premiers apologistes', *Revue de l'Université d'Ottawa*, XVII (1947), p. 88, denies this, but fails to offer any convincing evidence.

62. Cf. Busson, *Le Rationalisme dans la littérature française*, pp. 269-71. The passage quoted appears on p. 271.

63. For a survey of all the known information, plus some conjectures about the biography of Guy de Brués, see Panos Paul Morphos, *The Dialogues of Guy de Brués, A Critical Edition with a Study in Renaissance Scepticism and Relativism*, pp. 8-19.

64. On Ramus and de Brués, see Morphos, *op. cit.*, pp. 15-16, and sec. 88 and 113-14 of Morphos' edition of the *Dialogues* contained in this work; and Thomas

Greenwood, *'Guy de Brués'*, *Bibliothèque d'Humanisme et Renaissance*, XII (1951), pp. 80 and 181-4.

65. On de Brués and the Pléiade, see Morphos, *op. cit.*, pp. 19-25 and 71-3. Morphos concludes, 'In the presence of the available evidence, we conjecture that Brués reproduces the setting of the meetings and of the discussions held by Ronsard and his friends and perhaps the general nature of their talks rather than their real respective positions', p. 73. See also, Greenwood 'Guy de Brués', pp. 70-82.

66. De Brués, *Dialogues*, sec. 5-8.

67. *Ibid.*, sec. 9-10.

68. *Ibid.*, sec. 11ff.

69. *Ibid.*, Dialogue I, up to sec. 97.

70. *Ibid.*, sec. 50, 'all that men have invented, and thought that they knew, is only to be opinion and day-dreaming, except what is taught us by the Holy Scriptures.' Morphos insists that Baïf's view here is not true fideism, like that of Agrippa, but is merely an expedient and temporary conclusion since Baïf lacks the faith and the ardor of Agrippa and other ardent fideists. Cf. Morphos, *op. cit.*, pp. 35 and 77-78.

71. De Brués, *Dialogues*, sec. 131-6.

72. *Ibid.*, sec. 139ff.

73. *Ibid.*, Epistre and Preface, pp. 87-92 in Morphos edition.

74. Cf. Morphos. *op. cit.*, p. 7; and Busson, *Les Sources et le développement.*, p. 423. Another discussion of Brués book, in George Boas, *Dominant Themes of Modern Philosophy* (New York 1957), pp. 71-4, concludes with the suggestion that the thoroughness with which Brués outlined the tenets of scepticism may indicate that he was really advocating this view and not refuting it.

75. See, for instance, Greenwood, 'Guy de Brués', p. 268, and Greenwood, 'L'éclosion du scepticisme', pp. 97-8.

76. Pierre Villey, *Sources & L'evolution des Essais de Montaigne*, II, p. 173.

77. Busson, *Les Sources et le développement*, pp. 419-23; and Greenwood, 'L'éclosion du scepticisme,' pp. 95-8. (This article is almost all taken from Busson, without indicating this. Busson omits this section in his revised edition.)

78. The horrors of scepticism are a constant theme in Greenwood's 'L'éclosion du scepticisme.'

79. Busson, *Les Sources et le développement*, p. 425.

80. Villey, *op. cit.*, II, p. 172. The controversies of Talon, Galland and Brués are examined in detail in Schmitt, *Cicero Scepticus*, pp. 81-108.

81. Villey, *op. cit.*, II, p. 165.

82. This thesis is asserted throughout his *Sources et le développement du Rationalisme* and the revised version, *Le Rationalisme dans la littérature française*. See, for example, pp. 258 and 438-9 in the former, and pp. 233 and 410-11 in the latter. In a more extreme form, this is the thesis of Greenwood, in 'L'éclosion du scepticisme.' Both Villey and Strowski minimize the importance of pre-Montaignian sceptical thought. See Villey, *op. cit.*, II, p. 165 and Strowski, *Montaigne*, pp. 120ff.

83. Cf. preface by Henri Estienne to Sextus Empiricus, *Pyrrhoniarum hypotypωσεwn*, 1562 edition, pp. 2-8. This preface is translated into French in the *Oeuvres choisies* of Sextus Empiricus, trad. Jean Grenier et Geneviève Goron (Paris 1948), pp. 21-4.

84. A phrase attributed to the seventeenth century English Catholic philosopher, Thomas White, in the article on the 'Pyrrhonism of Joseph Glanvill', in *Retrospective Review*, I (1853), p. 106.

85. Preface of Hervet in 1569 edition of Sextus's *Adversus Mathematicos*, pp. a2–a3. This preface will be considered later in connection with scepticism and the Counter-Reformation in France.

86. Giordano Bruno, *La Cena de le Ceneri*, in *Opere Italiane*, 3 vols., edited by Giovanni Gentile (Bari 1925–7), I, p. 36.

87. Bruno, *Cabala del Cavallo Pegaseo*, in *Opere Italiane*, II, pp. 266–7, and 270.

88. *Ibid.*, II, pp. 289–91. This distinction between the two groups does not conform to the usage of either Sextus Empiricus or Diogenes Laertius. Sextus, in *P.H.* I, par. 7, makes 'sceptic', 'zetetic', 'ephectic', and 'Pyrrhonian', equivalent terms, and Diogenes, in I, par. 16, uses 'ephectic' to refer to the opposite of 'dogmatic', covering both Pyrrhonists and Academics.

89. Bruno, *Cabala*, II, p. 291, and Gentile's notes 4 and 6. The passage referred to in n. 6 is *P.H.* III, chaps. 27–29. pars. 252–256. especially par. 252 which appears almost literally translated.

90. Marsilio Cagnati, Veronensis Doctoris Medici et Philosophi, *Variarum Observationum Libri Quatuor* (Romae 1587), Lib. III, cap. vi, 'De Sexto, quem empiricum aliqui vocant,' pp. 203–6.

91. This vexing problem occurs throughout the literature on Sextus from the sixteenth through the eighteenth century. Cagnati rightly distinguishes Sextus Empiricus from Sextus Chaeroneae, Plutarch's nephew.

92. Juste Lipse, *Manuductionis ad Stoicam Philosophiam Libri Tres* (Antwerp 1604), Lib. II, dissert. III and IV, pp. 69–76. Isaac Casaubon also used Sextus for philological and historical information, and had his own Greek manuscript, now in the King's Library, British Museum, which he took from his father-in-law, Henri Estienne. Cf. Mark Pattison, *Isaac Casaubon 1559–1614*, 2nd ed. (Oxford 1892), pp. 30–1.

93. In the eighteenth century, Valentia's work appeared in the Durand edition of Cicero's *Académiques* as *Les Académiques ou des Moyens de Juger du Vrai: ouvrage puisé dans les sources; par Pierre Valence*. See for instance, the Paris 1796 edition of Cicero's *Académiques* where Valentia's book is pp. 327–464. The book was also abstracted and reviewed in the *Bibliothèque Britannique*, XVIII (Oct.-Dec. 1741), pp. 60–146.

94. Petrus Valentia (Valencia), *Academica sive De Iudicio erga verum, Ex ipsis primis frontibus* (Antwerp 1596).

95. *Ibid.*, p. 27.

96. *Ibid.*, p. 123. The discussion of Pyrrhonism is on pp. 27–33.

97. *Ibid.*, p. 123–4. 'Verum enimuerò illud interim his admonemur, Graecos humanumque ingenium omne sapientiam quaerere sibique & aliis promittere, quam tamen nec inuenire nec praestare unquam posse. Qui igitur vera sapientia indigere se mecum sentiet, postulet non ab huiusmodi philosophia; sed à Deo, qui dat omnibus affluenter & non improperat. Quod siquis videtur sapiens esse in hoc seculo, fiat stultus, ut sit sapiens: Abscondit enim Deus verum sapientiam à falsae sapientiae amatoribus, revelat verò paruulis. Ipsi soli sapienti per Iesum Christum gloria. Amen.' On Valentia, see Schmitt, *Cicero Scepticus*, pp. 74–76.

98. Francisco Sanches, *Quod Nihil Scitur* in Sanches, *Opera Philosophica*, edited by Joaquim De Carvalho (Coimbra 1955). In the literature the author's last name is given both in the Portuguese form, Sanches, and the Spanish form, Sanchez. He was apparently born in Portugal of Spanish Jewish parents who were *conversos*. He lived in France most of his life, where the name was spelled Sanchez.

99. Bayle, *Dictionaire*, art. 'Sanchez, François.' Anyone who reads this far in Bayle's *Dictionary* should read the following article on Thomas Sanchez, Jésuite Espagnol, before returning the work to the shelves. This is one of the most amazing articles in the whole *Dictionary*. The end of Rem. C may be the source of Hume's observations in *A Treatise of Human Nature*, Selby-Bigge ed., p. 114, Book I, Part III, sec. IX.

100. For biographical details, see the 'Prólogo' by Marcelino Menéndez' y Pelayo, pp. 7–9, to the Spanish translation of *Quod nihil scitur, Que Nada Se Sabe* (Colección Camino de Santiago no. 9) (Buenos Aires 1944). See also Carvalho's introductory material in his edition of the *Opera Philosophica*, where he indicates the date of birth may be in 1551. A good deal of biographical information is also given in John Owen's strange book, *The Skeptics of the French Renaissance* (London 1893), chap. IV, and in Emilien Senchet, *Essai sur la méthode de Francisco Sanchez* (Paris 1904). pp. i–xxxix. The most extensive collection of data about Sanchez is in the boxes of papers of Henri Cazac, located in the library of the Institut Catholique de Toulouse. These provide many biographical clues, plus suggestions about the sceptical influence amongst the Portuguese New Christians at the Collège de Guyenne that may have affected both Sanchez and Montaigne. Cazac's papers indicate that many professors and students at the Collège de Guyenne were Portuguese New Christians, and that many radical and sceptical ideas were considered there.

Also, on Sanchez, see Carlos Mellizo, 'La Preoccupacion Pedagogica de Francisco Sanchez', in *Cuadernos Salmantinos de Filosofia*, II (1975), pp. 217–229.

101. Sanches, *Quod Nihil Scitur*, Carvalho ed., p. 4. An extended summary with citations from the Latin is given in Strowski, *Montaigne*, pp. 136–44.

102. Sanches, *Quod Nihil Scitur*, pp. 4–5. See also Owen, *op. cit.*, pp. 630–631. Strowski claimed that this discussion of naming is the source of Mersenne's rather odd views on the subject in *La Verité des Sciences*. Strowski, *Montaigne*, pp. 137–8, n. 1. In his *Pascal et son temps*, Vol. I (Paris 1907), pp. 212–3, n.1, Strowski said that Sanchez was the sceptic that Mersenne had in mind in his work. That this is not the case will be shown in the discussion of Mersenne in a later chapter.

103. Sanches, *Quod Nihil Scitur*, pp. 5–6.

104. *Ibid.*, pp. 6–9.

105. *Ibid.*, pp. 13–4.

106. *Ibid.*, pp. 15–7.

107. *Ibid.*, pp. 17ff.

108. *Ibid.*, pp. 23ff.

109. *Ibid.*, pp. 47–53.

110. Cf. Joseph Moreau, 'Doute et Savoir chez Francisco Sanchez', in *Portugiesische Forschungen des Görresgesellschaft*, Erste Reihe, *Aufsätze zur Portugiesischen Kulturgeschichte*, I. Band (1960), pp. 24–50.

111. it is interesting that in a letter of Sanchez to the mathematician, Clavius, dealing with the problem of finding truth in physics and mathematics, Sanchez signed the document 'Carneades philosophus'. Cf. J. Irarte, 'Francisco Sánchez el Escéptico disfrazado de Carneades en discusión epistolar con Christóbal Clavio,' *Gregorianum*, XXI (1940), pp. 413–51. The text of this letter appears in Carvalho's edition of Sanchez, pp. 146–53.

112. Carvalho, introduction to Sanches, *Opera Philosophica*, pp. LVII-LIX.

113. Senchet, *Essai sur la méthode de Francisco Sanchez*, p. 1, 3, 72–96. The latter section compares the material in Sextus with that in Sanchez and claims that Sanchez employed and developed a good deal of it.

114. Cf. Owen, *op. cit.*, pp. 640-1; the *Dictionnaire des Sciences philosophiques*, ed. Ad. Franck, 2nd ed. (Paris 1875), art. Sanchez (François), pp. 1524-5; A. Coralnik, 'Zur Geschichte der Skepsis. I. Franciscus Sanchez', *Archiv für Geschichte der Philosophie*, classify him [Sanchez] as a Pyrrhonist' Strowski, *Montaigne*, pp. 136 and 143-5; and Senchet, *op. cit.*, pp. 89-146.

115. On Sanchez's role in the development of 'constructive scepticism', see Popkin, preface to H. Van Leeuwen's *The Problem of Certainty in English Thought*, 1630-80, (The Hague 1963); review of Sanches's *Opera Philosophica*, in *Renaissance News*, X (1957), pp. 206-8; and review of Gassendi's *Dissertations en forme de paradoxe, Isis*, LIII (1962), p. 414. There is an interesting discussion of the role of the scepticism of both Pedro Valencia and Francisco Sanchez in marcelino Menendez y Pelayo, *Ensayos de Critica Filosófica* (Madrid 1918) (Vol. IX of his *Obras completas*), in the chapter entitled, "De los orígenes del Criticismo y del Escepticismo y especialmente de los precursores españoles de Kant," pp. 119-221.

116. Ulrich Wild, *Quod aliquid scitur* (Leipzig 1664); and Daniel Hartnack, *Sanchez Aliquid Sciens* (Stettin 1665). Leibniz was apparently interested in Sanchez at this time, too.

117. The possible connections between Sanchez and Montaigne are examined in Villey, *Sources & Évolution*, II, pp. 166-9, coming to a rather negative conclusion. Villey here, and Strowski, in *Montaigne*, p. 145, indicate it is quite possible that Sanchez and Montaigne were related through Montaigne's mother. (From inspecting the data in the Cazac papers I would now conclude that Sanchez and Montaigne were distant cousins, since the Sanchez and Lopez families intermarried a great deal. Both families were prominent in Spain before the establishment of the Inquisition and the expulsion of the Jews and were involved in a plot to kill a leader of the Inquisition.)

118. Städlin, *Geschichte der Skepticismus*, II, pp. 53-7.

119. Owen, op. cit., p. 640.

120. Coralnik, *op. cit.*, pp. 193 and 195.

CHAPTER III: Michel de Montaigne

1. Donald Frame, in his recent biography, *Montaigne* (New York 1965), said that the 25% Jewish blood (Montaigne's mother was half Jewish) was probably in some measure responsible for his deep tolerance, 'his rather detached attitude typical of marranos and natural in them toward the religion he consistently and very conscientiously practiced; his tireless curiosity, mainly but not solely intellectual, the cosmopolitanism natural to the member of a far-flung family' (p. 28).

2. See Michel de Montaigne, *Journal de Voyage*, edited by Louis Lautrey (2nd edition), [Paris 1909].

3. Donald M. Frame, *Montaigne's Discovery of Man. The Humanization of a Humanist*, (New York 1955), Chaps. III and IV.
The scepticism in the early essays is treated in detail by Craig B. Brush, *Montaigne and Bayle, Variations on the Theme of Skepticism* (The Hague, 1966), chap. iii.

4. Villey, *Sources et Évolution*, I, p. 218 and 365, and II, p. 164-5.

5. See Jacob Zeitlin's edition of *The Essays of Michel de Montaigne* (New York

1935), Vol. II, pp. 481–7, especially p. 485, for a discussion of this matter. At the University of Toulouse Medical School, the portraits of Sanchez and Sebond have the places of honor. Sebond taught at Toulouse, and was probably, like Sanchez, an Iberian New Christian.

6. Montaigne, 'Apologie de Raimond Sebond', in *Les Essais de Michel de Montaigne*, edited by Pierre Villey, Tome II (Paris 1922), p. 147.

7. *Ibid.*, pp. 147–8.
8. *Ibid.*, pp. 148–9.
9. *Ibid.*, p. 150.
10. *Ibid.*, p. 155.
11. *Ibid.*, pp. 159–60.
12. *Ibid.*, p. 186.
13. *Ibid.*, p. 214.
14. *Ibid.*, p. 218.
15. *Ibid.*, p. 230.
16. *Ibid.*, pp. 236–7.
17. *Ibid.*, pp. 238–9.
18. *Ibid.*, pp. 239–66.
19. *Ibid.*, pp. 266–7.
20. *Ibid.*, p. 279.
21. *Ibid.*, p. 285.
22. *Ibid.*, p. 286.
23. *Ibid.*, pp. 287–8.
24. *Ibid.*, pp. 291–2.
25. *Ibid.*, p. 302.
26. *Ibid.*, p. 314.
27. *Ibid.*, p. 316.
28. *Ibid.*, pp. 324–5.
29. *Ibid.*, p. 325.
30. *Ibid.*, pp. 326–7.
31. *Ibid.*, pp. 329–49.
32. *Ibid.*, p. 349.
33. *Ibid.*, p. 353.
34. *Ibid.*, p. 361.
35. *Ibid.*, p. 364.
36. *Ibid.*, pp. 365–66.
37. *Ibid.*, p. 366.
38. *Ibid.*, pp. 366–7.
39. *Ibid.*, p. 367.
40. *Ibid.*, pp. 367 and 371. A much more detailed examination of the Pyrrhonian elements in the *Apologie* appears in Brush, *Montaigne and Bayle*, chap. iv, pp. 62–120.

41. Busson, *Sources et Développement*, pp. 434–49.

42. Along with what is said here, one should consider the recent article by Elaine Limbruck, 'Was Montaigne Really a Pyrrhonian?', in *Bibliothèque d'Humanisme et Renaissance*, XXXIX (1977), pp. 67–80.

43. Frederick Copleston, *A History of Philosophy, Ockham to Suarez*, Vol. III (Westminster, Maryland 1953), pp. 228–30; and Alfred Weber, *History of Philosophy*, (New York 1925), p. 218.

44. See, for instance, the discussion of Montaigne in Staüdlin's *Geschichte des*

Skepticismus,. Vol. II; or the evaluation of Montaigne in J. H. S. Formey's *Histoire Abrégée de la Philosophie* (Amsterdam 1760), in his chapter on 'De la Secte des Sceptiques moderns,' pp. 243-8.

45. Camille Aymonier, 'Un Ami de Montaigne, Le Jésuite Maldonat,' *Revue Historique de Bordeaux et du Départment de la Gironde*, XXVIII (1935), p. 25. The best known exposition of this interpretation appears in the Abbé Maturin Dréano's work, *La Pensée religieuse de Montaigne* (Paris 1936). See also Clément Sclafert, 'Montaigne et Maldonat,' *Bulletin de Littérature Ecclésiastique*, LII (1951), pp. 65-93 and 129-46. A quite different interpretation of Montaigne's view about religion is presented in Cassirer, *Erkenntnisproblem*, I, pp. 189-90. Frame, in his recent paper, "What Next in Montaigne Studies?" *French Review*, XXXVI (1963), p. 583, asserts "With all the talk about Montaigne's skepticism and all the debate over his religion, we should be further along here than we are. I think the debate is over—at least for the time—and that the burden of proof rests heavily on those who, in the Sainte-Beuve-Armaingaud-Gide tradition, think that Montaigne was a perfidious unbeliever." Then Frame points to the difficulties in determining what Montaigne's religious beliefs were.

After I had written this, the late Don Cameron Allen reasserted the irreligious interpretation of Montaigne in his *Doubt's Boundless Sea* (Baltimore 1964), where chapter III is entitled 'Three French Atheists: Montaigne, Charron, Bodin'.

46. Cf. David Hume, *Dialogues Concerning Natural Religion*, edited by Norman Kemp Smith, (2nd edition) (London & Edinburgh 1947), p. 228; Voltaire, *Dictionnaire Philosophique*, edited by Julien Benda and Raymond Naves (Paris 1954), art. 'Foi,' pp. 202-3; Blaise Pascal, *Pensées*, Brunschvicg ed., with intro. and notes by Ch.-Marc Des Granges, (Paris 1951). number 434, pp. 183-6; and Søren Kierkegaard, *Philosophical Fragments or A Fragment of Philosophy*, translated by David F. Swenson (Princeton 1946), esp. Chap. III and IV and 'Interlude.' See also, R. H. Popkin, 'Hume and Kierkegaard,' in *Journal of Religion*, XXXI (1951), pp. 274-81; and 'Theological and Religious Scepticism,' in *Christian Scholar*, XXXIX (1956), pp. 150-8.

47. Cf. Chap. IV and VI.

48. Recent researches lead me to believe that it will not be possible to assess the actual religious beliefs of either Montaigne or Sanchez until much more is known about the religious views and practices of the refugee New Christian families of Bordeaux and Toulouse. Were these families crypto-Jews, genuine Christians, nominal Christians, or what? Since Montaigne and Sanchez grew up and lived among the Spanish and Portuguese New Christians in southern France, their 'real' beliefs were probably related to those of the people around them. Some of the data I have come across suggests that crypto-Judaism was widespread in Southern France in the sixteenth century, *especially* in Bordeaux, and that almost all New Christian families were suspected of secretely Judaizing.

49. For a detailed study of Montaigne's impact, see Alan M. Boase, *The Fortunes of Montaigne: A History of the Essays in France*, 1580-1669 (London 1935); and for the period immediately following the publication of the *Essais*, Pierre Villey's *Montaigne devant la postérité* (Paris 1935).

50. He first met Montaigne, apparently in 1586.

51. For information about Charron, see Jean-Baptiste Sabrié, *De l'Humanisme au rationalisme: Pierre Charron* (1541-1603), *l'homme, l'oeuvre, l'influence* (Paris 1913). The copy of Ochino is in the Bibliothèque Nationale, Rés. D2, 5240.

Prof. Jean D. Charron has recently challenged the claim that Pierre Charron's views were all taken from Montaigne, and has insisted on the originality of Charron's thought. See his 'Did Charron Plagiarize Montaigne?; in *French Review*, XXXIV (1961), pp. 344–51. On this contention, see the answer by Prof. Floyd Gray, 'Reflexions on Charron's Debt to Montaigne', in *French Review*, XXXV (1962), pp. 377–82. On the basis of the evidence presented, I would still hold the view that Charron's scepticism is basically derived from Montaigne and that it is just presented in more organized form, a view that Prof. Gray seems to share.

52. Alfred Soman, 'Pierre Charron: A Revaluation', in *Bibliothèque d'Humanisme et Renaissance*, XXXII (1970), pp. 57–79.

53. See, for instance, the large number of editions listed in the Bibliothèque Nationale's printed catalogue. This list is by no means exhaustive.

54. Pierre Charron, *Les Trois Veritez* (Paris 1595), p. 17.

55. *Ibid.*, pp. 19–20.

56. Charron, *Les Trois Veritez*, Derniere edition (Paris 1635), p. 15, in *Toutes les Oeuvres de Pierre Charron* (Paris 1635).

57. *Ibid.*, p. 18.

58. Charron, *Trois Veritez* (Paris 1595 ed), p. 26.

59. Sextus Empiricus is numbered among the atheists, listed as 'Sextus Empyricus, grand professeur du Pyrrhonisme.' *ibid.*, p. 67 (p. 67 is misnumbered 76).

60. *Ibid.*, pp. 67–70.

61. *Ibid.*, Livre Troisieme, esp. pp. 215–49, 280, and 306.

62. *Ibid.*, pp. 552–8.

63. *Ibid.*, pp. 554–8.

64. Pierre Charron, *La Sagesse*, in *Toutes les Oeuvres de Pierre Charron* (Paris 1635), p. 1. (Each work in this volume has separate pagination.)

65. *Ibid.*, Book I, Chap. X, pp. 35–9.

66. *Ibid.*, Book I, Chaps. xiii–xl. The quotation is on p. 144.

67. *Ibid.*, Book II, Chaps. i–ii, pp. 10–32. See also Sabrié, *Humanisme au rationalisme*, chap. xii, esp. pp. 303–319; and R. H. Popkin, 'Charron and Descartes: The Fruits of Systematic Doubt,' in *Journal of Philosophy*, LI (1954), p. 832.

68. Charron, *La Sagesse*, Book II, chap. ii, p. 21.

69. *Ibid.*, Book II, chap. ii, p. 22.

70. *Ibid.*, loc. cit.

71. *Ibid.*, loc. cit.; and Charron, *Traicté de Sagesse* (Paris 1635), p. 225. (This work is also known as *Petit Traicté de Sagesse*.)

72. Charron, *Petit Traicté*, p. 226.

73. Cf. Popkin, 'Charron and Descartes', pp. 832–5.

74. Maryanne Cline Horowitz, 'Pierre Charron's View of the Source of Wisdom', in *Journal of the History of Philosophy*, IX (1971), pp. 443–457.

75. Julien-Eymard d'Angers, 'Le stoicisme en France dans la première moitié du siècle; les origines 1575–1616', in *Etudes franciscaines*, nouv. sér. II (Dec. 1951), pp. 389–410.

76. Alfred Soman, 'Methodology in the History of Ideas: The Case of Pierre Charron', in *Journal of the History of Philosophy*, XII (1974), pp. 495–501; reply by Maryanne Cline Horowitz, 'Complementary Methodologies in the History of Ideas', in same issue, pp. 501–09. See also L. Auvray, 'Lettres de Pierre Charron à

Gabriel Michel de la Rochemaillet', in *Revue d'Histoire Littéraire de la France*, I (1894), pp. 308-329.

77. The Cardinal du Perron, Bishop Claude Dormy, and Saint-Cyran, the Jansenist leader, approved of Charron's theology (though sometimes with reservations). This will be discussed in the next chapter.

78. It was so considered by Father François Garasse, S. J., who will be discussed in Chapter VI. Some of the criticisms of Charron are treated in Henri Bremond's 'La Folle "Sagesse" de Pierre Charron', in *Le Correspondant*, CCLII (1913), pp. 357-64.

79. On the problem of evaluating Charron, see my article on him in the latest edition of the *Encyclopedia Brittanica*. Jean Charron has argued for the sincerity and orthodoxy of Pierre Charron's views in his *the 'Wisdom' of Pierre Charron, An original and orthodox Code of Morality, University of North Carolina Studies in the Romance Languages and Literatures*, No. 34 (Chapel Hill 1961). And I have discussed this in some detail in my review of Eugene F. Rice, Jr's *The Renaissance Idea of Wisdom*, in *Renaissance News*, XII (1959), pp. 265-9.

80. Cf. Chap. IV, and the discussion of *l'affaire Garasse* in Chap. VI.

81. On Camus, cf. Boase, *The Fortunes of Montaigne*, pp. 114-34. (The defense of Montaigne against the charge of atheism is treated on p. 120); Villey, *Montaigne devant la postérité*, pp. 185-234; and Julien-Eymard d'Angers, *Du Stoïcisme chrétien à l'humanisme chrétien: Les 'Diversites' de J. P. Camus* (1609-1618) (n.p. 1952). Bayle's article on Camus has some amusing anecdotal material.

82. Jean-Pierre Camus, 'Essay Sceptique', in *Les Diversitez de Messire Jean-Pierre Camus, Evesque & Seigneur de Bellay, Prince de l'Empire*, Tome IV (Paris 1610), Livre XV, chap. iii, p. 187v.

83. Villey, *Montaigne devant la postérité*, p. 202.

84. Camus, 'Essay Sceptique', pp. 368r and 189r.

85. *Ibid.*, pp. 190r-335v. Copernicus is mentioned on pp. 268r and 319v.

86. *Ibid.*, pp. 336r-60r.

87. *Ibid.*, pp. 360r-70v. The comment on Sextus is on p. 368r.

88. Cf. Chapter II, p. 18, n. 3.

89. Camus, 'Essay Sceptique', p. 254r. See also pp. 224r-226r, 244v and 278r.

90. *Ibid.*, pp. 274v, 278r and 335v. See also Boase, *The Fortunes of Montaigne*, pp. 126-7.

91. Cf. Bayle, *Dictionnaire*, art. 'Camus'. In Stäudlin's *Geschichte des Skepticismus*, although Charron is treated at length, Camus is not discussed at all in the chapter on 'Von Montaigne bis la Mothe le Vayer'.

CHAPTER IV: Influence of New Pyrrhonism

1. Charles B. Schmitt, 'Philosophy and Science in Sixteenth-Century Universities: Some Preliminary Comments', in *The Cultural Context of Medieval Learning* edited by J. E. Murdoch and E. D. Sylla, (Dordrecht 1975), p. 501.

2. Joseph Mede, *The Works of Joseph Mede*, B.D. (London 1672), *The Author's Life*, p. II. .

3. Mede, *Works, Clavis & Commentationes Apocalypticae*, p. III.

4. John Aubrey, *'Brief Lives', chiefly of Contemporaries, set down by John

Aubrey, between the Years 1669 & 1696, edited by Andrew Clark (Oxford 1898), Vol. I, p. 173.

5. William Chillingworth, *Additional Discourses of Mr. Chillingworth, never before Printed* (London 1704).

6. Cf. Henri Busson, *La Pensée religieuse française de Charron à Pascal*, (Paris 1933); esp. Chaps. IV and V; Henri Gouhier, 'La Crise de la Théologie au temps de Descartes', in *Revue de Théologie et de Philosophie*, 3ᵉ Ser., IV (1954), pp. 19–54; and review of Gouhier's article by Julien-Eymard Chesneau in *Dix Septième Siècle*, No. 28, Juliet 1955, pp. 295–7.

7. This theme is also discussed in R. H. Popkin, 'Skepticism and the Counter-Reformation in France', in *Archiv für Reformationsgeschichte*, LI (1960), pp. 58–87, and in the French abridgement, 'Scepticisme et Contre-Réforme en France', *Recherches et Débats du centre catholique des intellectuals français*, cahier No. 40 (Oct. 1962), p. 151–84.

8. Gentian Hervet, preface to his edition of Sextus Empiricus, *Adversus Mathematicos*, pp. a2r–a2v.

9. Avmonier, 'Un Ami de Montaigne. Le Jésuite Maldonat', in *Rev. Hist. de Bordeaux*, XXVIII, (1935), pp. 5–25; and Sclafert, 'Montaigne et Maldonat', *Bull Litt. Ecclés*. LII, (1951) pp. 65–93, and 129–46; on Maldonat and Hervetus, see Joannis Maldonati, *Opera varia Theologica* (Lutetiae 1677), pp. 2–7 and 10–15 where two letters of Maldonat to Hervetus are given. Maldonat seems to have been troubled by some of the odd religious views of his friend, Hervetus. On Maldonat's career, see J. M. Prat, *Maldonat et l'Université de Paris* (Paris 1856). This work includes the interesting text of Maldonat's inaugural address at Paris, pp. 555–67, containing some suggestions of fideism.

10. St. François de Sales, *Les Controverses* in *Oeuvres*, Tome I (Annecy 1892), p. 73.

11. *Ibid.*, p. 335.

12. On Veron's career, see l'Abbé P. Feret, *La Faculté de Théologie de Paris et ses docteurs les plus célébres, Epoque moderne*, Tome IV, XVII Siècle, Revue littéraire (Paris 1906), chap. iii, 'François Veron', pp. 53–92; and art. 'Véron, François', in *Catholic Encyclopedia*, XV (New York 1912), pp. 359–60. Bayle, according to Haag et Haag, *La France protestante*, II, p. 319, called Veron, 'the licensed controversialist working the entire kingdom'.

13. François Veron, *Methodes de Traiter des Controverses de Religion* (Paris 1638), Part 1, p. 170. (This work is referred to as *Oeuvres*, since it is really a collection of works, and to avoid confusion with other titles by Veron. Also all references to this work are to Part I. St. Louis University has been kind enough to allow me to use their copy of this rare work.)

14. Veron, *La Victorieuse Methode pour combattre tous les Ministres: Par la seule Bible* (Paris 1621), pp. 45–6.

15. St. François de Sales, *Controverses*, p. 169. See also Charron, *Trois Veritez*, 1595 ed., livre III, Chap. II, pp. 216–21.

16. John Sergeant, *Sure-Footing in Christianity, or Rational Discourses on the Rule of Faith* (London 1665), p. 68.

17. Veron, *Oeuvres*, pp. 192–9. Actually these claims recur throughout Veron's text over and over again. The same sort of attack on Calvinism was made by Bishop Jean-Pierre Camus, the Montaignian, in his *La Demolition des fondemens de la doctrine protestante* (Paris 1639), p. 2. In his *L'Avoisinement des protestans vers l'Eglise Romaine* (Paris 1640), he suggested that if the Reformers

really believed their rule of faith, they would not write commentaries on Scripture, but would just go around quoting the Bible.

When Father Gontery was corresponding with the father of the sceptic, Bishop Pierre-Daniel Huet, in order to convert him to Catholicism, he pointed out that Scripture 'does not speak at all of rules of logic' so that the Reformers have no way of proving the articles of their faith from Scripture alone. Cf. Bibliothèque Nationale Ms. Fonds français 11909, No. 41.

18. Jean Daillé, *La Foy Fondée sur les Saintes Escritures: Contre les nouveaux Methodistes*, (2nd edition) (Charenton 1661), pp. 55–65; and Paul Ferry, *La Dernier désespoir de la tradition contre l'Escriture, ou est amplement refuté le livre du P. François Veron Iesiute, par lequel il pretend ensiegner à toute personne, quoy que non versee en Theologie, un bref & facile moyen de reietter la Parole de Dieu, & convaincre les Eglises reformees d'erreur & d'abus en tous & un chacun poinct de leur doctrine* (Sedan 1618), pp. 119–20 and 185.

19. Veron, *Oeuvres*, p. 169–70.

20. *Ibid.*, p. 169.

21. Pierre Du Moulin, *Elements de la Logique Françoise* (Geneve 1625), pp. 3–4.

22. Veron, *Victorieuse Methode*, p. 67.

23. Veron, *Oeuvres*, p. 177.

24. David Hume, *A Treatise of Human Nature*, edited by Selby-Bigge (Oxford 1949), Book I, Part IV, sec. 1, p. 180–3. An interesting version of this problem, which may be Hume's source, appears in Pierre Jurieu's, *Le Vray Systeme de l'Eglise & la veritable Analyse de la Foy* (Dordrecht 1686), pp. 277–80.

25. Veron, *Oeuvres*. The 8 moyens are stated in detail in the first part, each argued for, and then all objections to each answered in turn. A fascinating example of the application of Veron's method and the frustration it produced in the Calvinist opponent appears in the *Actes de la Conference tenue a Caen entre Samuel Bochart & Iean Baillehache, Ministre de la Parole de Dieu en l'Eglise Reformée et François Veron Predicateur des Controverses*, 2 tomes (Saumur 1630). (The copy at the Bibliothèque Nationale, D. 22117, belonged to the later French Catholic sceptic, Pierre-Daniel Huet, who had been a student of Bochart's.) Over and over again, the Protestants try to prove their case by appealing to Scripture, and Veron keeps pointing out that the Protestant claims are not identical with the words in Scripture, but are inferences from Scripture, that Scripture doesn't authorize these inferences, that reason can err in its inferences, etc. After trying and trying to prove their case, the Protestants finally say in despair. 'And as to the point that Mr. Veron raised that our reason is faulty, and can make mistakes in its conclusions: it was replied that if we ought to doubt of all of the conclusions which are drawn from Scripture, on the grounds that reason is faulty, we would also have to put in doubt all that we read in it in precise terms, in that it is also possible that our eyes deceive us, and that the same is the case with our ears, and thus the faith could not be from hearing of the Word of God; contrary to what the Apostle says in express terms, that "the faith is from hearing, and hearing the Word of God." In short, it would be necessary for us to doubt everything, and even that we are alive.

'That it is indeed reason which draws conclusions from the Word of God, but reason clarified by the light of faith, to which the conclusions are as much *spiritual and powerful demonstrations* as the Apostle describes them in *I Corinthians*, chap. 2, verse 4. It is the case that all of the articles of our faith that are directly necessary for salvation are proven by conclusions that are so clear, that there is no man of calm sense who is not obliged to accept this evidence, if passion has not already carried him away.' Tome I, pp. 404–5.

26. Veron, *Oeuvres*, p. 143.

27. *Ibid.*, p. 169.

28. Daillé, *La Foy Fondée sur les Saintes Escritures*, pp. 57–9.

29. *Ibid.*, p. 59.

30. *Ibid.*, p. 60.

31. *Ibid.*, pp. 63–5.

32. Daillé *Traité de l'Employ des Saincts Peres, pour le Iugement des differends, qui sont auiourd'huy en la Religion* (Geneve 1632), Chap. 1–2. Similar points were raised by the great Bible scholar, Father Richard Simon, in his *A Critical History of the Old Testament*, translated by Dodwell (London 1682), with regard to Biblical texts.

33. Daillé, *Employ des Saincts Peres*, pp. 62–3.

34. Veron, *Du Vray Juge et Jugement des Differents qui sont auiourd'huy en la Religion; où est respondu au sieur Daillé Ministre de Charenton, nouveau Pyrrhonien, & indifferent en Religion, contraire à ses Collegues & à son party.* (Paris n.d.).

35. Veron, *Oeuvres*, p. 178.

36. *Ibid.*, p. 177.

37. *Ibid.*, p. 178.

38. *Ibid.*, p. 177.

39. *Ibid.*, p. 170, 177 and 196–7, and 227.

40. Veron, *Du Vray Juge et Jugement*, p. 13.

41. *Ibid.*, p. 3.

42. Ferry, *Dernier Desespoir de la Tradition*, pp. 64–8.

43. *Ibid.*, pp. 146–8.

44. Veron, *Oeuvres*, p. 170.

45. Bayle, *Dictionaire*, art. 'Socin, Fauste,' closing comments.

46. Veron, *Oeuvres*, p. 197.

47. Veron, *La Victorieuse methode*, p. 58.

48. Cf. Gottfried Wilhelm Leibniz, *Essais de Theodicée sur la bonté de Dieu, la liberté de l'homme et l'Origine du Mal* (Amsterdam 1710), p. 74, par. 62.

49. Robert Ferguson, *The Interest of Reason in Religion, with the Import & Use of Scripture-Metaphors; and the Nature of the Union betwixt Christ & Believers* (London 1675), p. 190. See also Joseph Glanvill, ΛΟΓΟΥ ΘΡΗΣΚΕΙΑ: or, *A Seasonable Recommendation and Defence of Reason, In the Affairs of Religion; against Infidelity, Scepticism, and Fanaticisms of all sorts* (London 1670), pp. 32–3.

50. Bredvold, *Intellectual Milieu of Dryden*, p. 76 and seq.

51. John Maldonatus, *A Commentary on the Holy Gospels*, trans. by G. J. Davie (London 1888), esp. Vol. I, pp. xix-xx, and Vol. II, pp. 109–10.

52. Hervet, preface to Sextus Empiricus, *Adversus Mathematicos*.

53. Maldonatus, *A Commentary on the Holy Gospels*, Vol. II, pp. 420–1. In his inaugural address in Paris, Maldonat stressed the need for faith in order to gain understanding in theology, and the lack of importance of philosophers like Plato and Aristotle compared to Scripture and the Church in settling theological questions. Cf. Prat, *Maldonat et l'Université de Paris*, pp. 179, 185, 558–60 and 566.

54. In the life of Du Perron, prefixed to *Les diverses Oeuvres de l'illustrissime Cardinal Du Perron* (Paris 1622), it is reported that the Pope said on one occasion *'Let us pray to God that He inspire the Cardinal du Perron: for he will convince us of what he wishes.'* p. 22.

55. Jean Duvergier du Hauranne (Saint-Cyran), mentions Du Perron's admiration of Charron in *La Somme des Fautes et Faussetez Capitales contenues en la Somme Theologique du Pere François Garasse de la Compagnie de Jesus* (Paris 1626), Tome II, p. 324. On Du Perron's relations with Mlle. de Gournay, see Mario Schiff, *La Fille d'Alliance de Montaigne. Marie de Gournay* (Paris 1910), p. 37.

56. Pierre de l'Estoile, *Mémoires-Journaux*, 12 vols., Tome Deuxième, *Journal de Henri III*, 1581-1586 (Paris 1888), entry for Nov. 1583, p. 140-1.

57. St. François de Sales, letter to M. Celse-Bénigne de Chantal, 8 Décembre 1610, in *Oeuvres*, Tome XIV (Lettres, Tome IV) (Annecy 1906) p. 377. Boase, *Fortunes of Montaigne*, p. 61; and Schiff, *La Fille d'Alliance de Montaigne*, pp. 29-30.

58. St. François de Sales, *Controverses*, p. 328, and 'Notes préparatoires,' p. 17.

59. Montaigne, *Journal de Voyage*, pp. 250-2 and 274.

60. For example, Gabriel Naudé and François de La Mothe Le Vayer were protegés of Richelieu and Mazarin.

61. Cf. L. Auvray, 'Lettres de Pierre Charron à Gabriel Michel de la Rochemaillet', in *Revue d'Histoire Littéraire de la France*, I (1894), esp. pp. 323-7.

62. Cf. Boase, *Fortunes of Montaigne*, p. 186.

63. Cf. Joseph Dedieu, 'Survivances et Influences de l'Apologétique traditionelle dans les Pensées', in *Revue d'Histoire Littéraire de la France*, XXXVII (1930), p. 498-9. n.3.

64. By François Garasse, S. J. in his *La Doctrine curieuse des beaux esprits de ce temps, ou pretendus tels* (Paris 1623), and later works.

65. Cf. François Ogier, *Jugement et Censure du Livre de la Doctrine curieuse de François Garasse* (Paris 1623).

66. Saint-Cyran, *la Somme des Fautes et Faussetez*, Tome II, pp. 321-469. This matter will be discussed in detail later on in chap. 6.

67. Julien-Eymard d'Angers, 'Sénèque et le Stoïcisme dans l'oeuvre du cordelier J. du Bosc,' in *Dix-Septième Siècle*, No. 29, 1955, pp. 376.

68. Quoted in Boase, *Fortunes of Montaigne*, p. 61.

69. Cf. Jean Bodin, *De la Demonomanie des Sorciers* (Paris 1581), Preface, the 10th, 11th and 12th unnumbered pages.

70. John Chamber, *A Treatise against Judiciall Astrologie* (London 1601), pp. 16 and 23-4. Lynn Thorndike, in his *A History of Magic and Experimental Science*, Vol. VI (New York 1941), p. 205-6, says that Tommaso Giannini in a work published in 1618, also used materials from Sextus against the astrologers.

71. Sir Christopher Heydon, *A Defence of Judiciall Astrologie, In Answer to a Treatise lately Published by M. John Chamber. Wherein all those places of Scripture, Councells, Fathers, Schoolemen, later Divines, Philosophers, Historics, Lawes, Constitutions, and Reasons drawne out of Sixtus Empiricus, Picus, Pererius, Sixtus ab Heminga, and others, against this Arte, are particularly Examined: and the Lawfulnes thereof, by Equivalent Proofes Warranted* (Cambridge, 1603).

72. *Ibid.*, p. 127 and 135.

73. *Ibid.*, p. 134.

74. Pierre Le Loyer, *Discours, et Histoires des Spectres, Visions, et Apparitions des Esprits, Anges, Demons, et Ames, se monstrans visible aux hommes* (Paris 1605), Book I, chap. vi, pp. 35–46, '*Les Septiques & aporrhetiques Philosophes douteux, & ceux de la seconde academie refutez, qui disoient que les sens humains estoient faux & nostre imaginative fausse.*'

75. *Ibid.*, p. 39.

76. *Ibid.*, pp. 40–6.

77. Marin Mersenne, *La Verité des Sciences, contre les septiques ou Pyrrhoniens* (Paris 1625). The views in this work will be discussed in Chapter 7.

78. Petrus Gassendi, *Examen Philosophiae Roberti Fluddi Medici*, in *Opera*, Vol. III (the work was first printed in 1630), Gassendi's views will be discussed in chapters 5 and 7.

79. Mersenne, *La Verité des Sciences*, Book I, chap. xvi.

80. Gassendi, *Exercitationes paradoxicae adversus Aristoteleos*, first published in Grenoble, in 1624; and also in *Opera*, Vol. III.

81. See, for example, Joseph Glanvill, *A Blow at Modern Sadducism in some Philosophical Considerations about Witchcraft* (London 1668).

82. Cf. Pierre Pic, *Guy Patin* (Paris 1922), p. xixff.

83. Cf. François de La Mothe Le Vayer's essay, 'Discours pour montrer que les doutes de la Philosophie Sceptique sont de grand usage dans les sciences,' in *Oeuvres* (Paris 1669), XV, pp. 61–124.

84. Samuel Sorbière, *Discours sceptique sur le passage du chyle, & le mouvement du coeur* (Leyden 1648), pp. 153–4.

85. Wilhelm Langius, *De Veritatibus Geometricis, Libri II, prior, contra Scepticos & Sextum Empiricum &c. Posterior, contra Marcum Meibornium* (Copenhagen 1656). See also, Jean-Etienne Montucla, *Histoire des Mathematiques*, Vol. I, (Paris 1758), pp. 23–8. There is also an interesting letter of Lang's to Ismael Boulliard, unpublished, on Sextus and mathematics, dated 9 July 1657, The Hague, Bibliothèque Nationale, Ms. Franqis 13037, fol. 131.

86. Mersenne, *La Verité des Sciences*, Livres II-IV.

CHAPTER V: Libertins Érudits

1. Cf. Jacques Denis, *Sceptiques ou Libertins de la première moitié du XVIIe siècle: Gassendi, Gabriel Naudé, Gui-Patin, La Mothe-Le Vayer, Cyrano de Bergerac* (Caen 1884), pp. 5–16, and 52–4; François-Tommy Perrens, *Les Libertins en France au XVIIe siècle* (Paris 1899), pp. 1–27 and passim.; J.-Roger Charbonnel, *La Pensée italienne au XVIe siècle et le courant libertin* (Paris 1919), pp. 49–71; and René Pintard, *Le Libertinage érudit dans la première motié du XVIIe* (Paris 1943), Tome I, 2e Partie, chap. 1, and 3e Partie.

2. Perrens, *Les Libertins*, Chap. II; Charbonnel, *La Pensée italienne*, esp. pp. 49–71; Busson, *La Pensée religieuse française*, chaps. III and IV; Fortunat Strowski, *Pascal et son temps*, 1ere Partie, *De Montaigne à Pascal* (Paris 1938), chap. III; Pintard, *Le Libertinage érudit*, esp. Tome I, 2e Partie, chap. 1, and 3e Partie; and Julien-Eymard d'Angers, *L'Apologétique en France de 1580 à 1670; Pascal et ses précurseurs* (Paris 1954), chap. 1, 'Le courant libertin'.

3. Gui Patin, *lettres de Gui Patin*, edited by Paul Triaire, Tome I (Paris 1907), pp. 616–7.

4. On Théophile de Viau and Des Barreaux, see Antoine Adam, *Théophile de Viau et la libre pensée francaise en* 1620 (Paris 1935); and Frédéric Lachèvre, *Jacques Vallée Des Barreaux, Sa Vie et ses poésies* (1599-1673) (Paris 1907), and *Le Procès du poètie Théophile de Viau*, 2 vols. (Paris 1909).

5. Pintard, *Le Liberitnage érudit*, p. 177.

6. Gabriel Naudé, *Advis pour dresser une bibliotheque* (Paris 1627), pp. 49 and 75. (This work has recently appeared in English, *Advice on Establishing a Library*, intro. by Archer Taylor, [Berkeley and Los Angeles 1950]. The passages in question appear on pp. 23 and 36).

7. Charles A. Sainte-Beuve, 'Ecrivains critiques et Moralistes de la France, XI. Gabriel Naudé', in *Revue des Deux Mondes*, IV, 13ᵉ Anné N.S., 1843, pp. 755-6.

8. This is the title of the section on Naudé in Pintard, *Libertinage érudit*, 2ᵉ Partie, chap. 1, sec. v, p. 156.

9. Naudé, *Apologie pour les grands Hommes soupçonnez de Magie* (Amsterdam 1712), p. 4. This is hardly, as Rice claimed, exactly the same as Descartes' method of doubt. Cf. James V. Rice, *Gabriel Naudé* 1600-1653, in *Johns Hopkins Studies in Romance Literatures and Languages*, XXXV (Baltimore 1939), p. 63.

10. Naudé, *Advis*, p. 165 (English ed. p. 80).

11. *Naudaeana et Patiniana, ou Singularitez Remarquables, prises des Conversations de Mess. Naudé & Patin*, 2ᵉ ed. (Amsterdam 1703), p. 4. (The Bibliothèque nationale catalogue lists Pierre Bayle as the probable editor.)

12. *Patiniana*, p. 115.

13. According to Patin, one of his best friends was the fideist, Jean-Pierre Camus, Bishop of Bellay, Cf. Gui Patin, *Correspondance de Gui Patin*, edited by Armand Brette (Paris 1901), p. 102.

14. On La Mothe Le Vayer's career, see the introduction by Ernest Tisserand, to La Mothe Le Vayer's *Deux Dialogues faits à l'imitation des anciens* (Paris 1922); Boase, *The Fortunes of Montaigne*, chap. XVIII; and Pintard, *Libertinage érudit*, 2ᵉ Partie, chap. I, sec. iii, and 3ᵉ Partie, chap. III.

15. See, for example, the comments on La Mothe Le Vayer in 'Lettres de Jean-Louis Guez de Balzac', pub. by Philippe Tamizey de Larroque, in *Collection de Documents inédits sur l'histoire de France, publiées par les soins du Ministre de l'Instruction Publique. Mélanges Historiques*, Tome I (Paris 1873), pp. 393-820; the attack on La Mothe Le Vayer's work, *La Vertu des Payens*, in Antoine Arnauld's *De la necessité de la Foy en Jesus-Christ pour être sauvé* (Paris 1701), Tome II, esp. pp. 181-221; and Descartes' comments on a 'wicked book', in his letters to Mersenne of 15 Avril 1630 and 6 Mai 1630, in *Oeuvres de Descartes*, pub. by Charles Adam & Paul Tannery, Tome I (Paris 1897), pp. 144-5 and 148-9. Pintard has offered strong evidence that the book in question is La Mothe Le Vayer's *Dialogues*, in his 'Descartes et Gassendi', *Travaux du IXᵉ Congrès Internationale de Philosophie (Congrès Descartes)* II, part. ii, 1937 (*Actualitiés Scientifiques et Industrielles* no. 531), pp. 120-2.

16. Cf. Pintard, *La Mothe Le Vayer, Gassendi Guy Patin* (Paris n.d.) (*Publications de l'Université de Poitiers, Série des Sciences de l'Homme*, No. 5), pp. 5-13.

17. An example of this, is the closing statement in his 'Dialogue de la diversité des religions' where it is said, 'Therefore I have not been impertinent nor impious in maintaining that St. Paul taught us to believe and not to know, and that in terms of the truly aporetic views that Holy Scripture is full of, it has given us as explicit lessons on the vanity, even nullity, of all human sciences, as have ever come from our sceptical school. . . . Let us then boldly profess the honorable ignorance of our well-loved Scepticism, since it is this alone that can prepare the

way for us to revealed knowledge of the Divinity, and since all the other philosophical sects only take us further from it, tying us up in their dogmas, and mudd-
ling our minds with their scientific maxims, instead of enlightening us and purify-
ing the understanding,' *Cincq Dialogues faits à l'imitation des Anciens, par
Oratius Tubero* (Mons 1671), pp. 329–30.

18. This work appears in Volume IX of Francois de La Mothe Le Vayer,
Oeuvres de François de La Mothe Le Vayer, Conseiller d'Estat Ordinaire (Paris
1669), pp. 259–95. The quotation is on p. 287.

19. La Mothe Le Vayer, *Oeuvres*, Volume XV, p. 88.

20. *Ibid.*, pp. 91–5.

21. *Ibid.*, p. 103. The discussion of physics is on pp. 96–114.

22. *Ibid.*, pp. 115–20.

23. *Ibid.*, p. 124.

24. La Mothe Le Vayer, *Petit Traitté Sceptique sur cette facon de parler,* in
Oeuvres, Vol. IX, p. 280.

25. *Ibid.*, p. 228.

26. *Ibid.*, p. 290.

27. La Mothe Le Vayer, *Prose Chagrine*, in *Oeuvres*, Vol. IX, pp. 359–60.

28. *Ibid.*, pp. 361–2.

29. *Ibid.*, p. 361.

30. *Ibid.*, pp. 366–7.

31. La Mothe Le Vayer, *De la Vertu des Payens*, in *Oeuvres*, Vol. V, pp.
226–7.

32. See, for example, Busson, *La Pensée religieuse française*, pp. 210–4; Jean
Grenier, 'Le sceptique masqué: La Mothe Le Vayer,' *Table Ronde*, XXII (1949),
pp. 1511–2; Julien-Eymard d'Angers, 'Stoïcisme et "liberitnage" dans l'oeuvre de
François La Mothe Le Vayer', in *Revue des Sciences Humaines*, Fasc. 75
(Jul.-Sept. 1954), esp. pp. 281–3; and Pintard, *Le Libertinage érudit*, pp. 140–7
and 509–15.

33. Busson, *La Pensée religieuse française*, pp. 212–4; Grenier, 'Le sceptique
masqué', pp. 1505 and 1511; Julien-Eymard d'Angers, 'Sénèque et le Stoïcisme
dans l'oeuvre' du cordelier J. du Bosc', in *Dix-Septième Siècle*, no. 29 (Oct. 1955),
pp. 376–7; Popkin, 'Theological and Religious Scepticism', in *Christian Scholar*,
XXXIX (1956), pp. 151–2 and 155–6, and 'Kierkegaard and Scepticism', in
Algemeen Nederlands Tijdschrift voor Wijsbegeerte en Psychologie, I (1959), pp.
126–8.

34. Cf. the citation to works of Balzac and Arnauld given in note 2, p. 92, and
Grenier, 'Le sceptique masqué'; Julien-Eymard d'Angers, Stoïcisme et
'libertinage' dans l'oeuvre de François La Mothe Le Vayer'; and Pintard, *Libertinage érudit*, 2ᵉ Partie, chap. 1, sec. iii, 'Un voluptueux incrédule: La Mothe Le
Vayer'.

35. Cf. Popkin, 'Theological and Religious Scepticism', esp. pp. 155–7.

36. Julien-Eymard d'Angers, 'Stoïcisme et 'libertinage' dans l'oeuvre de
François La Mothe Le Vayer', pp. 259–84.

37. Grenier, 'Le sceptique masqué', esp. pp. 1509–12.

38. Pintard, *Le Libertinage érudit*, pp. 131–47 and passim.

39. Tisserand, in his introduction to La Mothe Le Vayer, *Deux Dialogues*, pp.
56–8.

40. L. M. Kahle's introduction to La Mothe Le Vayer's *Cinq Dialogues faits à
l'imitation des anciens, par Oratius Tubero. Nouvelle edition augmentée d'une*

refutation de la Philosphie Sceptique ou preservatif contre le Pyrrhonisme (Berlin 1744), pp. 9–10.

41. For information on Marandé, see Boase, *Fortunes of Montaigne*, chap. XV.

42. Abbé Léonard de Marandé, *Jugement des actions humaines* (Paris 1624), pp. 39 and 52–53.

43. *Ibid.*, p. 52.

44. *Ibid.*, pp. 53–59. The quotation is on p. 59.

45. *Ibid.*, pp. 59–60.

46. *Ibid.*, p. 60.

47. *Ibid.*, pp. 60–64.

48. *Ibid.*, p. 71. This case also worried Hume. Cf. *Enquiry Concerning Human Understanding*, Selby-Bigge ed. (Oxford 1955), Sec. XII, part ii, pp. 156–7.

49. Marandé, *op. cit.*, pp. 71–5.

50. *Ibid.*, pp. 76–87. The same year as Marandé's work appeared, Herbert of Cherbury's book came out, advocating a common consent criterion.

51. Marandé, *op. cit.*, p. 106.

52. The problem of the true name of the philosopher is discussed by Bernard Rochot in some introductory comments to his paper on 'La Vie, le caractère et la formation intellectuelle', in the Centre International de Synthèse volume, *Pierre Gassendi, 1592-1655, sa vie et son oeuvre* (Paris 1955), pp. 11–12.

53. For information about Gassendi's life, see Rochot, 'La Vie, le caractère'; and Pintard, *Le Libertinage érudit*, pp. 147–56.

54. Professor Rochot had undertaken this task. Since his unfortunate demise, this project has been halted. An English translation of a representative sample of Gassendi's work has been published by Craig Brush, *The Selected Works of Pierre Gassendi* (New York 1972).

55. Bayle's *Dictionaire*, art. 'Pyrrhon', Rem. B.

56. Cf. Gassendi's letter to Henricus Fabri Pybracii, April 1621, in Petrus Gassendi, *Opera Omnia* (Lyon 1658), Vol. VI, pp. 1–2.

57. This matter is discussed in Rochot's *Les Travaux de Gassendi sur Épicure et sur l'Atomisme*, 1619-1658 (Paris 1944), chap. 1, and in his article 'La Vie, le caractère', pp. 18–20; and in Gaston Sortais' *La Philosophie moderne depuis Bacon jusqu' à Leibniz* (Paris 1922), Tome II, pp. 32–36.

58. Gassendi, *Exercitationes Paradoxicae Adversus Aristoteleos*, in *Opera*, Vol. III, Praefatio, p. 99.

59. Cf. Gassendi's letter to Henricus Fabri Pybracii, April 1621, in *Opera*, Vol. VI, p. 1; the Praefatio to *Exercitationes Paradoxicae*, in *Opera*, Vol. III, pp. 98–104; and Gassendi's letter of 15 Juin 1629, in *Lettres de Peiresc*, Tome IV, publiées par Philippe Tamizey de Larroque (Paris 1893), in *Collection de Documents inédits sur l'histoire de France*, p. 196n.

60. Gassendi, *Exercitationes Paradoxicae*, Lib. I, in *Opera*, Vol. III, pp. 105–48. A summary of this is given in Sortais, *La Philosophie moderne*, Tome II, pp. 28–30.

61. Sortais, *op. cit.*, Tome II, pp. 23–4 and 32; and Rochot, *Travaux de Gassendi*, pp. 9–22, where the reasons for the delayed publication are discussed.

62. Cf. Sextus Empiricus, *Outlines of Pyrrhonism*, II, sec. 204.

63. Gassendi, *Exercitationes Paradoxicae*, II, in *Opera*, Vol. III, pp. 187–91. See also F. X. Kiefl, 'Gassendi's Skepticismus und seine Stellung zum Materialismus', *Philosophiches Jahrbuch der Görres-Gesellschaft*, VI (1893), pp. 27–34.

64. Gassendi, *Exercitationes Paradoxicae*, lib. II, Exer. vi, *Opera*, Vol. III, pp. 192–210.

65. Cf. Kiefl, 'Gassendi's Skepticismus', pp. 301–5.

66. Gassendi, *Exercitationes Paradoxicae*, Lib. II, *Opera*, Vol. III, p. 192.

67. *Ibid.*, Lib. II, Exer. vi.

68. *Ibid.*, Lib. II, Exer. vi, p. 192.

69. Quoted from the manuscript of Sorbière's *Discours de M. Sorbière sur la Comète*, in Gerhard Hess, 'Pierre Gassend. Der französische Späthumanismus und das Problem von Wissen und Glauben', in *Berliner Beiträge zur Romanischen Philologie*, Band IX, Heft 3/4 (1939), p. 77.

70. See, for instance, Gassendi's work against the Rosicrucian, Robert Fludd, *Examen Philosophiae Roberti Fluddi*, the answer to Herbert of Cherbury, 'Ad Librum, D. Edoardi Herberti Angli, de Veritate', and the *Disquisitio Metaphysica seu Dubitationes, et Instanciae adversus Renati Cartesii Metaphysicam*, all in Vol. III of *Opera*.

71. On Gassendi's scientific achievements, see Alexandre Koyré's paper, 'Le Savant', in the *Synthèse* volume, *Pierre Gassendi*, pp. 59–70; and Rochot, 'Gassendi et le Syntagma Philosophicum', in *Revue de Synthèse*, LXVII (1950), pp. 72–77, and Rochot, *Les Travaux de Gassendi*.

72. Cf. Rochot's paper, *Le philosophe* in *Synthèse* volume, *Pierre Gassendi*, pp. 74–94 and 104–6, and Rochot, *Les Travaux de Gassendi*, passim.

73. 'Media quadam via inter Scepticos & Dogmaticos videtur tenenda', Gassendi, *Syntagma philosophicum, Logica*, Lib. II, chap. V, in *Opera*, Vol. I, p. 79.

74. Cf. Gassendi's discussion of scepticism and knowledge in the second book of the *Syntagma philosophicum, Logica*, in *Opera*, Vol. I, pp. 69ff.; Henri Berr, *An Jure inter Scepticos Gassendus Numeratus Fuerit* (Paris 1898). This work has recently been translated into French by B. Rochot, with the title *Du Scepticisme de Gassendi*, (Paris 1960). Kiefl, 'Gassendi's Skepticismus', pp. 311 and 361–2; Rochot, 'Gassendi et le Syntagma Philosophicum', pp. 76–7; *Les Travaux de Gassendi*, pp. 79–80; 'Le philosphe', pp. 78ff; and Sortais, *La Philosophie moderne*, Vol. II, pp. 252–7. The most complete study now available of Gassendi's thought is Olivier R. Bloch, *La Philosophie de Gassendi* (The Hague 1971). Also see Tullio Gregory, *Scetticismo ed empirismo; studi su Gassendi*, (Bari 1961). Bloch tries to modify and expand some of Gregory's and my interpretations.

75. Gabriel Daniel, *Voyage du Monde de Descartes*, as quoted in Sortais, *op. cit.*, Vol. II, p. 257 n.1.

76. Cf. Rochot, 'Le philosophe' in *Pierre Gassendi*, pp. 98–9 and 102–3 (on p. 81–2, Rochot indicates that Gassendi had some empirical leanings in theology). See also Hess's chapter on 'Wissen und Glauben' in ' Pierre Gassend', pp. 108–58.

77. On Gassendi's friendship with Lullier and Bouchard, see Rochot 'La Vie et le caractère' in *Pierre Gassendi*, pp. 26–32; Gassendi, *Lettres familières à François Lullier pendant l'hiver* 1632-33, avec introduction, notes et index par Bernard Rochot (Paris 1944); and Pintard, *Le libertinage érudit*, pp. 191–5 and 200–3.

78. Pintard, *Le libertinage érudit*, esp. pp. 147–56 and 486–502, and also the various links between Gassendi and the *libertins* that are discussed throughout the book; and Pintard, 'Modernisme, Humanisme, Libertinage, Petite suite sur le

"cas Gassendi",' in *Revuew d'Histoire Littéraire de la France*, 48 Année (1948), pp. 1–52.

79. Rochot, *Travaux de Gassendi*, pp. 137–9 and 192–4; 'Le Cas Gassendi', in *Revue d'Histoire Littéraire de la France*, 47 Année (1947), pp. 289–313; and 'La vie et le caractère', pp. 23–54. See also Henri Gouhier's excellent discussion of 'le cas Gassendi' in his review of Pintard's *Le libertinage érudit* and *La Mothe le Vayer, Gassendi, Guy Patin*, in *Revue Philosophique de la France et de l'Étranger*, CXXXIV (Jan-Juin 1944), pp. 56–60.

80. Robert Lenoble, 'Histoire et Physique. A propos des conseils de Mersenne aux historiens et de l'intervention de Jean de Launoy dans la querelle gassendiste', *Revue d'Histoire des Sciences*, VI (1953), p. 125, n. 1.

81. So was Élie Diodati, the least philosophical member of the Tétrade. Cf. Pintard, *Le Libertinage érudit*, pp. 129–31.

82. On Sorbière, see André Morize, 'Samuel Sorbiere (1610-70)', in *Zeitschrift für französische Sprache und Litteratur*, XXXIII (1908), pp. 214–65; Pintard, *Le Libertinage érudit*, pp. 334–45; Popkin, 'Samuel Sorbière's Translation of Sextus Empiricus', pp. 617–8; and Sortais, *La philosophie moderne*, II, pp. 192–228.

83. Samuel Sorbière, *Lettres et Discours de M. de Sorbiere sur diverses matieres curieuses* (Paris 1660), letter to Du Bosc, pp. 151–2.

84. Sorbière, *Discours sceptique sur le passage du chyle, & le mouvement du coeur* (Leyden 1648), pp. 153–4. This passage is cited in Sortais, *La philosophie moderne*, II, p. 194.

85. Quoted in Vincent Guilloton, 'Autour de la Relation du Voyage de Samuel Sorbière en Angleterre 1663-1664', in *Smith College Studies in Modern Languages*, XI, no. 4 (July 1930), p. 21.

86. Thomas Sprat, *Observations on Monsieur de Sorbier's Voyage into England* (London 1665), pp. 275–6. 'But yet I must tell him, that perhaps this Rigid condemning of the *English* Cookery, did not so well suit his belov'd Title of *Sceptick*. According to the lawes of that profession, he should first have long debated whether there be any tast, or no; whether the steam of a pot be only a fancy, or a reall thing; whether the Kitchin fire has indeed the good qualities of rosting, and Boiling, or whether it be only an appearance. This had bin a dispute more becomming a *Sceptick*, then thus to conclude Dogmatically on all the *Intrigues of Haut gousts*; and to raise an endlesse speculative quarrel between those that had bin hitherto peaceful and practical *Sects*, the *Hasche's* and the *Surloiners*.

CHAPTER VI: Counter-Attack Begins

1. On this matter, see chapter 4, p. 83.

2. On Garasse, see Lachèvre, *Le Procès du poète Théophile de Viau*; Boase, *Fortunes of Montigne*, pp. 164–70; and Joseph Lecler, 'Un Adversaire des Libertins au début du VIIIᵉ siècle—Le P. François Garasse (1585-1631)', *Études*, CCIX (1931), pp. 553–72.

3. François Garasse, *La Doctrine curieuse des beaux esprits de ce temps, ou pretendus tels* (Paris, 1623).

4. François Ogier, *Jugement et Censure du livre de la Doctrine curieuse de François Garasse* (Paris 1623). The quotation is on p. vii.

5. Garasse, *Apologie du Pere François Garassus, de la Compagnie de Jesus, pour son livre contre les Atheistes & Libertins de nostre siecle, et reponse aux censures et calomnies de l'autur anonyme* (Paris 1624), p. 135.

6. *Ibid.*, chaps. 21–22.

7. Garasse, *La Somme Theologiques des veritez capitales de la Religion Chrestienne* (Paris 1625), 'Advertissements', p. 7.

8. *Ibid.*, 'Advertissemens', pp. 14 and 34.

9. *Ibid.*, Livre I, p. 15.

10. *Ibid.*, Livre I, p. 44.

11. *Ibid.*, Livre I, p. 45.

12. *Ibid.*, Livre I, p. 61.

13. *Ibid.*, Livre, I, pp. 60–5.

14. *Ibid.*, Livre I, pp. 81–111.

15. *Ibid.*, 'Advertissemens', p. 56.

16. Cf. Lecler, 'Un Adversaire des Libertins', p. 569; and Jean Orcibal, *Les Origines du Jansénisme*, Tome II (Paris and Louvain 1947), chap. V.

17. Cf. Gouhier's excellent study, 'La Crise de la Théologie au temps de Descartes', pp. 29–32, and 38.

18. Jean Duvergier du Hauranne (Saint-Cyran), *La Somme des fautes et faussetez capitales contenues en la Somme Theologique du Pere François Garasse de la Compagnie de Jesus* (Paris 1626), Tome I, Dedication to Cardinal Richelieu, 1st and 2nd pages. Although the title page claims this is a four volume work, only two and an abridgement of the fourth ever appeared. On this, see Orcibal, *Origines du Jansénisme*, II, p. 263 n. 3 and 280ff. On the appearance and reception of the work, see Orcibal, *op. cit.*, II, pp. 278–80, and Lecler, 'Un Adversaire des Libertins', p. 569.

19. Saint-Cyran, *Sommes des fautes*, Tome I, Dedication, 42nd page.

20. *Ibid.*, Tome II, Dedication to Richelieu, 10th and 11th pages.

21. *Ibid.*, Tome II, 'Advis a tous les sçavans & amateurs de la Verité, touchant la refutation de la Somme Theologique du Pere François Garasse, de la Compagnie de Jesus', 2nd page.

22. *Ibid.*, Tome II, p. 241.

23. *Ibid.*, Tome I, Dedication, 49th page.

24. *Ibid.*, Tome IV.

25. *Ibid.*, Tome II, pp. 321–4.

26. Cf. Orcibal, *Origines du jansénisme*, II, pp. 275–7; and Gouhier, 'Crise de la Théologie', pp. 29–31 and 51. Gouhier's presentation of the views of Jansen and Saint-Cyran makes the latter's defense of Charron perfectly intelligible. As Gouhier shows, the original Jansenists were advocating a simple and efficacious theology, removed from any philosophical base. They regarded philosophy as the source of errors and heresies, and rational theology as a road to complete uncertainty.

27. Saint-Cyran, *Somme des fautes*, II, pp. 321–469.

28. Anon., *Censure de la Sacree Faculté de Theologie de Paris, contre un livre intitulé La Somme Theologique des veritez capitales de la Religion Chrestienne, par R. P. François Garassus, &c.* (Paris 1626), pp. 3–14. The quote is on pp. 12–3. On the background of this condemnation, see Orcibal, *Origines du Jansénisme*, II, pp. 263–7.

29. Mersenne, *Verité des Sciences*, Dedicatory Epistle, 2nd-3rd pages. See also Mersenne's *Quaestiones celeberrimae in Genesim* (Paris 1623), and *L'Impieté des*

Deistes, Athees, et Libertins de ce temps, combattue, et renversée de point en point par raisons tirees de la Philosophie et de la Theologie (Paris 1624). Mersenne's general criticism of scepticism is discussed in the next chapter.

30. Jean Boucher, *Les Triomphes de la Religion Chrestienne* (Paris 1628), pp. 128-32.

31. *Ibid.*, pp. 99-100.

32. *Ibid.*, pp. 147-52.

33. *Ibid.*, p. 152.

34. Cf. Julien-Eymard d'Angers, 'Le "Fidéisme" de J. Boucher, Cordelier (1628)', in *Études franciscaines*, L, pp. 579-93. A more fideistic interpretation of Boucher appears in Busson, *La pensée religieuse*, pp. 257-9, and a less fideistic interpretation in Dedieu, 'Survivances et influences de l'Apologétique traditionelle dans les 'Pensées', in *Rev. d'Hist. litt.*, XXXVII (1930), pp. 507-8. See also Boase, *Fortunes of Montaigne*, pp. 174-8.

35. Cf., Balzac, 'Lettres de Jean-Louis Guez de Balzac'.

36. Balzac, *Socrate Chrestien*, Discours I, in *Les Oeuvres de Monsieur de Balzac* (Paris 1665), Tome II, p. 213. See also Busson, *La pensée religileuse*, pp. 266-9.

37. Charles Cotin, *Discours à Théopompe sur les Forts Esprits du temps* (n.p. 1629), pp. 4-28. Mersenne had claimed that Paris contained 60,000 atheists in 1623.

38. Pierre Chanet, *Considerations sur la Sagesse de Charon* (Paris 1643), Preface, 2nd and 3rd pages. Busson, *La pensée religieuse*, pp. 194-5, says that 'Chanet did not seem to know Montaigne' and did not know the *Apologie*, which is patently false. The reference to Montaigne was removed in the second edition of Chanet's work. Cf. Boase, *Fortunes of Montaigne*, p. 186 n. 4.

39. Chanet, *Considerations*, pp. 1-250. The various discussions in the seventeenth century of the merits of animals, including Chanet's, are treated in George Boas, *The Happy Beast in French Thought of the Seventeenth Century* (Baltimore 1933).

40. Chanet, *Considerations*, pp. 257-72.

41. *Ibid.*, p. 291.

42. *Ibid.*, pp. 288-304.

43. Yves de Paris, *La Theologie naturelle*, 3rd ed. (Paris 1641), Tome IV, pp. 393-403. (The first edition of Tome IV was in 1636.) In considering Yves de Paris here, I do not intend to imply that he was an Aristotelian in his philosophy, but only that this particular critique of scepticism illustrates the Aristotelian type of refutation of Pyrrhonism. Other kinds of reasons for rejecting scepticism are offered elsewhere in his writings. For a detailed picture of Yves de Paris's philosophy, see Charles Chesneau (Julien-Eymard d'Angers), *Le Père Yves de Paris et son temps* (1590-1678), 2 vols., (Paris 1946).

44. Jean Bagot, *Apologeticus fidei*, (Paris 1644), Liber I, p. 6.

45. *Ibid.*, Preface, Liber I, pp. 1-19 on scepticism, pp. 20-102 on Bagot's theory, and Liber II, pp. 17-8 deals with Charron.

46. Charles Sorel, *La Science des choses corporelles, premiere partie de la Science humaine* (Paris 1634), title page and preface.

47. *Ibid.*, pp. 15-27.

48. Sorel, *La Bibliotheque françois de M. C. Sorel* (Paris 1664), p. 392.

49. *Ibid.*, pp. 33-5, and the fourth volume of Sorel's *La Science universelle*, entitled *La Perfection de l'Ame.* . . . (Paris 1664), Part II, p. 30.

50. Sorel, *La Perfection de L'Ame*, pp. 21–30, gives a summary of the views of 'Des Pyrrhoniens ou Sceptiques'. The quote is on p. 30, where Sorel also said that these libertins are very few in number, and are afraid to avow their views in public.

51. Cf. Sorel, *La Science universelle de Sorel, où il est traité de l'usage & de la perfection de toutes les choses du monde*, Tome III (Paris 1647), pp. 257-69. Du Pleix, who was Sorel's predecessor as *Historiographe du Roy*, offered the same explanation of sense illusions, but did not refer at all to Pyrrhonism in this connection. Cf. Scipion Du Pleix, *Cours de Philosophie, reveu, illustré & augmenté* (Paris 1632), in the part entitled, 'La Physique ou Science des Choses Naturelles,' Livre 8, chaps. 14-9.

52. Sorel, *Science universelle*, Tome III, pp. 270-2.

53. *Ibid.*, pp. 272-4.

54. *Ibid.*, p. 277.

55. *Ibid.*, pp. 275-81.

56. This may be the attack La Mothe Le Vayer answered at the beginning of the second part of the *Prose Chagrine*, in *Oeuvres*, Tome IX, pp. 354-6.

57. Sorel, *Science universelle*, Tome III, p. 281.

58. Mersenne discussed Bacon in *La Verité des Sciences*, Livre I, chap. XVI.

59. Francis Bacon, *Of the Advancement and Proficiencie of Learning; or the Partitions of Sciences* (London 1674), Book V, chap. ii, pp. 144-5.

60. Bacon, *Instauratio Magna*, Eng. trans., in *The Works of Francis Bacon*, edited by Spedding, Ellis and Heath, Vol. VIII (Boston 1863), p. 52.

CHAPTER VII: Constructive or Mitigated Scepticism

1. The monumental work of the late Abbé Robert Lenoble has brought to light, for the first time, the tremendous achievement and importance of Mersenne. See, especially, Lenoble's *Mersenne ou la naissance du mécanisme* (Paris, 1943).

2. Cf. Marin Mersenne, *Quaestiones celeberrimae in Genesim* (Paris 1623); *L'Impieté des Deistes, Athees, et Libertins de ce temps, combatue, et renversée de point en point par raisons tirees de la Philosophie, et de la Theologie* (Paris 1624); and *La Verité des Sciences contre les Septiques ou Pyrrhoniens* (Paris 1625).

3. See, for instance, the questions treated in Mersenne's *Questions inouyes ou Recreation des Sçavans* (Paris 1634).

4. Mersenne, *Correspondance du P. Marin Mersenne*, publiée par Mme. Paul Tannery, editée par Cornelis de Waard avec la collaboration de René Pintard, Tomes I-IV (Paris 1932-55). Several more volumes are in preparation. The twelve published ones cover the period 1617-1643.

5. Cf. Lenoble, *Mersenne*, pp. 310-33.

6. Mersenne, *La Verité des Sciences*, dedicatory epistle. Part of this was quoted in chap. vi, pp. 117-8.

7. *Ibid.*, Preface, 2nd page.

8. *Ibid.*, Preface, 3rd page.

9. *Ibid.*, pp. 1-11.

10. *Ibid.*, p. 14.

11. The similarity of some of Mersenne's views to some of those of Charles Sorel, who was discussed in the previous chapter, is no doubt due to the fact that the latter used Mersenne's book as a source. The differences between their views will be discussed later in this chapter.

12. Mersenne, *La Verité des Sciences*, pp. 16-20.

13. *Ibid.*, p. 20.

14. *Ibid.*, p. 21.

15. *Ibid.*, pp. 22-74. The quotation is on p. 57.

16. *Ibid.*, pp. 150-1.

17. *Ibid.*, p. 153. The material dealt with in this paragraph occurs on pp. 130-56.

18. *Ibid.*, pp. 156-62.

19. *Ibid.*, pp. 179-89.

20. *Ibid.*, pp. 190-5.

21. *Ibid.*, pp. 196-204. The quotation is on p. 204.

22. *Ibid.*, p. 212. The discussion of Francis Bacon occurs on pp. 205-18.

23. *Ibid.*, pp. 219-20. The quotation is on p. 220.

24. *Ibid.*, p. 751.

25. Lenoble, *Mersenne*, p. 32.

26. Charles Adam, in his brief discussion of Mersenne's critique of Pyrrhonism, pointed out that Mersenne never questioned the truth of the scientific laws he employed in answering scepticism. Cf. Adam's *Vie de Descartes*, in *Oeuvres de Descartes*, Adam-Tannery ed., Vol. XII (Paris 1910), p. 131.

27. Cf. Bayle, *Dictionnaire*, art. Zenon d'Elée, Rem. K.

28. Mersenne, *Les Questions theologiques, physiques, morales et mathematiques* (Paris 1634), pp. 9-11. The quotation is on p. 11.

29. Mersenne, *Questions inouyes*, pp. 69-71. The quotation is on p. 71.

30. *Ibid.*, pp. 72-4.

31. Letters of Pierre Le Loyer to Mersenne, 13 February 1627, printed in *Correspondance du P. Marin Mersenne*, Tome I, p. 521, where Le Loyer said, 'I see that you are a follower of the second Academ;y and of Carneades, who believed that one could make probable judgments regarding matters proposed and put in dispute. And I embrace Varron's opinion, which was for the first Academy, which did not differ from the second except in words and not deeds. It was not like the second, which was that of Arcesilaus, and came very close to that of the Pyrrhonian philosophers, of whom I know you are as far removed as you are close to Platonic philosophy. . . .'

32. Gassendi's letter to Mersenne, 4 February 1629, which appeared as the preface to the former's attack on the Rosicrusian, Robert Fludd. This letter is printed in *Correspondance du P. Marin Mersenne*, Tome II, pp. 184-5, in which Gassendi said, 'And you are not unaware that my slight, sceptical talent (intelligence) is hardly able to come up with anything which would truly be satisfying to you . . .

'For although you prohibit that I be almost Pyrrhonian and are accustomed always to urge me thus, as if I might have something which I would publish dogmatically, on the other hand, on the basis of friendship, you have to concede that it is licit to have one's daily life and never to publish or expressly state anything save within the limits of mere probability.'

33. La Mothe Le Vayer, *Discours sceptique sur la musique*, printed in Mersenne, *Questions harmoniques. Dans lesquelles sont contenuës plusieurs choses remarquables pour la Physique, pour la Morale, & pour les autres sciences* (Paris 1634), pp. 161-2.

34. Letter of Mersenne to Sorbière, 25 April 1646, printed in the preface to Thomas Hobbes, *De Cive* (Amsterdam 1647), and in Sortais, *La Philosophie*

moderne, Vol. II, pp. 214–5, where Mersenne said, 'You will gladly renounce the suspension of judgment and the other idle talk of the Sceptics, when you will be forced to admit that dogmatic philosophy rests upon an unshakeable basis.' Mersenne had only the highest praise for Hobbes' *De Cive*, whereas Gassendi, though highly approving of the work, at least noticed its irreligious slant, and Descartes violently condemned the book because it was based on 'Maxims which are very bad and most dangerous.' Cf. Sortais, *op. cit.*, II, pp. 214–6; and Lenoble, *Mersenne*, pp. 576–8.

35. A more detailed consideration of this side of Mersenne appears in R. H. Popkin, 'Father Mersenne's War against Pyrrhonism', in *Modern Schoolman*, XXXIV (1956–7), pp. 61–78.

36. Blaise Pascal, *Pensées* (Classiques Garnier), no. 374, pp. 166–7.

37. Cf. Gassendi, *Syntagma philosophicum, Logica*, in *Opera*, Vol. I, p. 79. See also note 1, p. 106, chap. v.

38. Gassendi, *Syntagma, Logica*, Liber II, cap. ii-iii, in *Opera*, Vol. I, pp. 69–76.

39. *Ibid.*, Lib. II, cap. v. in *Opera*, Vol. I, pp. 79–81.

40. *Ibid.*, Lib. II, cap. v, in *Opera*, Vol. I, p. 81.

41. *Ibid.*, Lib. II, cap. v, in *Opera*, Vol. I, p. 79; see also George S. Brett, *The Philosophy of Gassendi* (London 1908), p. 8.

42. Gassendi, *Syntagma, Logica*, Liber II, cap. v, in *Opera*, Vol. I, esp. pp. 81–6.

43. Cf. Brett, *op. cit.*, p. 12.

44. See Sextus's discussion of indicative signs in *Outlines of Pyrrhonism*, II, chaps. x-xi.

45. Gassendi, *Syntagma, Logica*, Liber II, cap. v, in *Opera*, Vol. I, pp. 81ff. See also Sortais, *La Philosophie moderne*, II, pp. 91–6, Brett, *op. cit.*, pp. 10–13, and Rochot, 'Gassendi et le Syntagma,' pp. 76–7.

46. On the general characteristics of the positive views of Gassendi, see, besides the *Syntagma*, Berr, *An Jure Inter Scepticos Gassendus numeratus fuerit*, esp. Chap. ii; Brett, *Philosophy of Gassendi*; Kiefl, 'Gassendi's Skepticismus', pp. 361–73; Rochot, 'Gassendi et le Syntagma', 'Le Philosphe', pp. 72–84 and 104–5; Sortais, *La Philosphie moderne*, II, where a detailed summary and analysis of the *Syntagma* is given in art. II, chap. iv; and Bloch, *La Philosophie de Gassendi*, esp. IIe Partie.

47. The scientific value of Gassendi's type of qualitative atomism is discussed in Koyré's 'Le Savant'; and Rochot's *Les Travaux de Gassendi sur Épicure et sur l'atomisme.*

48. See chap. v, pp. 101–3.

49. Letter of Gassendi to Diodati, 29 August 1634, printed in Mersenne, *Correspondance du P. Marin Mersenne*, Tome IV (Paris 1955), p. 337.

50. Gassendi, 'Ad Librum D. Edoardi Herbeti Angli, De Veritate, *Epistola'*, in *Opera*, Vol. III, p. 413. See also Sortais, *Le philosophie moderne*, II, pp. 254–5.

51. Gassendi, *Objectiones Quintae*, in Descartes, *Oeuvres*, A. T., Tome VII, esp. pp. 257–8, and 277–9; Gassendi, *Disquisitio metaphysica seu Dubitationes, et Instantiae adversus Renati Cartesii Metaphysicam, et Responsa*, in *Opera*, Vol. III, esp. pp. 278–84 and 314–17; and *Syntagma, Logica*, Lib. I, cap. xi, and Lib. II, cap. vi, in *Opera*, Vol. I, pp. 65–6 and 90. See also, Rochot, 'Gassendi et la 'Logique' de Descartes', in *Rev. Philos. de la France et l'Etranger*, Année LXXX (1955), pp. 300–8.

52. Cf. Koyré, 'Le Savant, pp. 60-1; and Rochot, 'Gassendi. Sa place dans la pensée du XVIIe siècle', in *Revue de Synthèsè*, LX (1940-5), pp. 35-45, 'Le Philosophe', pp. 102-7; and Bloch, pp. 279-82 and 485-95.

53. Rochot, 'Gassendi. Sa place,' pp. 35-45.

54. Hence, Gassendi insisted on a qualitative rather than a mathematical atomism, and conceived of the atoms as having properties found in ordinary experience, rather than precise, abstract geometrical qualities. Cf. Rochot, *Travaux de Gassendi*, pp. 196ff. See also the discussion of Koyré, Rochot and Lenoble on Gassendi's atomism in the Centre International de Synthèse volume, *Pierre Gassendi*, pp. 108-13.

55. Rochot, 'Gassendi et le Syntagma', p. 77; *Travaux de Gassendi*, p. 196; and 'Le philosophe', p. 87. (An English version of some of this material appears in Brush, *Selected Writings of Gassendi*, pp. 157-278.)

56. See, especially, Rochot, 'Gassendi et le Syntagma', pp. 73ff, and 'Le philosophe', pp. 102-7.

57. Jacques Du Bosc, *Le philosophie indifférent*, 2 vols. (Paris 1643), 2 Partie, p. 1, 124. See also C. Chesneau (Julien-Eymard d'Angers), 'Un Precurseur de Pascal? Le Franciscain Jacques Du Bosc, in *XVIIe Siècle*, no. 15 (1952), pp. 426-48, where Du Bosc's views are discussed, and many citations, including this one, are given. According to the *Sorberiana ou les pensées critiques de M. de Sorbiere, recueillies par M. Graverol* (Paris 1695), art. 'Bosc', pp. 55-6, Du Bosc was an intimate friend of the 'nouveau Pyrrhoien', Samuel Sorbière.

58. Julien-Eymard d'Angers, 'Jacques du Bosc,' pp. 429-36.

59. *Ibid.*, pp. 436-44, and especially the citations given on pp. 443-4.

60. *Ibid.*, pp. 445-8.

61. William Chillingworth, *The Religion of the Protestants, A Safe Way to Salvation*, in *The Works of William Chillingworth* (London 1704), p. 108. 'For, my sense may sometimes possibly deceive me, yet I am certain enough that I see what I see, and feel what I feel. Our Judges are not infallible in their judgments, yet are they certain enough, that they judge aright, and that they proceed according to the Evidence that is given, when they condemn a Thief or a Murderer to the Gallows. A Traveller is not always certain of his way, but often mistaken: and doth it therefore follow that he can have no assurance that *Charing-Cross* is his right way from the *Temple* to *White-Hall*?'

62. *Ibid.*, Preface, 2nd page.

63. There are many similarities to Chillingworth's views in John Tillotson's *The Rule of Faith*, John Wilkins' *Of the Principles and Duties of Natural Religion*, and Joseph Glanvill's *Essays on Several Important Subjects in Philosophy and Religion*. Prof. Henry Van Leeuwen's book, *The Problem of Certainty in English Thought, 1630-80* (The Hague, 1963), deals in great detail with the development and influence of Chillingworth's theory. The impact of this view on English legal theory is discussed in Theodore Waldman, 'The Origin of the Concept of "Reasonable Doubt."' in *Journal of the History of Ideas*, XX (1959), pp. 299-316, and in Robert Todd Carroll, *The Philosophy of Bishop Stillingfleet in its Seventeenth Century Context* (The Hague, 1975).

64. Cf. Thomas Campanella, *The Defense of Galileo, Mathematician of Florence*, translated by Grant McColley, in *Smith College Studies in History*, XXII, Nos. 3-4 (1937); p. 70; and Galileo Galilei, *Dialogo sopra i due massimi Sistemi del Mundo* in *Le Opere de Galileo Galilei*, Edizone Nazionale, Vol. VII (Firenze 1933), Giornata Prima, p. 127 and Giornata Quarta, pp. 487-8; and in

the English edition, Galileo Galilei, *Dialogue on the Great World Systems*, ed. by Giorgio de Santillana (Chicago 1953), First Day, pp. 112-3, and Fourth Day, pp. 470-1.

65. James Collins, in his *A History of Modern European Philosophy*, (Milwaukee 1954), p. 82, quotes Galileo as having claimed that we cannot penetrate to 'the true and intrinsic *essence of natural substances.*' See also, Campanella, *op. cit.*, p. 21; and Descartes, *Meditations*, in *Oeuvres*, A.-T. Tome IX, Med. IV, p. 44.

66. Campanella, *op. cit.*, pp. 18, 24-5, 30 and 32; Galileo, *Massimi Sistemi*, Giornata Prima, pp. 128-9 (English ed., First Day, p. 114). See also the comments on this passage from Galileo in Edwin A. Burtt, *The Metaphysical Foundations of Modern Physical Science*, Anchor ed. (New York 1955), pp. 82-3; and the excellent discussion of Leonardo Olschki, in his 'Galileo's Philosophy of Science', in *Philosophical Review*, LII (1943), pp. 349-65, esp. p. 358, where he discusses why Galileo cannot be considered as a sceptic.

67. Descartes, letter to Mersenne, 11 October 1638, in *Oeuvres*, A. T. Tome II, p. 380.

68. At least people like Condillac, Condorcet, Hartley and Henry Home (Lord Kames) claimed this was the case.

CHAPTER VIII: Herbert of Cherbury

1. Edward, Lord Herbert of Cherbury, *De Veritate*, trans. Meyrick H. Carré (Bristol 1937), Intro. by Carré, pp. 10-11. The best study of Herbert of Cherbury is Mario Rossi, *La Vita, le opere, i tempi di Edoardo Herbert di Chirbury*, 3 vols. (Firenze 1947).

2. Cf. Lenoble, *Mersenne*, pp. 561-3.

3. Gassendi, Letter to Elie Diodati, 29 August 1634, in Mersenne, *Correspondance*, IV, pp. 335-40, and Letter to Herbert of Cherbury, in Gassendi, *Opera*, III, 411-19.

4. Hugo Grotius refers to Sextus in *De Jure Belli Ac Pacis*, trans. Francis W. Kelsey, (Oxford 1925), Book I, xii, p. 42, Book II, vii, p. 233, and xxviii, p. 256. Herbert in his *Autobiography*, ed. Sidney Lee, 2nd ed. (London n.d.), p. 133, mentions showing the manuscript of *De Veritate* to Grotius and Tilenus. There is a new edition of the *Autobiography*, edited by J. M. Shuttleworth (London 1976).

5. Herbert, *Autobiography*, Lee edition, pp. 133-4 and *De Veritate*, Introduction, p. 11.

6. Herbert, *De Veritate*, pp. 75-80. 'Those, then, who are so dubious on all subjects that they contend that it is impossible to know anything whatever, fail to understand the conditions by which our faculties are brought into conformity with objects.' p. 80.

7. *Ibid.*, p. 83. In the French edition of *De la Verité* (n.p. 1639), p. 10, this sentence reads 'I have no other intention in this proposition than to say that truth exists, against the impertinence and foolishness of the Sceptics.' The Latin text states, 'Ex propositione istá quae contra insanos & Scepticos instituitur.' *De Veritate* (n.p. 1656), p. 9.

8. Herbert, *De Veritate*, Carré, ed., p. 84.

9. *Ibid.*, p. 84.

10. *Ibid.*, p. 86.

11. *Ibid.*, p. 86.

12. *Ibid.*, pp. 90–100.
13. *Ibid.*, p. 101.
14. *Ibid.*, pp. 102–4.
15. *Ibid.*, p. 101.
16. *Ibid.*, pp. 105–6.
17. *Ibid.*, p. 106.
18. *Ibid.*, p. 115.
19. *Ibid.*, p. 116.
20. *Ibid.*, p. 117.
21. *Ibid.*, p. 118.
22. *Ibid.*, p. 121. See also pp. 119 and 139, where Herbert stated, 'Accordingly I take the chief criterion of Natural Instinct to be universal consent (putting aside persons who are out of their minds or mentally incapable).'
23. *Ibid.*, pp. 119 and 125. See John Locke, *An Essay Concerning Human Understanding*, in *Works of John Locke*, 11th ed. (London 1812), Vol. I, Book I, chap. 2, pp. 13–32.
24. Herbert, *De Veritate*, p. 126.
25. *Ibid.*, p. 131.
26. *Ibid.*, p. 135.
27. *Ibid.*, p. 140.
28. Gassendi reported that the Pope thought highly of it. See Gassendi's letter to Diodati, in Mersenne, *Correspondance*, IV, p. 336.
29. *Ibid.*, pp. 336–7.
30. *Ibid.*, p. 337.
31. *Ibid.*, p. 337.
32. *Ibid.*, p. 338.
33. Gassendi's letter to Herbert, Gassendi, *Opera*, III, p. 411ff.
34. René Descartes, letter to Mersenne, 16 Oct 1639, in Descartes, *Oeuvres*, edited by Adam-Tannery, Vol. II, pp. 596–7.
35. *Ibid.*, p. 597. Compare with Plato's *Meno* and Bayle's articles *Nicolle*, Rem. C, and *Pellisson*, Rem. D & E, in the *Dictionnaire*.
36. *Descartes, letter to Mersenne, 16 Oct. 1639, Oeuvres*, A.T., II, p. 597.
37. *Ibid.*, pp. 597–8.
38. *Ibid.*, p. 599.
39. Montaigne is always the villain in Silhon's discussions of scepticism. In his first work he had also made some nasty comments about Charron, but apologized for these on the *errata* slip, of his *Les Deux Veritez de Silhon. L'une de Dieu, et sa Providence, L'autre de l'Immortalité de l'Ame* (Paris 1626), where he said, 'Some respectable people have found it bad that I blame Charron a little in my Introductin to the second Truth, I am sorry about it, and wishing only that no one be offended by my writings, I would have eliminated the cause of it if it had been within my power.' Cf. Boase, *Fortunes of Montaigne*, pp. 165–6.
40. On Silhon's general apologetic plan, see Ernest Jovy, *Pascal et Silhon, (Études pascaliennes* II), (Paris 1927), pp. 9–16; Julien-Eymard d'Angers, *Pascal et ses Précurseurs*, (Paris 1954), p. 86; and Pintard, *Libertinage*, pp. 67–8.
41. For Strowski's interpretation, see his *Pascal et son Temps*, 3ᵉ Partie, pp. 282–6.
42. Jean de Silhon, *Les Deux Veritez*, p. 16.
43. *Ibid.*, pp. 16–7.
44. *Ibid.*, p. 18.
45. *Ibid.*, pp. 18–20.

46. On Silhon's relations with Descartes, see Charles Adam, *Vie & Oeuvres de Descartes* in Descartes, *Oeuovres*, A.-T., XII, pp. 463n–6n; Leon Blanchet, *Les Antécédents historiques du 'Je pense, donc je suis'* (Paris 1920), pp. 34–5.
47. Although his contemporaries are not mentioned, Silhon as an important government official probably knew La Mothe Le Vayer, Naudé and others.
48. Silhon, *De L'Immortalité de l'ame* (Paris 1634), p. 101. La Mothe Le Vayer also wrote a treatise on this subject, entitled, *Petit Discours Chrestien de l'Immortalité de l'Ame.*
49. *Silhon, Immortalité*, pp. 103–7.
50. *Ibid.*, pp. 107–8.
51. *Ibid.*, p. 108.
52. *Ibid.*, p. 108.
53. *Ibid.*, pp. 109–12.
54. *Ibid.*, p. 113.
55. *Ibid.*, p. 117.
56. *Ibid.*, pp. 117–22.
57. *Ibid.*, pp. 123–7.
58. *Ibid.*, p. 153.
59. *Ibid.*, p. 156.
60. *Ibid.*, p. 167.
61. *Ibid.*, pp. 168–76.
62. *Ibid.*, p. 178.
63. *Ibid.*, p. 178–9.
64. *Ibid.*, p. 179.
65. Silhon, *Le Ministre d'Estat*, 3e Part., *De la Certitude des Connoissances humaines* (Amsterdam 1662), p. 41. (The Bibliothèque Nationale also has an edition of his work from 1661.)
66. Silhon, *Immortalité*, p. 180; *De la Certitude*, p. 41.
67. On Silhon's *cogito*, see Blanchet, *Antécédents*, pp. 34–7.
68. Silhon, *Immortalité*, p. 184.
69. *Ibid.*, p. 184.
70. *Ibid.*, p. 186.
71. *Ibid.*, p. 189.
72. *Ibid.*, pp. 193–4.
73. *Ibid.*, pp. 195–6.
74. *Ibid.*, p. 204.
75. *Ibid.*, pp. 228–9. Cf. Jovy, *Pascal et Silhon*, pp. 39ff.
76. Silhon, *Immortalité*, pp. 230–232.
77. Descartes, *Meditations*, I, in *Oeuvres*, A.T. IX, pp. 13–18.
78. Blaise Pascal, *Pensées* (Classiques Garnier), no. 434, pp. 183–4.
79. Descartes, letter to *, March 1638, *Oeuvres*, A.-T. II, pp. 37–8.
80. Descartes, letter to *, March or April 1648, *Oeuvres*, A.-T. V, p. 138.

CHAPTER IX: Conqueror of Scepticism

1. Descartes, *Objectiones Septimae cum Notis Authoris sive Dissertatio de Prima Philosophia, Oeuvres*. A.-T. VII, p. 550.
2. L'Abbé François Para du Phanjas, *Théorie des êtres insensibles, ou Cours*

complet de Métaphysique, sacrée et profane, mise à la portée de tout le monde, 3 vols. (Paris 1779), I, p. xx.

3. Cf. Étienne Gilson, *Études sur le rôle de la pensée médiévale dans la formation du système cartésien* (Paris 1930?, and *La liberté chez Descartes et la théologie* (Paris 1913); Gouhier, *La pensée religieuse de Descartes* (Paris 1924), and *Essais sur Descartes* (Paris 1949); Koyré, *Essai sur l'idée de Dieu et les preuves de son existence chez Descartes* (Paris 1922); and Lenoble, *Mersenne*, introduction.

4. Cf. Descartes, *Discours de la Méthode, Texte et commentaire par Étienne Gilson* (Paris 1947), where throughout the commentary many indications are given of Descartes' use of Montaigne and Charron; and Léon Brunschvicg, *Descartes et Pascal, Lecteurs de Montaigne* (New York and Paris 1944). See also Adam, *Vie de Descartes*, in Descartes, *Oeuvres*, A.-T. XII, pp. 57 and 131; and J. Sirven, *Les Années d'apprentissage de Descartes 1596-1628* (Albi 1928), pp. 259-71.

5. Izydora Dąmbska, 'Meditationes' Descartes na tle sceptycyzmu francuskiego XVII wieku', in *Kwartalnik Filozoficzny*, XIX (1950), pp. 1-24 (French summary pp. 161-2): and Gouhier, 'Doute méthodique ou négation méthodique?,' in *Etudes Philosphiques*, IX, (1954), pp. 135-62, and *Les Premières pensées de Descartes: Contribution à l'histoire de l'anti-renaissance* (Paris 1958).

6. Descartes, *The Seventh Set of Objections with the Author's Annotations thereon, otherwise a Dissertation concerning First Philosophy*, in *Philosophical Works of Descartes*, Haldane-Ross ed. (New York 1955), Vol. II, p. 335. The original Latin is on pp. 548-9 of *Oeuvres*, A.-T. VII.

7. Lenoble, *Mersenne*, p. 192. No evidence is offered for this claim.

8. Cf. Gilson, *Liberté chez Descartes*, pp. 6-9 and 13; and Sirven, *Années d'apprentissage*, pp. 41-5. After a most careful consideration of the evidence available, Sirven concluded that Veron was never a teacher of a course that Descartes took at La Flèche.

9. Descartes, *Oeuvres*, A.-T. X, pp. 63-5 and 165; references to Charron and Montaigne in Gilson's commentary on Descartes' *Discours*; and Sirven, *Années d'apprentissage*, p. 271.

10. Descartes, *Reponses de l'avtevr avx secondes objections*, in *Oeuvres*, A.-T. IX, p. 103.

11. Cf. Pintard, 'Descartes et Gassendi,' pp. 120-2; and Descartes' comments on a 'meschant livre' in his letters to Mersenne of 1630 in Descartes, *Oeuvres*, A.-T. I, pp. 144-5 and 148-9.

12. Descartes, *Discours de la Méthode*, in *Oeuvres*, A.-T. VI, p. 32.

13. See Louis Moréri, *Le Grand Dictionnaire historique*, Tome III, (Paris 1759), art. Chandoux (N. de), p. 465.

14. *Ibid.*, p. 465.

15. Adrien Baillet, *Vie de M. Descartes* (Collection Grandeurs, La Table Ronde) (Paris 1946), p. 70.

16. *Ibid.*, p. 70.

17. Cf. the account given in Baillet, pp. 70ff; and Descartes' letter to Ville-bressieu, 1631, in Descartes, *Oeuvres*, A.-T. I, p. 213.

18. Baillet, *Vie de M. Descartes*, pp. 72-4. An analysis of the known information about the Chandoux affair and Descartes' relations with Cardinal Bérulle is given in Gouhier, 'La crise de la théologie au temps de Descartes,' *Rev. de Théol. et de la Phil.*, IV (1954), pp. 45-7.

19. Cf. Gouhier, *Pensée religieuse de Descartes*, p. 72; J. Millet, *Histoire de Descartes avant* 1637 (Paris 1867), p. 160; and Descartes' statement in the *Discours* in 1637 as to when he started employing his method and developing his system, in *Oeuvres*, A.-T. VI, pp. 30-1.

20. Cf. Descartes' survey of the various branches of learning that he was introduced to in school, in *Discourse, Oeuvres*, A.-T. VI, pp. 5-10.

21. Cf. Gouhier's comments on Bérulle and Descartes in his 'Crise de la théologie', p. 47.

22. Descartes, *Discours, Oeuvres*, A.-T. VI, p. 30. This whole passage seems to have echoes of the Chandoux episode.

23. *Ibid.*, pp. 30-1. The passage does not make too clear how Descartes started off, but mainly that this is when he began, and that the result was to render dubious much of what philosophers considered certain.

24. Although Gouhier and Cassirer have offered much evidence that this is a late work of Descartes, there are some indications that it may be quite early, perhaps from the 1630's. The demon hypothesis does not occur, which suggests the work may precede the *Meditations*. Also, the term 'Pyrrhoniens' occurs in this work, whereas, in the *Discourse* and *Meditations*, 'Sceptiques' is employed. In some of Descartes' early letters, 'Pyrrhoniens' are discussed. Lastly, the characters in *La Recherche* may be patterned after those in La Mothe Le Vayer's *Dialogues*, which Descartes probably read in 1630, in that they have similar names and somewhat similar views. La Mothe Le Vayer wrote a 'Dialogue traittant de la philosophie Sceptique,' whose personages are Eudoxus and Ephestion, whereas Descartes employed Polyander, Epistemon and Eudoxus as his characters. The author will treat the question of the possible date of *La Recherche* in a future study. For Cassirer's views, see his 'La place de la "Recherche de la Vérité par la lumière naturelle" dans l'oeuvre de Descartes,' in *Revue Philosophique de la France et de l'Étranger*, CXXVII, (1939), pp. 261-300; and for Gouhier's, his 'Sur la date de la Recherche de la Vérité de Descartes', in *Revue d'Histoire de la Philosophie*, III (1929), pp. 1-24.

25. Descartes, *Discours*, in *Oeuvres*, A.-T. VI, p. 18.

26. Cf. Charron, *Sagesse*, Book II, chap. ii; Sabrié, *De l'humanisme au rationalisme*, pp. 303-21; and Popkin, 'Charron and Descartes', *Jour., of Philos.*, LI (1954), p. 832.

27. Descartes, *La Recherche de la vérité par la lumière naturelle*, in *Oeuvres*, A.-T. X, p. 512.

28. Professor Alexandre Koyré has brought to my attention that this novel contribution of Descartes' to sceptical argumentation is attributed to Montaigne by Pascal in his 'Entretien de Pascal avec Saci sur Épictète et Montaigne', in *Oeuvres de Blaise Pascal*, edited by Brunschvicg, Boutroux et Gazier (Grands Ecrivains de la France), Tome IV (Paris 1914), p. 43.

29. Descartes, *Discours*, in *Oeuvres*, A.-T. VI, p. 32.

30. Descartes, *Meditations*, I in *Oeuvres*, A.-T. IX, p. 16.

31. Cf. Pascal, *Pensées* (Classiques Garnier), no. 434; and Hume, *Enquiry concerning Human Understanding*, Selby-Bigge ed. (Oxford 1951), Sec. XII, pp. 149-50.

32. Pascal, *Pensées* (Classiues Garnier), no. 434, p. 184. The late Professor A.G.A. Balz suggested to me that the possibility of God being a deceiver, discussed in Meditation IV, raises even more far-reaching doubt, and that only at this level are our rational faculties rendered dubious. It seems to me that the *malin génie* hypothesis and the deceptive God possibility differ in degree but not

in kind. The demon has sufficient power to accomplish a complete overthrowing of all standards. The deceptive God renders the situation cosmic and completely irremediable. The first is the misery of man without God; the second the eternal ruin of man if God is the Devil.

33. Descartes, *Entretien avec Burman* (Paris 1937), pp. 4–5; and *Oeuvres*, A.-T. V, p. 147.

34. Descartes, *Regulae ad directionem ingenii*, in *Oeuvres*, A.-T. X, pp. 362–6, and *Philosophical Works*, I, pp. 3–5.

35. Descartes, *Discours*, ed. Étienne Gilson, p. 290 of the commentary by Gilson.

36. Gouhier, *Essais sur Descartes*, pp. 146–8, and 294–6.

37. A completely contrary interpretation of Descartes' doubt and the nature of the Cartesian system appears in Willis Doney's interesting article, 'The Cartesian Circle', in *Journal of the History of Ideas*, XVI (1955), pp. 324–38, where it is contended that Descartes throughout his works maintained the view in the *Regulae*, that he never saw the necessity of a metaphysical justification of the use of reason, and that the highest level of doubt raised, even in the *Meditations*, is with regard to the reliability of memory rather than the truth of clear and distinct ideas. In Doney's interpretation, a radically different reading of many of the texts I have cited is offered. I do not think a definitive justification can be given for one interpretation rather than another, but that one has to examine the key passages in question and decide which reading is more in keeping with an overall interpretation of the nature and structure of Descartes' philosophy. My own views are obviously colored by placing the writings of Descartes' views in the light of the type of sceptical and counter-sceptical arguments then current. And, by and large, I believe that my interpretation of the radical nature of Descartes' scepticism of the First Meditation is in keeping with the analyses of Gilson, Gouhier, Koyré, and others, who have argued for several decades for the primacy of metaphysical and theological considerations in the philosophy of Descartes. (This is not to suggest that I believe any of these authorities would agree with my evaluation of the merits of Descartes' answer to scepticism.) As indicated by previous citaitons, these authorities find a development of radical scepticism with regard to reason in the *Discours* and *Meditations* that goes beyond the views of the *Regulae*, and which requires a radically different foundation for the certitude of human reason than that earlier proposed.

38. On the trial of Loudun, see Aldous Huxley, *The Devils of Loudun* (New York 1952); Bayle, *Dictionnaire*, art. 'Grandier', Mersenne, *Corespondance*, IV, pp. 192, 198 and 230; and the letter of Ismael Bouillard to Gassendi, 7 September 1634, published by P. Tamizey de Larroque in *Cabinet historique*, Series II, vol. III (1897), pp. 1–14. See also Michel de Certeau, *La possession de Loudun* (Paris 1970). It is interesting to note that in Pierre Du Moulin's *Elements de la logique françois* (of 1625), an example is given on p. 12 of an enunciation, 'God is not a liar.'

39. Cf. Gouhier, 'Doute méthodique ou négation méthodique?', in *Études Phil.*, IX, pp. 135–62. It is interesting in this regard that Gassendi, in commenting on the First Meditation, could not see why Descartes considered it necessary to regard everything as false, and to feign that God might be a deceiver, or that a demon might be on the loose, instead of merely indicating what things are uncertain. Cf. Gassendi, *Objectiones Quintae*, in Descartes, *Oeuvres*, A.-T. VII, pp. 256–7.

40. Descartes, *Discours*, in *Oeuvres*, A.-T. VI, p. 29.

41. Descartes, *The Search after Truth by the Light of Nature*, in *Philos. Works of Descartes*, I, p. 320. The Latin text is in *Oeuvres*, A.-T. X, pp. 519-20.
42. Descartes, letter to ***, March 1638, in *Oeuvres*, A.-T. II, p. 38.
43. Para du Phanjas, *Théorie des êtres insensibles*, p. 209.
44. Descartes, *Discours*, in *Oeuvres*, A.-T. VI, p. 32.
45. Cf. Descartes, *Reponses de l'avtevr avx secondes objections, Oeuvres*, A.-T. IX, pp. 110-1. This passage seems to be the most forceful one in favor of Doney's interpretation, in that Descartes asserts that knowledge of the existence of God is not required to know some truths with certainty. The sole example offered is the *cogito*, which Descartes insists is not the conclusion of a syllogism with the major premise, *'that everything that thinks is, or exists.'* Rather, the *cogito* is known by itself, by 'a simple act of mental vision.'
46. Descartes, 'Raisons qvi provvent l'existence de Diev & la distinction qvi est entre l'esprit & le corps hvmain, disposées d'vne façon geometrique', in *Reponses de l'avtevr avx secondes objections, Oeuvres*, A.-T. IX, pp. 124-32, esp. pp. 125-7.
47. Descartes, *Meditations*, III, *Oeuvres*, A.-T. IX, p. 27.
48. Descartes, *Les Principes de la Philosophie, Oeuvres*, A.-T. IX, Part I, sec. 45, p. 44.
49. Descartes, *Meditations*, III, *Oeuvres*, A.-T. IX, pp. 32-3, and *Reponses de l'avtevr avx secondes objections, Oeuvres*, A.-T. IX, p. 128.
50. Descartes, *Responses de l'avtevr avx secondes objections, Oeuvres*, A.-T. IX, pp. 127 (where Descartes contended that after following his method one would see that his axioms are 'true and indubitable'), and 128 (where axiom V is defended by stating, 'we have to note that the admission of this axiom is highly necessary for the reason that we must account for our knowledge of all things, both of sensuous and of non-sensuous objects).
51. Descartes, *Meditations*, III, *Oeuvres*, A.-T. IX, pp. 33-6, and *Reponses de l'avtevr avx secondes objections, Oeuvres*, A.-T. IX, p. 129 (Proposition II).
52. In Descartes' reply to the objections submitted by Mersenne, he said that after the proof of God's existence, and our realization of our total dependence on Him, the only way we can cast doubt on the ideas which we conceive clearly and distinctly is to suppose that God might be a deceiver. And if this were a serious possibility, then we could rely on neither our faculties nor our clear and distinct ideas. See *Reponses de l'avtevr avx secondes objections, Oeuvres*, A.-T. IX, p. 113.
53. Descartes, *Meditations*, IV, Oeuvres, A.-T. IX, pp. 42-3.
54. *Ibid.*, p. 42.
55. Cf. Descartes, *Meditations*, V and VI, *Oeuvres*, A.-T. IX, pp. 42-56.
56. Descartes, *Reponses de l'avtevr avx secondes objections, Oeuvres*, A.-T. IX, p. 111.
57. Doney offers a quite different interpretation of the passage about the atheist mathematician, in his 'Cartesian Circle', p. 337. He states that Descartes holds that the atheist can have certain knowledge of single truths, or simple demonstrations, but he could, 'have no real certainty about mathematics considered as a body of true propositions.' However, Descartes seems to me to go much further in asserting that the atheist 'cannot be sure that he is not deceived in the things that seem most evident to him.' Hence, even with regard to single truths and simple deductions, the atheist cannot be certain, since the demon has not been exorcised from his universe. The atheist knows that the three angle of a tri-

angle equal two right angles in a sense quite different from the religious mathematician, for whom this is true knowledge. The atheist may know this in the same sense that ordinary people know snow is white. They think it is so, they believe it, but it still may be false.

58. Descartes, *Principles, Oeuvres,* A.-T. IX, Part. I, sec. 43, p. 43.

59. Descartes, *Entretien avec Burman,* pp. 4–5, and *Oeuvres,* A.-T. V, p. 146.

60. I am using the term 'subjective certainty' to apply to one's mental state, one's psychic feelings when one knows or is certain that, e.g., 2 + 2 = 4. 'Objective truth' refers to whether, regardless how one feels, 2 + 2 does actually equal 4.

61. Jean-Baptiste Cochet, *La Clef des sciences & des beaux-arts, ou la logique* (Paris 1750), p. 58.

CHAPTER X: Sceptique Malgré lui

1. Adrien Baillet, in his *La Vie de M. Des Cartes* (Paris, 1691), 2ᵉ part., p. 92, reported that Voetius regarded his crusade against Descartes as a defense of religion in opposition to 'a Sceptic and an Atheist.' Voetius even tried to get Mersenne to join forces with him since the latter had been so outspoken against scepticism and atheism.

2. Letter of S.P. to Descartes, Feb. 1638, in Descartes, *Oeuvres,* A.-T. I, pp. 511-17.

3. The objections of Pierre Petit were printed from a manuscript in the Bibliothèque Nationale by Cornélis de Waard, in his 'Les objections de Pierre Petit contre le Discours et les Essais de Descartes', *Revue de Métaphysique et de Morale,* XXXII (1925), pp. 53-89.

4. De Waard, 'Les Objections de Pierre Petit', pp. 72-5. Descartes had a very low opinion of this criticism. Cf., *ibid.,* p. 64.

5. Descartes, Letter to Dinet, in *Philosophical Works,* II, p. 354. The Latin original is in *Oeuvres,* A.-T. VII, p. 573.

6. Father Bourdin, as cited in Descartes, *The Seventh Set of Objections,* in *Philos. Works,* II, pp. 318-9; *Oeuvres,* A.-T. VII, pp. 528-9.

7. Bourdin, in Descartes, *Philos. Works,* II, pp. 273-4 and 318; *Oeuvres,* A.-T. VII, pp. 469-70 and 528.

8. Bourdin, in Descartes, *Philos. Works,* II, p. 319; *Oeuvres,* A.-T. VII, p. 529.

9. Bourdin, in Descartes, *Philos. Works,* II, pp. 287-305 and 319-20; *Oeuvres,* A.-T., VII, pp. 488-509 and 529-30.

10. For details on this matter, see Descartes' Letter to Dinet, in *Philos. Works,* II, pp. 361-76; *Oeuvres,* A.-T., VII, pp. 582-603. For information about the philosophical views and careers of Voetius and Schoockius, see Paul Dibon, *La Philosophie néerlandaise au siècle d'or,* Tome I (Amsterdam 1954), and C. Louise Thijssen-Schoute, *Nederlands Cartesianisme* (Amsterdam 1954).

11. Martinus Schoockius and Gisbert Voetius, *Admiranda Methodus Novae Philosophiae Renati Des Cartes* (Ultraiecti 1643).

12. *Ibid.,* p. 2.

13. *Ibid.,* pp. 30 and 172-80.

14. *Ibid.,* p. 254.

15. *Ibid.*, pp. 245–54.
16. Martinus Schoockius, *De Scepticismo Pars Prior, sive Libri Quatuor* (Groningen, 1652), Lib. I, pp. 1–76.
17. *Ibid.*, Lib. II, pp. 88–9.
18. *Ibid.*, Lib. II, pp. 90–9.
19. *Ibid.*, Lib. III-IV.
20. The latter opponent seems to have bothered him most. Cf. Descartes' letter to Colvius, 23 April 1643, in *Oeuvres*, A.-T., III, p. 647, where Descartes said that after reading the *Admiranda*, 'I left the heavens for a few days, and used up a bit of paper to try to defend myself from the wrongs done to me on earth.'
21. Descartes, *Epistola Renati Des Cartes ad Celeberrimum Virum D. Gisbertum Voetium*, in *Oeuvres*, A.-T., VII B, pp. 169–71; and Letter to Dinet, in *Philosophical Works*, II, pp. 358–9; *Oeuvres*, A.-T., VII, pp. 578–80.
22. Gabriel Daniel, *A Voyage to the World of Cartesius*, translated by T. Taylor (2nd edition) (London 1694), p. 84. Descartes' method is discussed on pp. 76–92.
23. Cf. Pierre-Daniel Huet, *Censura Philosophiae Cartesianae* (Paris 1689); and *Censure de la reponse faite par M. Regis au livre inst\u0001tulé Censura Philosophie Cartesianae, par Theocrite De La Roche, Seigneur de Pluvigny*, Bibliothèque Nationale Mc. Fr. 14703, no. 3, chap. 1, fols. 22–113.
24. Although the second set of objections is listed as having been gathered by Mersenne, it may be by him, since it reflects his 'mitigated scepticism'.
25. Gassendi, *The Fifth Set of Objections*, in Descartes, *Philos. Works*, II, p. 152. The discussion of this topic is on pp. 151–2. The Latin original is in Descartes, *Oeuvres*, A.-T., VII, pp. 278–9.
26. Gassendi, *Fifth Objections*, in Descartes, *Philos. Works*, II, p. 152; and Descartes, *Oeuvres*, A.-T., VII, pp. 278–9.
27. Cf. the arguments of St. François de Sales against the Reformers, cited in Chap. IV.
28. Descartes, *The Author's Reply to the Fifth Set of Objections*, in *Philos. Works*, II, p. 214, and *Oeuvres*, A.-T., VII, p. 361.
29. *Ibid.*, *Philos. Works*, II, p. 226, and *Oeuvres*, A.-T., VII, p. 379. Craig Brush thinks Descartes can escape devastation by this objection. See his *Montaigne and Bayle*, p. 171, n. 1.
30. Descartes, *Seventh Set of Objections*, in *Philos. Works*, II, p. 279, and *Oeuvres*, A.-T., VII, p. 477.
31. Descartes, *Principles*, Partie I, sec. 43, in *Oeuvres*, A.-T., IX B, p. 43, 'we are by nature so disposed to give our assent to things that we clearly perceive, that we cannot possibly doubt of their truth. . . . ' See also Benedictus de Spinoza, *The Principles of Descartes' Philosophy* (La Salle, Ill., 1943), Part I, prop. xiv, p. 46; and Descartes, *Reponses de l'avtevr avx Secondes Objections*, in *Oeuvres*, A.-T., IX A, pp. 113–4.
32. Mersenne, *Secondes Objections*, in Descartes, *Oeuvres*, A.-T., IX A, pp. 99–10.
33. *Ibid.*, p. 100.
34. Descartes, *Reponses de l'avtevr avx Secondes Objections*, in *Oeuvres*, A.-T., IX A, p. 113. Descartes observes here that 'I here perceive that you are still entangled in the difficulties which I brought forward in the first Meditation, and which I thought I had in the succeeding Meditaitons removed with sufficient care.'
35. *Ibid.*, pp. 113–4.

36. *Ibid.*, p. 114.

37. Descartes, *Lettre de Monsievr Des-Cartes à Monsieur C.L.R.*, in *Oeuvres*, A.-T., IX A, pp. 211-2.

38. *Ibid.*, p. 212.

39. This appears in the ten volume English edition of Bayle's *Dictionary*, in the article on 'Cartes (René Des)' which is not by Bayle. The portion discussed here is taken from the sceptical work of Thomas Baker, *Reflections on Learning*, (4th edition) (London 1708), p. 73.

40. Bayle, *Dictionary*, Eng. edition (London 1734-40), art. 'Cartes (René Des),' Rem. AA.

41. Antoine Arnauld, *Quatriemes Objections*, in Descartes, *Oeuvres*, A.-T., IX A, p. 166.

42. On Descartes' rather perplexing answer to Arnauld's charge, and Descartes's contention that no circle actually occurs, see Descartes, *Réponses de l'avtevr aux Quatriémes Objections*, in *Oeuvres*, A.-T., IX A, pp. 189-90. Gouhier has recently published an interesting defense of Descartes on this point in the *Etudes Philosophiques*, XI (1956), 'La véracité divine dans la Méditation V,' pp. 296-310. See also Doney, 'The Cartesian Circle'.

43. Arnauld, *La Logique ou l'art de penser*, edited by L. Barré (Paris 1859), Part. IV, chap. vi, p. 329.

44. Nicholas Malebranche, *Reponse du Pere Malebranche, Prestre de l'Oratoire, a la troisième lettre de M. Arnaud, Docteur de Sorbonne, touchant les idées & les plaisirs*, in *Receuil de toutes les réponses du P. Malebranche à M. Arnauld*, Tome IV (Paris 1709), p. 51.

45. *Ibid.*, pp. 51-2. The quotation is on p. 52.

46. Descartes, *Seventh Set of Objections*, in *Philos. Works*, II, p. 279, *Oeuvres*, A.-T., VII, pp. 476-7; and *Entretien avec Burman*, pp. 4-5.

47. Descartes, *Troisième Objections faites par vn celebre Philosophe Anglois, avec les résponses de l'auteur*, in *Oeuvres*, A.-T., IX A, pp. 133-4; *Seventh Set of Objections*, in *Philos. Works*, II, p. 277, and *Oeuvres*, A.-T., VII, pp. 473-4; *Letter to Dinet*, in *Philos. Works*, II, p. 355, and *Oeuvres*, A.-T., VII, pp. 573-4; and *Notes Directed against a certain Programme published in Belgium*, in *Philos. Works*, I, p. 448, and *Oeuvres*, A.-T., VIII B, p. 367; and Johann Clauberg, *Opera Omnia Philosophica* (Amsterdam 1691), pp. 1311ff. See also Gouhier, 'Doute méthodique ou négation méthodique?', pp. 157-62.

48. Descartes, *Seventh Set of Objections*, in *Philos. Works*, II, p. 333, and *Oeuvres*, A.-T., VII, p. 546.

49. Hume, *Enquiry Concerning Human Understanding*, edited by Selby-Bigge, Sec. XII, pp. 149-50.

50. Descartes, Letter to Elisabeth, 28 June 1643, in *Oeuvres*, A.-T., III, p. 69.

51. Samuel Sorbière, *Lettre et Discours de M. Sorbiere sur diverses matieres curieuses* (Paris 1660), pp. 690-1.

52. Pascal, *Pensées*, Brunschvicg ed., nos. 374, 387, 395, 432 and 434.

53. Quoted in Christoph. Matt. Pfaff, *Dissertationes Anti-Baelius* (Tubingen 1719), I, pp. 3n-4n.

54. See, for instance, the review of Villemandy's *Scepticismus debellatus* in the *Histoire des Ouvrages des Savans*, Feb. 1697, pp. 240-50, esp. pp. 241-2.

55. Cf. Gabriel Wedderkoff, *Dissertationes duae quarum prior de Scepticismo profano et sacro praecipue remonstrantium. . . . posterior de Atheismo praeprimis Socinianorum* (Argentorati 1665), p. 3; Joh. Valent. Bützer, *Q.D.B.V. de Scepticorum Praecipuis Hypothesibus* (Kiloniens 1706), p. 4 ('The first author of

Scepticism is the devil'); and Ephraim Chambers, *Cyclopaedia*, Vol. II (London 1743), art. 'Scepticism.'

56. For a brief survey of the course of scepticism from the time of Descartes to Bayle, see Popkin, 'The High Road to Pyrrhonism' in *American Philosophical Quarterly*, II (1965), pp. 1–15.

CHAPTER XI: Isaac La Peyrère

1. See François Garasse's works discussed in chap. vi, pp. 114–16; and Jean Duvergier du Hauranne's (Saint-Cyran) answer, pp. 116–118.

2. The most detailed picture of La Peyrère's life appears in Jean-Paul Oddos. *Recherches sur la vie et l'oeuvre d'Isaac La Peyrère* (1596?–1676). Thése de 3ᵉᵐᵉ Cycle, (Grenoble 1974); see also Pintard, *Le Libertinage érudit*, pp. 355–61, 379, 399, 420–24, and 430; and R. H. Popkin, 'The Marrano Theology of Isaac La Peyrère', in *Studi Internazionali di Filosofia*, V (1973), pp. 97–126.

3. Early in his career, in 1626, he was accused of atheism and impiety, but was acquitted by the French Reformed Synod. No information is known about the charges. Cf. Bibliothèque Nationale Ms. Fonds Français 15827, fols. 149 and 162.

See the interpretations of Don Cameron Allen, *The Legend of Noah* (Urbana 1963), pp. 86–90 and 130–37; David R. McKee, 'Isaac de la Peyrère, a Precursor of the eighteenth Century Critical Deists', in *Publications of the Modern Languages Association*, LIX (1944), pp. 456–485; and Pintard, *Le Libertage érudit*, pages cited in Note 2.

4. Paul Oskar Kristeller, 'The Myth of Renaissance Atheism and the French Tradition of Free Thought', in *Journal of the History of Philosophy*, VI (1968).

5. A letttter of Gabriel Naudé to Cardinal Barberini in 1641, Bibl. Vat. Barberini, Latin 6471, fol. 22v, indicated that *Prae-Adamitae* had already been completed, and because Cardinal Richelieu had banned it, people were trying to obtain copies of it.

6. Cf. Popkin, 'The Marrano Theology of Isaac La Peyrère'.

7. La Peyrère's debt to Postel and the similarity of their universalistic message will be disucssed in a volume being prepared by Prof. Marion Daniels Kuntz and myself.

8. La Peyrère seems to have worried about whether Cain's wife could have been a descendent of Adam and Eve. See his "Proeme" to *A Theological System upon the Presupposition that Men were before Adam*, (the second part of *Men before Adam*) (n.p. 1656), and *Prae-Adamitae* (n.p. [Amsterdam] 1655).

In developing his case, especially in Book III, La Peyrère cited material he got from Boulliard, Gassendi, La Mothe Le Vayer, and especially from Julius Scaliger and Claude Saumaise. On his ancient and modern sources, see Popkin's 'The Development of Religious Scepticism and the Influence of Isaac La Peyrère's Pre-Adamism and Bible 'Criticism' in *Classical Influences on European Culture*, AD *1500–1700*, (Cambridge 1976); and Anthony Grafton, 'Joseph Scaliger and Historical Chronology: The Rise and Fall of a Discipline', in *History and Theory*, XIV (1975), esp. pp. 176–77 and note 83.

9. This Judeo-centric theory is developed principally in Books IV and V of *Prae-Adamitae*.

10. This is the central thesis of *Du Rappel des Juifs* (Paris 1643). It is summarized at the end of Book V of *Prae-Adamitae*.

11. La Peyrère, *Men before Adam*, Book III, chap. 1, p. 204-5. Since there are several different printings of *Prae-Adamitae*, it does not help to give the references to the original. They can easily be found since the chapter order is the same in the English translation as in the Latin original.

12. *Ibid.*, Book III, chap. 1, p. 208.

13. Thomas Hobbes, *Leviathan*, Part III, chap. xxxiii, p. 369 in Molesworth edition of the *English Works of Thomas Hobbes* (London 1839), Vol. III.

14. See books I-IV of *Prae-Adamitae*.

15. Menasseh ben Israel, *Conciliador* ([Frankfort] Amsterdam 1632). The remaining parts were published up to 1651.

16. On the earlier discussions of the pre-Adamite theory, see Popkin "The Pre-Adamite Theory in the Renaissance," in Edward P. Mahoney, ed. *Philosophy and Humanism, Renaissance Essays in Honor of Paul Oskar Kristeller* (Leiden 1976), pp. 50-54.

17. La Peyrère, 'A Discourse upon the twelfth, thirteenth, and fourteenth Verses of the Fifth Chapter of the Epistle of the Apostle Paul to the Romans', in *Men before Adam*, especially chap. viii, pp. 22, and chap. xxvi, pp. 60-61.

18. Cf. Popkin, 'The Marrano Theology of Isaac La Peyrère', pp. 104-05. Ismael Boulliard claimed, after the book was published, that he had advised La Peyrère not to print it. See his letter to Portnero, Dec. 3, 1655, Bibliotheque Nationale Fonds français 13041, fol. 179.

19. Popkin, 'Marrano Theology', pp. 104-05 and notes thereto.

20. Le Duc d'Aumale, *Histoire des Princes de Condé*, Tome VI (Paris 1892), p. 699; and Popkin, 'Marrano Theology', p. 105 and note 55.

21. Sven Stolpe, *Christina of Sweden* (New York 1966), p. 130. The author states that when Queen Christina read La Peyrère's manuscript, "she persuaded the author to have it printed without delay". Pintard, in *Le Libertinage Érudit*, pp. 399 and 420 suggests Christina was responsible for the publication of *Prae-Adamitae*.

22. La Peyrère, *Lettre de la Peyrère à Philotime* (Paris 1658), pp. 114-118.

23. Condemnation of the President and Council of Holland/Zeeland, The Hague, November 26, 1655. The British Library has a copy of this document.

24. La Peyrère's *Lettre à Philotime*, pp. 123-24. The work was also condemned in Rome and Paris. Cardinal Grimaldi said it was "un livre tres pernicieux [parce] que la doctrine qu'il contient est damnable, contraire à la parole de Dieu & à l'Escripture Sainte", Bibl. Nat. Coll. Baluze 325, fol. 63-66.

La Peyrère's friend, Gilles Menage, asked him to send him the book 'avant qu'il fût mis en lumière", *Menagiana*, Tome III (Paris 1729), p. 68.

25. No complete list of refutations has been compiled. Besides works that are totally devoted to refuting *Prae-Adamitae*, there are sections in a large variety of theological, historical and philosophical works offering answers.

26. Samuel Desmarets, *Refutatio Fabulae Prae Adamiticae* (Groningen 1656), which had two editions. This was the only criticism that La Peyrère answered, in a still unpublished work that Prof. Paul Dibon and I intend to edit.

27. This appears in Diderot's *Encyclopedie*, art. "Pré-Adamites".

28. Cited in Christian Huygens's *Journal de voyage à Paris et à Londres, Oct. 1660-Mai 1661*, and in H. L. Brugman's, *Le Sejour de Christian Huygens à Paris* (Paris 1935), entry for 21 Février 1661. La Peyrère told Huygens what he, La Peyrère, had been told by the General of the Jesuit order when he was in Rome.

29. Hugo Grotius, *Dissertatio altera de origine Gentium Americanarum adversus obtractatorem* (n.p., 1643), pp. 13-14. Grotius was apparently shown an early

manuscript by Father Mersenne, who admired La Peyrère's work including his theology.

La Peyrère answered Grotius in Book IV, chap. XIV, of *Prae-Adamitae* (p. 275 of *Men Before Adam*).

30. Letter of Richard Simon to La Peyrère, in Simon, *Lettres choisies de M. Simon*, Tome II (Rotterdam 1702), pp. 12–13.

31. Sir Matthew Hale, *The Primitive Origination of Mankind* (London 1677), p. 185.

32. Louis Ellies-Du Pin, *Nouvelle Bibliothèque des Auteurs Ecclesiastiques* (2nd edition), Tome I (Paris 1690), p. 4.

33. *Ibid.*, p. 30.

34. Louis Cappel, *Theses theologicae de summo controversiarium judice* (Sahn. [Sedan] 1635), sect. xxxiv, p. 107 and sect. xxxix, p. 109; *Arcanum punctationis revelatum* (n.p. 1624), Book II, chap xii reprinted in *Commentarii et notae criticae in Vetus Testamentum* (Amsterdam 1689), p. 794ff; and *Critica adversus injustem censorem, justa defensio* in *Critica sacra*, edited by Vogel (Halle 1775-1786), Tome III, p. 327.

I am grateful to Prof. Jean-Pierre Pittion of Trinity College, Dublin, for pointing out these passages to me, and for letting me see part of his unpublished study on Louis Cappel.

35. Thomas Paine, *The Age of Reason, Part the Second, being an Investigation of True and Fabulous Theology* (London 1795), p. 14.

36. David Levi, *Letters to Dr. Priestley in Answer to his Letters to the Jews, Part II, occasioned by Mr. David Levi's Reply to the Former Part* (London 1789), pp. 14–15.

37. Popkin, 'Marrano Theology', p. 107 and notes 73 and 74. While he was in jail a Papal letter declared La Peyrère was "un heritique detestable", cf. La Peyrère, *Lettre à Philotime*, p. 130.

38. This is reported in the biography of La Peyrère that Richard Simon wrote for a M.Z.S., in Simon's *Lettres choisies*, Tome II, pp. 24–25.

39. Pintard, *Le Libertinage érudit*, p. 422, based on Condé's papers.

40. La Peyrère, *Apologie de La Peyrère* (Paris 1663), pp. 1–7.

41. *Ibid.*, pp. 42–43.

42. La Peyrère, *Lettre à Philotime*, p. 139.

43. Cf. La Peyrère, *Recueil des lettres escrites à Monsieur le Comte de la Suze, pour l'obliger par raison à se faire Catholique* (Paris 1661), pp. 55–62, and 101–112, where La Peyrère lists the views he now abjures. See also La Peyrère, *Apologie*, pp. 40–58, and *Lettre à Philotime*, pp. 111–113.

When La Peyrère converted to Catholocism, it was said a large number of Protestants would also convert. Le Comte de Suze seems to have been the only actual convert.

44. La Peyrère, *Lettre à Philotime*, pp. 105–107; and *Apologie*, pp. 20–23.

45. La Peyrère, *Lettre à Philotime*, pp. 142–168.

46. Richard Simon, letter to M.Z.S., *Lettres choisies*, Tome II, pp. 24–25.

47. See Richard Simon's six letters to La Peyrère, 1670-71, in *Lettres choisies*, Tome II, pp. 1–23 and Tome IV, pp. 36–45; and Simon's letter to M.Z.S., Tome II, pp. 24ff.

48. La Peyrère's *Apologie* was published during this period, as was the letter to the Count de Suze. The work on Iceland, *Relation d'Islande*, (Paris 1663),

complements the earlier *Relation du Groenland* (Paris 1647), both written as letters to François de Mothe Le Vayer. These works were composed during La Peyrère's stay in Scandinavia, 1644-47, and made him the leading authority on the Eskimos of the time.

49. Simon, and Bayle's informant, Jean Morin du Sandat (Bayle's *Dictionnaire*, art. Peyrère, Isaac La, Rem. B.)

50. This is the letter to M.Z.S. Tome II.

51. Cf. Simon's letters to La Peyrère, 1670-71, *Lettres choisies*, Tome II, pp. 1-23, and IV pp. 36-45. The matter about Adam having dies of gout had already appeared in *Prae-Adamitae*.

52. Michel de Marolles, *Le Livre de Genese*, p. 2.

53. There are copies of this rare work at the Bibliothèque Nationale and the British Library. Details about its suppression are given in Niceron, *Memoires pour servir à l'histoire des hommes illustres*, Tome XX, (Paris 1732), p. 43. Although Marolles had given La Peyrère some data that appeared in *Prae-Adamitae*, Marolles did not accept the theory and claimed it was self-refuting. Cf. Michel de Marolles, *Memoires* (Amsterdam 1755), pp. 63-70, and 234-36.

54. La Peyrère sent Simon his manuscript in May 1670; Simon told him it was unprintable, in *Lettres choisies*, Tome II, pp. 12-13.

55. On this see Simon, letter to M.Z.S., Tome II, p. 26.

56. The manuscript of this interesting work is in the Prince of Condé's collection at Chantilly, Ms. 191 (698). Simon indicated that La Peyrère was afraid that after his demise the Fathers of the Oratory would sacrifice his opus to Vulcan. Therefore the manuscript was put away in the Prince de Condé's library. Simon, *Lettres choisies*, II, p. 26.

57. Quoted in Bayle, *Dictionnaire*, art. Peyrère, Isaac La, Rem. B. The original is in the Royal Library of Copenhagen in their collection of letters to Bayle.

58. Cited in Simon's letter to M.Z.S., *Lettres choisies*, II, p. 30.

59. Cited in Gilles Ménage, *Menagiana* (Paris and Amsterdam 1715), Vol. III, p. 69.

60. The earliest I can find is in Morgan Godwyn's, *The Negro's and Indian's Advocate* (London 1680) where he described the pre-Adamite theory being used by Virginia planters to justify their views towards Africans. The studies listed in note 62 discuss the latter use of pre-Adamism in racist theorizing and practice.

61. On Simon and Vico see Popkin, 'Bible Criticism and Social Science', in *Boston Studies in the Philosophy of Science*, XIV, pp. 344-45 and 347-350 and notes. The influence of La Peyrère on Spinoza is discussed below, and also in my article 'La Peyrère and Spinoza', in R. Shohan and J. Biro, eds., *Spinoza: New Perspectives* (Norman, Okla., 1978), pp. 177-195.

62. See Popkin, 'The Philosophical Bases of Modern Racism', in *Philosophy and the Civilizing Arts Essays presented to Herbert W. Schneider on his eightieth birthday*, edited by Craig Walton and John P. Anton (Athens, Ohio 1974), pp. 126-65; and 'Speculative Biology and Racism: Pre-Adamism in Early Nineteenth Century American Thought', in *Philosophia*, VIII (1978), 205-239.

63. Cf. Popkin, 'La Peyrère, the Abbé Grégoire and the Jewish Question in the Eighteenth Century', in *Studies in Eighteenth Century Culture*, Vol. IV (1975), pp. 209-222.

64. Winchell's book which was first published in Chicago in 1880, and

reprinted a couple of times thereafter, offers, facing the title-page, photographs of Pre-Adamites. The pictures are of a Dravidian, a Mongolian, a Negro, an Eskimo, a Hottentot, a Papuan, and an Australian aborigine.

65. I am preparing a volume on La Peyrère and the history of the pre-Adamite theory.

66. The Reverand Thomas Smyth, *The Unity of the Human Races proved to be the Doctrine of Scripture, Reason and Science* (Edinburgh 1851), p. 35.

67. Simon blamed La Peyrère for Spinoza's heresies. 'Il [Spinoza] ne parôit pas même qu'il ait fait beaucoup de reflexion sur la matière qu'il traitoît, s'étant contenté souvent de suivre le Système mal digére de la Peyrère Auteur des Préadamites', in Richard Simon, *De l'Inspiration des Livres Sacrés* (Rotterdam 1687), p. 48.

68. On Simon's theory see Popkin, 'Biblical Criticism and Social Science', pp. 347-50 and notes; and 'Scepticism, Theology and the Scientific Revolution in the Seventeenth Century' in *Problems in the Philosophy of Science*, edited by I. Lakatos and A. Musgrave (Amsterdam 1968), pp. 23-25.

69. See the list of Spinoza's books in Jacob Freudenthal, *Die Lebensgeschichte Spinoza's* (Leipzig 1899); Item 54 is "Prae-Adamitae 1655".

70. For a list of some of the borrowings, see Leo Strauss, *Spinoza's Critique of the Bible* (New York 1965), p. 264 and 327. Chapter three of this study is devoted to analyzing La Peyrère's contribution, concluding as I and Hans Joachim Schoeps do (in *Philosemitismus in Barok*, (Tugingen 1952), pp. 3-18) that La Peyrère's theory is basically that of a Marrano, i.e., a Jewish convert to Christianity, and that La Peyrère was probably himself a Marrano.

71. The only information about La Peyrère's stay in Amsterdam comes from a letter he wrote Ismael Boulliard in Feb. 16, 1661. The only person La Peyrère mentions meeting was the secretary to the Queen of Poland. Cf. Philippe Tamizey de Larroque, *Quelques lettres inédites d'Isaac de la Peyrère à Boulliau* (Paris and Bordeaux 1878), p. 24.

72. Menessah ben Israel's letter of Feb. 1, 1655, published in Paul Felgenhauer's *Bonum Nunciam Israeli quod offertur Populo Israel & Judae in hisce temporibus novissimus de MESSIAH* (Amsterdam 1655), pp. 89-90.

73. See the 'Beschluss' to Felgenhauer's *Anti-Prae-Adamitae*, pp. 89-90.

74. Felgenhauer's is the *Anti-Prae-Adamitae* identified in the previous footnote. In it Felgenhauer argued that only Jesus was a pre-Adamite, since he was before all men and after them.

Menasseh ben Israel listed in his *Vindiciae Judaeorum* (London 1656), in his works that are "ready for the Presse", p. 41, *Refutatio libri qui titulus Prae-Adamitae*. This work never appeared and no manuscript has been found.

75. Cf. Popkin, "Menasseh ben Israel and Isaac La Peyrère', in *Studia Rosenthalia*, VIII, pp. 59-63.

76. I. S. Révah, 'Aux Origines de la Rupture Spinozienne: Nouveaux documents sur l'incroyance d'Amsterdam à l'époque de l'excommunication de Spinoza', in *Revue des études juifs*, Tome III (XXIII) (1964), pp. 370-73 and 391-408.

77. I. S. Révah, *Spinoza et Juan de Prado* (Paris, The Hague 1959), esp. pp. 84-153.

78. Révah, 'Aux origines de la Rupture Spinozienne', pp. 378 and 393.

79. Révah, *Spinoza et Juan de Prado*, p. 43.

80. Révah, *Spinoza et Juan de Prado*, pp. 31-32 and 64 (where the Spanish text is given).

CHAPTER XII: Spinoza's Scepticism

1. Benedictus de Spinoza, *Opera Quotquot reperta sunt*, edited by J. Van Vloten and J. P. N. Land, Tomus secundus (The Hague 1914), *Tractatus Theologico-Politicus*, p. 89; *The Chief Works of Benedict de Spinoza*, translated by R. H. M. Elwes (New York 1955), *Tractatus*, p. 8.
2. Elwes translation, p. 9; Latin text, p. 90.
3. Elwes translation, p. 13; Latin text, p. 93.
4. Elwes translation, p. 25; Latin text, p. 106.
5. Elwes translation, p. 27; Latin text, p. 107.
6. Elwes translation, p. 25; Latin text, p. 107.
7. Elwes translation, p. 28; Latin text, p. 108.
8. Elwes translation, p. 28; Latin text, pp. 108-09.
9. Elwes translation, pp. 29-30; Latin text, pp. 110-111.
10. Elwes translation, p. 33; Latin text, p. 113.
11. Elwes translation, p. 40; Latin text, p. 120.
12. This school of English and Dutch theologians was given its theoretical foundation in Joseph Mede's *Clavis Apocalyptica* (Cambridge 1632). Many important English theologians including Sir Isaac Newton, in his *Observations upon the Prophecies of Daniel, and the Apocalypse of St. John* (London 1733), and William Whiston, Newton's successor, followed the interpretative framework laid down by Mede.
13. Elwes translation, p. 61; Latin text, p. 137.
14. Elwes translation, p. 61; Latin text, pp. 137-38.
15. Elwes translation, p. 83: Latin text, p. 158.
16. Elwes translation, p. 82; Latin text, p. 157.
17. Elwes translation, p. 85; Latin text, pp. 159-60.
18. Elwes translation, p. 99; Latin text, p. 172.
19. Elwes translation, p. 99; Latin text, p. 172.
20. See, for instance, Descartes's letter to the Doctors of the Sorbonne, prefixed to the *Meditaitons*, entitled 'To the most wise and illustrious the Dean and the Doctors of the Sacred Faculty of Theology', Haldane-Ross, Vol. I, pp. 133-37; A.-T., Vol. VII, pp. 1-6.
21. Pascal, *Oeuvres complètes* (Paris 1963), preface by Henri Gouhier, and notes of Louis Lafuma, 'Le Mémorial', p. 618. 'Dieu d'Abraham, Dieu d'Isaac, Dieu de Jacob, non des philosophes et des savants'.
22. Cf. Etienne Gilson, *Études sur le rôle de la pensée médiévale dans la formation du système cartésian*, and *La Liberté chez Descartes et la théologie*; Henri Gouhier, 'La Crise de la Théologie au temps de Descartes, and *La Pensée religieuse de Descartes*; and Alexandre Koyré, *Essai sur l'idée de Dieu et les preuves de son existence chez Descartes*.
23. See for example, the criticisms of Descartes by the Jesuit Father Bourdin and by the Calvinists Martinus Schook and Gisbert Voetius. Bourdin's criticism appears in 'Objectiones Septimae, cum notis authoris' A.-T., Vol. VII, pp. 451-561. Schook's and Voetius' criticism appears in *Admiranda methodus novae philosophiae Renati DesCartes*.
24. Descartes' answer to Father Bourdin appears in 'Objectiones Septimae cum notis authoris', A.-T., Vol. VII, pp. 451-561, and Descartes' complaining letter to Father Dinet, the Jesuit Provincial, A.-T. Vol. VII, pp. 563-603. His answer to Schook and Voetius is in 'Epistola Renati DesCartes ad Celeberremium virum D. Gisbertum Voetium', A.-T., Vol. VII-2 (Paris 1965).

Cartesians such as Geulincx, Arnauld, Malebranche and Bernard Lamy all claimed to be orthodox Catholics.

25. Cf. Footnote 79, chap. XI.

26. Cf. Spinoza, *Tractatus*, caput. vii, *"De Interpretatione Scripturae"*; and caput viii, 'In quo ostenditure, Pentateuchon et libros Josuae, Judicum, Rut, Samuëlis, et Regum non esse autographa, Deinde inquiritur, an eorum omnium Scriptores plures fuerint, an unus tantum, et quinam.'; Elwes translation, pp. 98-132.

27. Elwes translation, pp. 100-101, 119, 175-81 and 186-87; Latin text, pp. 173, 190, 237-243, and 247-48.

28. *Tractatus*, caps. vii-xiii.

29. Elwes translation, p. 190; Latin text, p. 250.

30. Elwes translation, pp. 114-118 and 190-191; Latin text, pp. 186-189, and 250-251.

31. Elwes translation, p. 197; Latin text, p. 256.

32. Elwes translation, pp. 192-199; Latin text, pp. 257-258.

33. On Simon, see A. Bernus, *Richard Simon et son Histoire Critique du Vieux Testament* (Lausanne 1869); Louis I. Bredvold, *The Intellectual Milieu of John Dryden* (Ann Arbor 1959), esp. pp. 98-107; Paul Hazard, *La Crise de la conscience européenne* (Paris 1935) Deuxième partie, chap. III, pp. 184-202; Henry Margival, *Essai sur Richard Simon et la critique biblique en France au XVIIe siècle* (Paris 1900); Jean Steinmann, *Richard Simon et les origines de l'exégèse biblique* (Paris 1960).

Simon's usual view about Spinoza was 'Spinoza a pû avancer dans son livre plusieurs choses veritables, qu'il aura mème prises de nos Auteurs mais il en aura tiré des consequences fausses et impies.' Richard Simon, *De l'Inspiration des Livres Sacrés* p. 43. One reason for Spinoza's bad results, according to Simon, was that Spinoza 'ne parôit meme qu'il ait fait beaucoup de reflexion sur la matière qu'il traitoît, s'étant contenté souvent de suivre le Système mal digeré de la Peyrere Auteur des Préadamites', p. 48.

34. Other false titles include *La Clef du Sanctuaire*, and *Reflexions curieuses d'un esprit des-interessé sur les matieres plus importantes au salut*. All these works were published in 1678 without any place of publication given.

35. See Spinoza's letter to Oldenburg, Summer of 1675, Elwes translation, Vol. II, pp. 296-97, letter xix (LXVIII); Latin text, Vol. III, pp. 218-219.

36. Henry More to Robert Boyle, letter of Dec. 4 [1670?], in *The Works of Robert Boyle*, edited by Thomas Birch (London 1772), Vol. VI, p. 514.

37. *Ibid.*, loc. cit.

38. As happened to Lessing and Jerusalem. See the article on Lessing by Henry Chadwick in the *Encyclopedia of Philosophy*, Vol. IV, pp. 443-446.

39. Pierre Bayle, *Dictionnaire historique et critique*, beginning of article 'Spinoza'.

40. *Ibid.*, main text just before Remark E.

41. Webster's *Third International Dictionary* gives as one of the three meanings of 'skeptic': 'a person marked by skepticism regarding religion or religious principles'; and one of the three meanings of 'skepticism': 'doubt concerning but not necessarily denial of the basic religious principles (as immortality, providence, revelation').

42. Letter LX (LVI) to Hugo Boxel, The Hague 1674, Elwes translation, Vol. II, p. 387; Latin text, Vol. III, p. 191.

43. Piero di Vona, 'Spinoza e lo scetticismo classico', in *Rivista critica di Storia della Filosofia*, Anno 1958, fasc. III, pp. 291-304.

44. Spinoza, *The Principles of the Philosophy of René Descartes*, in *Earlier Philosophical Writings*, translated by Frank A. Hayes (Indianapolis 1963), p. 13; Latin text, Vol. IV, p. 110.

45. Spinoza, *Principles of Descartes Philosophy*, Hayes translation, p. 13; Latin text, Vol. IV, p. 110.

46. Spinoza, *Principles*, Hayes translation, p. 13; Latin text, Vol. IV, p. 111.

47. *Ibid.*, Hayes translation, p. 17; Latin text, Vol. IV, p. 114.

48. *Ibid.*, Hayes translation, p. 20; Latin text, Vol. IV, p. 116.

49. *Ibid.*, Hayes translation, p. 33, Latin text, Scholium to Prop. VI, p. 126.

50. Spinoza, *Principles*, Part I, Prop. XIII and XIV.

51. Spinoza, *On the Improvement of the Understanding*, Elwes translation, Vol. II, p. 17; Latin text, *Tractatus de Intellectus Emendatione*, Vol. I, p. 14.

52. *Ibid.*, *loc. cit.*

53. *Ibid.*, *loc. cit.*

54. *Ibid.*, Elwes translation, p. 30; Latin text, I, p. 25.

55. *Ibid.*, Elwes translation, pp. 11-12; Latin text, I, pp. 10-11. I should like to thank Prof. J. N. Watkins of the London School of Economics for making me aware of the importance of these passages.

56. Spinoza, *Tractatus*, Elwes translation, p. 84; Latin text, II, p. 159.

57. *Tractatus*, Elwes translation, p. 270; Latin text, II, p. 315.

58. *Tractatus*, Elwes translation, pp. 84-85; Latin text, II, pp. 159-60.

59. Spinoza, *Ethica*, Elwes translation, pp. 114-15; Latin text, pp. 107-8.

60. *Ethics*, Elwes translation, p. 124; Latin text, I, p. 117.

61. This is the sixth axiom to the first book of Spinoza's *Ethics*.

62. Spinoza's letter to Albert Burgh, 1675, Elwes translation, Vol. II, p. 416; Latin text, III Epistola LXXVI, pp. 232-233.

63. *Ibid.*, Elwes translation, p. 416; Latin text, III, p. 233.

64. *Ibid.*, Elwes translation, pp. 416-417; Latin text, III, p. 233.

65. Spinoza, *Ethica*, Elwes translation, p. 77; Latin text, I, p. 69. (This and the following quote are from the appendix to Book I of the *Ethics*.)

66. *Ibid.*, Elwes translation, p. 80; Latin text, pp. 71-72.

67. The article, plus its long and numerous footnotes amounts to about three hundred ordinary pages.

68. Bayle, *Dictionnaire*, art 'Spinoza', remarks Q and T.

69. From 1792 onward the French Revolutionary government tried to eliminate all forms of traditional religion. The abbé Henri Grégoire, who fought for the 'liberté des cultes', claimed that this suppression was a social engineering experiment to create the society of atheists that Pierre Bayle had described, a society which would be more moral than a society of Christians. Cf. Grégoire, *Discours sur la liberté des cultes* (n.p. An III 1795) p. 1, and *Histoire des sectes religieuses*, Tome I (Paris 1828).

70. The final and best known version of the *Three Impostors* is attributed to Baron d'Holbach. On the *Three Impostors*, its history and possible authors see Don Cameron Allen, *Doubt's Boundless Sea* (Baltimore 1964), pp. 224-243; and Gerhard Bartsch, ed., *De Tribus Impostoribus* (Berlin 1960), 'Einleitung', pp. 5-38.

BIBLIOGRAPHY

A. PUBLISHED MATERIAL:

Adam, Antoine, *Theophile de Viau el la libre pensée française en* 1620, Paris: Librairie E. Droz, 1935.

Adam, Charles, *Vie de Descartes*, in *Oeuvres de Descartes*, edited by C. Adam & P. Tannery, Vol. XII, Paris: L. Cerf, 1910.

Agrippa von Nettesheim, Heinrich Cornelius, *Die Eitelkeit und Unsicherheit der Wissenschaften und die Verteidigungsschrift*, translated by Fritz Mauthner, München: G. Müller, 1913.

———, *Of the Vanitie and Uncertaintie of Artes and Sciences*, Englished by James Sanford, London: Henry Wykes, 1569.

Allen, Don Cameron, *Doubt's Boundless Sea: Skepticism and Faith in the Renaissance*, Baltimore: John's Hopkins Press, 1964.

———, *The Legend of Noah*, Urbana: Univ. of Illinois Press, 1963.

Anon., *Censure de la Sacree Faculté de Theologie de Paris, contre un livre intitulé La Somme Theologique des veritez capitales de la Religion Chrestienne, par R. P. François Garassus, & c.,* Paris: 1926.

Anon, 'Confession de Foi des Englises Protestantes de France-1559,' in Eug. et Em. Haag, *La France Protestante*, Tome X, Genève et Paris: J. Cherbuliez, 1858.

Anon., *De Tribus Impostoribus Anno MDICC*, edited by Gerhard Bartsch, Berlin: Akademie Verlag, 1960.

Anon., 'Pyrrhonism of Joseph Glanvill,' in *Retrospective Review*, I (1853) pp. 105-19.

Anon., Abstract and review of Valencia's *Academica, Bibliotheque Britannique*, XVIII (Oct.-Dec. 1741) pp. 60-146.

Anon., Review of Villemandy's *Scepticismus Debellatus*, in *Histoire des Ouvrages des Savans* (Feb., 1697) pp. 240-50.

Arnauld, Antoine, *La Logique ou l'art de penser*, edited by L. Barré, Paris: J. Delalain, 1859.

———, *De la necessité de la Foy en Jesus Christ pour étre sauvé*, Paris: C. Osmont (publié par L.-Ellies Dupin), 1701.

Aubrey, John, *'Brief Lives,' chiefly of Contemporaries, set down by John Aubrey, between the Years 1669 & 1696*, edited by Andrew Clark, Oxford: Clarendon Press, 1898.

Aumale, Henri d'Orléans, Duc de, *Histoire des princes de Condé*, Tome VI, Paris: Lévy frères, 1892.

Auvray, L., 'Lettres de Pierre Charron à Gabriel Michel de la Rochemaillet', in *Revue d'Histoire Littéraire de la France*, I (1894), pp. 308-29.

Aymonier, Camille, 'Un Ami de Montaigne: Le Jésuite Maldonat', in *Revue Historique de Bordeaux et du Départment de la Gironde*, XXVII (1935), pp. 5-29.

Bacon, Francis, *Of the Advancement and Proficiencie of Learning; or the Partitions of Sciences*, London: T. Williams, 1674.

———, *The Works of Francis Bacon*, edited by Spedding, Ellis, and Heath, Vol. VIII, Boston: Brown, 1863.

Bagot, Jean, *Apologeticus fidei*, Liber I, Parisiis: apud viduam N. Buon et D. Thierry, 1644.

Baillet, Adrien, *Vie de M. Descartes* (Collection Grandeurs, La Table Ronde), Paris: Table Ronde, 1946.

Balzac, Jean-Louis Guez de, 'Lettres de Jean-Louis Guez de Balzac,' pub. by Philippe Tamizey De Larroque, in *Collection de Documents inédits sur l'histoire de France, publiées par les soins de Ministre de l'Instruction Publique. Melanges historiques*, Tome I, Paris: (Imprimerie Impériale) Didot Frères, 1873.

———, *Les Oeuvres de Monsieur de Balzac*, Paris: T. Jolly, 1665.

Bayle, Pierre, *Dictionaire historique et critique*, Amsterdam, Leide, La Haye, Utrecht: P. Brunel, P. Humbert, etc., 1740.

———, *The Dictionary Historical and Critical*, English ed., (2nd edition), London: printed for J. J. and P. Knapton, etc., 1734-8.

Becker, Bruno, ed., *Autour de Michel Servet et de Sébastien Castellion*; *recueil*, Haarlem: H. D. Tjeenk Willink, 1953.

Bernus, Auguste, *Richard Simon et son Histoire Critique du Vieux Testament*, Lausanne: G. Bridel 1869.

Berr, Henri, *An jure inter Scepticos Gassendus numeratus fuerit*, Paris: Libraire hachette, 1898.

———, *Du Scepticisme de Gassendi*, trad. par B. Rochot, Paris: Albin Michel, 1960.

Bettenson, Henry, ed., *Documents of the Christian Church*, New York and London: Oxford Univ. Press, 1947.

Beza, Theodore, (Bèze), *A Discourse, of the True and Visible Marks of the Catholique Churche*, London: Robert Walde-Graue, 1582.

———, *De Haereticis a civili Magistratu puniendis libellus, adversis Martini Bellii farraginem, & Novorum Academicorum sectam*, n.p.: Oliva, R. Stephani, 1554.

Bierling, Friedrich W., *Commentatio de Pyrrhonismo Historico*, (Leipzig 1724).

Blanchet, Léon, *Les antécédents historiques du 'Je pense, donc je suis,* Paris: Alcan, 1920.

Bloch, Olivier, *La Philosophie de Gassendi*, International Archives of the Hhistory of Ideas, The Hague: Nijhoff, 1971.

Boas, George, *Dominant Themes of Modern Philosophy*, New York: Ronald Press, 1957.

———, *The Happy Beast in French Thought of the Seventeenth Century*, Baltimore: John Hopkins Press, 1933.

Boase, Alan Martin, *The Fortunes of Montaigne: A History of the Essays in France*, 1580-1669, London: Methuen & Co., 1935.

Bochart, Samuel, *Actes de la Conférence tenue à Caen entre Samuel Bochart & Iean Baillehache, Ministre de la Parole de Dieu en l'Église Réformée . . ., et François Véron, prédicateur des controverses, et Isaac Le Conte . . .,* 2 Tomes, Saumur: J. Lesnier et I. Desbordes, 1630.

Bodin, Jean, *De la Demonomanie des Sorciers . . .,* Paris: J. Du Puys, 1581.

Boucher, Jean, *Les Triomphes de la Religion Chrestienne*, Paris: L. Sonnius, 1628.

Boullier, David-Renaud, *Le Pyrrhonisme de l'Église Romaine . . .,* Amsterdam: J. F. Jolly, 1757.

Boyle, Robert, *The Works of Robert Boyle*, edited by Thomas Birch, London: J. and F. Rivington, 1772.

Bredvold, Louis I., *The Intellectual Milieu of John Dryden*, Ann Arbor: Univ. of Michigan Publications, Vol. XII, 1934–

Bremond, Henri, 'La Folle "Sagesse" de Pierre Charron', in *Le Correspondent*, CCLII (1913), pp. 357–64.

Brett, George S., *The Philosophy of Gassendi*. London: Macmillan, 1908.

Brugmans, Henri. L., *Le Sejour de Christian Huygens à Paris*, Paris: Libraire E. Droz, 1935.

Bruno, Giordano, *Çabala del Cavallo Pegaseo*, in *Opere Italienne . . .,* edited by Giovanni Gentile, 3 vols, Bari: Laterza, 1925-27.

———, *La Cena de le Ceneri*, in *Opere Italiane*, edited by Giovanni Gentile, 3 vols., Bari: Laterza, 1925-27.

Brunschvicg, Léon, *Descartes et Pascal, lecteurs de Montaigne*, New York and Paris: Brentano's, 1944.

Brush, Craig B., *Montaigne and Bayle, Variations on the Theme of Skepticism*, International Archives of the History of Ideas, Vol. 14, The Hague: Nijhoff, 1966.

Buckley, George T., *Atheism in the English Renaissance*, Chicago: University of Chicago Press, 1932.

Budé, Guillaume, *De Asse*, Paris: imprimebat M. Vascosanus Sibi, R. Stephano ac J. Roigny, affinibus suis, 1541.

Burtt, Edwin A., *The Metaphysical Foundations of Modern Physical Science*, New York: Doubleday (Anchor ed.), 1955.

Busson, Henri, *La Pensée religieuse française de Charron à Pascal*, Paris: Librairie Philosophique J. Vrin, 1933.

———, *Les Sources et le Développement du rationalisme dans la littérature française de la Renaissance* (1533-1601), Paris: Letouzey et Ané, 1922.

———, *Le Rationalisme dans la littérature française de la Renaissance* (1533-1601), Paris: J. Vrin, 1957. This is the revised edition of *Les sources et le développement.*

Bützer, Johann Valentin, *Q.D.B.V. de Scepticorum Praecipuis Hypothesibus*, Kiloniens: Litteris, B. Reutheri, 1706.

Cagnati, Marsilio, Veronesis Doctoris Medici et Philosophi, *Variarum Observationum Libri Quatuor . . .* , Romae: apud B. Donangelum, 1587.

Calvin, Jean, *Institution de la Religion Chrétienne*, edited by Frank Baumgartner, Genève et Paris: Beroud et Cie., 1888.

Campanella, Thomas, *The Defense of Galileo, Mathematician of Florence*, translated by Grant McColley, in *Smith College Studies in History*, XXII, Nos. 3-4, 1937.

Camus, Jean-Pierre, *L'Avoisinement des protestants vers l'Église romaine*, Paris: G. Alliot, 1640.

———, *La Démolition des fondemens de la doctrine protestante*, Paris: G. Alliot, 1639.

———, *Les Diversitez de Messire Jean Pierre Camus, Evesque & Seigneur de Bellay, Prince de l'Empire*, Tome IV, Paris: E. Foucault, 1610.

Cappel, Louis, *Arcanum punctationis revelatum*, (n. p. 1624).

———, *Critica sacra, sive de variis quae in Sacris Veteris Testamenti libris occurrunt lectionibus libri* VI, 3 vols., edited by J. L. Vogel, Halle: J. C. Hendel, 1775-86.

———, *Commentarii et notae criticae in Vetus Testamentum*, Amsterdam: P. and J. Blaeu, 1689.

———, *Theses theologicae de summo controversium judice*, Sedan 1635.

Carroll, Robert Todd, *The Common-Sense Philosophy of Religion of Bishop Stillingfleet 1635-1699*, International Archives of the History of Ideas, The Hague: Nijhoff, 1975.

Cassirer, Ernst, *Das Erkenntnisproblem in der Philosophie und Wissenschaft der neueren Zeit*, Berlin: Verlag Bruno Cassier, 1922.

———, 'La Place de la "Recherche de la Vérité par la lumière naturelle" dans l'oeuvre de Descartes,' *Revue Philosophique de la France et de l'Étranger*, CXXVII (1939), pp. 261-300.

Castellio, Sebastian (Castellion, Châteillon), *Concerning Heretics*, translated by Roland H. Bainton, New York: Columbia University Press, 1935-

———, (Martino Bellio, Pseud.), *De Haereticis* . . . , Magdeburgi: G. Rausch, 1554.

———, *De Arte Dubitandi*, in *Reale Accademia d'Italia, Studi e Documenti*, VII, *Per la Storia Degli Eretici Italiani del Secolo XVI in Europa*, edited by D. Cantimori e E. Feist, Roma (1937), pp. 307-430.

———, *De l'art de douter et de croire, d'ignorer et de savoir*, translated from Latin by Charles Baudouin and Pierre Raymond, Genève et Paris: Jeheber, 1953.

Centre international de synthèse, Paris, *Pierre Gassendi* 1592-1655, *sa vie et son oeuvre*, Paris: Éditions Albin Michel, 1955.

Certeau, Michel de, *La Possession de Loudun*, Paris: Juilliard, 1970.

Chadwick, Henry, 'Lessing, Gotthold Ephraim', in *Encyclopédia of Philosophy*, Vol. IV, New York: Macmillan Co., 1947, pp. 443-446.

Chamber, John, *A Treatise against Judicial Astrologie*, London: J. Harison, 1601.

Chambers, Ephraim, 'Scepticism,' in *Universal Cyclopedia*, Vol. II, London: D. Midwinter, Etc., 1743.

Chanet, Pierre, *Considerations sur la Sagesse de Charon*, Paris: C. Le Groult, 1643.

Charbonnel, J. Roger, *La Pensèe italienne au XVI siècle et le courant libertin*, Paris: Champion, 1919.

Charron, Jean D., 'Did Charron Plagiarize Montaigne?' in *French Review*, XXXIV (1961), pp. 344-51.

———, *The 'Wisdom' of Pierre Charron, An Original and Orthodox Code of Morality*, Univ. of North Carolina Studies in the Romance Languages and Literatures, No. 34, (Chapel Hill 1961).

Charron, Pierre, *Les Trois Véritez*, Paris: impr. de J. Du Corroy, 1595.

———, *Toutes les Oeuvres de Pierre Charron* . . . dernière edition, Paris: J. Villery, 1635.

Chesneau, Charles (Julien-Eymard d'Angers), *L'Apologétique en France de 1580 à 1670, Pascal et ses précurseurs*, Paris: Nouvelles éditions latines, 1954.

———, 'Le Fidéisme de J. Boucher, cordelier (1628),' *'Etudes franciscaines*, L., (1938), pp. 579-93.

————, *Le Père Yves de Paris et son temps* (1590-1678), 2 vols., Paris: Société d'histoire ecclésiastique de la France, 1946.

————, 'Un Précurseur de Pascal? Le Franciscain Jacques Du Bosc,' in *Dix-Septième Siécle*, No. 15 (1952), pp. 426-48.

————, 'Sénèque et le Stoïcisme dans l'oeuvre du cordelier J. Du Bosc,' in *Dix-Septième Siècle*, No. 29 (1955), pp. 353-77.

————, *Du Stoïcisme chrétien à l'humanisme chrétien: Les 'diversités' de J. P. Camus* (1609-1618), Meaux: Imprimerie André Pouyé, 1952.

————, 'Stoïcisme et "libertinage" dans l'oeuvre de François La Mothe Le Vayer', in *Revue des Sciences Humaines*, Fasc. 75 (Jul.-Sept. 1954), pp. 259-84.

————, 'Le stoicisme en France dans la première moitié du XVII siècle: les origines 1575-1616,' in *Études franciscaines*, II (1951), pp. 389-410.

————, Review of Henri Gouhier's article: 'La Crise de la théologie au temps de Descartes', in *Dix-Septième Siècle*, No. 28 (1955), p. 295-7.

————, Review of R. H. Popkin's *The History of Scepticism from Erasmus to Descartes*, in *Dix-Septième Siècle*, No. 59 (1963), pp. 105-09.

Chillingworth, William, *Additional Discourses of Mr. Chillingworth, never before Printed*, London: A. & J. Churchill, 1704.

————, *The Religion of the Protestants, a Safe Way to Salvation*, in *The Works of William Chillingworth*, London: A. Churchill, 1704.

Cicero, M. T. C., *Academiques*, Paris: Barbou Frères, 1796.

Clauberg, Johann, *Opera Omnia Philosophica*, Amsterdam: prostant apud Wolfgang, Janssonio-Waesbergios, Boom, A. Someron, et Goethals, 1691.

Clifford, Martin, *A Treatise of Humane Reason*, London: Henry Brome, 1675.

Cochet, Jean-Baptiste, *La Clef des sciences & des beaux- arts, ou la logique*, Paris: J. Desaint et C. Saillant, 1750.

Collins, James, *A History of Modern European Philosophy*, Milwaukee: Bruce Pub. Co., 1954.

Copleston, Frederick, *A History of Philosophy, Ockham to Suarez*, Vol. III, Westminster, Maryland: Newman Bookshop, 1953.

Coralnik, A., 'Zur Geschichte der Skepsis. I. Francisus Sanches', in *Archiv für Geschichte der Philosophie*, XXVII Neue Folge XX (1941), pp. 188-222.

Cotin, Charles, *Discours à Théopompe sur les Forts Esprits du temps*, n.p., 1629.

Daillé, Jean, *La Foy Fondée sur les Saintes Escritures: Contre les nouveaux methodistes* (2nd edition), Charenton: S. Périer, 1661.

————, *Traité de l'employ des Saints Pères, pour le jugement des differends qui sont aujourd'hui en la religion*, Genève: P. Aubert, 1632.

Dąmbska, Izydora, "Meditationes' Descartesa na tle Sceptycyzmu Francuskiego XVII Wieku,' in *Kwartalnik Filozoficny*, XIX (1950) pp.
1-24 (French summary, pp. 161-2).

————, *Sceptycyzm Francuski XVI i SVII Wieku, Towarzstwo Naukowe
Toruniv Prace Wydziału Fiologiczno-Filozoficznego*, Tom VII-Zeszyt
2 (Torun 1958).

Daniel, Gabriel, *A Voyage to the World of Cartesius*, translated by T.
Taylor, (2nd edition), London: T. Bennet, 1694.

Dedieu, Joseph, 'Montaigne et le Cardinal Sadolet,' in *Bulletin de Littérature Écclésiastique*, Ser. IV, vol. I (1909), pp. 8-22.

————, 'Survivances et influences de l'Apologétique traditionelle dans
les "Pensées,"' in *Revue d'Histoire Littéraire de la France*, XXXVII
(1930), pp. 481-513.

Degert, Antoine, 'Véron, Francois,' in *Catholic Encyclopedia*, Vol. XV,
New York: Robert Appleton Co., 1912, pp. 359-60.

Denis, Jacques, *Sceptiques ou libertins de la première moitié du XVIIe
siècle. Gassendi, Gabriel Naudé, Gui-Patin, La Mothe-Le Vayer,
Cyrano de Bergerac*, Caen: F. le Blanc-Hardel, 1884.

Descartes, René, *Discours de la Méthode, texte et commentaire par
Étienne Gilson*, Paris: J. Vrin, 1947.

————, *Entretien avec Burman*, Paris: Boivin et Cie., 1937.

————, *Oeuvres de Descartes*, pub. by Charles Adam & Paul Tannery,
12 vols., Paris: L. Cerf, 1897-1910.

————, *Philosophical Works*, edited by Haldane & Ross, 2 vols., New
York: Dover Publications, 1955.

Desmarets, Samuel, *Refutatio Fabulae Prae Adamiticae*, Groningen:
Bronchorst, 1656.

De Waard, Cornélius, 'Les Objections de Pierre Petit contre le Discours
et les Essais de Descartes,' in *Revue de Metaphysique et de Morale*,
XXXII (1925), pp. 53-89.

Dibon, Paul, *La Philosophie néerlandaise au siècle d'or*, Tome I,
Amsterdam: Elsevier, 1954.

Diderot, Denis, 'Pre-Adamites', in *Oeuvres complètes*, Vol. 16, Paris:
Garnier Frères, 1876.

Diogenes Laertius, *Lives of Eminent Philosophers*, translated by R. D.
Hicks, (Loeb Edition), vol. II, London: W. Heinemann, Cambridge,
Mass.: Harvard Univ. Press, 1950.

Di Vona, Piero, 'Spinoza e lo scetticismo classico', in *Rivista critica di
Storia della Filosofia*, Anno 1958, fasc III, pp. 291-304.

Doney, Willis, 'The Cartesian Circle', in *Journal of the History of Ideas*,
XVI (1955), pp. 324-338.

Dréano, Maturin, *La Pensée religieuse de Montaigne*, Paris: G. Beauchesne et ses fils, 1936.

Du Bosc, Jacques, *Le Philosophe indifférent*, Paris: A. De Sommaville et A. Courbé, 1643.

Du Moulin, Pierre, *Elements de la Logique Françoise*, Genève: P. Aubert, 1625.

Du Perron, Jacques Davy, *Les Diverses oeuvres de l'illustrissime Cardinal Du Perron . . .*, Paris: A. Estienne, 1622.

Du Pin, Louis Ellies, *Nouvelle Bibliothèque des Auteurs Ecclesiastiques* (2nd edition, Tome I, Paris: A. Pralard, 1690.

Du Pleix, Scipion, *Cours de philosophie. Reveu, illustré & augmenté*, Paris: C. Sonnius, 1632.

Duvergier de Hauranne, Jean (Saint-Cyran), *La Somme des fautes et faussetez capitales conteues en La Somme theologique de Pere François Garasse de la compagnie de Jesus*, Paris: J. Bouillerot, 1626.

Erasmus, Desiderius, *Inquisitio De Fide, Yale Studies in Religion, XV*, edited with introduction and commentary by Craig R. Thompson, New Haven: Yale Univ. Press, 1950.

———, *De Libero Arbitrio DIATRIBH*, Basileae: J. Frobenium, 1524.

———, *The Praise of Folly*, translation, introduction and notes by Leonard F. Dean, Chicago: Packard and Co., 1946.

Felgenhauer, Paul, *Anti-Prae-Adamitae*, Amsterdam: H. Betke, 1659.

———, *Bonum Nunciam Israeli quod offertur Populo Israel & Judae in hisce temporibus novissimus de MESSIAH*, Amsterdam: Typio Georii Trigge, 1655.

Feret, L'Abbé P., *La Faculté de Théologie de Paris et ses docteurs les plus célèbres, Époque moderne*, Tome IV, 'XVIIᵉ siècle, revue littéraire,' Paris: E. Picard et fils, 1906.

Ferguson, Robert, *The Interest of Reason in Religion, with the Import & Use of Scripture-metaphors; and the Nature of the Union betwixt Christ & Believers . . .*, London: D. Newmann, 1675.

Ferry, Paul, *Le Dernier désespoir de la tradition contre l'escriture, où est amplement refuté le livre du P. François Veron, iesuite, par lequel il prétend enseigner à toute personne, quoy que non versée en theologie, un bref & facile moyen de reietter la parole de Dieu et convaincre les églises reformees d'erreur et d'abus en tous et en chacun poinct de leur doctrine*, Sedan: Impr. de J. Jannon, 1618.

Formey, Jean-Henri-Samuel, *Histoire Abrégée de la Philosophe*, Amsterdam: H. Schneider, 1760.

Frame, Donald M., *Montaigne, A Biography*, New York, Harcourt Brace & World, 1965.

——, *Montaigne's Discovery of Man: The Humanization of a Humanist*, New York: Columbia Univ. Press, 1955.

——, 'What Next in Montaigne Studies?', in *French Review*, XXXVI (1963), pp. 577–87.

Frank, Adolphe, ed. *Dictionnaire des sciences philosophiques . . .* , (2nd edition) Paris: Hachette, 1875.

St. François de Sales, *Les Controverses* in *Oeuvres*, Tome I, Annecy: Impr. de J. Niérat, 1892.

——, *Lettres*, Vol. IV, in *Oeuvres*, Tome XIV, Annecy: Impr. J. Abry, 1906.

Freudenthal, Jacob, *Die Lebensgeschichte Spinoza's in Quellenscriften*, Leipsig: Konigl. Preussischen Akademie des Wissenschaften, 1899.

Galilei, Galileo, *Dialogo sopra i due massimi Sistemi del Mundi*, in *Le Opere de Galileo Galilei*, Edizione Nazionale; Firenze, G. Barbèra, 1929–39.

——, *Dialogue on the Great World Systems*, edited by Giorgio de Santillana, Chicago: Univ. of Chicago Press, 1953.

Galland, P., *Contra Novam Academicam Petri Rami Oratio*, Lutetiae: apud Vascos Anum, 1551.

Garasse, François, *Apologie du Pere Francois Garassus, de la Compagnie de Jesus, pour son livre contre les atheistes & libertins de nostre siecle, et reponse aux censures et calomnies de l'auteur anonyme*, Paris: S. Chappelet, 1624.

——, *La Doctrine curieuse des beaux esprits de ce temps, ou pretendus tels*, Paris: S. Chappelet, 1623.

——, *La Somme Theologique des veritez capitales de la Religion Chrestienne*, Paris: S. Chappelet, 1625.

Garin, Eugenio, *Der Italienische Humanismus*, Bern: A. Francke, 1947.

Gassendi, Pierre, *Lettres familières à François Lullier pendant l'hiver 1632–1633*, introduction & notes & index par Bernard Rochot, Paris: J. Vrin, 1944.

——, *Opera Omnia*, 6 vols., Lugduni: Sumptibus L. Anisson et J.-B. Devenet, 1658.

——, *Disquisito Metaphysica, seu Dubitationes et Instantiae adversus Renati Cartesii Metaphysicam et Responsa*, edited, with translation by Bernard Rochot, Paris: J. Vrin, 1959.

——, *Dissertations en forme de paradoxes contre les Aristoteliciens* (*Exercitationes Paradoxicae adversus Aristoteleos*), Book I and II, edited and translated by Bernard Rochot, Paris: J. Vrin, 1959.

———, *The Selected Works of Pierre Gassendi*, translated and edited by Craig Brush, New York: Johnson Reprint Corp., 1972.

Gilson, Étienne, *Études sur le rôle de la pensee médiévale dans la formation du système cartésien*, Paris: J. Vrin, 1930.

———, *La Liberté chez Descartes et la théologie*, Paris: F. Alcan, 1913.

Giran, Étienne, *Sébastien Castellion et la Réforme calviniste, les deux réformes*, Haarlem: Boisevain, 1913.

Glanvill, Joseph, *A Blow at Modern Sadducism in some Philosophical Considerations about Witchcraft*, London: Printed by E. C. for J. Collins, 1668.

———, *Essays on Several Important Subjects in Philosophy and Religion*, London: Printed by J. D. for J. Baker, etc., 1676.

———, ΛΟΓΟΥ ΘΡΗΣΚΙΑ *or, A Seasonable Recommendation and Defence of Reason, in the Affairs of Religion; against Infidelity, Scepticism, and Fanaticisms of all Sorts*, London: Printed by E. C. and A. C. for J. Collins, 1670.

———, *Scir^e tuum nihil est: or the Authors Defence of the Vanity of Dogmatizing; Against the Exceptions of the Learned Tho. Albius in his late Sciri . . . (A Letter to a Friend Concerning Aristotle)*, London: By E. Cotes for Henry Eversden, 1665.

Godwyn, Morgan, *The Negro's and Indian's Advocate*, London: Printed for the Author by J. D., 1680.

Gouhier, Henri, 'La Crise de la Théologie au temps de Descartes', in *Revue de Théologie et de Philosophie*, 3e Ser., IV (1954), pp. 19-54.

———, 'Doute méthodique ou négation méthodique?', *Études Philosophiques*, IX (1954), pp. 135-162.

———, *Essais sur Descartes*, Paris: J. Vrin, 1949.

———, *La Pensée religieuse de Descartes*, Paris: J. Vrin, 1924.

———, 'Sur la date de la Recherche de la vérité de Descartes,' *Revue d'Histoire de la Philosophie*, III (1929), pp. 1-24.

———, 'La Véracité divine dans la Méditation V,' in *Études Philosophiques*, XI (1956), pp. 296-310.

———, Review of Pintard's *Le Libertinage érudit* and *La Mothe Le Vayer, Gassendi, Guy Patin*, in *Revue Philosophique de la France et de l'Étranger*, CXXXIV (Jan.-Juin 1944), pp. 56-60.

———, *Les Premières pensées de Descartes, Contribution à l'histoire de l'anti-Renaissance*, Paris: J. Vrin 1958.

Grafton, Anthony;, 'Joseph Scaliger and Historical Chronology: The Rise and Fall of a Discipline,' in *History and Theory*, XIV (1975), pp. 156-185.

Gray, Floyd, 'Reflexions on Charron's Debt to Montaigne', in *French Review*, XXXV (1962), pp. 377-82.

Grégoire, Henri, *Discours sur la liberté des cultes*, n.p. An III (1795).

———, *Histoire des sectes religieuses*, Tome I, Paris: Baudouin Frères, 1828.

Gregory, Tullio, 'La Saggezza Scettica di Pierre Charron,' in *De Homine*, No. 21, pp. 163-182.

———, *Scetticismo ed empirismo; studio su Gassendi*, Bari: 1961 Editori Laterza.

Greenwood, Thomas, 'L'Éclosion du scepticisme pendant la Renaissance et les premiers apologistes,' *Revue de l'Université d'Ottawa*, XVII (1947), pp. 69-99.

———, 'Guy de Bruès', *Bibliothèque D'Humanisme et Renaissance*, XIII (1951), pp. 70-82, 172-86, and 266-69.

Grenier, Jean, 'Le Sceptique masqué: La Mothe Le Vayer,' in *Table Ronde*, XXII (1949), pp. 1504-13.

Grotius, Hugo, *De Jure Belli ac Pacis*, translated by Francis W. Kelsey, Oxford: Clarendon Press, 1925.

———, *Dissertatio altera de origine Gentium Americanarum adversus obtractatorem*, n.p., 1643.

Guilloton, Vincent, 'Autour de la Relation de voyage de Samuel Sorbière en Angleterre 1663-1664, in *Smith College Studies in Modern Languages*, XI, No. 4 (July 1930), pp. 1-29.

Haag, Eug. et Ém., *La France protestante* . . . , 10 vols., Paris, Genève: J. Cherbuliez, 1846-59.

Hale, Matthew, *The Primitive Origination of Mankind*, London: William Godbid for William Shrowsbury, 1677.

Hartnack, Daniel, *Sanchez Aliquid Sciens*, Stettin: apud J. Mamphrasium, 1665.

Hayer, Hubert, *La Règle de Foi vengée des Calomnies des Protestans et spécialement de celles de M. Boullier, Ministre Calviniste d'Utrecht*, Paris: Nyon, 1761.

Hazard, Paul, *La Crise de la Conscience européene, 1680-1715*, Paris: Boivin, 1935.

Herbert, Lord Edward, of Cherbury, *Autobiography*, (2nd edition), edited by Sidney Lee, London: G. Routledge & Sons, Ltd., 1906.

———, *De Veritate*, translated & introduction by Meyrick H. Carré, Bristol: pub. for the University of Bristol by J. W. Arrowsmith, Ltd., 1937.

Hess, Gerhard, 'Pierre Gassend. Der Französische Späthumanismus und das Problem von Wissen und Glauben,' in *Berliner Beiträge zur Romanischen Philologie*, Band IX, Heft 3/4 (1939), pp. 1-199.

Heydon, Sir Christopher, *A Defense of Judiciall Astrologie, In Answer to a Treatise lately Published by M. John Chamber. Wherein all those Places of Scripture, Councells, Fathers, Schoolemen, later Divines, Philosophers, Historics, Lawes, Constitutions, and Reasons drawne out of Sixtus Empiricus, Picus, Pererius, Sixtus Ab Heminga and others, against this Arte, are Particularly Examined: and the Lawfulness thereof, by Equivalent Proofes Warranted*, Cambridge: Printed by J. Legat, 1603.

Hirsch, Elizabeth Feist, 'Castellio's *De arte dubitandi* and the Problem of Religious Liberty,' *in Becker, Autour de Michel Servet et de Sebastien Castellion*, No. 23.

Hobbes, Thomas, *Elementa philosophica de Cive*, Amsterodami; L. Elzevirias, 1647.

——, *Leviathan*, in *English Works of Thomas Hobbes*, edited by Sir William Molesworth, London: J. Bohn, 1839.

Horowitz, Maryanne Cline, 'Complementary Methodologies in the History of Ideas', (a reply to A. Soman), in *Journal of the History of Philosophy*, XII (1974), pp. 501–509.

——, 'Pierre Charron's View of the Source of Wisdom', in *Journal of the History of Philosophy*, IX (1971), pp. 443–457.

Huet, Pierre-Daniel, *Censura Philosophiae Cartisianae*, Paris: apud D. Horthemels, 1689.

Hume, David, *Dialogues Concerning Natural Religion*, edited by Norman Kemp Smith, (2nd edition), London, New York, etc.: T. Nelson, 1947.

——, *Enquiry Concerning Human Understanding*, edited by Selby-Bigge, Oxford: Clarendon Press, 1955.

——, *A Treatise of Human Nature*, edited by Selby-Bigge, Oxford: Clarendon Press, 1949.

Huxley, Aldous, *The Devils of Loudun*, New York: Harpers, 1952.

Iriarte, J., 'Francisco Sánchez el Escéptico disfrazedo de Carneades en discusión epistolar con Cristóbal Clavio', *Gregorianium*, XXI (1940), pp. 413–451.

——, *Kartesischer oder Sanchezischer Zweifel*, Bonn: Bottrop, 1935.

Jovy, Ernest, *Pascal et Silhon (Etudes Pascaliennes II)*, Paris: J. Vrin, 1927.

Julien-Eymard d'Angers, See Chesneau, Charles (Julien-Eymard d'Angers).

Jurieu, Pierre, *Le Vray Système de l'Eglise et la veritable Analyse de la Foy*, . . . , Dordrecht: Vʳᵉ de Caspar et T. Goris, 1686.

Kibre, Pearl, *The Library of Pico Della Mirandola*, New York: Columbia Univ. Press, 1936.

Kiefl, F. X., 'Gassendi's Skepticismus und seine Stellung zum Material-ismus,' in *Philosophisches Jahrbuch der Görres-Gesellschaft*, VI (1893), pp. 23-34, 295-311, 361-73.

Kierkegaard, Søren, *Philosophical Fragments or a Fragment of Philosophy*, translated by David F. Swenson, Princeton: Princeton University Press, 1946.

Koyré, Alexandre, *Essai sur l'idée de Dieu et les preuves de son existence chez Descartes*, Paris: E. Leroux, 1922.

———, 'Le Savant', in Centre international de Synthèse, *Pierre Gassendi*, No. 63, pp. 59-70.

Kristeller, Paul Oskar, 'The Myth of Renaissance Atheism and the French Tradition of Free Thought', in *Journal of the History of Philosophy*, VI (1968), p. 233-43.

Lachèvre, Frédéric, *Le Prince des libertins du XVIIᵉ siècle: Jacques Vallée Des Barreaux, sa vie et ses poésies* (1599-1673), Paris: H. Leclerc, 1907.

———, *Le Procès du poète Théophile de Viau*, 2 vols., Paris: H. Champion, 1909.

La Mothe Le Vayer, François de, (Oratius Tubero, pseud.), *Cinq dialogues faits à l'imitation des anciens . . .* , par *Oratius Tubero*, Mons: P. De La Flèche, 1671.

———, *Cinq Dialogues faits à l'imitation des anciens, par Oratius Tubero. Nouvelle edition augmentée d'une refutation de la Philosophie Sceptique ou preservatif contre le Pyrrhonisme*, introduction by L. M. Kahle, Berlin: 1744.

———, *Deux dialogues faits à l'imitation des anciens*, intro. & notes by Ernest Tisserand, Paris: Editions Bossard, 1922.

———, *Oeuvres de François de La Mothe Le Vayer, Conseiller d'Estat Ordinaire*, 15 vols., Paris: L. Billaine, 1669.

Langius, Wilhelmus (Lang, Villum), *De Veritatibus geometricus, libri II. Prior contra Scepticos & Sextus Empiricum & posterior, contra Marcum Meibornium*, Copenhagen: literis P. Morsingii, 1656.

La Peyrère, Isaac, *Apologie de La Peyrere*, Paris: L. Billaine, 1663.

———, *Lettre de La Peyrère à Philotime*, Paris: A. Courbe, 1658.

———, *Men before Adam*, n.p. no printer, 1656.

———, *Prae-Adamitae*, n.p., 1655.

———, *Du Rappel des Juifs*, n.p., 1643.

———, *Recueil de lettres escrites à Monsieur le Comte de La Suze, pour l'obliger par raison à se faire Catholique*, Paris: S. Piget, 1661.

———, *Relation de l'Islande*, Paris: Billaine, 1663.

———, *Relation du Groenland*, Paris: Chez Augustin Courbe, 1647.

La Placette, Jean, *De Insanabili Romanae Ecclesiae Scepticismo, Dissertatio qua demonstratur nihil omnio esse quod firma fide persuadere sibi Pontificii possint*, G. Gallet, 1696.

———, *Of the Incurable Scepticism of the Church of Rome*, translated from French by T. Tenison, Archbishop of Canterbu;ry, London: Printed for R. Chiswel, 1688.

———, *Traité de l'autorité des Sens contre la Transsubstantiation*, Amsterdam, G. Gallet, 1700.

———, *Traité de la Conscience*, Amsterdam: G. Gallet, 1695.

Le Caron, Louis, *Le Courtisan second, ou de la vrai sagesse et des louanges de la philosophie*, in *Les Dialogues de Loys Le Caron . . .*, Paris: J. Longis, 1556.

Lecler, Joseph, 'Un Adversaire des libertins au début du XVIIᵉ siècle—Le P. François Garasse (1585-1631),' in *Études*, CCIX (1931), pp. 553-72.

Leclerc, J.-V., 'Sextus Empiricus,' in *Biographie Universelle*, Tome XLII, pp. 196-8, Paris: Michaud, 1825.

Leibniz, Gottfried Wilhelm von, *Essais de Théodicée sur la bonté de Dieu, la liberté de l'homme et l'Origine du Mal*, Amsterdam: I. Troyel, 1710.

Le Loyer, Pierre, *Discours et histoires des spectres, visions, et apparitions des esprits, anges, démons, et ames, se monstrans visible aux hommes*, Paris: N. Buon, 1605.

Lenoble, Robert, 'Histoire et physique. A propos des conseils de Mersenne aux historiens et de l'intervention de Jean de Launoy dans la querelle gassendiste', in *Revue d'Histoire des Sciences*, VI (1953), pp. 112-34.

———, *Mersenne ou la naissance du mécanisme* (Bibliothèque d'hishoirie de la philosophie), Paris: Vrin, 1943.

L'Estoile, Pierre de, *Mémoires-Journaux*, 12 vols., Tome Deuxième, *Journal de Henri III*, 1581-1586, Paris: Librairie des Bibliophiles. (A. Lemerre), 1888.

Levi, David, *Letters to Dr. Priestley in Answer to his Letters to the Jews, Part II, occasioned by Mr. David Levi's Reply to the Former Part*, London: Printed for the Author, 1789.

Limbruck, Elaine, 'Was Montaigne really a Pyrrhonian?', in *Bibliothèque d'Humanisme et Renaissance*, XXXIX (1977), pp. 67-80.

Lindeboom, J., 'La place de Castellion dans l'histoire de l'esprit,' in Becker, *Autour de Michel Servet et de Sebastien Castellion*, No. 23.

Lipse, Juste (Lipsius, Justus), *Manuductionis ad Stoicam Philosophiam libri tres . . .*, Antverpiae: ex Officina Plantiniana, apud J. Moretum, 1604.

Locke, John, *Works of John Locke*, London: W. Otridge and Son, etc., 1812.

Luther, Martin, *D. Martin Luther's Werke*, Weimar: H. Böhlau, 1883-1948.

Maldonatus, John (Maldonado, Juan), *A Commentary on the Holy Gospels*, (2nd edition), translated by G. J. Davie, London: J. Hodges, 1888.

———, *Opera varia Theologica*, Lutetiae Parisiorum: A. Praland, 1677.

Malebranche, Nicolas, *Reponse du Pere Malebranche, prestre de l'Oratoire, à la troisième lettre de M. Arnaud, Docteur de Sorbonne, touchant les idées & les plaisirs*, in *Recueil de toutes les réponses du P. Malebranche à M. Arnaud*, Tome IV, Paris: M. David, 1709.

Malvezin, Théophile, *Michel de Montaigne, son origine, sa famille*, Bordeaux: C. Lefebvre, 1875.

Marandé, Léonard de, *Jugement des actions humaines*, Paris: C. Cramoisy, 1624.

Margival, Henri, *Essai sur Richard Simon et la critique biblique en France au xviie siècle*, Paris: Maillet 1900.

Marolles, Michel de, *Le Livre de Genese*, n.p., n.d.

———, *Memoires*, Amsterdam (Paris), 1755.

McKee, David R., 'Isaac de la Peyrère, a Precursor of the Eighteenth Century Cricial Deists', in *Publications of the Modern Languages Association*, LIX (1944), pp. 456-485.

Mede, Joseph, *Clavis Apocalyptica*, Cambridge: Thomas Buck, 1632.

———, *The Works of Joseph Mede*, B.D., London: R. Norton for R. Royston, 1672.

Mellizo, Carlos, 'La Preoccupacion Pedagogica de Francisco Sanchez,' in *Cuadernos Salmantinos de Filosofia*, II (1975), pp. 217-229.

Ménage, Gilles, *Menagiana*, 4 vols., Paris: Chez la Veuve Delaulne, 1729.

Menasseh ben Israel, *Conciliador*, (Frankfort) Amsterdam, 1632.

———, *Vindiciae Judaeorum*, London: Printed by R. D., 1656.

Menendez y Pelayo, Marcelino, *Ensayos de Critica Filosofica*, (Vol. IX of his *Obras completas*), Madrid: 1918.

Mersenne, Marin, *Correspondance du P. Marin Mersenne*, publiée par Mme. Paul Tannery; editée et annotée par Cornelis De Waard; avec la collaboration de René Pintard, Tome I-Paris: G. Beauchesne et ses fils, 1932, Tome II—Paris: G. Beauchesne et ses fils, 1936, Tome III —Paris: Presses Universitaires, 1946, Tome IV—Paris: Presses Universitaires, 1955.

———, *L'Impieté des deistes, athees, et libertins de ce temps, com-*

battuë, et renversée de point en point par raisons tirees de la philosophie et de la theologie, Paris: P. Bilaine, 1624.

———, *Quaestiones celeberrimae in Genesim* . . . , Lutetiae Parisiorum: sumptibus S. Cramoisy, 1623.

———, *Questions Harmoniques. Dans lesquelle sont contenues plusieurs choses remarquables pour la morale, & pour les autres sciences*, (includes *Discours sceptique sur la musique*, by La Mothe Le Vayer), Paris: J. Villery, 1634.

———, *Questions inouyes ou recreation des scavans*, Paris: J. Villery, 1634.

———, *Les Questions theologiques, physiques, morales et mathematiques*, Paris: H. Guenon, 1634.

———, *La Verité des Sciences contre les septiques ou pyrrhoniens*, Paris: T. Du Bray, 1625.

Millet, J., *Histoire de Descartes avant* 1637, Paris: Didier & Cie, 1867.

Molière, Jean-Baptiste Poquelin, *Le Mariage Forcé*, in *Oeuvres de Molière* (*Les Grands Ecrivains de la France* series), Tome IV, Paris: Librairie Hachette, 1878.

Montaigne, Michel E. de, 'Apologie de Raymond Sebond', in *Les Essais de Michel de Montaigne*, edited by Pierre Villey, Paris: F. Alcan, 1922.

———, *The Essays of Michel de Montaigne*, translated & edited by Jacob Zeitlin, New York: A. A. Knopf, 1935.

———, *Journal de Voyage* . . . , edited & translated by Louis Lautrey, Paris: Hachette, 1909.

Montucla, Jean-Étienne, *Histoire des mathematiques*, 2 vols., Paris: A. Jombert, 1758.

Moreau, Joseph, 'Doute et Savoir chez Francisco Sanchez', *Portugiesische Forschungen des Görresgesellschaft*, Erste Reihe, *Aufsätze zur Portugiesischen Kulturgeschichte*, I. Band, (1960), pp. 24–50.

Moréri, Louis, *Le Grand Dictionnaire historique*, Paris: Les Libraires Associés, 1759.

Morize, André, 'Samuel Sorbière (1610-70)', in *Zeitschrift für französische Sprache und Literatur*, XXXIII (1908), pp. 214–65.

Morphos, Panos Paul, *The Dialogues of Guy de Brués, A Critical Edition with a Study in Renaissance Scepticism and Relativism, Johns Hopkins Studies in Romance Literatures*, Extra Volume XXX, Baltimore: Johns Hopkins Press, 1953.

Mutschmann, Hermann, 'Die Uberlieferung der Schriften des Sextus Empiricus', in *Rheinisches Museum für Philologie*, LXIV (1909), pp. 244–83.

Nashe, Thomas, *The Works of Thomas Nashe*, 5 vols., edited by Ronald B. McKerrow, London: Sedgwick, 1910.

Naudé, Gabriel, *Advice on Establishing a Library*, introduction by Archer Taylor, Berkeley & Los Angeles: Univ. of Calif. Press, 1950.

———, *Advis pour dresser une bibliotheque* . . . , Paris: F. Targa, 1627.

———, *Apologie pour les grands Hommes soupçonnez de Magie*, (dernière édition . . .), Amsterdam: P. Humbert, 1712.

———, *Naudaeana et Patiniana, ou Singularitez remarquables prises des conversationes de Mess. Naudé & Patin* (2nd edition) (ed. Pierre Bayle?), Amsterdam: F. van der Plaats, 1703.

Nauert, Charles G. Jr., 'Magic and Scepticism in Agrippa's Thought,' in *Journal of the History of Ideas*, XVIII (1957), pp. 161–82.

———, *Agrippa and the Crisis of Renaissance Thought*, Illinois Studies in the Social Sciences, Vol. 55, Urbana: Univ. of Illinois Press, 1965.

Newton, Isaac, *Observations upon the Prophecies of Daniel, and the Apocalypse of St. John*, London: J. Darby and T. Browne, 1733.

Niceron, Le P. Jean-Francois, *Memoires pour servir à l'histoire des hommes illustres*, Tome XX, Paris: Briasson, 1732.

Nicole, Pierre, *Les Prétendus Réformez convaincus de schisme*, . . . , Paris: G. Desprez, 1684.

Oddos, Jean-Peaul, *Recherches sur la vie et l'oeuvre d'Isaac La Peyrère, (1596?-1676)*, These de 3ème Cycle, Grenoble, 1974.

Ogier, François, *Jugement et censure du livre de La Doctrine curieuse de François Garasse*, Paris: n.p., 1623.

Olaso, Ezequiel de, review article of Schmitt's *Cicero Scepticus*, 'Las Academica de Cicerion y la Filosofia Renacentista', in *International Studies in Philosophy* VII (1975), pp. 57–68.

Olschki, Leonardo, 'Galileo's Philosophy of Science,' *Philosophical Review*, LII (1943), pp. 349–65.

Orcibal, Jean, *Les Origines du Jansénisme*, Tome II, Paris: Vrin & Louvain: Revue d'Histoire Ecclésiastique, 1947.

Owen, John, *The Skeptics of the French Renaissance*, London: S. Sonnenschein & New York: Macmillan, 1893.

Paine, Thomas, *The Age of Reason, Part the Second, being an Investigation of True and Fabulous Theology*, London: H. D. Symonds, 1795.

Para du Phanjas, Abbé François, *Théorie des êtres insensibles, ou cours complet de métaphysique, sacrée et profane, mise à la portée de tout le monde*, 5 vols., Paris: L. Cellot et A. Jombert, 1779.

Pascal, Blaise, *Oeuvres de Blaise Pascal*, edited by Brunschvicg, Boutroux et Gazier (*Grands Écrivains de la France*), Tome IV, Paris: Librairie Hachette, 1914.

————, *Pensées*, edited by Brunschvicg; introduction & notes by Ch.-Marc Des Granges, Paris: Éditions Garnier Frères, 1951.

————, *Oeuvres complètes*, preface by Henri Gouhier; edited by Louis Lafuma, Paris: Éditions de Seuil, Macmillan, 1963.

Patin, Gui (Guy), *Lettres de Gui Patin*, Tome I, edited by Dr. Paul Triaire, Paris: H. Champion, 1907.

————, *Correspondance de Gui Patin, extraits publiés, avec une notice bibliographique*, edited by Armand Brette, Paris: A. Colin, 1901.

————, *Naudaeana et Patiniana* . . . (same as no. 238).

Pattison, Mark, *Isaac Casaubon, 1559–1614* . . . , second edition, Oxford: Clarendon Press, 1892.

Peiresc, Nicolas-Claude Fabri de, *Lettres de Peiresc*, . . . , publiées par Philippe Tamizey de Larroque, Tome IV in *Collections de documents inédits sur l'histoire de France, 2ᵉ sér., Paris: Impr. nationale, 1893.*

Pellisson-Fontanier, Paul, Réflexions sur les différends de la religion . . . , Paris: G. Martin, 1686.

Perrens, François-Tommy, *Les Libertins en France au XVIIᵉ siècle*, Paris: C. Levy, 1899.

Pfaff, Christoph. Matt., *Petrus Baelius . . . in Dictionario historico et critico . . . evidentiam veritatis criterium haud esse probaturus . . . provocat*, Tubingen: n.p., 1719. (Also called *Dissertationes Anti-Baelius*).

Pic, Pierre, *Guy Patin*, Paris: G. Steinheil, 1911.

Pico Della Mirandola, Gian Francesco, Joannis Francisci Pici Mirandulae Domini, et Concordiae Comitis, *Examen Vanitatis Doctrinae Gentium, et Veritatis Christianae Disciplinae. Distinctum in Libros Sex, quorum Tres omnen Philosophorum Sectam Universim, Reliqui Aristoteleam et Aristotelis Armis Particulatim Impugnant Ubicunque Autem Christiana et Asseritur et Celebratur Disciplina*, Mirandulae: Impressit I. Maciochus Bundenius, 1520.

Pico Della Mirandola, Gian Francesco, *Opera Omnia*, Basle: ex officina H. Petrina, 1572–73.

Pico Della Mirandola, Giovanni, *Disputationes Adversus Astrologiam Divinatricem*, edited by Eugenio Garin (Edizione Nazionale), Firenze: Vallecchi, 1946–52.

Pintard, René, 'Descartes et Gassendi', *Travaux du IXᵉ Congrès internationale de philosophie* (Congrès Descartes), II, part. ii, 1937, (*Actualities scientifiques et industrielles*, No. 531), pp. 115–22.

————, *La Mothe le Vayer, Gassendi, Guy Patin, Études de biographie et de critique suivies de textes inédits de Guy Patin*, Paris: Furne, Boivin et Cⁱᵉ, 1943.

318   Bibliography

—————, *Le Libertinage érudit dans la première moitié du XVIIe siècle*, Paris: Boivin, 1943.

—————, 'Modernisme. Humanisme, Libertinage, Petite suite sur le "cas Gassendi",' *Revue d'Histoire Littéraire de la France*, 48 année (1948), pp. 1-52.

Pinvert, Lucien, 'Louis Le Caron, dit Charondas, (1536-1613)', in *Revue de la Renaissance*, II (1902), pp. 1-9, 69-76 and 181-8.

Popkin, Richard H., 'Bible Criticism and Social Science', in *Boston Studies in the Philosophy of Science*, XIV (1974), pp. 339-360.

—————, 'Charron and Descartes: The Fruits of Systematic Doubt', in *Journal of Philosophy*, LI (1954), pp. 831-7.

—————, 'Charron, Pierre', in *Encyclopedia Britannica, Micropedia*, (15th edition), 1975, II, p. 770.

—————, 'A curious Feature of the French Edition of Sextus Empiricus', in *Philological Quarterly*, XXXV (1956), pp. 350-2.

—————, 'The Development of Religious Scepticism and the Influence of Isaac La Peyrère: Pre-Adamism and Biblical Criticism', in *Classical Influences on European Culture*, edited by R. R. Bolgar, Cambridge: Cambridge Univ. Press, 1976, pp. 271-80.

—————, 'Father Mersenne's War against Pyrrhonism', in *Modern Schoolman*, XXXIV (1956-7), pp. 61-78.

—————, 'The High Road to Pyrrhonism', in *American Philosophical Quarterly*, II (1965), pp. 1-15.

—————, articles in *The Encyclopedia of Philosophy*, ed. Paul Edwards, New York: The MacMillan Co. & The Free Press, 1965; 'Henricus Cornelius Agrippa von Nettesheim', I, pp. 60-61; 'Pierre Charron', II, pp. 81-83; 'Desiderius Erasmus', III, pp. 42-44; 'Pierre Gassendi', III, pp. 269-273; 'François de La Mothe Le Vayer', IV, pp. 382-383; 'Marin Mersenne', V, pp. 282-283; 'Michel Eyquem de Montaigne', V, pp. 366-368; 'Francisco Sanches', VII, pp. 278-280; and 'Skepticism', VII, pp. 449-61.

—————, introduction to Olms photoreproduction edition of Heinrich Cornelis von Nettesheim, *Opera*, Col. I, pp. v-xxii, Hildesheim: Georg Olms Verlag, 1970.

—————, 'Hume and Kierkegaard', in *Journal of Religion*, XXXI (1951), pp. 274-81.

—————, 'Kierkegaard and Scepticism', in *Algemeen Nederlands Tijdschrift voor Wijsbegeerte en Psychologie*, LI (1959), pp. 123-41.

—————, 'La Peyrère and Spinoza', in R. Shahan and J. Biro, *Spinoza: New Perspectives* (Norman, Okla. 1978), pp. 177-195.

—————, 'La Peyrère, the Abbé Grégoire and the Jewish Question in the

Eighteenth Century', in *Studies in Eighteenth Century Culture* IV (1975), pp. 209-222.

———, 'The Marrano Theology of Isaac La Peyrère', in *Studi Internazionali di Filosofia*, V (1973), pp. 97-126.

———, 'Menasseh ben Israel and Isaac La Peyrère', in *Studia Rosenthalia*, VIII, pp. 59-63.

———, 'The Philosophical Bases of Modern Racism', in *Philosophy and the Civilizing Arts: Essays presented to Herbert W. Schneider on his eightieth birthday*, edited by Craig Walton and John P. Anton, pp. 126-165. Athens, Ohio: Ohio Univ. Press, 1974.

———, 'The Pre-Adamite Theory in the Renaissance', in *Philosophy and Humanism, Renaissance Essays in Honor of Paul Oskar Kristeller*, edited by E. P. Mahoney, pp. 50-69. Leiden: Brill, 1976.

———, Review of Gassendi's *Dissertations en forme de paradoxes contre les Aristoteliciens, (Exercitationes Paradoxicae Adversus Aristoteleos)*, in *Isis*, LIII (1962), pp. 413-5.

———, Review of Eugene F. Rice, Jr.'s *The Renaissance Idea of Wisdom*, in *Renaissance News*, XII (1959), pp. 265-9.

———, Review of Sanches's *Opera Philosophica*, Carvalho ed., in *Renaissance News*, X (1957), pp. 206-8.

———, 'Samuel Sorbière's Translation of Sextus Empiricus', in *Journal of the History of Ideas*, XIV (1953), pp. 617-21.

———, *'Scepticisme et Contre-Reforme en France,'* Recherches et Debats du Centre Catholique des intellectuels français, Cahier No. 40 (*Essais sur Teilhard de Chardin*), Oct. 1962, pp. 151-84.

———, 'Skepticism and the Counter-Reformation in France,' *Archiv für Reformations-geschichte*, LI (1960), pp. 58-87.

———, 'Scepticism, Theology and the Scientific Revolution in the Seventeenth Century', in *Problems in the Philosophy of Science*, edited by I. Lakatos and A. Musgrave, Amsterdam: North-Holland, 1968, pp. 1-39.

———, 'Speculative Biology and Racism: Pre-Adamism in Early Nineteenth Century American Thought', in *Philosophia*, VIII (1978) 205-239.

———, 'Theological and Religious Scepticism', in *Christian Scholar*, XXXIX (1956), pp. 150-8.

Prat, J.-M., S. J., *Maldonat et l'Université de Paris au xvie siècle*, Paris: Julien, Lanier, et Cie, 1856.

Den President ende Raden ober Holland/Zeelant The Hague, Nov. 26, 1655. (Condemnation of La Peyrère's *Prae-Adamitae*.

Rabelais, François, *Le Tiers Livre*, edited by Jean Plattard, Paris: Fernand Roches, 1929.

————, *Oeuvres de François Rabelais*, edition critique publiée sous la direction de Abel Lefranc, texte et notes par H. Clouzot, P. Delaunay, J. Plattard et J. Porcher, Paris: H. Champion, 1931.

————, *The Urquhart-Le Motteux Translation of the Works of Francois Rabelais*, edited by A. J. Nock and C. R. Wilson, New York: Harcourt, Brace and Co., 1931.

Révah, I. S., 'Aux Origines de la Rupture Spinozienne: Nouveaux documents sur l'incroyance dans la communauté judéo-portugoise d'Amsterdam a l'époque de l'excommunication de Spinoza', in *Revue des Études juifs*, III (CXXIII), 1964, pp. 357-431.

————, *Spinoza et Juan de Prado*, Paris and the Hague: Mouton, 1959.

Rice, James Van Nostrand, *Gabriel Naudé 1600-1653*, in *Johns Hopkins Studies in Romance Literatures and Languages*, XXXV, Baltimore: The Johns Hopkins Press, 1939.

Richter, Raoul, *Der Skeptizismus in der Philosophie und seine Überwindung*, Vol. II Leipzig: Verlag der Dürr'schen Buchhandlung, 1908.

Rochot, Bernard, 'Le Cas Gassendi', in *Revue d'Histoire Littéraire de la France*, 47e année (1947), pp. 289-313.

————, 'Gassendi et la "logique" de Descartes', in *Revue Philosophique de la France et de l'Étranger*, année LXXX (1955), pp. 300-8.

————, 'Gassendi et le Syntagma Philosophicum', *Revue de Synthèse*, LXVII (1950), pp. 67-79.

————, 'Gassendi: Sa Place dans la pensée du XVIIe siècle', in *Revue de Synthèse*, LX (1940-5), pp. 27-45.

————, 'Le Philosophe', in Centre international de synthèse, *Pierre Gassendi*, No. 63, pp. 71-107.

————, *Les Travaux de Gassendi sur Épicure et sur l'Atomisme*, 1619-1658, Paris: J. Vrin, 1944.

————, 'La Vie, le caractère et la formation intellectuelle', in Centre international de synthèse, *Pierre Gassendi*, No. 63, pp. 9-54.

Rossi, Mario, *La Vita, le opere, i tempi di Edoardo Herbert di Chirbury*, 3 vols., Firenze: G. C. Sansoni, 1947.

Sabrié, Jean-Baptiste, *De l'Humanisme au rationalisme: Pierre Charron* (1541-1603), *l'homme, l'oeuvre, l'influence*, Paris: F. Alcan, 1913.

Sadoleto, Jacopo, *Elogio della Sapienza (De Laudibus philosophiae)*, trad. and edited by Antonio Altamura, intro. Giuseppe Toffanin, Naples: R. Pironti, 1950.

————, *Opera quae exstant omnia*, Veronae: ex typ. J. A. Tumermani, 1738.

Sainct-Gelays, Melin de (Saint-Gelais, Mellin de), *Advertissement sur les jugemens d'astrologie*, Lyon: J. de Tournes, 1546.

———, *Oeuvres complètes de Melin de Sainct-Gelays*, edited by Prosper Blanchemain, Paris: P. Daffis (Bibliothèque Elzévirienne), 1873.

Sainte-Beuve, Charles A., 'Ecrivains critiques et moralistes de la France, XI. Gabriel Naudé', in *revue des Deux Mondes*, IV, 13ᵉ année N.S., 1843, pp. 754–89.

Sanches, Francisco, *Quod Nihil Scitur*, in *Opera Philosophica*, Nova Ediçao, precedida de introduçao por Joaquim De Carvalho, Coimbra: Inedita Ac Rediviva, Separata de *Revista da Universidade de Coimbra*, vol. XVIII, 1955.

———, *Que Nada Se Sabe . . .* , (Prólogo by Marcelino Menéndez y Pelayo), (Coleccion Camino de Santiago No. 9), Buenos Aires: Editorial Nova, 1944.

Savonarola, Girolamo, *Prediche Sopra Ezechiele*, edited by Roberto Ridolfi, (Edizione Nazionale, Vol. I), Rome: Belardatti, 1955.

Schiff, Mario, *La Fille d'alliance de Montaigne. Marie de Gournay*, Paris: H. Champion, 1910.

Schmitt, Charles B., *Cicero Scepticus*, International Archives of the History of Ideas, the Hague, Nijhoff, 1972.

———, 'Filippo Fabri and Scepticism; A Forgotten Defense of Scotus', *Storia e Cultura al Santo* a cura di Antonio Poppi, (Vincenza 1976), pp. 308–312.

———, *Gianfrancesco Pico della Mirandola (1469-1533) and his Critique of Aristotle.* International Archives of the History of Ideas, Vol. 23, The Hague: Nijhoff, 1967.

———, 'Guilio Castellani (1528-1586): A Sixteenth-Century Opponent of Scepticism', in *Journal of the History of Philosophy*, V (1967), pp. 15–39.

———, 'Philosophy and Science in Sixteenth-Century Universities: Some Preliminary Comments', in *The Cultural Context of Medieval Learning*, edited by J. E. Murdoch and E. D. Sylla, Dordrecht, D. Reidel Publishing Co., 1975, pp. 485–537.

———, 'An Unknown Seventeenth-Century French Translation of Sextus Empiricus', in *Journal of the History of Philosophy*, VI (1968), pp. 69–76.

———, 'An Unstudied Fifteenth Century Latin Translation of Sextus Empiricus by Giovanni Lorenzi', in *Cultural Aspects of the Italian Renaissance, Essays in Honour of Paul Oskar Kristeller*, edited by Cecil H. Clough, (Manchester 1976), pp. 244–261.

Schoeps, Hans Joachim, *Philosemitismus in Barok*, Tübingen: J. C. Mohr (Paul Siebeck), 1952.

Schoockius, Martinus (Schoock, Martin), *De Scepticismo Pars Prior, sive Libri Quatuor*, Groningen: ex officina H. Lussinck, 1652.

Schoockius, Martinus (Schoock, Martin), and Gisbert Voetius, *Admiranda Methodus Novae Philosphiae Renati Des Cartes*, Ultraiecti: ex officina J. Van Waesbergae, 1643.

Sclafert, Clément, 'Montaigne et Maldonat', *Bulletin de Littérature Ecclesiastique*, LII (1951), pp. 65–93 and 129–46.

Senchet, Émilien, *Essai sur la méthode de Francisco Sanchez*, . . . Paris: V. Giard et E. Brière, 1904.

Sergeant, John, *Sure-Footing in Christianity, or Rational Discourses on the Rule of Faith*, London: J. Sergeant, 1665.

Sextus Empiricus, *Adversus Mathematicos . . . , graece nunquam, Latine nunc primum editum, Gentiano Herveto Avrelio interprete. Eivsdem Sexti Pyrrhoniarum HYPOTYPΩSEWN libri tres . . . interprete Henrico Stephano*, Paris: Martinum Juvenem, 1569.

―――, *Les Hipotiposes ou Institutions pirroniennes, (pyrrhoniennes)*, (Amsterdam): n.p., 1725, and London: aux depens de la Compagnie, 1735.

―――, *Oeuvres choisies*, . . . trad. Jean Grenier et Geneviève Goron, Aubier: Montaigne, 1948.

―――, *Opera, graece et latine . . . notas addidit Jo. Albertus Fabricus*, Leipzig: J. F. Gleditschii, 1718.

―――, *Sexti Empirici Opera quae extant . . . Pyrrhoniarum Hypotypwseωn libri III . . . Henrico Stephano interprete. Adversus Mathematicos . . . libri X, Gentiano Herveto Aurelio interprete, graece nunc primus editi . . .* , Paris, Geneva: P.&J. Chouet, 1621.

―――, *Outlines of Pyrrhonism*, by Rev. R. G. Bury, translated Cambridge, Mass. and London: Loeb Classical Library, 1933–49.

―――, *Sexti Philosophi Pyrrhoniarum Hypotypωsewn libri III*, Paris: excudebat idem H. Stephanus, 1562.

Silhon, Jean de, *Les Deux veritez de Silhon: l'une de Dieu et de sa providence, l'autre de l'immortalité de l'ame . . .* , Paris: L. Sonnius, 1626.

―――, *De L'Immortalité de l'ame*, Paris: P. Billaine, 1634.

―――, *Le Ministre d'Estat*, 3ᵉ part, *De la Certitude des connoissances humaines*, Amsterdam: A. Michiels, 1662.

Simon, Richard, *A Critical History of the Old Testament*, translated by Dodwell, London: printed for Jacob Tonson, 1682.

―――, *De l'Inspiration des Livres Sacrés*, Rotterdam: Reinier Leers, 1687.

―――, *Lettres choisies de M. Simon*, Rotterdam: Renier Leers, 1702–05.

Sirven, Joseph-Emmanuel, *Les Années d'apprentissage de Descartes 1596–1628*, Albi: Impr. Coopérative du Sud-Quest, 1928.

Smyth, Thomas, *The Unity of the Human Race proved to be the Doctrine of Scripture, Reason and Science*, New York: G. Putnam, 1850.

Soman, Alfred, 'Methodology in the History of Ideas: The Case of Pierre Charron,' in *Journal of the History of Philosophy*, XII (1974), pp. 495–501.

——, 'Pierre Charron: A Revaluation', in *Bibliothèque d'Humanisme et Renaissance*', XXXII (1970) pp. 57–79.

Sorbière, Samuel, *Discours sceptique sur le passage du chyle, & le mouvement du coeur*, . . . Leyden: impr. de J. Maire, 1648.

——, *Lettres et Discours de M. de Sorbière sur diverses matieres curieuses*, Paris: F. Clousier, 1660.

——, *Sorberiana ou les Pensées critiques de M. de Sorbière, recueillies par M. Graverol* (2nd edition) Paris: F. and P. Delaulne, 1695.

Sorel, Charles, *La Bibliotheque françoise de M. C. Sorel*, Paris: Compagnie des Libraires du Palais, 1664.

——, *La Perfection de l'ame* . . . , Paris: T. Quintet, 1664. Tome IV of *La Science Universelle de Sorel*.

——, *La Science des choses corporelles, premiere partie de la Science humaine*, Paris: P. Billaine, 1643.

——, *La Science universelle de Sorel, où il est traité de l'usage & de la perfection de toutes les choses du monde* . . . , Tome III, Paris: T. Quintet, 1647.

Sortais, Gaston, *La Philosophie moderne depuis Bacon jusqu'à Leibniz*. Tome II, Paris: P. Letheilleux, 1922.

Spinoza, Benedictus de, *The Chief Works of Spinoza*, 2 vols., edited by R. H. M. Elwes, New York: Dover, 1955.

——, *Earlier Philosophical Writings*, translated by Frank A. Hayes, Indianapolis: Bobbs-Merrill, 1963.

——, *Opera Quotquot reperta sunt*, edited by J. Van Vloten and J. P. N. Land 4 vols., (3rd edition), The Hague: Nijhoff, 1914.

——, *The Principles of Descartes' Philosophy*, La Salle, Ill.: Open Court Pub. Co., 1943.

Sprat, Thomas, *Observations on Monsieur de Sorbier's Voyage into England*, London: printed for J. Martyn, & J. Allestry, 1665.

Stanley, Thomas, *The History of Philosophy*, London: printed for T. Bassett, D. Newman, and T. Cockerill, 1687.

Stäudlin, Carl Fridrich, *Geschichte und Geist des Skepticismus* . . . , 2 vols., Leipzig: S. L. Crusius, 1794.

Steinmann, Jean, *Richard Simon et les origines de l'exégèse biblique*, Paris: Desclée de Brouwer, 1960.

Stolpe, Sven, *Christina of Sweden*, New York: The Macmillan Co., 1966.

Strathmann, Ernest A., *Sir Walter Ralegh, A Study in Elizabethan Skepticism*, New York: Columbia Univ. Press, 1951.

Strauss, Leo, *Spinoza's Critique of Religion*, New York: Schocken Books, 1965.

Strowski, Fortunat, *Montaigne*, (2nd edition), Paris: F. Alcan, 1931.

———, *Pascal et son temps*, Vol. I, Paris: Plon-Nourrit, 1907.

Tamizey de Larroque, Philippe, 'Document relatif à Urbain Grandier', (Lettre d'Ismael Boulliau à Gassendi), *Cabinet historique*, XXV, (Série II), Vol. III (1879), pp. 1–14.

———, *Quelques lettres inédites d'Isaac de la Peyrère à Boulliau, Paris and Bordeaux*, Plaquettes gontaudaises, No. 2, 1878.

Thijssen-Schoute, C. Louise, *Nederlands Cartesianisme*, Amsterdam: N.V. Noord-Hollandsche Uitgevers, 1954.

Thorndike, Lynn, *A History of Magic and Experimental Science*, Vol. VI, New York: Macmillan Co., 1941.

Johannes Turretin, A., Pyrrhonismus Pontificus, Leiden 1692.

Valence, Pierre (Valentia), *Les Académiques ou des moyens de juger du vrai ouvrage puissé dans les sources; par Pierre Valence*, in Cicero, M. T. C., *Academiques* (Durand edition), London: P. Vaillant, 1740.

Valentia, Petrus (Valencia), *Academica sive de iudico erga verum, ex ipsis primis fontibus*, Antwerp: 1596.

Van Leeuwen, Henry, *The Problem of Certainty in English Thought, 1630–1680*, The Hague: Nijhoff, 1963.

Veron, François, *Methodes de Traiter des Controverses de Religion . . .*, (Oeuvres), Paris: Chez Louys de Heuquiville, 1638.

———, *La Victorieuse Methode pour combattre tous les Ministres: Par la seule Bible*, Paris: 1621.

———, *Du Vray Juge et jugement des Differents qui sont auiourd'huy en la religion; où est respondu au Sieur Daillé Ministre de Charenton, nouveau pyrrhonien, & indifferent en religion, contraire à ses colleagues & à son party*, Paris: n.d.

Villey, Pierre, (Villey-Desmeserets), 'Montaigne a-t-il lu le Traité de l'éducation de Jacques Sadolet?', in *Bulletin du Bibliophile et du Bibliothécaire*, (1909), pp. 265–78.

———, *Montaigne devant la posterité*, Paris: Ancienne Librairie Furne, Boivan, et Cⁱᵉ, Éditeurs, 1935.

———, *Les Sources & l'Evolution des Essais de Montaigne*, Paris: Hachette & Co., 1908.

Voetius, Gisbert, (Voet, Gisbert), and Schoockius, Martinus, *Admiranda methodus novae philosophiae Renati Des Cartes*, 1643.

Voltaire, François Marie Arouet de, *Dictionnaire philosophique*, edited by Julien Benda & Raymond Naves, Paris: Garnier Frères, 1954.

Waldman, Theodore, 'Origins of the Legal Doctrine of Reasonable Doubt,' *Journal of the History of Ideas*, XX (1959), pp. 299-316.

Weber, Alfred, *History of Philosophy*, translated by Frank Thilly, New York, Chicago, etc.: C. Scribner's Sons, 1925.

Wedderkopff, Gabriel, *Dissertationes duae quarum prior de Scepticismo profana et sacro praecipue remonstrantium, posterior de Atheismo praeprimus Socinianorum*, Argentorati: 1665.

Wilbur, Earl Morse, *A History of Unitarianism*, Cambridge: Harvard University Press, 1945-52.

Wild, Ulrich, *Quod aliquid scitur*, Leipzig: 1664.

Winchell, Alexander, *Preadamites: or a Demonstration of the Existence of Men before Adam*, (5th edition), Chicago: S. C. Griggs & Co., 1890.

Yves de Paris, *La Theologie naturelle*, (3rd edition), Tome IV, Paris: 1641.

Zambelli, Paola, 'A propositio della'de vanitate scientiarum et artium de Cornelio Agrippa', in *Rivista critica di storia della filosofia*, XV (1960), pp. 166-80.

———, 'Corneille Agrippa, Érasme et la Théologie humaniste', in *Douzième Stage International d'Études humanistes*, Tours 1969, Vol. I, pp. 113-59, (Paris 1972).

———, 'Magic and Radical Reformation in Agrippa of Nettesheim', in *Journal of the Warburg and Courtauld Institutes*, XXXIX (1976), pp. 69-103.

B. MANUSCRIPT MATERIAL:

Boulliau, Isaac, Letter to Portnero, Dec. 3, 1655, Bibl. Nationale, Fonds français 13041, fol. 179.

Cardinal Grimaldi, Bibl. Nationale Collection, Baluze 325, for. 63-66.

Cazac, Henri, Papers on Sanchez, deposited in the library of the Institut Catholique de Toulouse.

Gontery, Jean, S. J., Letter to Daniel Huet, (the latter was the father of P. D. Huet), Bibliothéque Nationale, Paris, Ms. Fonds française 11909, No. 41.

Huet, Pierre-Daniel, *Censure de la reponse faite par M. Regis au livre intitulé Censura philosophiae cartesianae, par Theocrite de la Roche,*

Seigneur de Pluvigny, Bibliothéque Nationale Paris, Ms. Fr. 14703, No. 3.

Langius, Wilhelmus (Lang, Villum), Letter to Ismaël Boulliau, 9 July 1657, The Hague, Bibliothéque Nationale Paris, Ms. Fr. 13037, fol. 131.

La Peyrère, Isaac, Les Juifs élus, reiettés et rapellés, Chantilly Ms. 191 (698).

——, Notes concerning his being accused in 1626, Bibliothèque Nationale Ms. Fonds française, 15827, fols. 149 and 162.

Naudé, Gabriel, Letter to Cardinal Barberini, 1641, Bibl. Vat. Barberini, Latin 6471, fol. 22ᵛ.

Sextus Empırıcus, *Adversus Mathematicos*, Latin trans. by Joh. Laurentius, Vatican library, Ms. 2990 fols. 266-381.

——, *Hypotyposes* and parts of *Adversus Mathematicos*, Latin translation by Petr. de Montagnana, Biblioteca Nazionale Marciana (Venice), cod. lat. x267 (3460) fols. 1-57.

——, *Pyrrhoniarum Hypotyposeon*, Bibliothèque Nationale, Paris, Ms. Fonds latin 14700, fols. 83-132.

——, *Pyrrhoniarum Hypotyposeon*, Biblioteca Nacional, Madrid, Ms. 10112, fols. 1-30.

INDEX

Abraham, 233, 297
Adam, 216, 218, 224, 292, 295
Adam, Antoine, 271
Adam, Charles, 271, 279, 284, 285
Agrippa von Nettesheim, Henricus Cornelius, 21, 23-26, 39, 89, 102, 173, 198, 255, 258
Albizzi, Cardinal, 222
Alexander VII, Pope, 222-223
Alexander the Great, 223
Al-Ghazzali, 18
Allen, Don Cameron, 263, 292, 299
Anaxagoras, 257
Antiochus of Ascalon, xiv
Anton, John P., 295
Arcesilas, xiii, xiv, xv, 28, 36, 40, 279
Archimedes, 64
Aristotle, 19, 20, 26, 28, 29, 31, 38, 50, 53, 60, 64, 72, 83, 84, 85, 92, 100-103, 108, 110-111, 118-121, 123, 126-128, 132, 135, 144, 153, 166, 199, 254, 268
Arnauld, Antoine, 90, 94, 105, 202, 207, 208, 291, 298
Aubert, John, 30
Aubrey, John, 66, 265-266
Augustinus (Augustine) Aurelius, Saint, xiii, xiv, xvi, xx, xxi, 36, 70, 114-115, 121, 218
Aumale, le Duc d', 293
Aurispa, Giovanni, 20
Auvray, L., 264
Aymonier, Camille, 263, 266

Bacon, Francis, 40, 41, 84, 89, 92, 101, 126, 136, 159, 174, 278
Bagni, Cardinal Jean-François, 87, 90, 174
Bagot, Jean, 121
Baïf, Jean-Antoine, 30-31
Baillehache, Jean, 267
Baillet, Adrien, 285, 289

Bainton, Roland H., 251
Baker, Thomas, 291
Balz, A. G. A., 286
Balzac, Jean Louis Guez de, 90, 94, 117, 161
Bangius, Thomas, 215
Barberini, Cardinal Francesco, 90, 222, 292
Bartsch, Gerhard, 299
Bayle, Pierre, xvii, xviii, xx, 21, 37, 65, 76, 88, 89, 100, 137, 207, 212, 213, 214, 225, 238, 247, 251, 252, 255, 260, 261, 266, 268, 271, 283, 287, 290, 292, 295, 298, 299
Becker, Bruno, 251
Bellarmino, Roberto, Saint, 68
Berkeley, George, 98, 214
Bernus, A., 298
Berr, Henri, 274, 280
Bérulle, Cardinal Pierre de, 55, 80, 113, 175-176, 186, 286
Beza, Theodore, 10, 11, 26
Bierling, Friedrich, 254
Birch, Thomas, 298
Blanchemain, Prosper, 257
Blanchet, Léon, 286
Bloch, Olivier R., 274, 280, 281
Boaistuau, Pierre, 32
Boas, George, 258, 277
Boase, Alan M., 263, 265, 269, 271, 273, 277, 283
Bochart, Samuel, 267
Bodin, Jean, 82, 263
Bonaparte, Napoleon, 225
Bosc, Jacques du, 129, 146, 272, 275, 281
Bouchard, Jean-Jacques, 88, 104
Boucher, Jean, 115-117
Bouillard, Ismael, 215, 270, 287, 292, 293, 296
Boullier, David-Renaud, 15, 16, 251, 252

Haag, Émile, 250, 266
Haag, Eugene, 250, 266
Hale, Matthew, 220, 294
Halevi, Judah, 18, 218
Hamann, J. G., 248
Hartley, David, 282
Hartnack, Daniel, 261
Hayer, Humbert, 16
Hayes, Frank A., 299
Hazard, Paul, 298
Henri III, 79
Henri, IV, de Navarre, 43, 56
Herbert, Edward, Lord Herbert of
    Cherbury, 121, 130, 144, 150-161,
    163, 170, 178, 185, 273, 274, 282-
    283
Hervet, Gentian, 19, 21, 26, 34-35, 36,
    68, 78-79, 259
Hess, Gerhard, 274
Heydon, Christopher, 83, 111, 269
Hirsch, Elisabeth Feist, 251
Hobbes, Thomas, 107, 130, 139, 174,
    214, 215, 217, 221, 293
Home, Henry (Lord Kames), 282
Horowitz, Maryanne C., 61, 264
Huart, Claude, 20, 253
Huet, Pierre-Daniel, xviii, 200, 212,
    214, 267, 290
Hume, David, xviii, xxi, 55, 72, 95,
    104, 129, 179, 210, 213, 214, 232,
    247, 260, 263, 267, 273, 291
Huxley, Aldous, 287
Huygens, Christian, 293

Iriarte, J., 260
Isaac, 233, 297

Jacob, 233, 297
Jerusalem, Karl, 298
Jesus, 216, 217, 230, 247, 296
Joshua, 217
Jovy, Ernest, 283, 284
Jude, Saint, 225
Julien-Eymard d'Angers. *See* Ches-
    neau, Charles (Julien-Eymard
    d'Angers)
Jurieu, Pierre, xx, 267

Kahle, L. M., 96, 272
Kant, Immanuel, xviii, 21
Kelsey, Francis W., 282

Kepler, Johannus, 108
Kibre, Pearl, 254
Kiefl, F. X., 273-274, 280
Kierkegaard, Søren, xviii, xx, 55, 94,
    95, 248, 263, 272
Koyré, Alexandre, 233, 274, 280, 285,
    286, 297
Kristeller, Paul O., 215, 252, 292, 293
Kuntz, Marion Daniels, 292

Lachèvre, Frédéric, 271, 275
Lafuma, Louis, 297
Lakatos, Imre, 296
Lamennais, Felicité Robert de, 248
La Mothe Le Vayer François, 85, 87,
    90-97, 104-106, 108, 125, 138-139,
    143, 164, 173, 181, 215, 252, 278,
    284, 286, 292, 295
Lamy, Bernard, 298
Land, J. P. N., 297
Langius, Wilhelm (Lang, Villum), 85,
    270
La Peyrère, Isaac, xviii, 87, 93, 108,
    130, 215-231, 233, 236, 238, 247,
    248, 292, 293, 294, 295, 296, 298
La Placette, Jean, 14, 15
Launoy, Jean, 105
Laurentius, Joh., 252
Le Caron, Louis, 27
Lecler, Joseph, 275, 276
Lee, Sidney, 282
Le Ferron, Arnould (Du Ferron), 25,
    256
Lefranc, Pierre, 253
Leibniz, Gottfried W., 21, 261, 268
Le Loyer, Pierre, 83, 111, 138, 279
Lenoble, Abbé Robert, 136, 275, 278,
    279, 280, 281, 282, 285
Leo X, Pope, 2
Lessing, Gotthold Ephraim, 298
L'Estoile, Pierre de, 269
Levi, David, 221, 294
Lilith, 218
Limbruck, Elaine, 262
Lindeboom, J., 251
Lipsius, Justus, 36
Locke, John, 157, 214, 283
Lorraine, Charles, Cardinal de, 31, 34,
    68
Loyola, Ignatius, Saint, 4
Lucian, 23